The Environmental History
of the Near and Middle East
Since the Last Ice Age

The Environmental History of the Near and Middle East Since the Last Ice Age

Edited by

William C. Brice

School of Geography, University of Manchester
Manchester, England

1978

Academic Press   London   New York   San Francisco

A Subsidiary of Harcourt Brace Jovanovich, Publishers

ACADEMIC PRESS INC. (LONDON) LTD
24/28 OVAL ROAD
LONDON NW1

U.S. Edition Published by
ACADEMIC PRESS INC.
111 FIFTH AVENUE
NEW YORK, NEW YORK 10003

Library of Congress Catalog Card Number: 77–81377
ISBN: 0–12–133850–9

Printed in Great Britain by
Willmer Brothers Ltd, Birkenhead

Contributors

Al-Asfour, T., *Department of Geography, The University of Kuwait, P.O. Box 23558, Kuwait, Arabia*

Allchin, B., *Wolfson College, Cambridge CB3 9BB, England*

Ambraseys, N. N., *Department of Civil Engineering (Seismology), Imperial College of Science and Technology, London SW2 2A2, England*

Bottema, S., *Biologisch-Archaeologisch Instituut, Rijksuniversiteit, Poststraact 6, Groningen, The Netherlands*

Brice, W. C., *School of Geography, University of Manchester M13 9PL, England*

Butzer, K. W., *Department of Geography, University of Chicago, Chicago, Illinois 60637, USA*

Clutton-Brock, J., *Department of Zoology, British Museum of Natural History, Cromwell Road, London SW7 5BD, England*

Costantini, L., *Istituto Italiano per il Medio ed Estremo Orienti, Via Merulana 248, Rome, Italy*

Eisma, D., *Netherlands Institute for Sea Research, Postbox 59, Den Burg-Texel, The Netherlands*

Erinç, S., *Department of Geography, The University of Istanbul, Istanbul, Turkey*

Erol, O., *Birinci Cadde 26/13, Bahçelievler, Ankara, Turkey*

Evans, G., *Imperial College of Science and Technology, Prince Consort Road, London S.W.7., England*

Ganji, M. H., *Department of Geography, Faculty of Letters and Human Sciences, The University, Tehran, Iran*

Gerasimov, I. P. *Academy of Sciences of the USSR, Institute of Geography, Staromonetny per. 29, Moscow, USSR*

Goudie, A., *School of Geography, Mansfield Road, Oxford, England*

†Higgs, E. S.

Larsen, C. E., *Gilbert/Commonwealth, 209 E. Washington Avenue, Jackson, Ml. 49201, USA*

† Deceased.

v

Raphael, C., *Eastern Michigan University, Ypsilanti, Michigan 48197, USA*

Seth, S. K., *Inspector General of Forests, Ministry of Agriculture and Irrigation, New Delhi, India*

Stevens, J., *Knight, Frank and Rutley, 20 Hanover Square, London W1R 0AH, England*

Tosi, M., *Istituto Italiano per il Medio ed Estremo Oriente, Via Merulana 248, Rome, Italy*

Vita-Finzi, C., *Department of Geography, University College London, Gower Street, London WC1 E, England*

Wilkinson, T. J., *24 Swallowcroft, Eastington, Stonehouse, Gloucestershire, England*

Preface

My archaeological friends at the annual Arabian Seminar once asked me, after I had delivered some unconvincing speculations about natural conditions in early Arabia, "Can you please tell us firmly whether it was wetter or drier, or where exactly was the shoreline, in a certain place at such a time?". In truth, I could not; nor probably could anyone else. But it occurred to me that it might be useful to collect the conclusions of a number of experts working in this field in the Eastern Mediterranean and Western Asia, and to arrange, to digest, and to correlate them for the benefit of my inquisitors. Hence this book. The spur to write it came from the generous suggestion of my friend and colleague, Dr James Mellaart. My twenty-two collaborators have shown magnanimity, forebearance and patience to a degree that I had no right to expect. Beyond them, I would like to pay tribute to one who would certainly have been the twenty-third, if he had still been alive, my courageous friend Jim (H. R.) Cohen. During the seven months of his last illness, we often ranged over his work in the plain of Konya and wondered what life was like there in the Neolithic. Anything useful which I may have been able to do here will have owed much to those happy meetings.

Cherry Tree Cottage,   *W.C.B.*
Didsbury
April 1978

Contents

List of contributors v
Preface vii
List of illustrations xvi
Introduction 1

Part I: General

1
The Late Prehistoric Environmental History of the Near East
K. W. BUTZER 5
History of investigations 5
The three sub-regions 7
General conclusions 11
References 12

Part II: The Balkans, The Aegean and The Levant

2
The Late Glacial in the Eastern Mediterranean and the Near East
S. BOTTEMA 15
Introduction 15
The Late Pleistocene and Early Holocene in the area of
Lake Xinias in Greece 17
Other Late Glacial diagram sections 19
Discussion 26
Acknowledgements 28
References 28

3
Early Domestication and the Ungulate Fauna of the Levant during the Prepottery Neolithic Period

J. CLUTTON-BROCK 29

Topography 29

Fauna 29

The aceramic Neolithic culture 30

References 38

4
Environmental Changes in Northern Greece

E. HIGGS. 41

Vegetational changes 41

Lake levels 42

Cave climates 44

Erosional and depositional changes 44

Fauna 45

Location of archaeological sites 46

Human ecology 46

Bibliography 48

5
The Erosional History of the Plain of Elis in the Peloponnese

C. N. RAPHAEL 51

Introduction 51

The physical landscape of coastal Elis 54

A chronology for coastal Elis 56

The association between archaeology and geomorphology . 57

Causes of deposition and erosion in Elis 62

References 65

6
Stream Deposition and Erosion by the Eastern Shore of the Aegean

D. EISMA 67

Introduction 67

Alluvial fans and valley infill 69

The river deltas 70

Synchronicity of stream deposition and erosion . . . 73

Relative sea-level in historic times 75

Soil erosion and climatic changes   76
References   79

Synopsis of Part II   82

Part III: The Plateaux of Anatolia and Iran

7
Changes in the Physical Environment in Turkey Since the End of the Last Glacial

S. ERINÇ.   87
Introduction   87
Conditions during the last Ice Age   88
Climatic changes and their consequences   89
Changes in the physical environment due to exogenous processes   99
Changes in the physical environment due to endogenous
processes   106
Changes in the physical environment due to human activities .   107
References   108

8
The Quaternary History of the Lake Basins of Central and Southern Anatolia

O. EROL.   111
Introduction 111
The lake basins of eastern, northern and south-eastern Anatolia 112
The lake basins of south-central Anatolia and the west Taurus
lake district   113
The tectonic history of the Turkish lake district and
south-central Anatolia 120
The Tuzgölü Basin 122
The Konya-Ereğli Basin   126
The Burdur Basin 130
A comparison of the Tuzgölü, Konya and Burdur Basins .   . 135
References   136

9
The Desiccation of Anatolia

W. C. BRICE   141
Degeneration of the flora and fauna since Classical times   . 141

Changes of vegetation through the Holocene   .   .   . 143
Recent experiments in restoration   146
References   146

10
Post-Glacial Climatic Changes on the Iranian Plateau
M. H. GANJI   149
Introduction 149
Geographical background 151
The nature of the problem   152
Climatological evidence   153
Chronology of contributions   156
Conclusion   160
References   162

11
The Environment of Southern Sistan in the Third
Millennium B.C., and its Exploitation by the Proto-Urban
Hilmand Civilization
L. COSTANTINI AND M. TOSI   165
The Hilmand culture   165
Sistan: position and geographic characteristics   .   .   . 167
Climate   171
Hydrography 173
Flora and fauna   176
Ecosystems   179
Notes 181
References   182

12
Studies in Historical Seismicity and Tectonics
N. N. AMBRASEYS   185
Scope of studies   185
Development of studies   186
Seismic activity   190
Historical seismicity and tectonics in the Middle East   .   . 194
Speculations 207
References   209

Synopsis of Part III.   212

Part IV: Mesopotamia and the Gulf

13
Erosion and Sedimentation along the Euphrates Valley in Northern Syria
T. J. WILKINSON 215
    Introduction 215
    Present fluvial activity 216
    Stages in the evolution of the landscape 221
    Discussion and conclusions 224
    Acknowledgements 225
    Notes 225
    References 226

14
The Holocene Geological History of the Tigris-Euphrates-Karun Delta
C. E. LARSEN and G. EVANS 227
    Introduction 227
    Early studies 227
    Environmental background 231
    Geological evidence from the delta region 234
    Discussion 236
    Conclusion 239
    References 242

15
The Marine Terraces of the Bay of Kuwait
T. AL-ASFOUR 245
    The field-work 245
    Interpretation and comparisons 248
    References 253

16
Recent Alluvial History in the Catchment of the Arabo-Persian Gulf
C. VITA-FINZI 255
    The alluvial record 255
    Discussion 258
    References 260

17

Post-Pluvial Changes in the Soils of the Arabian Peninsula
J. H. STEVENS 263
  The palaeosols of Arabia 263
  Indications of past pluvial episodes 263
  Evidence from south-east Arabia 264
  Reddened soils 265
  Processes elsewhere in Arabia 271
  Conclusion 273
  References 273

Synopsis of Part IV 275

Part V: The Deserts of the Indus and of Trans-Caspia

18

**The Desiccation of the Thar Desert and its Environs during
  the Protohistorical and Historical Periods**
S. K. SETH 279
  Introduction 279
  Present conditions 280
  Climate 281
  Past conditions 285
  The desert in history 296
  The decline of the Harappan civilization 297
  Has the climate changed? 299
  Conclusions 301
  Notes 302
  References 302

19

**Climatic Change in the Indian Desert and North-West India
  during the Late Pleistocene and Early Holocene**
B. ALLCHIN and A. GOUDIE 307
  Background 307
  River terraces 307
  Sand dunes 310
  Miliolite deposits 312
  Fossil river-courses 313
  Glacial deposits and landforms 313

Acknowledgements 314
References   314
Appendix   314

20A
Ancient Rivers in the Deserts of Soviet Central Asia
I. P. GERASIMOV   319
Natural phenomena 319
Early irrigation   324
The Sarykamysh lake and its phases   326
Causes of shifts of rivers 329
Conclusion   332
References   333

20B
The Past and the Future of the Aral and the Caspian Seas
I. P. GERASIMOV   335
General history and geography 335
The Caspian Sea   336
The Aral Sea 345
References   349

Synopsis of Part V 350

Conclusion
W. C. BRICE   351

Subject Index 357

List of illustrations

Chapter 1
Fig. 1: Regional conditions 7

Chapter 2
Fig. 1: Geographical map of the area with the location of the
coring sites 16
Fig. 2: Simplified diagram of Lake Vico 20
Fig. 3: Simplified diagram of Trstenik 21
Fig. 4: Simplified diagram of Ioannina 22
Fig. 5: Simplified diagram of Lake Xinias 23
Fig. 6: Simplified diagram of Tenagi Philippon . . . 24
Fig. 7: Simplified diagram of the Ghab Valley 25
Fig. 8: Simplified diagram of Lake Zeribar 26

Chapter 3
Fig. 1: Map of Western Asia to show the localities of the
archaeological sites mentioned in the text 32
Fig. 2: Percentages and absolute numbers of the remains of the
main food animals from the Prepottery Neolithic levels
of the Jericho Tell 37

Chapter 4
Fig. 1: Section of deposits at Kastritsa cave showing beach levels 43

Chapter 5
Fig. 1: Coastal and fluvial geomorphology of coastal Elis . . 52
Fig. 2: The association between archaeological sites and
geomorphology north of the Peneus River 53
Fig. 3: Cross-section and relationship of the alluvial
deposits and the archaeology of the Sachia river valley . . 55

Fig. 4: Chronology of late historical deposits in the
eastern Mediterranean   64

Chapter 6
Fig. 1: The four major rivers in western Turkey   .   .   .   68
Fig. 2: The flood plains of the Büyük Menderes and the
Küçük Menderes   71

Chapter 7
Fig. 1: Geomorphic and geological evidence of repeated changes
of level during the Quaternary   92
Fig. 2: The İncesu Valley   94
Fig. 3: The deltaic plain of Çukurova   101
Fig. 4: The deltaic plain of the Küçük Menderes   .   .   .   102
Fig. 5: Coastal changes in the post-Glacial epoch in the Meander
plain   103
Fig. 6: The deltaic plain of Troy   105

Chapter 8
Fig. 1: The lake basins of eastern, northern and south-eastern
Anatolia   113
Fig. 2a: The former extent of some Anatolian lakes.   .   .   114
Fig. 2b: The maximum extent of Tuzgölü and Lake Konya   .   115
Fig. 3: The lake basins of south-central Anatolia
and the west Taurus lake district   116
Fig. 4: The large swallow-cave of Lake Suğla which is dried
out today   118
Fig. 5: The coastal spit belonging to the older Pluvial
levels of Lake Suğla and the erosional notches of the
recent lake at its edge   118
Fig. 6: Comparison of heights and ages of the terraces
of the Anatolian lakes   121
Fig. 7: The Tuzgölü Basin   123
Fig. 8: The Tuzgölü Lake   125
Fig. 9: The Konya-Ereğli Basin   126
Fig. 10: The pediment-like footplains at the foot of Bozdaglar
in the north-west of the Konya lake basin   127
Fig. 11: The inner basin of Konya   128
Fig. 12: Coastal traces east of Dinvanlar   .   .   .   129
Fig. 13: The Burdur Basin   131

Fig. 14: The Burdur Basin: morphology 132
Fig. 15: Lake Burdur—middle section of west coast.   .   . 133
Fig. 16: Lake Burdur—west coast near northern extremity   . 134

Chapter 10
Fig. 1: Map of Iran showing places named in this chapter .   . 151

Chapter 11
Fig. 1: Resources and trade in the vicinity of Shahr-i Sokhta
in the third millennium B.C.   166
Fig. 2a: Photograph by Earth Resources Technological
Satellite of the irrigable area of the Iranian Sistan .   . 168
Fig. 2b: Guide-trace to accompany Fig. 2a   .   .   . 169
Fig. 3: Mean monthly temperatures at three places in Sistan   . 172
Fig. 4: Monthly rainfall totals at three places in Sistan   . 173
Fig. 5: Average total monthly discharge of the lower
Hilmand River   173
Fig. 6: Changes through time in the relative proportion of
sheep and goats in Sistan 177

Chapter 12
Fig. 1: Regional seismicity—first to seventeenth centuries A.D. . 191
Fig. 2: Ground deformations of tectonic origin   .   . 192
Fig. 3: The eruptions of the Santorin volcano related to
E. Mediterranean seismicity   198
Fig. 4: Fault-break near Dorud   199
Fig. 5: Fault-break near Dasht-e-Bayaz (Iran) .   .   . 200
Fig. 6: Faulting associated with event no. 4 (Gediz).   . 201

Chapter 13
Fig. 1: Location of Dibsi Faraj   217
Fig. 2: The geomorphology of the Dibsi Basin.   .   . 218
Fig. 3: The course of incision in Wadi el Safa.   .   . 219
Fig. 4: The Euphrates Valley above Dibsi Faraj   .   . 220

Chapter 14
Fig. 1: Past shorelines of the Mesopotamian Delta Region .   . 229
Fig. 2: The stratigraphy of Lower Iraq, from borings   . 237

Fig. 3a: Satellite picture of the head of the Gulf
taken on 23 December 1972   240
Fig. 3b: Guide-trace to accompany Fig. 3a   241

Chapter 15
Fig. 1: Location map: Kuwait   246
Fig. 2: The marine terraces along the north side of the
Bay of Kuwait   247
Fig. 3: Bay of Kuwait, showing the general fall in
elevation from West to East   247
Fig. 4: Tentative correlation of Late Pleistocene and
Holocene sea-level changes in the Arabian Gulf   .   .   . 250

Chapter 16:
Fig. 1: The catchment of the Gulf   256

Chapter 17
Fig. 1: The sand-seas and highlands of Arabia 266
Fig. 2: Outwash deposits of the Oman Mountain Ranges   .   . 267

Synopsis Part IV
Fig. 1: The irrigation and drainage system of Mesopotamia
in Abbasid times *c.* A.D. 800–1200   276

Chapter 18
Fig. 1: The Thar Desert: four types of physiography   .   . 280
Fig. 2: The Thar Desert: annual rainfall.   283
Fig. 3: Evidence of changes in the drainage of Sind .   .   . 292
Fig. 4: Former drainage channels of the Punjab   .   .   . 294

Chapter 19
Fig. 1: Gujarat and Rajasthan   308

Chapter 20A
Fig. 1: *Takyrs* in the Karakum Desert   320
Fig. 2: The major regions of Turan where *takyrs* and
takyr-like formations are common   321
Fig. 3: Areas of ancient and modern irrigation in the
basins of the Amu-Darya and Syr-Darya   325

Fig. 4: The lower reaches of the Uzboi 328
Fig. 5: The four phases of abundant water in the Sarykamysh
hollow 330

Chapter 20B

Fig. 1: The lower Khvalyn Basin: dated to the end of the
Pleistocene   338
Fig. 2: The late Khvalyn Basin: dated to the beginning of
the Holocene.   339
Fig. 3: The New Caspian Basin c.4000–5000 B.P.   .   .   . 342
Fig. 4: The fluctuations of level of the Caspian over the
period from A.D. 1760 to the present.   342
Fig. 5: The Aral Sea: recent fluctuations of level and intake   . 347

Conclusion

Fig. 1: Wind-circulation in the Old World under glacial and
interglacial conditions   352
Fig. 2: Synoptic table.   353
Fig. 3: Conditions about 10,000 B.P.   354
Fig. 4: Conditions about 5000 B.P.   355

Introduction

W. C. Brice

The constant danger in this subject is that of circular argument. C. E. P. Brooks (1926) in his classic and still valuable book *Climate through the Ages*, though not guilty himself, sets a trap for the unwary when he deduces episodes of drought or excess rain from records of human migration, by awarding negative or positive marks according to whether the movement was from a wet area to a dry, or from a dry area to a wet. It is all too easy thereafter to take his graphs of climatic change and to use them to explain the migrations of peoples!

There is also the risk of coming across a tempting theory and pressing it to bear too much. A case in point is Rhys Carpenter's use in his lectures (''Discontinuity in Greek Civilization'': Cambridge, 1966) of Willetts's 1850-year cycle of drought to explain the migrations of the Dark Age of the Aegean. It could be that whole peoples were disturbed by the beginning of the ''deterioration'' of climate towards the ''sub-glacial'' conditions of the sub-Atlantic period: but is there yet stratigraphic evidence from any branch of natural history that conditions changed about this time either in the districts they left behind or at their destination?

So throughout this collection the object is to record what is known to have happened, where and when, without regard to why it happened or to what its consequences. Of course, this is a counsel of perfection. The human population can never be ignored, for it is always influencing its own environment, sometimes drastically. Likewise, any attempt to correlate natural happenings in different places must have an eye to possible causes. But the general brief to the writers has been to set down simply what occurred, where and when. Some significant comparisons may have emerged in consequence; but even if these are not accepted, the independent records in each essay may prove useful. At present the time-scale must be marked in millennia rather than centuries, though data will doubtless some time appear that make it possible to consider changes of a shorter wavelength in historical times. But changes of the term here considered must have had a bearing on the conditions of life as Mesolithic cultures were replaced by Neolithic, and they in turn by more elaborate ways of life.

The studies are grouped into four parts (II–V), and each of these parts is introduced and summarized by a short note. Part I consists of a general review of the subject by Professor Karl Butzer. All unattributed contents are of course editorial.

I

General

1
The Late Prehistoric Environmental History of the Near East

Karl W. Butzer

History of Investigations

For almost a century the history of climatic changes in the Near East has had an unusual interest for historians and archaeologists. Here Western scholars first saw signs of former fertility on the margins of the present arid zone, and sought for explanations. Quaternary studies began in the 1880s, and the conclusions drawn from the accumulating evidence for Pleistocene climates substantially different from those of the present were, during the first quarter of the twentieth century, blithely extended to apply to the Holocene and even to historical times. The paradigm of environmental determinism was first formulated here, and the riposte of the "possibilists" was illustrated from the same ground so fertile in examples. In the end, much of this controversy was reduced to divergent interpretations of the empirical evidence for climatic change.

The phase of field-studies which terminated with World War II did not produce much incontrovertible evidence, despite many extensive regional studies and some details from specific sites. This was partly because the lack of chronometric aids rendered most stratigraphic correlations ingenuous if not incorrect: moreover, conclusions were almost exclusively based upon geological interpretations, at a time when sedimentological studies were few, and geomorphic systems almost unknown. I attempted to compile, discuss and evaluate these earlier data (Butzer, 1958), shortly before a new phase of economic affluence allowed Western scholars to approach the same problems again, but with more evolved techniques, and with the assistance of radiocarbon dating.

The last fifteen years have consequently seen a proliferation of new regional or local studies, essentially geomorphological, but now complemented by varied paleo-biological investigations, the range of which can be gauged from the chapters of this volume. Unquestionably, a great deal has been learned. But, as I have also emphasized in a recent critical review (Butzer, 1975a), the available information is still unsatisfactory, incomplete and often inconclusive. The actual number of field studies is still small, compared with those in Europe and North America, and their scope is often extensive. Remarkably few stratigraphic events have been radiometrically fixed outside Israel and the Nile Valley. Changes within environmental systems in the Mediterranean Basin and in the arid zones generate features that more often than not remain difficult to interpret: in particular, minor climatic variations are only discernible, let alone explicable, with some degree of subjectivity. Above all, the quality of the work has been uneven. Many researchers apply ever more discriminating criteria to their subject matter, as they learn by experience and seek to improve their conceptual modes. Some, however, persist in using *a priori* theoretical frameworks or outmoded technologies, sometimes in the guise of "scientism", and continue to subject their colleagues to conclusions that are no less simplistic and subjective than those of an earlier generation. Even in matters of dating we find that isolated lithic artefacts are still being employed to correlate and "fix" Pleistocene phenomena in time.

By all acceptable standards, the Near Eastern evidence is still fragmentary and frequently of variable quality, and chronological data are inadequate for a stratigraphy of the region as a whole. At the general rather than local level, one can still do little more than outline and discuss the present state of regional information from different categories of evidence. The broad, generalized impressions that emerge are intriguing but remain elusive in their details. This brief paper will only attempt to summarize some of these generalizations. For a specific enumeration and analysis of the data, the reader is referred to Butzer (1975a, b, 1976a), as well as to the individual chapters of this volume.

The information falls logically within three regional contexts:
  A. the highland perimeter (Anatolia, Armenia, Kurdistan, Iran);
  B. the hills and plains of the "Fertile Crescent" (the Levant and Mesopotamia);
  C. the lower Nile Basin (including the north-eastern Sahara).

The Three Sub-regions

The Northern Highlands

The record of the highland belt between the Late Pleistocene and the Mid-Holocene can at present be synthesized as follows.

1. Glacial vestiges are widespread in Turkey, Transcaucasia, Iran and the adjacent parts of Iraq, as well as in the high Lebanon. They all serve to indicate a colder climate during the Würm Full Glacial. Mean summer temperatures may have been in the order of 6–7°C lower than at present. The multiple minor ("recessional") moraines found in association with most of these Late Pleistocene glaciers afford evidence of one or more re-

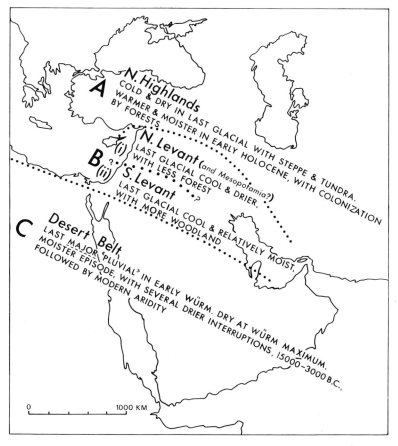

Fig. 1: Regional conditions. The design and the wording are editorial. The Northern Zagros sites fall within Region A.

advances during the Late Glacial as well as of one or more stages of temporary readvance or re-glaciation during the Holocene.

2. Pollen diagrams and associated evidence, particularly from Lake Zeribar, suggest that an open vegetation of steppe and mountain tundra, perhaps with scrub-steppe in more favoured localities, was characteristic of Turkey, north-eastern Iraq, and most of Iran, during the Full Glacial. The warm-up during the Alleröd, and particularly during the Early Holocene, appears to have been accompanied by an increase in precipitation which led to a gradual re-forestation of the highlands.

3. Other categories of geomorphologic evidence from the highlands do not appear to contradict these conclusions from Lake Zeribar. Few lacustrine deposits have been dated, and many but not all seem to be of Early Würm or of Holocene date. In no case do the higher lake levels indicate a very appreciable increase in rainfall, and those of Glacial age are readily explained by reduced evaporation alone. The alluvial deposits of the highlands are dated, on rather indirect criteria, as Late Pleistocene: some, or even the majority, may turn out to be of Early Würm age; others may belong to the Full Glacial and reflect seasonally concentrated stream-discharge and accelerated morphogenesis under a more severe climate. Although dissected Holocene alluvia appear to be infrequent or lacking, there is at least a strong possibility of higher lake levels during some parts of the Holocene, in Lake Burdur for example.

4. The available evidence argues that the Near Eastern Highlands, north of about latitude 35°, did not experience "pluvial" conditions during the last 50,000 years or so. The Full and Late Glacial were conspicuously cold and comparatively dry. The Holocene environment appears to have remained fairly constant, with conditions similar to what might be expected today without human disturbance. Perhaps the only significant post-Pleistocene changes in this regional setting have been those accompanying and following intensive or rapacious land-use. Under any circumstances, considerable environmental changes must have accompanied the Pleistocene–Holocene transition, but unfortunately the exact nature of these changes can only be conjectured at the moment.

The Levant and Mesopotamia

The climatic vicissitudes of the late Pleistocene and Early Holocene are documented by several categories of evidence in the hill country and plainlands of Syria, Lebanon, Israel, Jordan and Iraq.

1. It is somewhat surprising that there are no imposing lake deposits

outside the Jordan Valley, and geomorphologic changes are mainly reflected in the fairly widespread alluvial fills that accompany many streams both large and small. The implications of these now-dissected alluvia are not unequivocal, and they may be a result of one or more of the following factors: more torrential rains; more concentrated discharge and/or precipitation; greater precipitation; more detritus as a result of accelerated weathering; and, in areas with an effective vegetation mat today, changes of the vegetative cover through differing temperatures and evaporation rates. Until more detailed work has been done and isotopic dating has become available, the geomorphic environment of the Levant and Mesopotamia in recent geological times will remain somewhat enigmatic. Important exceptions are the Damascus Basin and the Jordan Valley, where several moist interludes can be clearly recognized in the time-range from the Late Pleistocene to the Holocene. Such an interpretation of the lacustrine beds and massive spring-deposits seems to be clear in this area; but further sedimentological study of the alluvial terraces will be necessary.

2. A number of cave sequences show that most of the Early Würm, and parts of both the Full and Late Würm, were sufficiently cold and moist to generate significant frost-weathering. The resulting angular rubbles are interrupted by horizons which reflect chemical weathering or fine-grained sedimentation under more temperate conditions. The state of studies of cave sedimentology, although encouraging, still leaves much to be desired.

3. Biological evidence from the Levant and Mesopotamia includes both faunas and some pollen. Although the Full Glacial cave-deposits of the Levant show a number of intrusive Palaearctic forms, the Glacial age faunas everywhere suggest ecological conditions remarkably similar to those of today.

Far more impressive are the pollen data, which show that forest vegetation was generally diminished during the Glacial periods. This was much more the case in northern Syria and Lebanon, where absolute rainfall must have decreased markedly during the Full Glacial, than in Israel, and notably in the Negev, where rainfall did not decline appreciably but where reduced evaporation favoured expansion of existing woodlands. There may also be some biological evidence that conditions were moister during part of the Early and Middle Holocene in Israel and the Damascus Basin; but the paucity of evidence for change elsewhere should be taken to imply that there has been little alteration of climate of ecological significance in post-Pleistocene times north of perhaps 32° latitude.

4. The available evidence provides no support for theories once current that agriculture originated through post-Pleistocene desiccation. There is no evidence for a deterioration of conditions in lands suitable for agriculture in the Levant or Mesopotamia during the transition from the Pleistocene to the Holocene. Rather, at the close of the Pleistocene extensive arable lands were opened up in the high country. Similarly, there is no reason whatsoever to believe that agricultural dispersals were affected or aided by progressive desiccation of the nuclear agricultural area in south-western Asia (Butzer 1971, Chapters 32–33).

Egypt–Arabia

Modest increases of precipitation have had disproportionately great effects on geomorphic equilibrium and ecological conditions in a hyper-arid environment such as Egypt. Yet even here true "pluvial" conditions were last experienced during the first half or so of the Würm. In the later, Full Glacial, period Egypt was as dry as it is today.

1. There is evidence of increased discharge down wadis in Egypt and Nubia somewhat prior to 25,000 years ago. Stream activity in these deserts was also more significant than now during much of the period between 15,000 and 3000 B.C., except for three major dry interludes centered at approximately 9500 B.C., 5500 B.C. and 4500 B.C.: the relevant geomorphologic evidence, substantiated by fragmentary biological data, suggests that rains became more frequent and perhaps of greater duration during much of this time. A reddish palaeosol, bearing distinctive evidence of biochemical weathering, can be dated to 5000 B.C. In Arabia as well, lake-beds and spring-deposits seem to show that one or more moist spells occurred in Mid-Holocene times.

2. The effects of "sub-pluvial" intervals on the fauna of Egypt during late prehistoric times has long been of interest. There is no evidence, however, that episodes of Late Pleistocene desiccation in Egypt forced prehistoric settlement to concentrate in the Nile Valley, as was once claimed. Lower and Middle Paleolithic habitation seems to have been confined already to the vicinity of reliable sources of water, and the Late Paleolithic settlers of the Nile Valley did not expand into the nearby deserts during moister intervals. However, the biomass and diversity of game resources outside the riverine zone would have varied significantly, with potential implications for at least some of the activities of certain prehistoric groups.

3. Present-day ecological conditions were finally established in Old

Kingdom times, and a long arid phase, during which dunes became more active and the floods of the Nile were comparatively low, had begun by the end of the Fifth Dynasty (c. 2350 B.C.). This period of drought was probably responsible in part for the ultimate breakdown of the Old Kingdom (Butzer 1976b).

General Conclusions

The available evidence allows several broader conclusions:

a. The last Interglacial period is poorly recorded in most areas, but was apparently more often than not characterized by environmental conditions similar to those of today. Nonetheless, wherever there is detailed information it is becoming equally evident that climates changed through time.

b. During the last Glacial there were three distinct paleoclimatic provinces in the Near East: the highlands of Anatolia and Iran, intensely cold most of the time and very dry during the Full Glacial, with next-to-no tree growth possible; the Levant, moderately cold and relatively dry in the north, cool and comparatively moist in the south (this distinction possibly extended eastwards across Mesopotamia and southern Iran); Egypt, which experienced long periods of increased rainfall, except during the maximum of the Würm Glacial (a pattern possibly repeated in Sinai and Arabia). Different trends again are apparent in the southern Sahara and East Africa (Butzer et al., 1972).

c. During Mid-Holocene times there were repeated moister episodes in Egypt and Arabia, comparable to those in sub-Saharan Africa. These moister spells affected Israel too, but are not evident farther north.

d. The Early-to-Middle Pleistocene period, although not discussed here, is, in fact, virtually intangible in view of the fragmentary evidence, and above all in consideration of the almost total lack of those radiometric and palynological criteria that are proving to be essential for unravelling the environmental history of Late Pleistocene and Holocene times in the Near East.

e. All of the climatic changes recorded were of relatively short "wavelength", and none exceeded the duration of the standard Late Pleistocene substages used in European geochronology. This makes direct correlations with the European sequences difficult if not undesirable, particularly in default of radiometric dating.

f. Except for Egypt, there is no sound evidence for pluvials as such in the

Near East—and in any case the term "pluvial" is best used only as an adjective to describe a specified range of phenomena.

References

Butzer, K. W. 1958. Quaternary Stratigraphy and Climate in the Near East. *Bonn. Geog. Abh.* **24**; 1969 Bonn and New York: Johnson Reprint Corporation, pp. 1–157.

Butzer, K. W. 1971. *Environment and Archeology: and ecological approach to prehistory.* London: Methuen, and Chicago, Aldine, 705 pp.

Butzer, K. W. 1975a. Patterns of environmental change in the Near East during late Pleistocene and Holocene times. *In: Problems in Prehistory: North Africa and the Levant* (F. Wendorf and A. E. Marks, eds), pp. 389–410. Dallas: Southern Methodist University Press.

Butzer, K. W. 1975b. Pleistocene littoral-sedimentary cycles of the Mediterranean Basin. *In: After the Australopithecines.* (K. W. Butzer and G. L. Isaac, eds), pp. 25–71. The Hague: Mouton; and Chicago: Aldine.

Butzer, K. W. 1976a. Pleistocene climates. *In: The Ecology of the Pleistocene* (R. C. West, ed.), Baton Rouge; *Geosci. Man* **13** (in press).

Butzer, K. W. 1976b. Early hydraulic civilization in Egypt: a study in cultural ecology. *Prehist. Archeol. Ecol.* **3**, 1–134.

Butzer, K. W., Isaac, G. L., Richardson, J. L. and Washbourn-Kamau, C. K. 1972. Radiocarbon dating of East African lake levels. *Science* **175**, 1069–1076.

II

The Balkans, The Aegean and The Levant

Geographical changes have been remarked and discussed more frequently with regard to this than to any other part of the region, doubtless because of its interest for both Classical and Biblical history. The Victorian scholar and traveller, H. Swainson Cooper, was struck by the widespread traces of abandoned cultivation in Cyrenaica, which, in his book *The Hill of the Graces*, he attributed to climatic desiccation; while in his famous essay on ''The burial of Olympia'' in the *Geographical Journal* for 1910 (**36**, 657) Ellsworth Huntington assigned the massive accumulation of silt in this valley of the Peloponnese to a similar cause, a marked diminution of the rainfall of Greece after 400 B.C. The great Pauline scholar and explorer of Anatolia, W. M. Ramsay, remarked on the widespread and often catastrophic deterioration of the landscape of Asia Minor around the turn of the era, and in his book *The Cities of Saint Paul* (p. 19) particularly he connected some of Paul's ideas about the state of creation with the evident changes in the physical world in which he was living. Ramsay, however, did not attempt to explain these changes.

More recently, palynological sections, archaeological stratification and historical records have made it possible to approach these questions with more precise dates and with more hope of ascertaining causes and effects. The following six essays offer some examples of changes in the area of the Eastern Mediterranean with respect to flora, fauna and the deposition of coastal alluvium, beginning in Late Glacial times and leading up to the Classical period and beyond.

2
The Late Glacial in the Eastern Mediterranean and the Near East

Sytze Bottema

Introduction

In this chapter the Late Glacial history of the climate and vegetation of the area between Italy and Iran will be discussed on the basis of pollen diagrams. The information available for the period from about 14,000 to 10,000 B.P. is still rather scanty, as pollen diagrams covering this period are very scarce, at least from most of the countries in that area. In north-west Europe, however, the palynological characteristics of the same period are quite well defined, and it may therefore be very useful to compare the two areas in this respect.

Indeed, in the diagrams from north-west Europe the Late Glacial pollen zones can be synchronized over large distances, and it is for this reason tempting to correlate these zones with those from other parts of the world, with reference to the many fluctuations often found in diagrams. Such correlations may, however, be premature if the fluctuations are based only on a few spectra. If there is a small number of dominating pollen types, and their values are presented as percentages of a sum, the fluctuations in the diagrams become exaggerated. However, a careful study of spectra from samples taken at close intervals, combined with radiocarbon dates, will make possible a reliable correlation.

In Table I simplified portions of diagrams from the Mediterranean and the Near East are presented as a basis for a study of the history of vegetation in the Late Glacial period (Figs 2–8). The pollen percentages from which these diagrams are constructed are, in general, based upon a sum which includes the pollen of trees, shrubs, *Artemisia*, and Chenopodiaceae. In

Table I: Tentative correlation scheme of the Late Glacial in north-western Europe, the eastern Mediterranean and the Near East

BP	pollen zones	NW EUROPE	ITALY Lake Vico	YUGOSLAVIA Trstenik	GREECE Ioannina	GREECE Xinias	GREECE Tenagi	SYRIA Ghab	IRAN Zeribar
10.000	IV	Preborial	forest	forest	forest 10.190 ●	forest	forest	10.080 ●	savanne
	III	Younger Dryas		Artemisia / Chenopod. steppe	few pines incr. pine forest	10.680 ●	incr. conifers/ decr.conifers/ incr. conifers	forest	
11.000	II	Alleröd	Artemisia / Chenopodiaceae steppe			Chenopod. veget. Artemisia/Chenopodiaceae steppe		Artemisia / Chenopodiaceae steppe	Artemisia / Chenopodiaceae steppe	Chenopodiaceae/Artemisia steppe
12.000				Artemisia/Chenopod. steppe few pines	Artemisia / Chenopodiaceae steppe	incr. conifers/ decr.conifers/ incr. conifers			
13.000	I	Older Dryas							
14.000							14.600 ●		13.650 ●

some cases other, non-local, herb pollen is included. The cores have been taken at localities where forest would constitute the natural vegetation nowadays: only in the Ghab Valley would a transition from forest to forest-steppe be found under natural conditions.

In Table I the Late Glacial of north-west Europe is divided into the classical sequence of Older Dryas (I), Alleröd (II), Younger Dryas (III), the

Fig. 1: Geographical map of the area with the location of the coring sites.

subdivision of the Older Dryas into Bölling etc. being omitted; and alongside this sequence are ranged for comparison simplified descriptions of vegetation abstracted from Figs 2–8.

In the figures the various pollen zones are designated where possible according to the classical numbering; otherwise the designation used by the relevant author is given. All these sites have this in common, that during the Upper Full Glacial (about 27,000–14,000 B.P.) steppe vegetation prevailed; though steppe forest occurred in the southern part of Europe in favourable locations at elevations of between 500 and 800 m (Bottema, 1974).

In pollen diagrams from north-west Europe, the beginning of the Late Glacial is marked by an increase in the percentages of tree pollen, which is doubtless to be explained by an important rise in temperature as well as precipitation. However, to the south and the east this increase in the percentages of tree pollen may be weaker or even absent, and in the Near East especially the beginning of the Late Glacial period may show an increase in the values of herbaceous pollen.

Since the section from Xinias is new, it will be discussed first and in detail.

The Late Pleistocene and Early Holocene in the Area of Lake Xinias in Greece

The Pollen Diagram

From a core taken in the former Lake Xinias, 500 m above sea-level (39° 4' 0"N, 22° 15' 30"E), a pollen diagram was made which covers approximately the last 50,000 years. A part of this diagram is reproduced in Fig. 5, to show some pollen-types which may be taken as typical of the last part of the Würm Glacial and the beginning of the post-Glacial in Greece. The pollen percentages in this figure refer to a sum which includes all types apart from those of local marsh- and water-plants. The diagram is divided into the following zones:

Zone V shows low percentages of arboreal pollen, mainly of *Pinus* and *Quercus*, but relatively high values for *Artemisia* and Chenopodiaceae.

Zone W starts with an increase in the values of arboreal pollen, mainly caused by *Pinus*. This zone is subdivided into three subzones on the basis of the AP/NAP (arboreal/nonarboreal pollen) ratio. During subzone W 1, *Pinus* pollen shows relatively high values, whereas during subzone W 2 AP values decrease considerably. At the same time, Chenopod pollen becomes dominant over all other types, whereas *Artemisia* decreases. The third subzone, W 3, shows increasing percentages of tree pollen, whereas Chenopods decrease rapidly. At the close of this subzone, *Pinus* shows a clear decrease, while the type of *Quercus robur* (deciduous oak) now becomes important. This leads to the establishment of the next zone, X, which is characterized by high AP values, including, among others, *Pistacia*: this same zone is also defined by high values of *Sanguisorba minor*-type.

The Reconstruction of the Vegetation

During zone V the pollen spectra reflect a steppe vegetation, and *Artemisia*, Chenopods and other herbs must have covered the area. Trees would have been scarce or completely absent in the neighbourhood and restricted to the mountains, quite probably to the higher levels of the Pindus. The climate must have been cold and dry. For the level between 370 and 380 cm a radiocarbon date of $21,390 \pm 430$ B.P. was obtained.

At the beginning of zone W, the percentages of *Pinus* pollen increase, while Chenopodiaceae also become more important. Values of oak pollen remain constant, so one may conclude that the change in conditions which favoured trees was most marked at higher elevations. This observation points to a rise in temperature, which at lower elevations would not have favoured tree growth, as drought would there have been the limiting factor for trees as against steppe. An increase in Chenopod pollen may have been caused by a proliferation of members of the Goose-foot family in a steppe vegetation but these plants also may have grown on the shore of Lake Xinias during summer drought (Wasylikowa, 1967). At higher elevations where moisture was not the limiting factor, a slight increase in temperature possibly enabled the conifers to expand a little.

During the next subzone, W 2, conditions seem to have been very unsuitable for tree-growth. In the Xinias area there would have been few trees if any, and only steppe vegetation. A decrease in the percentages of *Artemisia* pollen suggests that the share of this genus was much smaller than in the previous subzone. At the same time, Chenopodiaceae show very high pollen values, for the reasons explained above.

During subzone W 3, conditions which inhibited the growth of trees were less extreme: at lower and middle elevations open vegetation prevailed, as indicated by the high percentages of herb pollen, but at higher elevations some conifer stands were formed.

The first important increase in this area in the percentages of tree pollen is dated by radiocarbon to $10,680 \pm 90$B.P. The climate at that time evidently changed quite suddenly in favour of forest. Oaks increased rapidly in numbers, the role of conifers became restricted, and steppe-plants mostly disappeared. New plants, including *Pistacia* and *Sanguisorba minor* or *Poterium spinosum* (both Rosaceae have an identical type of pollen) became important during zone X. These plants played a role during the development of post-Glacial vegetation not only in Greece (Bottema, 1974), but also in the Near East (Niklewski and van Zeist, 1970; van Zeist, 1967).

Other Late Glacial Diagram Sections

Lake Garda

The shape of the pollen curves in the diagrams from the area of Lake Garda (Grüger, 1968), which is situated more or less in between the two main regions here compared, still shows affinities with that of those from north-west Europe. Table II shows the successive stages in the vegetation for three zones of elevation.

Table II

	Saltarino 194 m	Fiavè 654 m	Bondone 1.550 m
III	open mixed-oak forest	open birch-pine larch forest	above upper forest line
II	mixed-oak forest birch-pine forest	pine forest	upper forest line
Ic	open forest	open forest	steppe

In this part of Italy Period III was not only colder than II, but also drier, as steppe plants (*Artemisia*) then again became more dominant. According to Grüger, there was a sharp contrast of climate between the southern foothills of the Alps and the edge of these mountains, and it is reasonable to suppose that such differences of climate were altitudinal as well as latitudinal.

Lake Vico

With reference to west-central Italy, a diagram (Fig. 2) is provided by Frank (1969). The lower spectra (zones I . . . III) are dominated by types of nonarboreal pollen, especially *Artemisia* and Chenopodiaceae. Frank ascribes the first and sudden increase of AP percentages to the Late Glacial, but since the values which are then established for the various trees are just as high as those of the Lower post-Glacial, the contrast is too great for a transition from Full Glacial to Late Glacial: and for that reason I have attributed these earliest high AP values to the post-Glacial.

Thus, in my opinion, steppe vegetation was found around Lake Vico during the Late Glacial. Such an interpretation is supported by pollen diagrams and radiocarbon dates from the Greek sites of Ioannina, Edessa,

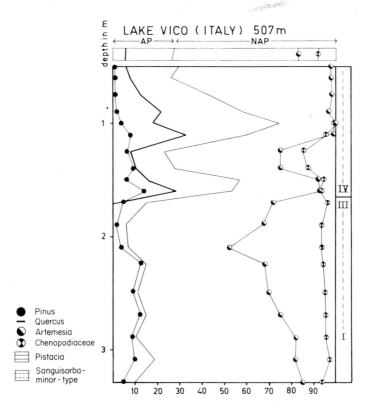

Fig. 2: Simplified diagram of Lake Vico (after Frank). The Key is the same for Figs 2–8.

and Khimaditis (Bottema, 1974), and by the new information from Xinias which has been presented here.

Slovenia

In Slovenia, Sercelj's investigations at Ljubljanska Barje (1966) and Pokljuka, Kostanjevica and Trstenik (1971), correspond more with the north-west European sequence than with the Greek.

In the diagram from Trstenik I (Fig. 3) which is presented here, the pollen percentages are recalculated on the basis of a pollen sum which includes the pollen of trees, *Artemisia*, Chenopodiaceae, and Gramineae, in order to make the values comparable with those of the other diagrams. As in the other Slovenian diagrams, a division into Late Glacial periods I, II and III is proposed by Sercelj, but radiocarbon dates are needed to confirm

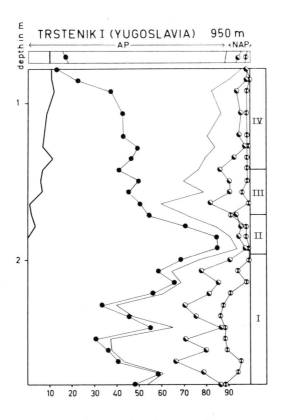

Fig. 3: Simplified diagram of Trstenik (after Sercelj).

this division. Periods I and III were dominated by steppe vegetation, while pine forest was present somewhere in the region. During period II (the Alleröd) pine forest was dominant. Oaks started to spread during the Younger Dryas, while at the same time an increase in *Artemisia*, indicating rather dry conditions, is found, just as in Saltarino (Table II).

Greece

The situation in Greece is somewhat different from that described for the previous sites. During the Würm Glacial steppe vegetation was found in Greece, with scattered trees on favourable locations at higher elevations. Towards the end of the Glacial conifers expanded on the slopes of the Pindus, as can be concluded from the Ioannina and Xinias diagrams (Figs 4 and 5). The first and the last part of zone W, which can be regarded as

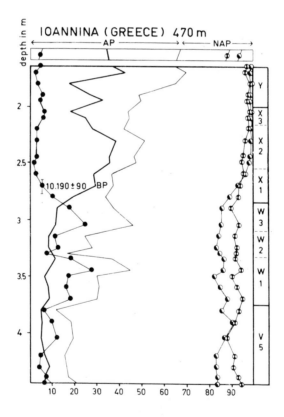

Fig. 4: Simplified diagram of Ioannina.

identical with the Late Glacial periods I and III, show an increase in percentages of *Pinus* pollen, whereas the middle part (subzone W 2, which could have been contemporaneous with the Alleröd) shows a decrease. This decline of forest must have been effected by a rise in temperature in a rather dry period, conditions unsuitable for tree growth.

On the border of Greek Macedonia and Thrace in Tenagi Philippon (Wijmstra, 1969) (Fig. 6; Table I), at 40 m above sea-level, NAP values during the Full Glacial are higher than in the other Greek diagrams, doubtless because tree-stands at elevations of 500 to 800 m in the mountains would have been more distant from Tenagi Philippon than from the other Greek sites included in this chapter. The first increase of trees must have taken place at these higher elevations, and it was not until a further improvement of the climate that trees expanded to lower levels. It is for this reason that I draw the boundary of the Late Glacial and the post-

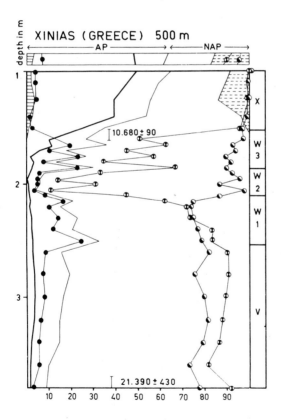

Fig. 5: Simplified diagram of Lake Xinias.

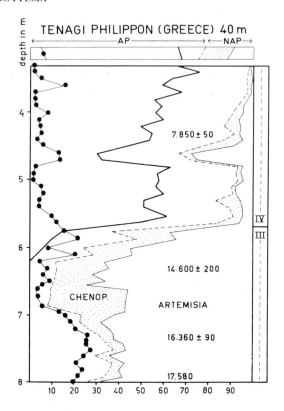

Fig. 6: Simplified diagram of Tenagi Philippon (after Wijmstra).

Glacial at about 5·80 m instead of at 4·50 as Wijmstra did. In the Tenagi diagram an increase in *Pinus* percentages is only visible in a few spectra towards the end of period III.

The Near East

From the Near East not much information is available. Leroi-Gourhan's study (1973) on Syrian and Lebanese material does not provide many details on the Late Glacial in that area.

From north-west Syria a diagram (Fig. 7) has been published by Niklewski and van Zeist (1970). On the west side of the Ghab Valley, where the core was taken, forest would be the natural vegetation at the present time, whereas steppe forest would be found on the east side.

As (from the evidence of the diagrams) did Xinias and Lake Vico, the

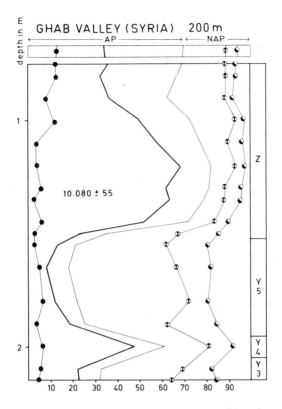

Fig. 7: Simplified diagram of the Ghab Valley (after Niklewski and van Zeist).

Ghab too at the end of the Würm Glacial experienced conditions more extreme than ever before during the last Glacial. The increase of AP percentages (zone Z) was given an estimated date of about 11,400 B.P. by Niklewski and van Zeist. If AP values had increased already during the Late Glacial (they did so at least some time before 10,080 B.P.), then no signs are visible of a deterioration of climate in the Younger Dryas.

Finally, the most easterly information comes from Lake Zeribar in western Iran. Here the investigations by van Zeist (1967) reveal that values for tree pollen were very low not only during the Glacial period but also during a large part of the post-Glacial (Fig. 8). Values for *Artemisia* decrease at about 13,650 B.P. and Chenopodiaceae become the most important type. The course of both types of herb pollen is closely similar to that in the Xinias diagram. Towards the end of the Late Glacial only a very slight increase in AP values can be observed, and it was not until about 5500 B.P. that tree-pollen reached its post-Glacial maximum.

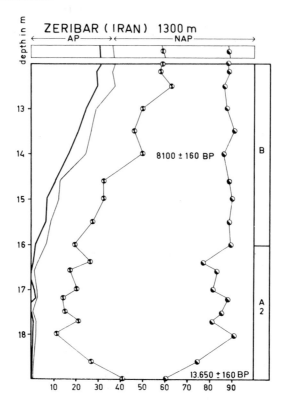

Fig. 8: Simplified diagram of Lake Zeribar (after van Zeist).

Discussion

It is the object of this chapter to compare the development of vegetation in the Late Glacial period in north-west Europe with that in the Mediterranean Basin and the adjacent area to the east.

The Late Glacial history of vegetation directly south of the Alps and in north-western Yugoslavia still seems to be comparable to that in the same period north of the Alps. The climatic changes obviously favoured an extension of forest. The limiting factor for the growth of trees was probably the temperature, although an increase in *Artemisia* during the Younger Dryas indicates that precipitation also played a part.

Nearer the Mediterranean, central Italy and the mainland of Greece seem to have suffered from a shortage of precipitation, for there the increase of forest either did not occur or was of limited extent. As at present, average temperatures must have been higher than in the north, where forest did develop, and this makes it clear that precipitation was the main limiting factor. The increase of coniferous forest in Greece during the first part of the Late Glacial must be ascribed to the rise in temperature mentioned above. This amelioration would have favoured only species of montane forest, as oaks show no increase. It is true that oaks need less moisture than pine, but at lower levels an increase in temperature caused even more dryness, while at higher elevations it was too cold for oaks. During the second period, possibly the Alleröd, even pines decreased, or moved to higher elevations, as conditions became too dry for them. The situation was in fact the reverse of that of north-west Europe, where the Alleröd was more suitable for the growth of trees than the two Dryas periods.

In the Younger Dryas, coniferous forest expanded again, while the conditions for deciduous oaks, growing at lower elevations, became more favourable, and formed the starting-point for the dominant oak-forests in the first part of the post-Glacial in Greece.

Over most of the Near East, the small total of rainfall and its uneven distribution during the year are responsible for a summer drought even more pronounced than in the Mediterranean. On lower levels this results at present in steppe or desert vegetations, whereas forest or savanna occur only in the mountains. On the slopes bordering the Ghab Valley, trees, especially oaks, had already reached an optimum at 10,080 B.P., after a marked increase that may have started already during the Younger Dryas. The earlier part of the Late Glacial must have had a climate more unsuitable for the growth of trees than any time during the Würm Glacial. As already mentioned, this is in sharp contrast with what happened during the Older Dryas and the Alleröd in western Europe.

In north-west Iran the influence of a possible Late Glacial change of climate cannot be observed in the behaviour of tree pollen, but the decrease of values for *Artemisia* and the parallel increase of Chenopodiaceae point to a change in conditions. Precipitation must have been the limiting factor for tree growth, while increasing temperatures did more harm than good to such vegetation. Whereas the present lower limit of forest theoretically stands at sea-level in all the other sites, oak forest in the Zagros Mountains only grows above 800 m. The conditions at the beginning of the post-Glacial were so bad that the expansion of such oak forest reached an optimum only at about 5500 B.P. It is clear that in this case we need not expect a palynological picture comparable with its counterpart in Europe during Late Glacial times.

Acknowledgements

I am much indebted to Professor W. van Zeist for his many discussions on the subject and to Dr J. J. Butler for his corrections and improvement of the English. The drawings have been prepared by Mr J. M. Smit.

References

Bottema, S. 1974. Late Quaternary vegetation history of northwestern Greece. Thesis, Groningen.

Frank, A. H. E. 1969. Pollen stratigraphy of the Lake of Vico (Central Italy). *Palaeogeog. Palaeoclimatol. Palaeoecol.* **6**, 67–85.

Grüger, J. 1968. Untersuchungen zur spätglazialen und frühpostglazialen Vegetationsentwicklung der Südalpen in Umkreis des Gardasees. *Bot. Jb.* **88**–2, 163–199.

Leroi-Gourhan, A. 1973. Les possibilités de l'analyse pollinique en Syrie et au Liban. *Paléorient.* **1**, 39–47.

Niklewski, J. and van Zeist, W. 1970. A late Quaternary pollen diagram from northwestern Syria. *Acta Bot. Neerl.* **19**(5), 737–754.

Sercelj, A. 1966. Pelodne analize Pleistocenskih in Holocenskih sedimentov Ljubljanskega Barja (Pollenanalytische Untersuchungen der pleistozänen und holozänen Ablagerungen von Ljubljansko Barje). *Razpr. 4.r. Slov. akad. znan. umetn.* **9**, 431–472.

Sercelj, A. 1971. Postglazialni razvoj gorskih gozdov v severozahodni Jugoslaviji (Die postglaziale Entwicklung der Gebirgswälder im nordwestlichen Jugoslawien). *Razpr. 4. r. Slov. akad. znan. umetn.* **9**, 267–293.

Wasylikowa, K. 1967. Late Quaternary plant macrofossils from Lake Zeribar, western Iran. *Rev. Palaeobotan. Palynol.* **2**, 313–318.

Wijmstra, T. A. 1969. Palynology of the first 30 meters of a 120 meter deep section in northern Greece. *Acta Bot. Neerl.* **18**(4), 511–528.

van Zeist, W. 1967. Late Quaternary vegetation history of western Iran. *Rev. Palaeobotan. Palynol.* **2**, 301–311.

3
Early Domestication and the Ungulate Fauna of the Levant during the Prepottery Neolithic Period

Juliet Clutton-Brock

Topography

South-western Asia is a region that has a large number of contrasting environments in a limited geographical area. There are great altitudinal differences and local changes in climate that are unmatched in their extremes. Combined with these varied environments the Levant has been a junction for biological invasions from tropical Africa, the Mediterranean, the Middle Eastern alpine zone, and from eastern Asia. The broad area that will be considered in this chapter includes southern Turkey and extends southwards to Sinai and Arabia. In the north it is bounded by the mountains of Kurdistan and in the east by the Zagros Mountains of Iran. Within this region there are four main environmental zones, these being the coastal wooded Mediterranean strip, the Jordan rift valley, the arid steppe zone, and the high mountain and plateau areas.

Fauna

Elements

The tropical element in the conglomerate fauna that inhabits the Middle East and the Levant is the most ancient and it is represented today by a relatively few relict species. Whatever order of animals is studied it is found that the assemblage consists of a small number of tropical forms mingled with larger numbers of species that belong to the Mediterranean and Asiatic subregions of the Palaearctic. This has been shown for the history of the rodents in Palestine since the Upper Pleistocene by Tchernov (1968) and for the reptiles by Haas (1952). The same composition holds for the large mammal fauna.

Shifts

Since the middle of the Pleistocene period there has been an overall decline and withdrawal of the tropical fauna towards the Ethiopian region whilst those species that remained became ecologically separated from those of North Africa, and new endemic species and genera evolved (Tchernov, 1968). Concurrently, and particularly during the Late Pleistocene at periods of glacial maxima, the Mediterranean fauna was forced southwards into Africa and eastwards into the Levant, Sinai, and Arabia. To complicate the situation further it is possible that the higher precipitation that occurred at intervals during the glacial phases had the contradictory effect of temporarily preserving the tropical elements in the fauna of the Levant by producing a warm damp environment.

The Aceramic Neolithic Culture

Date

Any examination of the changes in the zoogeography that have occurred since the end of the Pleistocene has to be undertaken in the context of this intermixing of the climatic and biotic zones. At first, man was only one element in this juxtaposition of ecosystems but his extending influence over the fauna and flora gradually made an impact that had an irreversible effect on the environment of the Middle East. This impact first becomes discernible at the crucial period when man changed from a semi-wandering way of life to that of settled village communities with cultivated plants and controlled livestock. This is the period that has been described by Flannery (1969) as that of "early dry farming and caprine domestication"; it lasted from approximately 8000 B.C. to 5500 B.C. The villagers built houses of mud brick and on some sites they used a hard lime plaster on their floors and as lining for their storage pits and roasting ovens but they made no pottery. The period is therefore known as the prepottery or aceramic Neolithic.

Distribution

Figure 1 shows the localities of the principal sites of this period that have provided data for the present work. The probable environments of these sites at approximately 7000 B.C. are summarized below:

Southern Turkey Hacılar, Aşıklı Hüyük, and Can Hasan III (Payne, 1972). Alluvial plains close to rivers or intermontane lakes that would have supplied perennial water. Mediterranean wooded country.

Çayönü (Braidwood et al., 1974). An early village-farming site in south-east Turkey.

Çatal Hüyük (Perkins, 1969). Deciduous mixed forests bordering on desert grasslands. (Butzer, 1972, Fig. 89.)

Suberde (Perkins and Daly, 1968). The Konya Plain, 914 m (3000 ft) above sea-level.

Levant Nahal Oren (or Wadi-Fallah. Ducos, 1968; Legge, 1972) and Munhatta 3–6 (Ducos, 1968). These sites are in the Mediterranean zone with subtropical woodlands.

Jericho (Clutton-Brock, 1969; 1971) and Beidha (Perkins, 1966). The semi-arid Jordan rift valley with grasslands and semi-desert but with perennial water supplies.

Kurdistan Jarmo (Braidwood and Howe, 1960; Reed, 1959). Grasslands bordering on subtropical woodlands in hill country in north-eastern Iraq. There was probably a perennial water supply from a stream which is drier at the present day.

Iran The Bus Mordeh and Ali Kosh phases of the Deh Luran complex (Flannery, 1969; Hole et al., 1969). Like Jarmo, the site of Ali Kosh is in desert grassland country on the edge of subtropical woodlands. It is situated at the foothills of the Zagros Mountains and as today would have been subjected to long hot summers and warm wet winters.

Economy

Descriptions of the faunal remains from these sites have been published and will not be repeated in detail here. Nor will the controversial topic of speciation within the genus Gazella be discussed (see Clutton-Brock, 1971; Groves and Harrison, 1967; Harrison, 1968; Lange, 1972). I should like, however, to make some general comments on the probable composition of the large mammal fauna of the region in the early prepottery Neolithic period and on the dramatic change that took place in the faunal remains from archaeological sites once domestication was established, and wild prey were exchanged for domestic livestock.

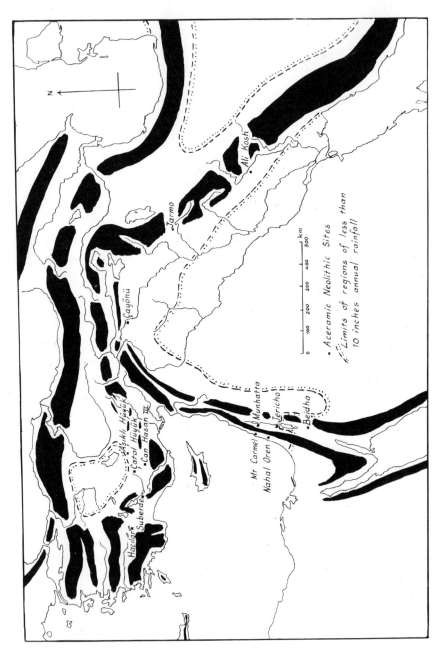

Fig. 1: Map of Western Asia to show the localities of the archaeological sites mentioned in the text.

Food Storage

Many theories have been put forward to explain the fundamental change from wandering hunter to settled farmer; a change that has occurred in different parts of the world at varying times from 10,000 years ago to the present day. As stated by Flannery (1969, p. 75) it is unlikely that the mobile hunters of the Middle East altered their way of life during the immediate post-Pleistocene period for the reason that they were unable to obtain enough food for survival. It seems more likely that an expanding human population found that it could extend its habitat from the optimal areas by storing food that could be eaten during hard times. The long dry summers of the Levant meant that the inhabitants could not subsist off the land the whole year round except in the wooded coastal zone which had a relatively high rainfall. The storage of grain transported from its natural habitat and artificially grown near a perennial supply of water such as a spring, and the storage of meat by means of tethered animals would greatly widen the limits of marginal habitats even in a climate which was increasing in dryness. This theory was first put forward in a discussion on the origin of domestic cereals by Harlan and Zohary (1966). The discovery of storage pits at several Natufian and later sites supports the theory that the practice of food storage was inherent in the beginnings of domestication.

Neglect of Desert Species

None of the sites listed above had a truly desert environment and in reviewing the species of wild animals that were exploited by the hunters of the early Holocene in the Levant it is noteworthy that so few are of tropical or desert origin. Amongst the ungulates the species whose bones might be expected are:

Equus asinus, African wild ass
Camelus sp.
The desert antelopes, *Oryx leucoryx*, *Addax nasomaculatus* and *Alcelaphus buselaphus*
Ammotragus lervia, the Barbary sheep
Hemitragus jayakari, the Arabian tahr (see Harrison, 1968).
In fact, only *Alcelaphus buselaphus*—and possibly *Equus asinus*—have been identified from prepottery Neolithic and later sites outside Africa. The possible implications of this observation are, first that the species listed above were already rare and localized in their distribution in the Levant despite the possibility that the climate may have been drier in the steppe

desert than it is today (van Zeist, 1969, p. 43); or, second, that the hunters were familiar with a number of mammals that were "preferred game" and that they did not kill any others; or, thirdly and most likely that the people had no need to penetrate into the desert areas on their hunting expeditions because of the abundance of game close by.

The hartebeest, *Alcelaphus buselaphus* is, of all the desert antelopes the least well adapted to an arid environment. It has been recorded from a number of post-Pleistocene sites and was identified from the Bronze Age site of Tel Gat by Ducos (1968, p. 49). It is now restricted to Africa south of the Sahara.

Species of Equid

The position of *Equus asinus* in the Levant is anomolous and the possibility of its presence there as an indigenous, wild species was not recognized until the last few years. Zeuner (1963, p. 368) believed that the domestic ass, throughout the Near East in prehistoric times, was derived from the onager, or Asiatic wild ass, *Equus hemionus*, and this theory was generally adhered to until the recent reports of Ducos (1968, 1970, 1975) suggested that it could be incorrect.

It now appears that *E. hemionus* may never have been domesticated and the equid remains from early sites in the prehistoric levant could be from wild *E. asinus*, whilst those from Bronze Age and later sites are from domesticated donkeys, perhaps also of local origin. Careful examination of the pictorial evidence from friezes and figurines in western Asia, of the first and second millennia B.C., shows that the domesticated equids, other than the true horses, are as likely to be asses and mules as onagers (the mule being either a hybrid between the ass and the onager, or the ass and the horse).

The true horse, *Equus caballus*, was present in the upper Pleistocene levels of Mount Carmel (Bate, 1937, p. 218) but it has not been recorded again with certainty in western Asia until the Bronze Age, by which time it may be assumed to be a domestic introduction. Other equids that have been identified from the Near East are *Equus hydruntinus*, a small species possibly more closely related to the zebras than to the asses, which became extinct in the early Holocene, and the Syrian onager, *Equus hemionus hemippus*. This is the smallest and most westerly subspecies of onager and it too is now extinct. The five subspecies of onager are Asiatic in origin and form a geographical cline that ranged from the Levant to Tibet, with the largest subspecies in the east. Bate (1937) recorded the remains of *E. hemionus* from all levels of the Wadi el-

Mughara caves at Mount Carmel in Palestine, but this animal was considerably larger than the equid remains that are found in post-Pleistocene levels; it approached the size of *E. hemionus kiang* Moorcraft, 1841, the Tibetan onager which is the largest of the hemione asses. A very small equid from Tabun C and B and from Skhul was identified as *Equus hydruntinus* Regalia by Bate (1937). This identification seems to be correct; certainly the tooth characters are very different from those of the *E. asinus* from the prepottery Neolithic and later periods, in that the external sulcus in the lower molars penetrates the metaconid and metastylid. This feature is not found in *E. asinus* or *E. hemionus*.

Ducos (1974) states that the main area where *E. asinus* was living in the early Holocene was the steppe plains of northern and western Syria; this evidence being based on the relative abundance of finds from sites in this area. He asserts that the wild ass constituted an endemic subspecies rather than an immigrant race from the Ethiopian region. I, however, subscribe to the latter view and can only see this ass as part of the relict tropical fauna, which like *Alcelaphus buselaphus* may have been extinct in the Levant by the end of the Bronze Age.

Apart from *Equus asinus* all the species of large mammal that were hunted and domesticated by man in the Levant were of Mediterranean or Asiatic origin.

Hunting of Ungulates

A characteristic of the early phases of the prepottery Neolithic, for example Bus Mordeh from Ali Kosh and the prepottery A levels at Jericho, is a broad-based hunting economy that relied on a large number of food resources. Within each area of the region described here, however, a different game animal provided a high proportion of the meat. In southern Turkey the majority of the animal remains from Çayönü and Çatal Hüyük came from cattle (in the earliest levels wild *Bos primigenius* and in the later, domesticated ox), red deer, sheep and goat. In the Levant the greatest number of animal remains came from gazelle with fox also an important source of meat. At Jarmo and in the Deh Luran sites the people hunted mainly wild sheep and goat, but also gazelle, fox, aurochs, and pig. Beidha is the only site from which the Nubian ibex (*Capra ibex nubiana*) has been identified.

Gazelle

Both Zeuner (1955) and Legge (1972) believed that the gazelle may have been at least herded if not domesticated by man in the Levant during the eighth millennium B.C. Hole *et al.* (1969) have suggested that at Ali Kosh the abundant wild gazelle may have been hunted along known gazelle trails, and I would rather believe that this was the case than that these animals were subject to any direct control by man, for I am sure that the clues to the history of domestication must be looked for in the behaviour patterns of the potential domesticates. All species of gazelle are likely to be strongly territorial in their behaviour and therefore unlikely to breed successfully in large numbers when constrained. Flocks of sheep and goat, on the other hand, are based on hierarchical systems but are not markedly territorial (Geist, 1971; Jewell *et al.*, 1974).

Shifts to Domestication of Caprines

A small community of people living in a hot dry country with a restricted supply of water around which a few precious crops were planted would soon lose their harvest if a herd of gazelle were encouraged to graze nearby. But a few sheep and goats could be tethered and thereby act as a store of meat and a breeding stock without destruction of the growing crops. This is a new side to Zeuner's theory of "crop robbers" (1963, p. 199) as potential domesticates. Zeuner believed that goats and sheep were domesticated before the cultivation of cereals and that it was wild cattle and pigs that were the raiders of cultivated crops. It is now believed that plants were cultivated in western Asia during the early post-Pleistocene before the domestication of any of the herd animals. I therefore see the dramatic exchange between gazelle bones in the prepottery Neolithic A levels at Jericho and those of goat/sheep in the prepottery Neolithic B (Fig. 2) as the response of a settled community to an economy that was becoming dependent on the harvesting of cultivated cereals rather than on the gathering of wild plants. Controlled livestock would be as essential to the arable farmer in 7000 B.C. as at the present day. Despite evidence quoted by Legge (1972) for the stalling of gazelles by the Ancient Egyptians, I think it is unlikely that tethered gazelle could be as easily managed or would mate and breed as freely as goat and sheep.

Conditions of Dry Farming

Van Zeist (1969, p. 44) has claimed that the climate would have been too dry (with an annual precipitation of 140 mm) in the prepottery Neolithic A at Jericho to allow the cultivation of the barley, wheat, and pulses that have been found there, and that this grain must have been imported. Kenyon, on the other hand, (1970, p. 45) maintains that almost 4·5 Ha (10

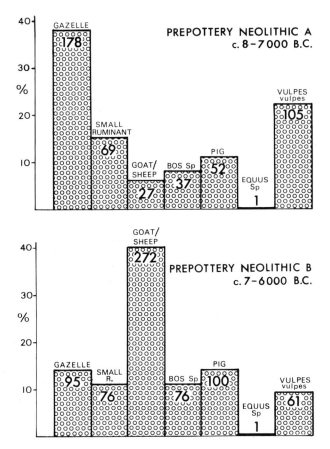

Fig. 2: Percentages and absolute numbers of the remains of the main food animals from the prepottery Neolithic levels of the Jericho Tell. The category "small ruminant" contains the numbers of fragments of bone that could not be identified closer than this. The numbers are only provisional as the final work on the material is not yet complete.

acres) of land were occupied by about 2000 people as early as 8000 B.C. and that these farmers must have had an irrigation system to water their crops. This theory makes much more sense to me and I do not see why, in the so-called period of "dry-farming" the people could not have used simple systems of irrigation, for it has been shown for all the sites involved that there was a perennial water-supply in the vicinity.

The theory of "the birth of civilization in the Fertile Crescent" has perhaps led to a misunderstanding of the environmental conditions in western Asia that caused man to change from a hunter-gatherer to a settled farmer. It is most probable that small populations of humans were widely established in many parts of the world in the early Holocene but that, because they were living in groups that were well adapted to their environment and to their food resources, they have left little to mark their presence in the archaeological record. In the semi-arid zone of western Asia the balance between the widely differing faunal elements was tenuous and easily became unstable. The climate was harsh for a large part of the year and food was often scarce. The migrant human populations found that marginal habitats could be exploited as long as there was a perennial supply of water. The early farmers at Jericho and Beidha, for example, surely learned very early that water could be used to cultivate cereal crops, the seeds of which were brought from the hilly regions of the north where there was a higher rainfall.

The remains of sheep and goats that have been identified from the early levels of the prepottery Neolithic may also have been imported as the first domesticated animals or they may have been present in small numbers as wild indigenous flocks. Both sheep and goat have been identified from the prepottery Neolithic A of Jericho but there is no osteological evidence to suggest that the bones are from domesticated animals (Clutton-Brock and Uerpmann, 1974). By the prepottery Neolithic B levels at Jericho, however, there is more certain evidence for domestic goat, as there is for caprines at all the other sites of this period. At this time the exploitation of gazelle falls off dramatically, and it may be stated that by 7000 B.C. the primary method of subsistence of the village farmers in the Levant, southern Turkey, and as far east as the Zagros Mountains had become so specialized as to be dependent on cultivated einkorn and emmer wheat, barley, sheep and goats. It need not be stressed how successful this dependence has become.

References

Bate, D. M. A. 1937. *In: The Stone Age of Mount Carmel* I. Part II *Palaeontology: The fossil fauna of the Wady el-Mughara Caves.* (D. A. E. Garrod and D. M. A. Bate eds), pp. 139–240. Oxford: Clarendon Press.

Braidwood, R. J. and Howe, B. 1960. Prehistoric investigations in Iraqi Kurdistan. *Stud. Anc. Orient. Civil.* **31**.

Braidwood, R. J., Cambel, H., Lawrence, B., Redman, C. L. and Steward, R. B. 1974. Beginnings of village-farming communities in southeastern Turkey—1972. *Proc. Nat. Acad. Sci. USA.* **71**, 568–572.

Clutton-Brock, J. 1969. Carnivore remains from the excavations of the Jericho

Tell. In: the Domestication and Exploitation of Plants and Animals (P. J. Ucko and G. W. Dimbleby, eds), pp. 337–345. London: Duckworth.

Clutton-Brock, J. 1971. The primary food animals of the Jericho Tell from the Proto-Neolithic to the Byzantine period. Levant III, 41–55.

Clutton-Brock, J. and Uerpmann, H.-P. 1974. The sheep of early Jericho. J. Arch. Science, I. No. 4, 261–274.

Ducos, P. 1968. L'Origine des Animaux Domestiques en Palestine. Publ. de l'Inst. Prehist. de l'Univ. de Bordeaux. Mém. No. 6.

Ducos, P. 1970. The Oriental Institute excavations at Mureybit, Syria: preliminary report on the 1965 campaign. Part IV: Les restes d'Equidés. J. Near Eastern Stud. 29, 273–289.

Ducos, P. 1975. A new find of an equid metatarsal bone from Tel Mureibet in Syria and its relevance to the identification of equids from the early Holocene of the Levant. J. Arch. Science, 2, No. 1, 71–73.

Flannery, K. V. 1969. Origins and ecological effects of early domestication in Iran and the Near East. In: The Domestication and Exploitation of Plants and Animals. (P. J. Ucko and G. W. Dimbleby, eds), pp. 73–100. London: Duckworth.

Geist, V. 1971. Mountain Sheep: A Study in Behaviour and Evolution. Chicago: University Press.

Groves, C. P. and Harrison, D. L. 1967. The taxonomy of the gazelles (genus Gazella) of Arabia. J. Zool. Lond. 152, 381–387.

Haas, G. 1952. Remarks on the origin of the herpeto-fauna of Palestine, Rev. Fac. Sci. Univ. Istanbul. 17, B. (2), 95–105.

Harlan, J. R. and Zohary, D. 1966. Distribution of wild wheats and barley. Science 153, No. 3740, 1074–1080.

Harrison, D. L. 1968. The Mammals of Arabia. Vol. II. London: Benn.

Hole, F., Flannery, K. V. and Neely, J. A. 1969. Prehistory and human ecology of the Deh Luran Plain. Mem. Mus. Anthrop. Univ. Michigan, Ann Arbor, Vol. I.

Jewell, P. A., Milner, C. and Boyd, J. M. (eds), 1974. Island Survivors, the Ecology of the Soay Sheep of St Kilda. London: Athlone Press.

Kenyon, K. M. 1970. Archaeology in the Holy Land. London: Benn.

Lange, J. von. 1972. Studien an gazellenschädeln. Ein beitrag zur systematik der kleineren gazellen, Gazella (de Blainville. 1816). Sauget. Mitt. Munchen, 20, 193–249.

Legge, A. J. 1972. Prehistoric exploitation of the gazelle in Palestine. In: Papers in Economic Prehistory (E. S. Higgs, ed.), pp. 119–124. Cambridge: University Press.

Payne, S. 1972. Can Hasan III, the Anatolian aceramic, and the Greek Neolithic. In: Papers in Economic Prehistory (E. S. Higgs, ed.), pp. 191–194. Cambridge: University Press.

Perkins, D. 1966. The fauna from Madamagh and Beidha. In: Five seasons at the pre-pottery Neolithic village of Beidha in Jordan (D. Kirkbride), Palestine Exploration Quarterly 98, 56–67.

Perkins, D. 1969. Fauna of Çatal Hüyük: evidence for early cattle domestication in Anatolia. *Science* **164**, 177–179.

Perkins, D. and Daly, P. 1968. A hunters' village in Neolithic Turkey. *Scient. Am.* **219**, 97–106.

Reed, C. A. 1959. Animal domestication in the prehistoric Near East. *Science* **130**, 1629–1639.

Tchernov, E. 1968. Succession of rodent faunas during the Upper Pleistocene of Israel. *Mammalia Depicta* Hamburg: Paul Parey.

van Zeist, W. 1969. Reflections on prehistoric environments in the Near East. *In: The Domestication and Exploitation of Plants and Animals* (P. J. Ucko and G. W. Dimbleby, eds), pp. 35–46. London: Duckworth.

Zeuner, F. E. 1955. The goats of early Jericho. *Palestine Exploration Quarterly* April, 70–85.

Zeuner, F. E. 1963. *A History of Domesticated Animals*. London: Hutchinson.

4
Environmental Changes in Northern Greece

Eric Higgs †

Vegetational Changes

The best evidence for vegetational change comes from a pollen core from Tenagi Philippon (*c.* 50 m O.D.) east of Saloniki and near to Kavallia (Wijmstra, 1969; Van der Hammen *et al.*, 1971). The lowest part of the core, which is believed to be of Rissian age, shows a high proportion of steppe plants. It is followed by interglacial deposits, characterized at first by pistacio and *Quercus ilex* pollen: later, deciduous oaks are dominant: but towards the end of the period there is a decrease in oak and an increase in pine.

The last glaciation begins with a rapid increase of open vegetation; there are three forest interstadials and reversions to steppe conditions in the stadials. These interstadials are believed to be contemporaneous with the more northerly European Amersfoot (Doxaton), Brørup (Drama) and Odderade (Elevtheroupolis) interstadials.

About 60,000 years ago there begins a vegetation with steppe elements dominant and trees almost absent. This is considered to be an extension of the cool-to-cold steppe zone of Central Asia (Van der Hammen *et al.*, 1971). Steppe conditions continue, but with interruptions by a number of interstadials which are believed to be contemporaneous with similar phenomena observed either in France or Holland. They have been named as follows: Philippi (Lascaux), Photolivos (Tursac), Krinides II and Krinides I (Denecamp), Kalabaki II and Kalabaki I (Hengelo), Heraklitsa II and Heraklitsa I (Moershoofd).

At the beginning of the Late Glacial period, oak increases and the steppe plants decrease; but at its end there is a marked rise in herbaceous pollen, which is thought to have been contemporaneous with the Younger Dryas. This phase is followed by the Xanthi interstadial, which has been

†Deceased.

correlated with both the Allerød and Bølling oscillations. Thereafter, about 10,000 years ago, the post-Glacial forest begins (Fig. 6, p. 24).

The Ioannina pollen cores (Bottema, 1967, 1974), although taken from sites at 470 m O.D. and only about 300 km and one degree of latitude away from Tenagi Philippon, show only a fair measure of agreement. This may be expected in such areas where today there are great altitudinal and therefore vegetational differences within a few kilometres. Such differences are not likely to have been completely over-ridden by climatic change, as they were in lowland countries nearer to the ice sheet. Further, pollen, which in a uniform topography may be dispersed laterally over short distances, may travel long distances vertically, as at Ioannina where there is an immediately adjacent mountain massif. The two core sites are in very different situations and therefore are not likely to have other than broad similarities (Figs 2 and 4, pp. 22 and 24).

The two diagrams do agree in that there is evidence for a deciduous forest followed by a long steppe interval and then a forested post-Glacial, and Epirus seems to have been a refuge in glacial conditions for a variety of trees. Van der Hammen is of the opinion that in the Balkan Mountains during the Pleniglacial there was a belt of montane forest, probably narrow, with a cool steppe vegetation below and an alpine steppe above. The difficulties of inferring climate from the presence of such widely tolerant plants as *Artemisia* are apparent. There is in the palynological record, however, an observable vegetational change in the Late Glacial around 14,000 years ago when there was an increase of trees and a fall in steppe pollen.

From this evidence it is held that the climate in Greece during the last Glacial was cooler and drier than now, a situation which appears to differ from that in most other areas in the eastern Mediterranean at that time (Farrand, 1971). However, in view of the evidence from lake levels, the former view may need to be modified.

Lake Levels

An excavation of a 10 m square down to 8 m below the surface in the lake deposits at Ioannina has been informative, for some of the lake stratigraphy was directly related by extended excavation to the Kastritsa cave stratigraphy (Higgs *et al.*, 1967). There were seven superimposed beach levels separated by terrestrial deposits. Four of the beaches reached to the cave itself (Fig. 1). The highest beach was 3 m above the present lake level and has the following C^{14} dates,

I 2465   19,900 ± 370   immediately above the beach
I 2468   20,200 ± 480   at the top of the beach
I 2466   20,200 ± 810   in the beach
I 2467   21,800 ± 470   below the beach.

Below the lowest beach there were Upper Palaeolithic artefacts both in the lacustrine and the cave deposits. They cannot have been older than 40,000 years, but were probably older than *c.* 22,000 years. Beyond doubt there was a series of rises in the level of the Ioannina Lake after 40,000 years ago, and the highest level was reached some 20,000 years ago, contemporaneously with the peak of the Last Glacial. Such a change could be due either to a change in inflow or in outflow. There is, however, no

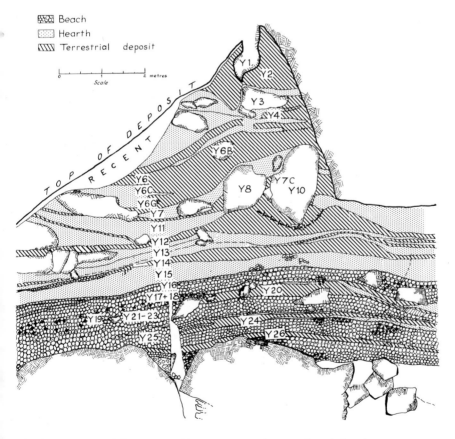

Fig. 1: Section of deposits at Kastritsa cave showing beach levels.

reason to think that a topographical change in this area could have restricted an outlet, and indeed the outlet of Ioannina Lake is believed to be underwater.

The simplest explanation is that during the last Glacial the run-off from the surrounding mountains increased some time before 21,800 B.P., and that this was due to an increase in pluviation. The rainfall, other things being equal, would have been greater than that of today, though the pollen record over this period does not indicate vegetational changes due to rainfall. However, these two observations are not necessarily in conflict; for there could have been an increase (perhaps seasonal) in rainfall, though insufficient to give rise to vegetational changes clear enough to show up in the pollen diagrams.

It is interesting to note that the earliest reference in the historical record to the Ioannina Lake is dated to the twelfth century A.D., and it has therefore been presumed by historical geographers that it did not exist in Classical or Hellenistic times (Hammond, 1967).

Cave Climates

Legge (1972) has shown that during the Last Glacial in Epirus there was probably a marked difference between the cave environments of the hinterland and those of the foothills adjacent to the littoral. Considerable frost-shattering of the cliff-faces was noted at Kastritsa inland, but not in the area of Asprochaliko and Alexopoulos (Higgs et al., 1967; Higgs and Webley, 1971). This contrast may have been due to the different aspects of the rock faces at the two sites: nevertheless, considerable frost-shattering of rocks did take place in Greece, as elsewhere in the eastern Mediterranean, during the Last Glacial. Further scree formation in the Louros gorge has been attributed by Hey (Dakaris et al., 1964) to a phase of the Last Glacial contemporaneous with a similar phase in North Africa. Such phenomena are an indication of the presence of a quantity of moisture during the Last Glacial, but the amount cannot be assessed.

Erosional and Depositional Changes

At least some of the erosion so evident in Greece is of considerable antiquity. Plato in the *Critias* regarded it as a phenomenon of some thousands of years' duration before his time. At Kokkinopilos, the Middle

Palaeolithic sites of *c.* 40,000 years ago were on Red Beds of fluvial origin which had been deposited earlier and which were subsequently covered by further similar sediments which contained Upper Palaeolithic artefacts (Dakaris *et al.*, 1964). Harris and Vita-Finzi (1968) consider that the lithology and form of the Red Bed fans around the Ioannina Lake indicate that at the time of the high lake-level there was heavier frost-shattering and more intense rain, the distribution of which was probably strongly seasonal with summers if anything drier than those of today. Erosion and subsequent deposition, massive and at least up to 50 m in depth in some areas, continued intermittently in the Middle and Upper Palaeolithic periods (Leroi-Gourhan and Chavaillon, 1963). There may have been a period of relative stability in Bronze Age times (Higgs, 1968) and deposition had ceased at Kokkinopilos by Roman times at latest (Harris and Vita-Finzi, 1968).

There has been recorded in Greece and other Mediterranean countries a phase of extensive deposition which occurred in post-Classical times. The plain of Arta was laid down then, and no doubt there was similar coastal deposition elsewhere (Vita-Finzi, 1969). This phenomenon has been attributed to the "Little Ice Age", but it seems probable that a factor which was at least contributory was the increase at that time in the human and domesticated animal populations, consequent indirectly upon village and urban developments.

Fauna

The evidence from the cave sites indicates that a Middle Palaeolithic fauna about 40,000 years ago which included rhinoceros was replaced at least by 24,000 years ago by a more modern fauna. During the Last Glacial, *Equus hydruntinus*, the steppe ass, was common in the upland areas inland and rarer on the coast and coastal foothills. This species has not been recognized in Neolithic faunal assemblages dated to *c.* 8000 years ago (Boessnek, 1962; Rodden, 1962), whence it may be inferred that it was by that time either rare or extinct in Greece. Red deer (*Cervus elaphus*) were the most common animal recorded at cave-sites throughout the glacial periods, and have along with fallow deer persisted in Greece up to the present. There is no evidence of reindeer, and Greece may be considered to have been even in Glacial times beyond the climatic or vegetational range of that animal: in fact the environment of Greece in Glacial times has been compared with that of northern Scotland today.

C

Beaver (*Castor fiber*) has been recognized in the faunal assemblage from the Kastritsa cave and dated to Late Glacial times.

It is evident that by 8000 years ago the domestication of animals had developed in Greece at Argissa Magula (Boessnek, 1962) and Nea Nikomedeia (Rodden, 1962), though how much earlier than that domestication began is not known: some thousands of years before that time, however, cattle in Kastritsa evolved to a smaller size. By the sixth millennium B.C. domesticated cattle were spread over the area from Greece to Anatolia and they were accompanied by domesticated sheep, goats and pigs; but though the domestication of animals and plant-agriculture must have been widely spread in the sixth and fifth millennia B.C., there is no evidence in the pollen spectrum to indicate a consequent vegetational change over the 3000 years until the Bronze Age.

Location of Archaeological Sites

The study of the whereabouts of archaeological sites has indicated that, whatever were the climatic or vegetational changes in Greece in Glacial and post-Glacial times, the environment of the coastal regions remained very different from that of the upland interior, and that climatic changes over this period did not obliterate such differences (Higgs *et al.*, 1967; Higgs and Webley, 1973).

Human Ecology

We now consider the relationship between environmental changes and changes in the human record.

Up to the onset of the Last Glacial, there is evidence that Middle Palaeolithic peoples occupied the coast and the foothills of the mountain ranges, but there is little indication of the exploitation of the interior and the upland regions. There is similar evidence from Germany (Gamble, pers. comm.) and Italy (Barker, 1974).

During the Last Glacial, Upper Palaeolithic peoples exploited both low coastal and high interior areas in a pattern of transhumant exploitation which brought together distant resources at different altitudes. Such mobile economies were necessary, if anything like the full exploitation of available resources was to be achieved. In the long term, the geographic distribution of resources directed the human activities.

The post-Glacial climatic amelioration did not at first greatly affect this situation. By the seventh millennium B.C. crop agriculture had developed, especially in the lowlands where the soil was tillable and retained sufficient moisture; but such lowland areas probably amounted to no more than 10% of the surface area of Greece. In consequence, settlements appeared only sporadically, most of them probably only occupied seasonally, and the palynological record gives no evidence for a consequent disturbance of the environment until thousands of years later, in the Bronze Age. Mobile economies based on pastoralism still followed the migration routes of Palaeolithic times, and although the animals exploited became different, the purpose of the economies, to make use of complementary resources, distant from each other, within efficient economic units, remained the same. The routes of movement, such as those between northern and southern Greece, and between Yugoslavia and Thessaly, can still be traced through the record of the artefacts (*vide* Hammond, 1967; 1972). Such mobile economies, though of steadily decreasing importance, continued to be the dominant style of livelihood in Greece until very recent times, and they can still be seen in the existing Vlach populations whose history goes back to at least the sixth century A.D.

Another important phenomenon which needs explanation is the evident massive and persistent erosion. Throughout the Last Glacial and up to the present day the environment of Greece has been ''brittle''. Any changes in climate or in the biotope were likely to upset a delicate balance. The introduction of the exotic sheep and goat in Neolithic times may have increased erosion and deposition, but capra-ovines were indigenous to the area and we do not know if their numbers were increased by domestication. According to one opinion (Hutchinson, 1969), agriculture was on the whole a force for conservation rather than destruction, certainly before the beginning of urbanism: so it is probable that the human factor in environmental change up to and even since that time has been greatly overestimated.

The erosion of the uplands led to the transportation of sediments down to the coastal regions which were by climate and topography more suited to settlement; and this process was therefore, by contrast with what happened in Bulgaria (Dennell and Webley, 1974), in total and in the long term, probably advantageous. The deposition in mediaeval times of such areas as the Arta plain gave rise to a considerable increase in agricultural potential, which was eventually put to use and is being increasingly exploited through developing technology.

References

Barker, G. W. W. 1974. Prehistoric territories and economies in central Italy. *In: Palaeoeconomy*, (E. S. Higgs, ed.), pp. 111–177. Cambridge: University Press.

Boessnek, J. 1962. Die Tierreste aus der Argissa-Magula vom präkeramischen Neolithicum bis zur Mittleren Bronzezeit. *In:* "Die deutschen Ausgrabungen auf der Argissa-Magula in Thessalien" (V. Milojcić, J. Boessnek and M. Hopf, eds), *Beitr. urgesch. frühgesch. Archäeol. Mittelmeer-Kulturraumes* **2**, 27–99.

Bottema, S. 1967. A Late Quaternary pollen diagram from Ioannina, northwestern Greece. *Proc. Prehist. Soc.* **32**, 26–29.

Bottema, S. 1974. *Late Quaternary Vegetation History of Northwestern Greece.* Groningen.

Dakaris, S. I., Higgs, E. S. and Hey, R. W. 1964. The climate, environment and industries of Stone Age Greece: Part I. *Proc. Prehist. Soc.* **30**, 199–245.

Dennell, K. W. and Webley, D. 1974. Prehistoric settlement and land use in Southern Bulgaria. *In: Palaeoeconomy* (E. S. Higgs, ed.), pp. 97–111. Cambridge: University Press.

Farrand, W. 1971. Late Quaternary Palaeoclimates of the Eastern Mediterranean area. *In: The Late Cenozoic Glacial Ages* (Karl K. Turekian, ed.), pp. 529–564. Yale: University Press.

Hammen, T. van der, Wijmstra, T. and Zagwijn, W. H. 1971. The floral record of the Late Cenozoic of Europe. *In: The Late Cenozoic Glacial Ages* (Karl K. Turekian, ed.), pp. 391–425. Yale: University Press.

Hammen, T. van der, Wijmstra, T. and Molen, W. H. van der. 1965. Palynological study of a very thick peat section in Greece and the Würm Glacial vegetation in the Mediterranean region. *Geologie en Mijnbouw.* N. S. **44**, 37–40.

Hammond, N. G. L. 1967. *Epirus.* Oxford: University Press.

Hammond, N. G. L. 1972. *A History of Macedonia.* Oxford: University Press.

Harris, D. R. and Vita-Finzi, C. 1968. Kokkinopolis—a Greek badland, *Geog. Journ.* **134**, 537–543.

Higgs, E. S. and Vita-Finzi, C. 1966. The climate, environment and industries of Stone Age Greece: Part II, *Proc. Prehist. Soc.* **31**, 1–29.

Higgs, E. S., Vita-Finzi, C., Harris, D. R. and Fagg, A. 1967. The climate, environment and industries of Stone Age Greece: Part III, *Proc. Prehist. Soc.* **32**, 1–30.

Higgs, E. S. 1968. The stone industries of Greece. *In: La Préhistoire, Problèmes et Tendances* (F. Bordes and D. de Sonneville Bordes, eds), pp. 223–235. Paris: Centre National de Recherche Scientifique.

Higgs, E. S. and Webley, D. 1971. Further information concerning the environment of Palaeolithic man in Epirus. *Proc. Prehist. Soc.* **27**, 367–380.

Higgs, E. S. 1974, *Palaeoeconomy*. Cambridge: University Press.
Hutchinson, J. 1969. Erosion and land use in the Epirus region of Greece. *Agric. Hist. Review* **17**.
Legge, A. J. 1972. Cave climates. *In: Papers in Economic Prehistory* (E. S. Higgs, ed.), pp. 119–125. Cambridge: University Press.
Leroi-Gourhan, A. and Chavaillon, J. and N. 1963. Paléolithique du Péloponèse. *B.S.P.F.* **60**.
Rodden, R. J. 1962. Excavations at the early Neolithic site at Nea Nikomedeia, Greek Macedonia, *Proc. Prehist. Soc.* **28**, 267–288.
Vita-Finzi, C. 1969. *The Mediterranean Valleys*. Cambridge: University Press.
Wijmstra, T. 1969. Palynology of the 30 m of a 120 m deep section in Northern Greece. *Acta Botan. Neerl.* **18**, 4, 511–527.

5
The Erosional History of the Plain of Elis in the Peloponnese

C. Nicholas Raphael

Introduction

To judge from the distribution of archaeological sites, man's prehistoric and historic development, in varying conditions of climate and geology, has taken place particularly in coastal areas. A maritime environment is still appealing; in the United States, for example, about 75% of the population lives within the coastal zone. Following such close and continuous occupation, sequences of artifacts from districts near the sea, and chronologies based thereon, are usually quite complete.

Perhaps no other type of geomorphic region is so subject to rapid modification as a low-lying coastal plain; for marine landforms such as beach-ridges and other barriers are not particularly stable and can quickly prograde, erode or subside. Rivers contributing sediments to such coastal plains, and, continuously striving after steeper gradients, shift from place to place and bring about readjustments in the sediment budgets which are reflected in coastal changes.

Coastal areas, therefore, where archaeological sites are abundant, chronologies relatively complete, and physical changes rapid, provide good conditions for identifying and documenting geomorphic changes, and for relating them to human activity. In the United States, the changing association between man and his coastal habitat has been worked out in great detail, notably in south Louisiana where settlement has followed the courses of the shifting Mississippi River delta (McIntire, 1958). Similarly, though on a larger scale, in the coastal plains of the eastern Mediterranean, an association between cultural and physical history is manifest.

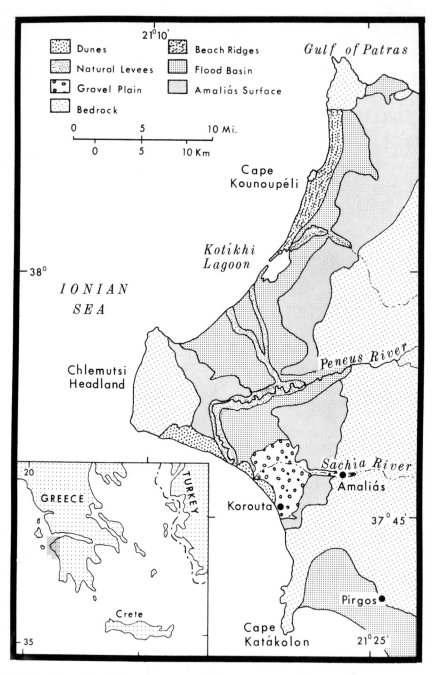

Fig. 1: Coastal and fluvial geomorphology of coastal Elis.

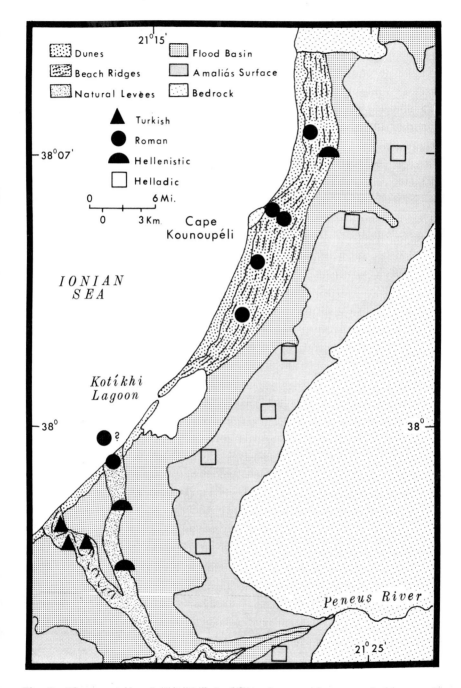

Fig. 2: The association between archaeological sites and geomorphology north of the Peneus River.

The Physical Landscape of Coastal Elis

Geomorphic field studies which relate coastal and fluvial geomorphology to archaeology in the Peloponnesus are few (see Kraft, 1972). However, the use of travel accounts and maps, in addition to aerial photographs, has greatly extended the evidence available for the Elis project. This study was undertaken in four steps: fluvial and coastal landforms of the project area were identified and mapped; all archaeological sites discovered were charted, and artifacts from them collected in order to determine their absolute age; sites noted by previous investigators were also visited for the purpose of confirmation; and finally the changes of coastal and fluvial landforms were correlated with events in human history as revealed by archaeological and palaeographic evidence.

The coastal plain of Elis is composed of the most extensive Late-Quaternary deposit in the Peloponnesus (Fig. 1). Although the alluvial plain is only about 35 km long and at most some 12 km wide, it exhibits a variety of landforms. The shore is composed of a series of crescentic barriers which tie into high limestone headlands. The barrier between the Chlemutsi Headland and Kotíkhi Lagoon is composed of a single low sand-ridge occasionally breached by wash-over fans deposited by winter storms. From Kotíkhi northward, the barrier is represented by a series of well defined beach-ridges paralleling the present shoreline. The beach-ridge complex, like the simple barrier to the south, is at present being eroded as mobile dunes encroach inland. Landward, the landscape is occupied by lagoons, many of which are intermittent and abut against the higher terrain to the east. This last is a broad upland surface composed of well oxidized fluvial sands and gravels, and will be referred to as the Amaliás surface. The principal river is the Peneus which, originating in the Erimanthos Mountains to the east, flows on to the alluvial surface and debouches into the sea south of the Chlemutsi Headland.

In winter, flooding occurs periodically and well defined natural levees have been deposited. Strabo in his *Geography* (8.3.5) noted that "It is between Chelonatas (Chlemutsi) and Cyllene (Kounoupéli) that the River Peneius empties". Pre-nineteenth century maps also depict the river flowing to the north of that headland, whereas more recently cartography illustrates the Peneus in its present approximate position. The diversion seems therefore to have occurred in the late 1700s or early 1800s A.D. That the Peneus formerly flowed north of the headland is confirmed by the two ancestral levee systems which have been identified and mapped (Figs 1, 2). Of the two, the southern appears to be the younger, as vestiges of a channel and point-bar topography are evident as far as the point of bifurcation several kilometres inland. South of the Peneus River, the Elian plain is composed of coarse fluvial gravels and sands which fan seaward from Amaliás. This alluvial surface stands above the flood basin and below the equally obvious Amaliás surface. Beneath the gravel wedge, the Amaliás surface is encountered. The stratigraphic relationship of this fan-shaped wedge of coarse sediment, which thickens in a seaward direction, is similar to that between the Pleistocene surfaces and the Recent alluvium encountered on many depositional coasts throughout the world.

The Sachia Valley west of Amaliás (Fig. 3) shows distinct phases of deposition and erosion. Here the Amaliás surface was initially entrenched and a valley 700 m wide and 55 m deep was incised. Subsequent filling has deposited 50 m of alluvial gravels. This more recent alluvium is now being entrenched, and vertical sections as much as 7 m thick are exposed. At the shoreline, north of Korouta, this gravel plain is truncated by the sea, and in places is capped by active parabolic dunes.

Owing to their unconsolidated nature, coastal plains such as that of Elis are characterized by relatively rapid geomorphic change, which may be effected or accentuated by tectonic instability. The present coastal process

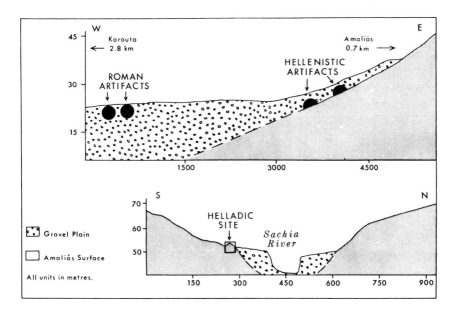

Fig. 3: Cross-section and relationship of the alluvial deposits and the archaeology of the Sachia river valley, west of Amaliás.

in Elis is one of erosion, as is substantiated by the following observations:
1. the gravel plain truncated by the Ionian Sea has been retreating for several decades. A calculation of the seaward projection of this surface, which does not take into account tectonic instability, suggests that it intersected the sea some 500 m beyond the present shoreline;
2. north of Kotíkhi Lagoon, mobile sand dunes are invading the beach-ridges, burying the woody vegetation of the ridges, and exposing the swales on the shoreline;
3. natural levee systems normally decrease in elevation as they approach sea-level and are scarcely discernible on the shore. Both the ancestral Peneus levee systems stand out as low sea cliffs on the present shoreline and thus clearly indicate coastal erosion. If the older levee scarp immediately south of the Kotíkhi Lagoon is projected seaward, it intercepts the level of the sea 1·2 km offshore;
4. sherds of Roman age washed up on many beaches, especially in the vicinity of the Kotíkhi Lagoon, suggest coastal retreat during post-Roman time.

This tectonic instability, observed by ancient writers and by modern scholars, has been documented by Galanopulos (1940). More recently, oceanographic investigations (Hsu, 1972) have revealed a deep sea-trench and island-arc complex extending from the heel of Italy to Crete and to Cyprus. Adjacent to such convex trenches and island arcs, earthquakes and volcanic activity are normally encountered; it is no surprise, therefore, that the western coasts of the Peloponnese and the adjacent Ionian Islands have the highest incidence of earthquake activity in Greece (*British Admiralty Handbook*, 1945). Tectonic activity has continued, even though on a subdued scale, ever since the Tertiary (Alpine) orogeny (Temple, 1968).

In addition to the evidence of horizontal shifts along the Elian coast, wave-cut notches bear witness to vertical instability. Fossil wave-cut notches at Cape Katákolon are incised in upper Tertiary fossiliferous limestone; but their discontinuity and southerly dip, the absence of similar features on other and older limestone headlands, and the tectonic record, all indicate clearly that this coastal area is unstable.

A Chronology for Coastal Elis

The patterns of prehistoric and historic settlement in Elis have only recently been investigated. The first regional survey appears to be that of

Sperling (1942). More recently, archaeological teams have concentrated on specific cultures and periods of time: Leroi-Gourhan *et al.* (1963) and Servais (1961) on prehistoric settlements; McDonald and Hope-Simpson (1964) and Loy (1970), in the south-western Peloponnese, on the reconstruction of the palaeogeography of Messenia in the Bronze Age (the Helladic period). The chronology has been incomplete and it has only begun to fall into place within the last decade, but it is now evident that the north-western Peloponnesus has been continuously occupied since prehistoric time. The chronology presented here (Table I) is based on discoveries of artefacts, and like any preliminary chronology, it will undoubtedly be refined in the future. The earlier dates are, of course, approximate.

Table I: Chronology of the north-west Peloponnesus

Period	Age
Turkish	A.D. 1354–A.D. 1821
Mediaeval	A.D. 326–A.D. 1354
Roman	146 B.C.–326 B.C.
Hellenistic	338 B.C.–146 B.C.
Classical	550 B.C.–338 B.C.
Archaic	1100 B.C.–800 B.C.
Helladic	3000 B.C.–1100 B.C.
Pre-Helladic	before 3000 B.C.

Physical geographers interpreting changes in the landscape can use settlement patterns and archaeological remains as geologists use fossils. Equally, historians and archaeologists with some knowledge of the geomorphology of an area can often predict where sites of some particular age will occur; for human occupation of coastal areas is invariably associated with particular geological terrain.

The Association between Archaeology and Geomorphology

The prehistoric sites range in age from Palaeolithic to Neolithic and terminate with the introduction of metals. All prehistoric sites mapped and identified occupy the oxidized sands and gravels of the Amaliás surface and the older and higher geologic surfaces (Fig. 3). After the conclusion of my fieldwork in Elis, 49 additional sites were discovered by Chavaillon *et al.* (1969): but all these locations confirm what Leroi-Gourhan (1963, p. 324) and others have noted:

> De Patras à Pyrgos et tout particulièrement dans les régions de Kato Achaia, de Kastron, de Néochori, d'Amaliás et du Cap Katákolon, nous avons découvert, en place, dans formations pleistocènes continentales, les vestiges d'industries appartenant à trois périodes du Paléolithique grec . . .

Artefacts, in part representing Mousterian and Levalloisian industries, consist of white and reddish-brown flakes of chert which are not indigenous to the area, and their locations frequently overlook the sea or the modern flood basin.

Helladic sites are represented by mounds, locally called *magoula*, which stands as much as 4 m above their surroundings and are composed of locally derived oxidized sand and gravel. The sherds from *magoula* in the northwest Peloponnesus have been dated as late Helladic, from 1800 to 1500 B.C. Although no excavations have been undertaken in this area to determine the precise function of the *magoula*, the larger mounds are probably tombs, whereas the lower mounds were habitation sites, many of which are located on scarps that overlook the Ionian Sea or river valleys (Fig. 2). Intensive field work in the adjacent province of Messenia has revealed a similar pattern (Loy, 1970). In fact McDonald and Hope-Simpson (1964, p. 240) concluded that:

> The lowest sites so far identified seem to set precisely at the line of demarcation between the slightly sloping Pliocene sediments and the Recent alluvium.

Other occupational sites of the pre-Helladic and Helladic cultures may lie beneath the coastal plain and have been covered by the Flandrian transgression. Archaic sites, though few, were also established on the pre-modern surfaces, which suggests that settlement on the present coastal plain did not take place before early Classical times.

The remarkable absence from the coastal plain of pre-Classical sites may be explained by subsequent burial by Recent alluvium. Immediately after the sea level reached its present "still-stand" about 3500 years ago, the coastal plain would be marshy and subsidence active. Any site then established on the marshy plain may subsequently have subsided beneath the surface and been concealed under deposits of river alluvium. By way of analogy, it may be remarked that in south Louisiana, where subsidence is active, mounds have been known to disappear beneath the unconsolidated surface over a period of 20 years (McIntire, 1958, p. 27). Thus a sequence of events—rising sea-level, subsidence, and alluviation— may have obliterated these sites. As Leake (1830, Vol. II, p. 220) noted:

> . . . it may be some consolation . . . to consider, that the soil subject like that of the *Eleia*, to alluvial changes, was the best adapted speedily to conceal, and may still therefore preserve some of the works of art which survived the fury of the persecutors of idolatry.

Post-Archaic sites are the most important for dating the Recent landforms. The classical city of Elis, located on the left bank of the Peneus River valley, organized and managed the Olympic games. Although Classical sites are few, contemporary accounts hint at a relatively dense population. Archaeological evidence on the coastal plain is, however, more abundant for the Hellenistic period. Evidently it was at this time that the beach-ridges and the flood basin were first occupied (Fig. 2). Sherds identified and dated as Hellenistic were noted on the levee system immediately south of the Kotíkhi Lagoon and on the most landward beach ridge.

The Sachia River near Amaliás has cut a gorge exposing the oxidized Amaliás surface where it plunges beneath the gravel plain. At the contact of the two dissimilar alluvia, well preserved Hellenistic sherds were abundant (Fig. 3). This pottery, with decorative painting characteristic of the period, was found on both walls of the river channel, and was often associated with charcoal, an indication that the finds are *in situ* and not transported or deposited by alluvial or colluvial processes.

Perhaps the most abundant historic sites in the north-west Peloponnesus are those of Roman age, when settlement was evidently both dense and well distributed (Fig. 2). Roman sites are associated with all landforms: beach-ridges, levees, dunes and upland topography. Sherds washed up on many beaches, and cemented in beach rock at the present shoreline, suggest that some Roman sites are submerged offshore. At Cape Katákolon, limestone foundations and abundant Roman sherds may mark the site of the ancient Pheia described by Strabo (8.3.12). In the mediaeval period this part of Greece lay under Byzantine and Frankish domination and most of the sites characterized by the *palaeokastra* of feudal landlords occupied easily defended headlands such as Chlemutsi and Cape Kounoupéli. The majority of the place-names of the region are non-Hellenic and reflect ten centuries of foreign influence and control. The

Ottoman Turks, who followed the Franks, occupied Greece for approximately 500 years. Several sites of the Turkish period have been identified, of which the more significant occur on the abandoned levee system 5 km south of the Kotíhki Lagoon (Fig. 2). Sherds are so plentiful here that the local inhabitants refer to the area as "Turkopolis". In addition to pottery, abandoned wells, of presumably Turkish design, are also located on this levee.

Table II illustrates the relation of human occupance to geomorphology. The Helladic and prehistoric settlements were primarily established on the higher and older geological surfaces; but the earliest settlements on the modern coastal plain were Classical in age. Thereafter, settlement increased through time, so that the most abundant sites on the modern coastal plain range from the Hellenistic through to the Turkish period.

Table II: Association between archaeological sites and landforms

Age	Dates	Frequency	Landform Association
Turkish	A.D. 1354–A.D. 1821	5	Abandoned levee 5 km south of Kotíkhi Lagoon
Mediaeval	A.D. 326–A.D. 1354	5	Headlands, one possible site on flood basin
Roman	146 B.C.–A.D. 326	14	Dunes, beach-ridges, gravel plain, levee 1 km south of Kotíkhi Lagoon, offshore (beach rock), bedrock surface
Hellenistic	338 B.C.– 146 B.C.	7	Most landward beach-ridge flood basin, abandoned levee 1 km south of Kotíkhi Lagoon, Amaliás surface
Classical	550 B.C.– 338 B.C.	3	Peneus Valley flood plain, bedrock surface
Archaic	1100 B.C.– 800 B.C.	1	Amaliás surface
Helladic	3000 B.C.–1100 B.C.	14	Amaliás surface and bedrock
pre-Helladic	–3000 B.C.	12	Amaliás surface and bedrock

Archaeological sites on the beach-ridge complex reveal that settlement on the lowland had occurred by Hellenistic times (Fig. 2). Although only one site from that period was identified on the oldest beach-ridge, it does imply that the minimum age of the barrier is 2300 years. Roman sites, abundant on the younger beach-ridges, indicate that the coastline prograded continuously through Roman times to its present position at least. The calculated rate of accretion was in the order of 170 m per century, and the principal source of sediments for the beach ridges was the ancestral channels of the Peneus River. This is, however, a minimum value, since sherds of Roman age washed up on to the shore suggest that the shoreline was once farther seaward and has been eroded back to its present position.

Both morphology and archaeology indicate that periods of erosion have occurred during historical time. For instance, an examination of the truncated levee south of the Kotíhki Lagoon shows that it has Roman sherds incorporated within it, to depths of 40 cm.

This is clear evidence that flooding of the channel was active during and after Roman times. The second abandoned channel, 5 km south of Kotíhki Lagoon was occupied during Turkish times, so that its minimum age is about 200 years. This levee system, standing well above the flood basin at the shoreline, reveals that the shore lay further seaward during the Middle Ages and has retreated since then. Whether a second distinct phase of coastal progradation took place cannot be determined, since the Ionian Sea has encroached over the youngest beach-ridges, which could be sites of Turkish occupation.

Another area that illustrates erosion and deposition during historical time is the Amaliás surface, which has been alluviated by a gravel surface west of Amaliás (Fig. 3). In several localities on this gravel plain, Roman grave sites, which lie a few centimetres beneath the surface, suggest that deposition was completed by the Roman period, and that this surface has not been significantly degraded by sheetwash or channelled flow since that time. At the contact of the gravel surface and the Amaliás surface, several well preserved sites of Hellenistic age, including charcoal *in situ*, indicate that alluviation was active after the Hellenistic occupation. Thus alluviation, which was apparently confined to Roman times, occurred on the Amaliás surface as well as on the coast. After the interval of deposition, incision by the Sachia River exposed alluvial gravels up to 25 m in thickness. Since the sea-level has been fairly stable since the end of the Roman period, the dissection of this aggradational surface is probably related to coastal erosion and perhaps to the tectonic instability of the region. The incision into the gravel plain and the erosion of the shoreline post-date the Roman occupation.

The broad sequence of events which has led to the development of the coastal plain of Elis is illustrated in Table III. It is evident from the human and physical history that the progradation of the coastal plain and its subsequent recession are confined to definite cultural periods. The episode of deposition, and hence of coastal progradation, began just before or during the Hellenistic times, and the bulk of the alluviation appears to have taken place prior to the Mediaeval period.

Causes of Deposition and Erosion in Elis

The factors responsible for depositional and erosional events along the Ionian coast cannot be precisely determined. During the Roman occupation, enough sediment was contributed by the Peneus River to cause a rapid build-out of this coastal region. At present, coastal and fluvial erosion, including the retreat of the modern outlet of the Peneus River, suggest that insufficient sediment is being transported to the coastal region to cause coastal accretion.

Some writers suggest that, during mediaeval times, the European storm-tracks lay farther to the south and caused an increase in precipitation in the Mediterranean. These periods of climatic stress have been referred to as the "Secondary Climatic Optimum" (A.D. 1000–1200) and the "Little Ice Age" (A.D. 1430–1850) (Lamb, 1966). Evidence from alluvial valleys in several widely separated localities in the Mediterranean suggests a mediaeval fill (Fig. 4). In fact, Vita-Finzi (1969) concludes that stream deposition occurred after Roman times throughout the Mediterranean: for example, in Greece, 30 km south of Elis, where deposits of this age have been confirmed along a tributary of the Alpheus near Olympia (Vita-Finzi, 1966). There are, however, historical deposits in the Mediterranean which do not fit into this general picture. In east-central Sicily, for example, the greatest alluviation occurred between 1700 and 325 B.C. (Judson, 1963). The north-western Peloponnesus too, does not conform to the regional pattern postulated by Vita-Finzi, for it does not appear to have been significantly influenced by a post-Roman fluvial period. In general, the coastal evidence suggests accretion in the eastern Mediterranean prior to A.D. 1000. In the Küçük Menderes delta at Ephesus in Turkey the accumulation of sediment was greatest during Hellenistic times, and contemporary with the diffusion of Hellenic culture

TABLE III: Summary of major events related to the development of the Plain of Elis

Period	Event	Evidence
Turkish	Peneus River occupied channel 5 km south of Kotíkhi Lagoon; Peneus diverted southward in late 1700s; coastal retreat	Turkish sherds and wells on relict levee; map data and literature; dune-ridges, exposed beach-ridge swales, truncation of gravel plain
Mediaeval	Coastal progradation (?)	Questionable Byzantine site exposed on present shoreline
Roman	Coastal progradation of beach-ridges; deposition of gravel plain completed	Roman occupance of beach-ridges, and levee 1 km south of Kotíkhi Lagoon; offshore sites; Roman grave sites on surface of gravel plain
Hellenistic	Peneus River flowing north of Chlemutsi Headland; beach-ridges established; initiation of gravel plain	Sherds on premodern levee 1 km south of Kotíkhi Lagoon and oldest beach-ridge; also at contact of gravel plain and Amaliás surface

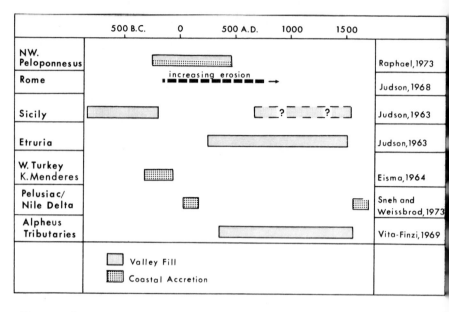

Fig. 4: Chronology of late historical deposits in the eastern Mediterranean.

to Anatolia (Eisma, 1964). In the north-west Peloponnesus, coastal progradation occurred during Hellenistic times or shortly thereafter (Raphael, 1973). In the Pelusiac/Nile delta also, beach-ridges were deposited about A.D. 25 (Sneh and Weissbrod, 1973).

Tectonic deformation in the Mediterranean during historic times has been documented by Flemming (1969). The submergence of several archaeological sites in the western Mediterranean is attributable to downward displacement of the land rather than to eustatic change of sea-level. In Elis, the beach-ridge system and the gravel plain which has alluviated the Sachia Valley and spread over at least part of the Amaliás surface were initiated no later than Hellenistic times, and deposition continued through the Roman occupation. Thus the building out of the coast and the filling of the valley were synchronous. Progradation of beach-ridges is most likely to happen during a period of relatively stable or slowly dropping sea-level: conversely, the optimum condition for valley filling is a rising sea-level or a level that has been stable over a long period. Although the beach-ridges are about 35 km north of the gravel plain, tectonic activity acting in opposite vertical directions at this distance apart may have influenced the development of these two depositional landforms of approximately the same age.

Many writers have commented on the decay of the physical environment of the Mediterranean which is thought to have resulted from centuries of human misuse. During the Classical Age in Greece, commissioners of woods and forests (Aristotle, *Politics* 6.5.4., 7.11.4.) were appointed to see to the proper administration of the woodlands.* We may, therefore, speculate that deterioration of the landscape was brought about by human occupation, and has accelerated during or since Classical and Roman times. As we have seen, judging from the archaeological data "goodly Elis" was well populated during most prehistoric and historic periods. Pollen data from a lagoon near Pylos in Messenia shows a decrease in the distribution of Aleppo pine (*Pinus halepensis*) after 2000 B.C. which was due to deforestation, not to climatic change (Wright, 1968). Palynological studies in Macedonia reveal no proper, pluvial conditions in the northern Mediterranean during the Würm glacial (van der Hammen, 1965). More recently, pollen analysis of post-Glacial sapropell muds south of Crete points to the devastation of the vegetation by man and domesticated animals during the last 8000 years (Rossignol and Pastouret, 1971).

Data from Catalonia (Butzer, 1964) reveal that increased runoff and stream discharges, due to human disuse during historical times, produce features similar to those associated with pluvial alluviation, particularly in the coastal region. Only in recent years have physical geographers fully realized that man is a significant modifier of the landscape. It appears that, in coastal regions of the Mediterranean, man's diffusion and settlement patterns may indeed be closely associated with changes of land use and subsequent erosion and deposition. However, more detailed valley and coastal studies are still required to unravel the complex and fascinating problems of the last few thousand years in the Mediterranean.

---

*Judson (1968) noted near Rome increased erosion rates with intensified occupation during and since Roman times.

References

British Admiralty. 1945. *Greece*, Geogr. Handbook Ser., B.R. 516, 3.

Butzer, K. W. 1964. Pleistocene geomorphology and stratigraphy of the Costa Brava region (Catalonia). *Akad. Wissensch. Lit.* **1964**, 3–51.

Chavaillon, J. *et al.* 1969. Industries paléolithiques de l'Élide. *Bull. Correspond. Hellén.* **93**, 97–151.

Eisma, D. 1964. Stream deposition in the Mediterranean area in historical times. *Nature* **203**, 1061.

Flemming, N. C. 1969. Archaeological evidence for eustatic change of sea-level and earth movements in the western Mediterranean during the last 2000 years. *Geol. Soc. Amer. Spec. Paper* 109.

Galanopulos, A. 1940. Du seismizität von Elis. *Gerlands Beitr. Geophys.* **56**, 92–107.

Hammen, van der, T. 1965. Palynological study of a very thick peat section in Greece, and the Würm-Glacial vegetation in the Mediterranean region. *Geol. Minjnb.* **44**, 37–39.

Hsu, K. J. 1972. When the Mediterranean dried up. *Scient. Am.* **227**, 27–36.

Judson, S. 1963. Erosion and deposition of Italian stream valleys during historic times. *Science* **140**, 898–899.

Judson, S. 1968. Erosion rates near Rome, Italy, *Science* **160**, 1444–1445.

Kraft, J. C. 1972. *A Reconnaissance of the Geology of the Sandy Coastal Areas of Eastern Greece and the Peloponnese.* Univ. of Delaware Tech. Rept. No. 9, Newark.

Lamb, H. H. 1966. *The changing Climate: Selected Papers.* London: Methuen.

Leake, W. M. 1830. *Travels in the Morea*, 3 vols. London.

Leroi-Gourhan, A. *et al.* 1963. Premiers résultats d'une prospection de divers sites préhistoriques en Élide occidentale. *Ann. Géol. Pays Hellén.* **14**, 324–329.

Loy, W. G. 1970. *The Land of Nestor: A Physical Geography of the Southwest Peloponnese.* National Academy of Sciences Rept. No. 34, Washington, D.C.

McDonald, W. A. and Hope-Simpson, R. 1964. Further exploration in Southwestern Peloponnese: 1962–1963. *Am. J. Archaeol.* **68**, 229–245.

McIntire, W. G. 1958. *Prehistoric Indian Settlements of the Changing Mississippi River Delta*, Louisiana State Univ. Coastal Studies Ser. No. 1, Baton Rouge.

Raphael, C. N. 1973. Late Quaternary changes in coastal Elis, Greece. *Geogr. Rev.* **63**, 73–89.

Rossignol, M. and Pastouret, L. 1971. Analyse pollinique de Niveaux Sapropéliques Post-Glaciaires dans une carotte en Méditerranée orientale. *Rev. Palaeobotan. Palynol.* **11**, 227–238.

Servais, J. 1961. Outils paléolithiques d'Élide. *Bull Correspond. Hellén.* **85**, 1–9.

Sneh, A. and Weissbrod, T. 1973. Nile Delta: the defunct Pelusiac branch identified. *Science* **180**, 59–61.

Sperling, J. 1942. Explorations in Elis. *Am. J. Archaeol.* **46**, 77–89.

Strabo. c. A.D. 50, *Geography,* 4 (trans. Jones, H. L. 1964, London: Heinemann).

Temple, P. G. 1968. Mechanics of large-scale gravity sliding in the Greek Peloponnesos. *Geol. Soc. Amer. Bull.* **79**, 687–700.

Vita-Finzi, C. 1966. The New Elysian Fields. *Am. J. Archaeol.* **70**, 175–178.

Vita-Finzi, C. 1969. *The Mediterranean Valleys: Geological Changes in Historical Times.* Cambridge: University Press.

Wright, H. E. 1968. Climatic change in Mycenaean Greece. *Antiquity* **42**, 123–127.

6
Stream Deposition and Erosion by the Eastern Shore of the Aegean

Doeke Eisma

Introduction

The four major rivers in western Turkey that run westwards towards the Aegean—the Büyük Menderes, the Gediz, the Küçük Menderes, and Bakır Çay*—have their sources in the western Anatolian mountains and in the uplands that separate the central Anatolian plain from the coast. The Gediz and the Büyük Menderes are large rivers, draining together about one-third of western Anatolia; the Bakır Çay and Küçük Menderes are much smaller and have their sources only some 80 km from the coast. They flow through broad east-west *graben*, formed since the Late Tertiary, which have flat alluvial valley floors, interrupted only by small hills of Tertiary or older rocks and by the incisions of the river itself and its tributaries. The small rocky hills are the vestiges of a more lively topography, carved out when sea-level was low during the Pleistocene glacial stages and now buried below the river alluvium. All four rivers turn towards the south-west near the coast, following mainly SW–NE directions of faulting, and have each formed a broad deltaic coastal plain. The coastal plains of the Küçük Menderes, the Gediz and Bakır Çay are connected with the main valleys by a narrow passage. Only the broad *graben* of the Büyük Menderes extends without interruption from the sea to more than 150 km inland.

During the rise in sea-level that began about 14,000 years ago (Milliman and Emery, 1968) the sea entered the valleys to a point far deeper inland, that is further east, than the present coastline: by contrast, even during

* Respectively the ancient Maiandros, Hermos, Kaystros and Kaïkos.

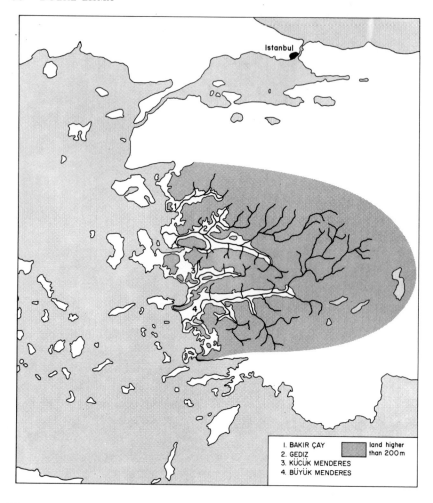

Fig. 1: The four major rivers in western Turkey.

historical times the coastline has been seen to move westwards over a considerable distance due to stream deposition, and this process undoubtedly began much earlier. At the same time, the valleys further inland were filled up with mostly fine-grained river alluvium and with coarser sands and gravels from the surrounding hills, so that usually the following features are present in the lower valleys:

    a. alluvial fans, spreading out from the hillsides;

    b. a flat alluvial plain, rarely flooded by the river, at 5–10 m above the present river bed;

c. a broad flood plain near the river mouth which is flooded during the winter;

d. lagoons, beach-ridges and dunes along the coast.

Alluvial Fans and Valley Infill

Alluvial fans have been observed in many parts of western Turkey (Philippson, 1910, 1911, 1920; Chaput, 1936). They are very conspicuous, especially along the northern edge of the Büyük Menderes Valley from the mouth to above Nazilli (Grund, 1906a, b; Philippson, 1911; Russell, 1954), along the Gediz, and between the Büyük Menderes Valley and Izmir (Philippson, 1920; Eisma, 1960). Often present at the termini of small tributary valleys, they may rise steeply to more than 100 m above the alluvial plain. The higher parts are often cultivated and inhabited, and the railway between Cellat and Belevi is cut through such a fan, so it would appear that their formation has ceased by now. Nowhere, however, have the alluvial fans been dated. They are at least contemporaneous with, and probably often older than, the river alluvium in the valleys; but they are certainly younger than the red and grey, often gravelly, deposits that lie on top of the Neogene marls, chalks and sandstones. These deposits are very prominent along the northern edge of the Büyük Menderes *graben* and south of the Gediz, where they were called Tmolosschutt by Philippson (1911). They can easily be distinguished from the light yellow and buff alluvial fans, not only by their colour, but also through their being usually broken, tilted and dissected. Philippson (1911) assumed the Tmolosschutt to be Neogene, and similar reddish deposits elsewhere to be Quaternary, while Chaput (1936) dated them as Pliocene or Old Quaternary. Nebert (1955) called them Pliocene, but according to Erinç (1955b) they were formed during the Lower or Middle Pleistocene, and Birot (Birot and Dresch, 1956) called them Villafranchian. It follows that the younger alluvial fans may have been formed at any time during the Quaternary. Vita-Finzi (1969b), lumping together a number of similar-looking alluvial fan deposits and tentatively correlating them with Middle Palaeolithic remains, arrives at a Würm age, but this correlation is very speculative. The fans may actually be very young, because soil formation has not proceeded very far on them, and many still carry an active stream bed (which in some cases is cut into the fan — Philippson, 1920): but this bed may be in equilibrium and not contributing new deposits to the fan. It is also conceivable that the formation of the fans started early in the

Pleistocene and has proceeded in stages, of which the present surface represents only the latest.

Alluvial valley infill, cut by the present river, is a very common feature in western and northern Turkey. Its thickness, where it has been measured (near the Büyük Menderes, the Küçük Menderes and the Gediz), has been found to be 5–10 m (Vita-Finzi, 1969b). In Ephesus and Sardis the valley infill buries parts of the ancient buildings. Similar deposits in northern Turkey (near Sinop, Bafra and Boyabat) contain Roman pottery. In contrast to the alluvial fans, which have been formed by intermittent streams and may be associated with torrential winter rains, the valley infill has been deposited by a continuously flowing river similar to that which flows at present. After the deposition of the valley infill, a period of erosion began and the present river bed was cut.

The River Deltas

At the mouth of each river there is a flood plain which is relatively flat, rising slowly inland to $+10$–20 m. It is characteristically closed towards the sea by a complex of lagoons, beach ridges and low dunes, breached only by the outflowing river. The river flows through it between levees at approximately the same level as the plain, often changing its course and leaving numerous old channels. Sand from old bars and levees is blown locally into small dunes which may reach a height of 3 m. Deposition on the flood plain is still continuing.

The flood plains of the Büyük Menderes and the Küçük Menderes have progressed seaward in historical times over large distances. Archaeological and historical evidence has shown that between 750 and 300 B.C. the Küçük Menderes progressed slowly over not more than 1 km (Fig. 2); then in the period 300–100 B.C. it moved forward rapidly over about 5 km, the speed later decreasing in Roman times (about 2 km between 100 B.C. and A.D. 200), and still more during the Early Middle Ages (about 1·5 km between A.D. 200 and 700). Since then the coast has remained stationary (Eisma, 1962). The present beach-ridges and dunes were formed between approximately A.D. 100 and 720, but after the cutting of the canal in 1934/35 (the Yeni Menderes) a new beach-ridge was formed north of the canal mouth.

Data for the Büyük Menderes delta are less complete, but suggest a similar history. Priene of early Classical times was situated on the sea, but its exact location is not known. A new city of Priene, marked by the

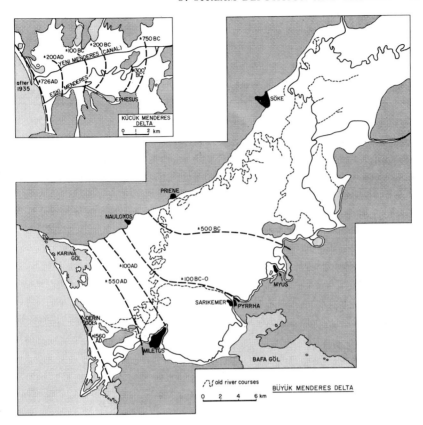

Fig. 2: The flood plains of the Büyük Menderes and the Küçük Menderes.

present ruins, was founded in the fourth century B.C. (Schede, 1964) with a harbour, Naulochos, 5 km distant (Strabo, 12.8.17), which has been identified with some ruins at a small former bay at the appropriate distance west of Priene. On the southern border of the Maeander plain, Myus had an open harbour in about 500 B.C. (Herodotus, V, 36) but was deserted in Hellenistic times: there are no Roman ruins. In the first century B.C. the coast was at Sarıkemer near ancient Pyrrha (Strabo, 12.8.15; 14.1.10); in about A.D. 100 the level of the pavement in the streets in the lower parts of Miletus had to be raised, which suggests that the river mouth had already reached the area between the city and the former island of Lade. Philippson (1936) suggests from archaeological data that in the fourth century A.D. the former Latmian Gulf (now Bafa göl) was definitely closed and that around the sixth century A.D. the area around Miletus had been silted up; after the fourth century A.D. no new buildings were erected in the city. The old Maeander course, probably active until the Early Middle Ages, was subsequently replaced by the newer southern course which closed the Latmian Gulf: the charters of the Patmos cloister mention the "old" Maeander in the eighteenth century. A Greek seaman's description from around A.D. 1560 locates the coast at about eight miles from Miletus (Wiegand, 1929), which is approximately its present position if we discount the pointed delta which protrudes seaward at the southern end beyond Lade. This mouth of the river was active until 1945, and according to Philippson (1936) there was still some deposition going on when he visited the area in 1909. In 1945/46 during a winter flood the river again changed its course, followed an old bed north of Batmaz (the former Lade island), and now has its mouth just south of Derin göl, a large coastal lagoon where another river mouth was formerly located (Russell, 1954). From this account it follows that the delta progressed rapidly in late Classical and Hellenistic times until about A.D. 100, and then slowed down. After the Middle Ages delta-building was restricted to the formation of the southern part, which is probably a very young feature, built up rather quickly and not yet eroded.

On the history of the deltas of the Gediz and Bakır Çay far less data are available. The main Greek city on the Gediz delta, Aeolian Larissa, did not have a harbour, as the inhabitants were mainly farmers, not sailors. The descriptions of Pliny (*NH.V.* 119) and Evliya Çelibi (Erinç, 1955a) do not permit a conclusion on the progression of the delta. In the early nineteenth century A.D. the Gediz began to form at its main mouth a narrow extension which pointed southward and attained a length of about 3 km in 1886: a second extension was then forming at a more eastern mouth of the river. Since these advances threatened the shipping channel to Izmir, a canal was cut in 1886 from the Gediz to a former bed which still carried water flowing from the hills along the northern edge of the plain (Kiepert, 1887). This westerly course was later changed again, so that the mouth is now situated very near to the northern hills. A comparison of Kiepert's map of 1887 with a topographic map of 1944 shows that since 1886 the Gediz has built a delta plain about 5 km in length.

On the progression of the Kaïkos delta even less is known. A Roman bridge of the first century A.D. which crosses the river between Elaia and Pitane indicates that the inner plain at least must have been silted up before A.D. 100. Since then the front of the delta has progressed at most 5 km.

Besides the four deltas discussed already, there are other Anatolian deltas that are known to have been progressing actively in historical times. That of the Sakarya has extended by about 100 m in the last 30 years and possibly by 2 km in the last 2000 years (Russell, 1954). Perge, Sillyon and Aspendos, all inland cities of Pamphylia, whose economy was based on agriculture and trade, could each be reached from the sea by a river which is now completely silted up: since the last century B.C. the coast has progressed by from 4 to 5 km (Strabo, 14.4.2; Blumenthal, 1963). The Ceyhan and the Seyhan deltas progressed rapidly in the first century B.C. (Strabo, 12.2.4) but unfortunately no exact data are available. The delta of the Skamander near Troy, however, has hardly progressed at all in historical time, for the distance given by Skylax in the fourth century B.C. from Troy to the sea was only slightly less than it is now; moreover, the descriptions of Homer, Strabo and Pliny accord with the present conditions (Schliemann, 1881; Dörpfeld, 1902). Forchhammer (in Schliemann, 1881) mentions strong currents of up to 1 m sec^{-1} in the Dardanelles and strong north-east winds and waves during most of the year, which would together prevent any lasting progression of the coast: when a small delta is formed in front of one of the mouths of the Skamander, it is destroyed again when the river shifts to another mouth. In summary, if we leave out of consideration the river deltas for which no, or only a few, data are available, we may conclude that the deltas of the Küçük Menderes and Büyük Menderes show roughly the same pattern of growth up to the Early Middle Ages. The Büyük Menderes, however, has a post-mediaeval extension, as also has the Gediz, but not the Küçük Menderes, whereas the Skamander delta has since early Classical times advanced not at all or only slightly. The presence of beach-ridges, dunes and lagoons is related to a decrease or standstill of delta-growth.

Synchronicity of Stream Deposition and Erosion

Vita-Finzi (1969b, 1972) has suggested the following general sequence regarding stream deposition and erosion in the Mediterranean:

20,000–10,000 B.P. : deposition of the older valley deposits (Fill I)

10,000–2000 B.P.   : erosion and downcutting, with increasing deposition of deltaic material between 5000 B.P. and 2000 B.P.

2000–300 B.P.   : deposition of the younger valley alluvium (Fill II)

300–0 B.P.   : erosion and increased delta-building.

Post-Roman deposits with C^{14} ages ranging from 1950 B.P. to 500 B.P. and containing Roman and mediaeval potsherds have been found in many areas around the Mediterranean. Their deposition coincides more or less with the alluvial plain-deposits in western Turkey (in so far as these have been dated) and with the slowing down of delta-progression on the Küçük and Büyük Menderes Rivers. After the mediaeval period of accumulation, the present channels were cut, a process which started in Italy and Greece in the sixteenth century, and probably much later elsewhere in the Mediterranean (Vita-Finzi, 1969a, b). This would be roughly con-temporaneous with a postulated increase in delta-building after 300 B.P.: the sudden local progression of the Gediz in the nineteenth century, the growth of the Sakarya delta in the last 30 years, and the formation after the sixteenth century of the southern part of the Büyük Menderes delta may be regarded as more-or-less synchronous, but as long as it is not known why these new accumulations took place such correlations are tentative at best.

During the period of erosion which preceded the deposition of the post-Roman valley-infill, down-cutting and bulk erosion resulted (according to Vita-Finzi, 1969b, 1972) in high sediment loads within the rivers and in delta-building. Although in general this may be true, it does not explain the acceleration in the progression of the Küçük Menderes delta in Hellenistic times (300–100 B.C.) nor, for example, the lack of accumulation at the Skamander mouth. In trying to explain these events the following broad processes are to be considered:

a. fluctuations in relative sea-level, caused either by eustatic sea-level changes or by tectonic movements;

b. soil erosion and/or historical changes in regional climate either of which might have brought about the deposition of the valley infill as well as the subsequent erosion;

c. local circumstances: the deltas of the Büyük Menderes, the Küçük Menderes, the Bakır Çay, the Skamander, and probably also the Gediz, while growing seawards, gradually reached deeper and more exposed open water, with stronger currents and waves, which may have slowed down delta-progression.

The question is whether stream deposition and erosion in the Mediterranean in historical times are indeed mainly determined by world-wide (or Mediterranean-wide) changes in climate and sea-level, or principally by the local or regional effects of tectonic movements, soil erosion and topographic changes, soil characteristics, currents, wave conditions and the like.

Relative Sea-level in Historical Times

Over historical times the sea-level around western Turkey has risen steadily, as is evident from the present position of many coastal ruins; and a similar movement has also been observed in other parts of the Mediterranean (Hafemann, 1960a, b, 1961; Flemming, 1969, 1972). Hafemann (1960a, 1961) concluded from a large number of observations that since around A.D. 800 sea-level has risen eustatically by 2 m ± 30 cm, and since approximately 500 B.C. by about 2·5–2·8 m. These estimates, however, were based on observations made in a region which is tectonically very active, while also, as Flemming (1969) has pointed out, the selection of the sites was biased. Pongratz (1972), measuring in Latium the position of Roman fish tanks which were placed directly in connection with the sea, deduced a relative rise of sea-level since c. 2000 B.P. of c. 1 m. Shepard's (1964) estimate for the eustatic sea-level rise in the same period is 1·5 m. Flemming (1972) calculated from many observations on coastal ruins in south-western Anatolia that the eustatic rise in sea-level since Classical times has only been very small, but that the coast between Izmir and Finike has been sinking since about 3000 B.P. at an average rate of 0–0·5 m per 1000 years. Sea-level, Flemming concludes, was in 3000 B.P. within a few centimetres of the present, dropped gradually to − 30 cm in 1300 B.P., and subsequently rose again. This agrees with his conclusions (Flemming, 1969, 1972) for other parts of the Mediterranean, and with those of Mörner (1969) based on observations in southern Scandinavia; but less well with those of Fairbridge (1961), Shepard (1964) and others (vid. Flemming, 1969), who, however, apart from other uncertainties, were not able to measure the influence of small tectonic movements on their sea-level curves.

The main post-Glacial rise in sea-level ended about 4,000 years B.P. when sea-level was near the present level (Mörner, 1969). Apart from the small rise of sea-level since Classical times, virtually no indications have as yet been found on the west Anatolian coast of other fluctuations, such as a postulated high post-Glacial sea-level resulting in a wave-cut terrace at + 3–4 m which has been observed in neighbouring areas—the Dardanelles, the Black Sea, the Levant, northern Egypt, Corinth, Silifke (Butzer, 1958; Fink and Schröder, 1971; Brunnacker, 1973) and elsewhere (Fairbridge, 1961). Only near Foça has an old cliff at + 3 m been observed (Philippson, 1911). The lowest coastal (wave-cut) terrace that has been found in western Turkey south of the Dardanelles, at + 7 m near Selçuk (Ephesus) and Çeşme (Grund, 1906a, b; Erinç, 1955a), probably dates from the latest interglacial (Monastir II). There are very few indications that the small relative rise in sea-level in historical times has influenced stream deposition or erosion in western Turkey. Near the Büyük Menderes mouth there may be some recent flooding of the coastal plain due to a relative subsidence of the valley floor, but this is probably due to tectonic movements: a comparison of the 1906/09 map of Philippson (1936) with topographic maps of 1936 and 1949 suggests that the largest lagoon (Karina göl) has grown in size during the first half of this century, and that the wave-eroded gaps that connect the lagoon with the sea have become wider (Russell, 1954). Tectonic movements may also have caused the Büyük Menderes to change its western course for a southern one below Söke.

Soil Erosion and Climatic Changes

Agriculture and animal husbandry started about 10,000 years B.C. in Iran in the Kurdish foothills, and by 7000 B.C. farming was firmly established in several parts of the Near East (Butzer, 1964, 1965). In Turkey, including the western part, wild wheats and barley are endemic, and the very early agricultural settlements in south-western Turkey and Greece (Hacılar, Çatal Hüyük and Sesklo, beginning already at 7000–6000 B.C.) indicate that farming and husbandry (sheep, goat and pig) have been practised in this area for more than 8000 years. The necessary clearance of forests, the widespread use of fire (plot-burning), grazing and overgrazing, the agricultural use of the soil leading to changes in soil structure and composition, the chopping of wood for fuel, and gradually also the increasing use of wood for the construction of houses and ships, caused in the long-run large-scale destruction and alteration of the natural vegetation. The destruction of the protective vegetational cover resulted in degradation and often erosion of the soil; and especially where this soil was already poor and thin—as on limestones and many loose and permeable sandy and loamy deposits—this process is irreversible.

The natural vegetation in western Turkey in the early period of agriculture consisted of subtropical woodlands in the coastal areas (mainly pinewoods and maquis) and of deciduous mixed forests of pine, oak and juniper on the higher hills and mountains (Louis, 1939; Butzer, 1965; Krause, 1917, 1929). This is also approximately the present vegetational pattern so that, apart from human interference, probably only small changes have occurred. From pollen records preserved in a peat deposit in northern

Turkey (near Yeniçağa göl, north-west of Ankara; Beug, 1967) some minor vegetational changes have been deduced: around 2000 b.c. there was a decrease in the proportion of beech and fir pollen and an increase in pine with an admixture of juniper, heather and chestnut. This may have been due to the onset of the drier period which Butzer (1957, 1958) has postulated for the Near East between 2400 and 850 b.c.: but also perhaps to human activity, for Beug (1967) has pointed out that many Indo-European people migrated to Anatolia at that time; and near Abant Göl it can still be seen that cutting of the beech and fir forest and heavy grazing leads to increased growth of juniper.

In western Turkey remnants of the original forest (of pine, oak and juniper) are found solely in the more remote mountain areas, and even there only in small locations which are difficult of access. The former woodlands have in large part been replaced by maquis, evergreen bush with hard and leathery leaves, and loose groups of trees. In the Mediterranean littoral zone, which is very dry in summer and where winter temperatures are nearly always above 0°C, maquis is the normal vegetation; but it has often been replaced by a degraded form, the phrygana, with smaller, thornier and more xeromorph shrubs. Krause (1929) has pointed out that since in Italy and Greece extensive deforestation occurred in Classical times, this undoubtedly also took place in western Turkey, although it is less well documented: the effects are evident in the form of denuded limestone hills, dissected bad-lands, phrygana, and the isolated remains of the original forest. In the pollen records of Yeniçağa the increase in the pollen of walnut and chestnut also points to intensifying human interference. Evidence for an extension of agriculture, however, has not yet been found in the Anatolian pollen diagrams.

It is probable that the rapid acceleration in the advance of the delta of the Küçük Menderes between the period of 300–100 b.c. was due to soil erosion, as it corresponds with a period of extensive colonization and devastation by wars in Hellenistic times when, after the conquest of Alexander the Great, Greek influence reached far into Asia Minor (Eisma, 1964). Similarly, the progression of the Büyük Menderes delta may be related to the intensive cultivation of its catchment area, as was already pointed out by Pausanias (VIII, 24, 11). The slowing down of delta growth could be an after-effect of soil erosion: when most of the available soil has been removed, there is little left on the nearly bare slopes to be transported, while the process of soil formation is far too slow to supply as much sediment to the streams as was transported when the soils were

D

being eroded. It is clear, however, that in the case of both rivers local factors may also have been involved: for during the Middle Ages both streams reached deeper and more open water, as had been the case at the Skamander mouth already since around 1000 B.C. Vita-Finzi (1969a, 1969b) has correlated the retarding of delta growth with the deposition of the alluvial fill further upstream. This depositional change would be due to a slight change in climate resulting in rainfall being more evenly distributed throughout the year, which would effect a more regular stream regime than at present. Butzer (1958, 1959) found indications of a moister period in Asia Minor between A.D. 800 and 1000, and relatively moister winters again at the end of the thirteenth and the beginning of the fifteenth and seventeenth centuries. Descriptions by Arab geographers of North African streams in the Middle Ages point to silt-laden floods building up the valley floor, where now the stream bed is incised and no such floods occur (Vita-Finzi, 1969a). But, although a somewhat different stream regime during the Middle Ages seems likely, the formation of the thick alluvial deposits is hardly compatible with the presence of a closed vegetational cover, so that de-vegetation and soil erosion must have been important. In these post-Roman times also a certain measure of coincidence of events could be supposed, as soil erosion may have increased more-or-less simultaneously in many regions of the Mediterranean due to the disorganization and neglect which followed the break-up of the Roman Empire. Moreover, a period of incision and lowering of the stream bed would logically have followed a period of accumulation, since the decrease in the sediment load of the streams, after most of the soil had been removed, would increase their capacity to erode and to cut a new river bed. Thus soil erosion too would to a large extent account both for the observed Mediaeval accumulation and for the subsequent erosion.

Soil erosion has occurred, however, since the early Classical period—in Greece on a particularly wide scale—and has continued until very recent times: in the western Mediterranean it increased during the nineteenth century in a degree not known before (Houston, 1964), and in Pamphylia there are now bare hills and mountain-sides where descriptions from as late as 1915 mention an open forest (Blumenthal, 1963). There exists, however, no systematic history of soil erosion in western Turkey, and the indications of climatic changes are also few, the data being still insufficient to come to any definite conclusions. A comparative study of the data on the west Anatolian rivers, however, makes it clear that delta building especially has to a large extent been influenced by local circumstances.

References

Beug, H. J. 1967. Contributions to the post glacial vegetational history of northern Turkey. *Quaternary Paleoecology. Proc. VII Congress Int. Assoc. Quat. Res.* **7**, 349–356.

Birot, P. and Dresch, J. 1956. *La Méditerranée et le Moyen Orient* Vol. II. Paris: Serie Orbis.

Blumenthal, E. 1963. Die altgriechische Siedlungskolonisation im Mittelmeerraum unter besonderer Berücksichtigung der Südküste Kleinasiens. *Tübinger Geogr. Studien* **10**.

Brunnacker, K. 1973. Bemerkungen zu quartären Strandterrassen des Mittelmeers. *N. Jahrb. Geol. Paläont.* **3**, 129–135.

Butzer, K. W. 1957. Late glacial and post glacial climatic variation in the Near East. *Erdkunde* **11**, 21–35.

Butzer, K. W. 1958. Quaternary stratigraphy and climate in the Near East. *Bonner Geogr. Abh.* **24**, 1–157.

Butzer, K. W. 1959. Contributions to the Pleistocene geology of the Nile valley. *Erdkunde* **13**, 46–67.

Butzer, K. W. 1964. *Environment and Archeology, an introduction to Pleistocene geography.* Chicago: University Press.

Butzer, K. W. 1965. Physical conditions in Eastern Europe, Western Asia and Egypt before the period of agricultural and other settlement. *The Cambridge Ancient History* (revised ed.) Vol. I, Ch. II. Cambridge: University Press.

Chaput, E. 1936. *Voyages d'études géologiques et géomorphogeniques en Turquie* Vol. II. Paris: Mém. de l'Inst. Fr. d'arch. d'Istanbul.

Cold, C. 1886. *Küsten—Veränderrungen im Archipel.* Thesis, Marburg.

Dörpfeld, W. 1902. *Troja und Ilion.* Athens.

Eisma, D. 1960. *Het berg- en bekkenland tussen Selçuk en Söke.* Unpublished report, Geogr. Inst. University of Utrecht.

Eisma, D. 1962. Beach ridges near Selçuk, Turkey. *Tijdschrift Kon. Ned. Aardr. Gen.* **79**, 234–246.

Eisma, D. 1964. Stream deposition in the Mediterranean area in historical times. *Nature* **203** (4949), 1061.

Erinç, S. 1955a. Gediz ve Küçük Menderes deltalarinin morfolojisi. *9uncu Coğr. Meslek Haftasi, 22–29 Aralik 1954.* Türk Coğrafya Kurumu.

Erinç, S. 1955b. Ueber die Entstehung und morphologische Bedeutung des Tmolosschuts. *Rev. Geogr. Inst. Univ. Ist. (Int. ed.)* **2**, 57–72.

Erinç, S. 1955c. Die morphologische Entwicklungsstadien der Küçük Menderes Masse. *Rev. Geogr. Inst. Univ. Ist. (Int. ed.)* **2**, 93–95.

Fairbridge, Rh. W. 1961. Eustatic changes in sea level. *In: Physics and Chemistry of the Earth* Vol. 4, pp. 99–185. Oxford: Pergamon Press.

Flemming, N. C. 1969. *Archaeological evidence for eustatic change of sea level and* earth movements in the western Mediterranean during the last 2000 years. Geol. Soc. of America, Special paper 109.

Flemming, N. C. 1972. Eustatic and tectonic factors in the relative vertical displacement of the Aegean coast. In: The Mediterranean Sea (D. J. Stanley, ed.), pp. 189–201. Stroudsberg, Penn.: Dowden, Hutchinson and Ross.

Flemming, N. C., Czartorysk, N. M. G. and Hunter, P. M. 1971. Archaeological evidence for eustatic and tectonic components of relative sea level change in the South Aegean. In: Marine Archaeology (D. J. Blackman, ed.), pp. 1–66. London: Butterworth.

Fink, R. and Schröder, B. 1971. Anzeichen eines holozänen Meereshochstandes an der Landenge von Korinth. N. Jb. Geol. Paläont. Mh. 265–270.

Grund, A. 1906a. Vorläufiger Bericht über physiogeographische Untersuchungen im Deltagebiet des Kleinen Mäander bei Ajasoluk (Ephesos). Sitz. Ber. Kais. Akad. Wiss. Math.—Naturw. Kl. 115, 241–262.

Grund, A. 1906b. Vorläufiger Bericht über physiogeographische Untersuchungen in den Deltagebieten des Grossen und Kleinen Mäander. Sitz. Ber. Kais. Akad. Wiss. Math.—Naturw. Kl. 115, 1757–1769.

Hafemann, D. 1960a. Die Frage des eustatischen Meeresspiegelanstiegs in historischer Zeit. Tagungsber, D. Geografentag Berlin 1959, pp. 218–231.

Hafemann, D. 1960b. Anstieg des Meeresspiegels in geschichtlicher Zeit. Umschau 7, 193–196.

Hafemann, D. 1961. Art und Ausmass des Meeresspiegelanstiegs in den letzten zweieinhalb Jahrtausenden. Ber. deutsche Landesk. 27, 229–234.

Houston, J. M. 1964. The Western Mediterranean World. London: Longmans.

Kiepert, H. 1887. Veränderungen im Mündungsgebiete des Flusses Hermos in Kleinasien. Globus 51, 150–152.

Krause, K. 1917. Die Wälder Kleinasiens. Archiv. Wirtschaftsforschung im Orient 2, 161–201.

Krause, K. 1929. Die Vegetationsverhältnisse der Milesischen Halbinsel, In: Milet (Th. Wiegand, ed.) Vol. II, p. 2.

Louis, H. 1939. Das natürliche Pflanzenkleid Anatoliens. Stuttgart.

Milliman, J. D. and Emery, K. O. 1968. Sea levels during the past 35,000 years. Science 162, 1121–1123.

Mörner, N. A. 1969. Eustatic and climatic changes during the last 15,000 years. Geol. en Mijnb. 48, 389–399.

Nebert, K. 1955. Die Braunkohlenvorkommen nördlich Nazilli. Report-Maden Tetkik ve Arama Enstitüsü, Ankara.

Philippson, A. 1910. Reisen und Forschungen im westlichen Kleinasien I. Petermanns Mitt. Erg. 167.

Philippson, A. 1911. Reisen und Forschungen im westlichen Kleinasien II. Petermanns Mitt. Erg. 172.

Philippson, A. 1920. Zur morphologischen Karte des westlichen Kleinasien. Petermanns Mitt. 66, 197–202.

Philippson, A. 1936. Das südliche Ionien. *In: Milet* (Th. Wiegand, ed.), Vol. III, p. 5.

Pongratz, E. 1972. Historische Bauwerke als Indikatoren für Küsten-morphologische Veränderungen (Abrasion und Meeresspiegelschwankungen) in Latium—Feldbegehung und Luftbildauswertung. *Münchener Geogr. Abh.* **4**.

Rayet, O. and Thomas, A. 1877. *Milet et le Golfe Latmique*, Vol. I. Paris: J. Bawdry.

Russell, R. J. 1954. Alluvial morphology of Anatolian rivers. *Ann. Assoc. Amer. Geogr.* **44**, 363–391.

Schliemann, H. 1881. *Ilios, Stadt und Land der Trojaner.* Leipzig: Brockhaus.

Schede, M. 1964. *Die Ruinen von Priene.* Berlin: De Gruyter.

Shepard, F. P. 1964. Sea level changes in the past 6000 years: possible archaeological significance. *Science* **143**, 574–576.

Vita-Finzi, C. 1964. Synchronous stream deposition throughout the Mediterranean area in historical times. *Nature* **202**, 1324.

Vita-Finzi, C. 1969a. *The Mediterranean Valleys.* Cambridge: University Press.

Vita-Finzi, C. 1969b. Late Quaternary continental deposits of central and western Turkey. *Man* **4**, 605–619.

Vita-Finzi, C. 1972. Supply of fluvial sediment to the Mediterranean during the last 20,000 years. *In: The Mediterranean Sea* (D. J. Stanley, ed.), pp. 43–46.

Wiegand, Th. 1929. Die Milesische Landschaft. *In: Milet.* (Th. Wiegand, ed.), Vol. II, p. 2.

Synopsis of Part II

There is a broad coincidence between the conclusions of Higgs from his work in northern Greece and those of Bottema drawn from palynological sections from a wider area of the eastern Mediterranean and the Levant: the prevailing vegetation of the Last Glacial period was dry cold steppe with an association of Artemisia; forest began to spread in the early part of the Late Glacial and, after a brief revival of steppe, the post-Glacial tree-cover took general hold after 10,000 B.P.

This approximate date of 10,000 B.P is taken by Clutton-Brock to mark the start of the "Aceramic Neolithic" period in the Levant, when the hunting of gazelle gradually gave place to the keeping of domesticated caprines.

Higgs remarks that the habit of domestication was firmly established in northern Greece by 8000 B.P. at latest, but notices no trace of any consequent deterioration in the vegetation over the succeeding three millennia. Raphael, by contrast, blames the damage to the vegetation of the Peloponnese after 8000 B.P. for the supply of excessive alluvium which in Roman times accumulated in the lower valley of the Sachia, burying Hellenistic remains, and supplied the beach-ridges. On the other side of the Aegean, too, Eisma assembles impressive evidence for a rapid acceleration in the extension of deltas in the period of three or four centuries just around the turn of the era. This phase of valley erosion and the expansion of deltas followed an earlier period of the accretion of alluvial fans and valley fill. On the evidence of Schliemann and Dorpfeld (p. 73) the Skamander delta appears to be an exception; but the more recent study by Bilgin evidently shows that it has indeed expanded during the last 3000 years (pp. 104–5).

Both Raphael and Eisma draw attention to the instability of the shores of the Aegean, and to the isostatic movements, studied by Flemming in particular, which must have had local effects on coastal processes. In addition to Flemming's work, the acute observations of George Bean should be noted, in his *Aegean Turkey* (pp. 106, 142) and *Turkey's Southern Shore* (1968, pp. 154–5, 160, 171, 173). It seems that while the Lycian coasts of southern Anatolia have risen relative to the sea since Classical times, the western shores have sunk generally by some 1·5–1·8 m. The question of tectonic instability will be considered again by Erinç in regard to the shores of Turkey, by Ambraseys with reference to the high plateaux, and in a discussion of the processes at work in the contentious region of the delta of Lower Iraq.

At this point, as a link with what will be discussed in Parts IV and V (see p. 278) we may notice a three-fold sequence of climate and stratigraphy established recently in the region of the Wadi Gaza below the hills of South Judaea (David Price–Williams, The British Western Negev Expedition, *Quest* **31,** Summer 1976, 32–34). First, between 60,000 and 40,000 B.P. this was a land of braided streams, with a climate of "North Mediterranean" type, cooler and probably hotter than now, and a riverine vegetation of juniper, willow and poplar where the Mousterian population hunted primaeval cattle and wild ass. Second, from about 40,000 to 10,000 B.P., when sea-level fell and more land was exposed to the west, conditions grew more arid, silts washed down by desert floods accumulated to great depths, and the region was virtually deserted. Thirdly, after about 10,000 B.P. winter rains increased, and the silts were rapidly cut away; Neolithic farmers moved in, but occupation remained erratic as the climate was never better than semi-arid. This succession accords broadly with that postulated by Butzer for the "Desert Belt" (p. 7, Zone C.).

III

The Plateaux of Anatolia and Iran

As in East and North Africa, so in the plateaux of Anatolia and Iran, the fluctuations of levels of water in the great lake-basins, if they can be dated, should help in defining the degree of aridity at different periods: and, as in the Alps, the advance and retreat of the glaciers of the Anti-Taurus and Anti-Caucasus ranges must also reflect changes of climate. It is at first sight paradoxical that this region where seasonal changes are now so extreme should have witnessed some of the earliest attempts to apply the arts of farming and domestication; and it is reasonable to ask whether these attempts were related to contemporary changes of climate or topography. Further, it is evident from literature and archaeology that these plateaux supported some two or three millennia ago a considerably larger population and a more productive rural economy than they do now, and the further questions arise of whether the natural conditions at that time were different from those of today, and, if they were, in what measure and why. These are the main concerns of the first four studies which follow. The fifth sets out in summary fashion the conclusions so far of an attempt to compile the seismic history of the region, work of manifest value both for understanding past calamities and for predicting those which unfortunately will happen in time to come.

7
Changes in the Physical Environment in Turkey Since the End of the Last Glacial

Sirri Erinç

Introduction

Although discussion on the Pleistocene–Holocene boundary continues and although the last deglaciation began at different times in different regions, there is a general agreement that roughly 20,000 years have elapsed since the Last Würm Maximum. Therefore it seems best to ignore local differences in the duration of the "post-Glacial" epoch, and to study it instead on a world scale. It has been a time of complex changes, involving a transition from the completely different environment of the Last Glacial to that of the present, and most noticeably from a low sea-level to that of the present day.

In a study of changes of physical environment during this post-Glacial epoch, Turkey merits special attention for several reasons. Lying as it does between generally arid and generally humid areas, this country is extremely sensitive to even minor changes of atmospheric circulation. Moreover, in districts of markedly different climate, there survive traces of both glacial and pluvial phases. Turkey is of course located in a tectonically and seismically very active zone; and, finally, it has experienced continuous settlement for at least 10,000–12,000 years, and possesses a rich record of human occupation, in the form both of archaeological remains and of written documents, which enables us to evaluate man's role in modifying the environment.

Changes in the physical environment within Turkey during the post-Glacial epoch have been extremely complex and varied, and have involved climate, vegetation, drainage, hydrology, crustal deformations, pedogenesis and shifts of coastline. The story is complicated by the wide differences of climate and morphology within the different parts of the country. Nevertheless, most changes were, and still are, linked by chain-reactions, and, therefore, it seems possible to group them, according to their first causes, into four main categories:

1. changes in climate and their consequences;
2. changes due to exogenous processes;
3. changes due to endogenous processes;
4. changes resulting from human activities.

Conditions during the Last Ice Age

In the following pages, changes of physical environment in Turkey during the last 20,000 years will be outlined in accordance with the above grouping, but, first, a short description of the geography of Turkey during the Last Glacial may serve as a basis for comparison.

During the Last Glacial in Turkey, there was a fall of mean annual temperatures by 4° to 5°C, probably accompanied by a slight increase in precipitation, and certainly by a considerably higher percentage and longer duration of snowfall. There followed inevitably a reduction of ablation and evaporation, an increased accumulation of ice, and a general lowering of the snow line of between 600 and 800 m. There is, however, a striking parallelism between the isolines of the Last Glacial snow lines and those of the present. Indeed, during the Last Glacial, the snow line was, as now, lowest on the outer slopes of the northern (2200 m) and southern (2400 m) marginal mountains, and became gradually higher towards the interior (because of increasing continentality), to reach its maximum in eastern Anatolia (3400 m). This indicates that the general pattern of atmospheric circulation, as well as regional differences in the distribution of precipitation, following on differences of exposure, were, during the Last Glacial, very similar to what we see now, and that the changes leading to glacial conditions in Turkey were mainly caused by a lowering of temperature. It follows that the general distribution of ice during the last glaciation was like that which obtains at present (Erinç, 1952a). More specifically, the former maximum of glaciation was reached, as today, in the east Pontic Mountains in the north, and in the Cilo and Sat Mountains in the south-east, where glaciers of a thickness of more than 500 m, and of a length exceeding 10 km, accumulated and descended to a height of

2000–1500 m above sea-level. During this same period, the whole length of the Taurus ranges, and several mountains of the interior which rose sufficiently high above the snow line, carried small valley and cirque glaciers or ice caps. In the ranges which cross eastern Anatolia, glaciation was much more intense than was once assumed, and led, for example in the Munzur Mountains, to the formation of glaciers 15 km long descending from mountain ice-sheets. Extensive glaciation in such extremely continental areas of relatively low rainfall is another indication that a lowering of temperature was the main cause of the Last Ice Age.

Changes of climate, and especially the reduced evaporation, had also affected the hydrological balance, and resulted in considerable rises of level in existing lakes (Van, Tuz, Burdur, İznik, Acıgöl, Hazar), or in the formation of new lakes, such as the pluvial Konya Lake, a body of water 25 m deep which extended over 9100 km^2. River discharges were considerably higher than before, and streams therefore were very active in cutting down and reaching back, with the result that there occurred successive captures of the drainage of closed basins, and the total area of interior drainage shrank. The timber line was 600–700 m lower than at present, the zones of Mediterranean and Colchic floras became narrower, and true steppes were much reduced in extent. Laterization, which, during the preceding Interglacial period, had been the prevailing process of soil formation up to 1000 m above the sea in the outer slopes of east Pontic Mountains, was replaced by podsolization. To complete the picture of conditions during the Last Glacial, we should remember that the level of the sourrounding seas was lowered by 90 m, and that the Bosporus and Hellespont were converted to broad land-bridges connecting the two continents.

Climatic Changes and their Consequences

In the present state of our knowledge it is almost impossible to give a complete and systematic picture of the climatic changes in Turkey during the post-Glacial period. In what follows an attempt will be made to outline the climatic evolution during the post-Glacial epoch by assembling scattered observations which may serve as indirect evidence, such as variations in glacier stands, in lake and sea-levels, in drainage, and in vegetation. The picture will be completed by an analysis of historical and meteorological records, and of some results of dendro-climatological work. Nevertheless, due to the scarcity of absolute determinations of age, and of palynological studies, it cannot be assumed that correlations of time are all satisfactorily established; and, for the same reasons, we think that it is too early to compile all the regional results in a comparative table.

Glacial Variations as Evidence of Climatic Changes

Studies carried out in the areas of past and present glaciation in Turkey indicate a remarkable general parallelism between the variations of extent of glaciers in the Pontic Mountains, the Taurus, north-western Anatolia and even the isolated mountains and ranges of the interior (see the references at the end of this chapter). In all the areas mentioned, the retreat of the Pleistocene glaciers is marked by recessional stages, varying in number between two and five. This general shrinkage seems to have ended in the total extinction of the Pleistocene glaciers. Indeed, moraines resulting from post-Glacial phases of extension of ice overlie on a considerable scale morainic deposits dating from the Last Glacial epoch, which indicates that ''post-Glacial'' glaciers are not the direct survivors of the Pleistocene glaciers, but were regenerated in a cold stage of post-Glacial times (Erinç, 1952b; Klaer, 1962). During the maximum post-Glacial advance, glaciers covered an area roughly twice as large as that over which they now extend.

Unfortunately, we cannot as yet date exactly these glacial events in the post-glacial epoch. From comparative studies, however, it seems highly probable that the complete disappearance of the retreating Pleistocene glaciers should be placed in the post-glacial Optimum (7000–5000 years B.P.). This phase was followed by a continuous expansion of the regenerated glaciers, most probably in a colder period, around 4500–4000 years B.P. The situation then reverted through a general glacial shrinkage, interrupted by several stages of recession and re-advance during historical times. Indeed, there are widespread indications of glacial advances in the seventeenth century (around A.D. 1600 and 1680), and in the early eighteenth (1720?) and the mid-nineteenth (around 1850). Since then, the general trend has been towards shrinkage, possibly interrupted by a less marked short episode of expansion at the turn of century. A study of pictures taken at different dates, confirmed by a comparison of observations, indicates that recession has continued for the last 70 years, though both the time of the start and the rate of shrinkage varied from district to district.

Changes in Lake Levels

Climatic changes during the post-Glacial epoch were reflected also in a series of changes in the lake levels. These changes affected the prehistoric inhabitants more directly than did the variations in the glaciers, which happened well above the levels favourable for living. Geomorphic and geological evidence indicates repeated changes of level during the Quaternary (Fig. 1) in the basins of several Turkish lakes, including Van, İznik, Acıgöl and Hazar. In most cases, however, it is at the moment hardly possible to make a clear distinction between post-Glacial and earlier levels. The two exceptions are the Konya and Burdur Basins, where Pleistocene and younger terraces may be distinguished thanks to prehistoric finds and C^{14} determinations.

In both basins, the general trend has been towards a lowering of lake level, interrupted by humid stages during which younger fill terraces were deposited. The general lowering of level resulted in the total drying out of the former Konya Lake, whereas the Burdur Basin is still occupied by a lake of a maximum depth of 45 m. According to Erol (1971) and Sungur (1974), the pluvial terraces of the former Burdur Lake are clearly divided into an older (Pleistocene) and a younger (post-Glacial) set. The younger (post-Glacial) terraces are developed below the 935 m terrace on which are located the Neolithic site of Hacılar (earliest occupation 7050 B.C.) and the Mesolithic artifacts found by Louis (1938) at Baradiz. The younger terraces of the basin are composed of three fills, according to Erol and Sungur, though these two differ on the question of terrace altitudes. They agree, however, on two essential points—that the climate has undergone considerable variations during the last 9000 years, with a general trend to the semi-arid conditions of the present day; and that the formation of the lowest of the Pleistocene terraces (that at 935 m above sea-level) was followed by a considerable and apparently long-lasting regression which may, in our opinion, be correlated with the arid interval of the post-Glacial Climatic Optimum (7000–5000 B.P.). The younger and less marked three terraces should be linked to high stands of the Burdur Lake, and were most likely caused by further periods of relative cold, as reflected in the stages of re-expansion and recession of mountain glaciers during the last 4000 years.

The general trend of changes in the Konya Basin, which is today partly occupied by patches of swamps and sand dunes, seems to have followed essentially the same pattern as that observed in the Burdur Basin. But, here again, opinions differ as to the number of terraces and their altitudes.

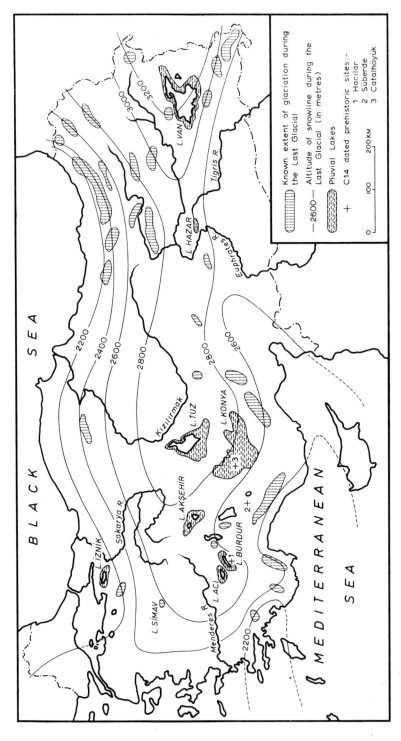

Fig. 1: Geomorphic and geological evidence of the repeated changes of level during the Quaternary

Sungur (1967) was the first to put forward evidence of three well-marked pluvial high levels of the former Konya Lake at 1010, 995 and 990 m above sea-level. Subsequently, however, Erol (1971) outlined a more complex picture, assuming a high level at 1017 m (and a 1010 level, ascribed to the Pleistocene), and adding three intermediate terraces at 1006, 1002 and 1000 m. The matter is, at present, open to question, and requires further investigation. One observation, however, stands beyond any doubt, namely that the latest two (according to Sungur) or three (Erol) of the younger terraces are certainly of post-Glacial age. Indeed, the prehistoric site of Çatalhüyük, dated back by C^{14} to 6400 B.C., is located on a fill surface at 1000–1006 m. Thus, the general pattern of climatic changes in the Konya Basin seems to have followed the same line as in that of Burdur. Geomorphologic evidence described by Sungur indicates that extremely dry conditions prevailed in the Konya Basin following the last stand of the lake. Indeed, the lake was completely dried out, and loose sandy material of its former floor was subjected to an intense deflation, leading to the formation of typical hair-pin dunes of a length of between 2 and 4 km. These desert conditions, which prevailed during the post-Glacial Climatic Optimum, between 7000 and 5000 years ago, were later succeeded, around 4000 B.P. by a relatively cooler and moister period, which resulted in the stabilization and fossilization of the hair-pin dunes through a denser vegetation. In later centuries, the climate has continued to fluctuate, finally to reach the semi-desert character of recent times, when the former sandy deposits of the pluvial lake have been again picked up and transported by wind to form the small chains of barchans around Karapınar.

Climatic variations during recent centuries have continued to effect oscillations of lake levels. The longest available record on this subject, analysed by Erinç (1953), is based on descriptions dealing with the level of Lake Van. It indicates a considerable rise of level in the years A.D. 1740, 1810, 1850 and 1875–80, and a lowering in 1852 and 1892.*

Changes in Drainage

Variations of climate in post-Glacial times have naturally affected the hydrological balance of the terrain, and in this way have brought about some changes of drainage. The general effect of climatic changes has been a decrease in discharge, which has impoverished the river systems and led to an expansion of the areas of interior drainage. A typical example is provided by the İncesu Valley to the south-east of Ankara (Fig. 2). This is a

*Quaternary Lake Van; see Postscript, p. 108.

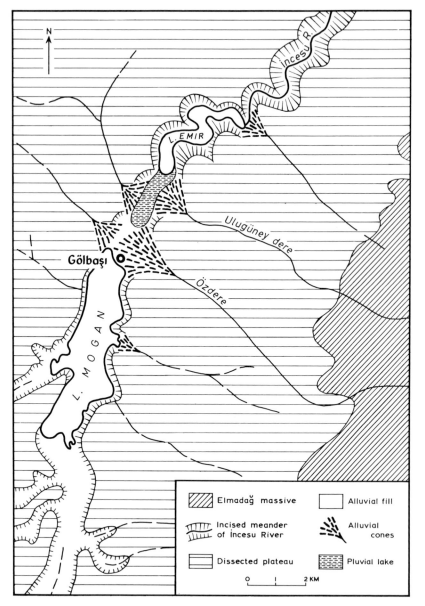

Fig. 2: The former southward extension of Lake Emir is now occupied by swamps.

connecting gorge with incised meanders, and used to link its catchment area to the coast. In the post-Glacial epoch, however, the stream discharge was considerably reduced. This resulted in the blocking of the valley by alluvial cones and the formation of two lakes (Emir and Moğan) without natural outlet. A similar expansion of interior basins during the post-Glacial epoch is reported from the area between the upper courses of the Sakarya River and the Sultan Mountains in south-western central Anatolia (Darkot, 1936), where there is a well developed system of dry valleys. The more arid conditions of post-Glacial times also account for the extension of interior drainage to include the basins of the Burdur and Acıgöl Lakes further to the west. This deterioration of the hydrological balance has also indirectly affected the physical environment of man during the post-Glacial by bringing about changes in the chemical and biological properties of some lakes and by expanding the range of saline soils.

Changes in Sea-level

As a consequence of the world-wide eustatic movement during the Last Glacial, when much of the water of the Planet was removed from the oceans and sealed in land ice, the sea-level around Turkey was about 90–100 m lower than at present. Thus, some 20,000 years ago the Straits were transformed into land, the Sea of Marmara was occupied by a lake, and the Black Sea was in a state of regression and desalinization (the so-called New Euxine stage), while streams were actively cutting down their beds because of their increased gradients (Erinç, 1954). Following the peak of the Last Glacial, sea-level started to rise almost simultaneously both in the Mediterranean and Black Sea Basins. But there are several indications that the subsequent rise of sea-level was not a regular and continuous transgression: it was interrupted temporarily by several still-stands, and even by minor regressions. For example, studies of cores in the deltaic deposits of the Meriç River (Göçmen, 1973) and the Black Sea provide convincing evidence of a post-Glacial sea-level at around − 40 m. In the Black Sea Basin, disconnected from the Mediterranean but responding exactly in the same way to the glacio-eustatic movements, the rise in level, marking the second part of the New Euxine stage, was a result of post-Glacial conditions developing in the catchment area and over the Black Sea itself. It took the form of a freshwater transgression, and was later followed by the final intrusion of the waters of the Mediterranean into the Black Sea. It is widely believed that the salinization of the Black Sea Basin began simultaneously with the onset of the upward movement of the level of the ocean. In fact, the intrusion of the Mediterranean into the Black Sea was considerably delayed because of topographic and hydrologic conditions in the Straits, and the salinization of the Euxine Basin must have begun only at a time when the Mediterranean Sea rose to a level close to, or even higher than, that where it now stands. This deduction is proved positively by the C^{14} dates from cores obtained in the Black Sea Basin (Degens, 1971). They indicate that the mass intrusion of saline waters into the Black Sea started 7140 ± 180 years ago, and lasted up to 3000 years before the present, during which period there were drastic changes in the physical and biological conditions of the Black Sea. Several pieces of evidence indicate that, during this stage, roughly coinciding with the post-Glacial Climatic Optimum, sea-level all along Turkey's coasts stood 2–3 m higher than it does at present. Proofs of such a higher sea-level during the post-Glacial Climatic Optimum and in later centuries include widespread and well developed terraces (Erinç, 1954), corrasion notches and coastal caves with marine sands and prehistoric remains (Erol, 1963), and old beach-rock formations lying 2 m above the present sea-level and containing broken fragments of Hellenistic columns and jars (Bener, 1970). Then followed a slow regression, until the present sea-level was reached around 3000–2000 years B.P.

Changes in Vegetation

Throughout the Pleistocene, the alternation of glacial and inter-glacial conditions greatly affected both the territorial extension and the floristic structure of vegetation in Turkey. During glacial (or pluvial) periods, vertical vegetation zones were lowered by several hundred metres, and the strip of Mediterranean vegetation became narrower, while the Palaeoboreal forests expanded in the north and the steppes retreated towards the south-east. Interglacials (or interpluvials) were characterized by changes in the opposite sense. Repeated displacements to and fro of vegetation during the Pleistocene account for the very mixed flora of Turkey, and for the survival in several parts of the peninsula of Glacial, Mediterranean and Colchic relics.

The climate has been subjected to similar, though considerably less extreme, changes during the post-Glacial, and the present character of the vegetation in Turkey is chiefly the result of these changes, though it has been affected too by the long human occupance of the land. It is a completely safe assumption that, at the start of post-Glacial epoch, forests covered a considerably larger, and true steppes a much smaller, area than now. Unfortunately, there are no findings that provide positive confirmation of this picture. However, palynological analysis made at the prehistoric site of Süberde (C^{14} date 6570 B.C. ± 140 years) clearly support such an assumption (Aytuğ, 1967). They indicate a climate markedly cooler and moister than now, and the existence in this part of south-western interior Anatolia at roughly 8500 years B.P. of large tracts of forests, including *Pinus silvestris* and *Betula*, of a kind that is at present restricted to the northern and north-eastern region of Turkey. This relatively humid stage was followed by the extremely dry conditions of the post-Glacial Climatic Optimum between 7000 and 5000 B.P., as indicated by changes in glaciers, lake levels, and drainage. During this dry stage the former forests would shrink in size and change in composition, while the steppes would become more pure in form and more wide in extent. Subsequently, the climate has continued to fluctuate, and we may assume that these oscillations have led eventually to at least a partial recovery of the forest vegetation. Indeed, botanical and archaeological investigations at Gordion in central Anatolia, lying in the heart of the present steppes, have proved that 2500 years ago well developed non-deciduous forests (*Taxus baccata, Pinus silvestris, Cedrus libanii,* etc.) flourished there and were exploited (C^{14} date 2500 ± 60 B.P.; Kayacık and Aytuğ, 1968). Thereafter, the exploitation of forests, which continued at an accelerating pace, for the purposes of obtaining materials for construction, mining and export, resulted during the pre-Hellenistic, Hellenistic and Roman epochs in considerable changes in the natural vegetation of the country. Already at Strabo's time central Anatolia was completely deprived of its forests (Strabo, *Geography*, 6. 1), and by the end of the tenth century A.D. the vegetational wealth of most of this region had been thoroughly exhausted (Brice, 1966, pp. 48–51, 53, 283). Through the devastation by man in later centuries, the forested area continued to shrink, even in the humid coastal strip of the eastern Black Sea, resulting in the disappearance of several dense forests admiringly described by the travellers of the nineteenth century. It is clear that large tracts of the central Anatolian steppe landscape are not a direct result of past and present climates, but have been converted to treeless anthropogene steppes through the reckless exploitation by the inhabitants of the former mostly park-like forest vegetation (Uslu, 1960).

Evidence of Climatic Changes in Historical, Dendroclimatological and Meteorological Records

In the preceding paragraphs, the indirect evidence of climatic variations through the post-Glacial period has been summarized. In the following, an attempt will be made to complete the picture by analysing some historical, dendroclimatological and meteorological records.

Documents maintained in the Turkish archives have not yet been systematically perused for evidence of climatic conditions in historic times; but it would not be wise to expect such studies to provide an unbroken record of former climate. Moreover, the evaluation of and generalization from such records require a particular quality of caution, because of the subjective and for the most part parochial character of descriptions of periods of drought and extreme cold. At present, we are best informed about the climatic conditions of the historical past which prevailed in and around İstanbul. An analysis of data related to temperature variations enables us to distinguish the following periods.

1. Around the first century A.D., temperature was close to, or perhaps a little lower than, that of the present. There was a possible slight increase in temperature up to the beginning of the eighth century.

2. A colder period extending from the middle of the eighth century to the thirteenth, during which the Bosporus, and even parts of the Black Sea, were repeatedly frozen, and floating ice masses were driven about in the Sea of Marmara (e.g. in the years 739, 753, 755, 762, 928, 934, 1011 and 1213).

3. A period of markedly mild winters for 400 years from the middle of the thirteenth century to the middle of the seventeenth.

4. A relatively colder period with severe winters starting in the middle of the seventeenth century and lasting up to the present day (with freezing of the Bosporus, the Golden Horn and parts of the Black Sea in A.D. 1620, 1669, 1849 and 1893). However, the intensity of the winter cold has gradually diminished during this period.

In historical records, droughts are given particular attention because of their adverse effects on agricultural activities and crop yields. It is evident from Herodotus's description (I. 94) of western Anatolia that periodic or non-periodic severe droughts occurred here also during early Classical times. In the Middle Ages central Anatolia was hit several times by destructive arid conditions. The only dendroclimatological study available (Gassner and Christiansen-Weniger, 1948) shows that the climate has continued to oscillate between moist and arid conditions during the last few centuries, and that central Anatolia repeatedly suffered from severe droughts in the years 1770–73, 1779–82, 1792, 1799–1803, 1819–22, 1845, 1853, 1873–74, 1882, 1890–92, 1894, 1898–1900, 1916–18 and 1927–30. The disastrous effects of the drought of 1873–74, which led to the total failure of crops, to the loss of several hundreds of thousands of domestic animals, and to the death and dispersion of thousands of the farming population are described by Naumann (Erinç, 1950), while the similar consequences of arid conditions in 1916–18 and 1927–30 are still alive in memory.

Only the meteorological records maintained in İstanbul over a period of nearly 130 years are long enough to be useful for detecting climatic variations (Erinç and Bener, 1961). An analysis of rainfall from data here has shown that precipitation, both annual and seasonal, has been subject to marked periodic and nonperiodic changes; and also that there have occurred remarkable deviations from the present precipitation regime in such a way that normally dry summers have alternated with remarkably wet summers during the last 100 years.

Changes in the Physical Environment due to Exogenous Processes

Considerable changes in the physical environment since the Last Glacial in Turkey have been brought about by exogenous processes such as fluvial aggradation, coastal development, karstification, mass movements and deflation. Most of these phenomena are closely related to and reflect changes in climate.

The major part of the alluvial fills which form both the smaller and the larger plains of the country is the outcome of fluvial deposition during post-Glacial times. These flat lowlands, as well as the former floors of shrinking post-Glacial lakes, covered with rich alluvial deposits, have provided the most favourable terrain for settlement and agriculture since Prehistoric times. At the beginning, they must have had an indeterminate drainage and, most probably, have been infested by malaria, so that settlements were mainly located on the relatively higher alluvial fans and piedmont plains on the peripheries.

However, the role of fluvial aggradation, jointly with thalassogene processes, in changing the coastline has been more significant, and has deeply affected both the landscape and the destiny of several important settlements. Deltas and deltaic fills all along the coast of Turkey owe their formation and present shape to fluvial and marine processes which have been operating since the present sea-level was reached, that is in the last 7000 years. Further, the post-Glacial rise of sea-level had resulted in the formation of a wide variety of types of submerged shoreline all along the coasts of Turkey, with both large and small gulfs and embayments, and in the transformation of former stream valleys within the Bosporus and Hellespont into the present sea passages linking the Mediterranean and the Black Sea. All these changes are so recent as to have been witnessed by prehistoric man, so that it is quite understandable why the origin of Bosporus was explained, in early Antiquity, as due to an overspilling of the Black Sea.

The coastal types which took shape through the initial post-Glacial submergence have been preserved almost intact in areas where streams are only small or where the sedimentary load is not great enough to change the coastline significantly. The coasts of Dalmatian type and *rias* of the southwest Anatolia, the *liman* coasts and *rias* of the northern shores of the Sea of Marmara, and the typical *rias* formed by the Bosporus and the Golden Horn may be cited as instances where initial submergence features have been preserved without any substantial change.

On the other hand, a rapid alteration has taken place in coastal areas where powerful streams have been depositing their heavy load along with marine sediments. The results of this joint process are either the typical large protruding deltas of the Yeşilırmak, Kızılırmak, Göksu and Gediz, and the coalesced deltas of the Seyhan and Ceyhan Rivers, or deltaic plains with smoothed fronts such as those of the Great Meander, the Lesser Meander, and the Bakırçay, depending on variations of the submarine topography and on the relative efficiency of the marine currents.

A typical example of these rapid coastal changes is provided by the deltaic plain of Çukurova (Cilicia) (Fig. 3). It is the joint work of the Tarsus, Seyhan and Ceyhan Rivers and has a more complex history than is usually thought. Indeed, it is composed of three slightly tilted fill terraces of Pleistocene age, surrounded at a lower level by a deltaic plain *sensu stricto* (Erinç, 1960). This plain, which carries no prehistoric mounds, is of post-Glacial age, and is bounded landwards by the front of the lowest Pleistocene terrace and seawards by saline marshes and lagoons. The width of the deltaic plain varies between 10 and 20 km. It follows that the rate of coastal progradation during the post-Glacial epoch must have been of the order of 150–300 m per century. River channels have shifted frequently in the deltaic plain, with the result that the area of maximum deposition has been displaced. It is a common belief that the ancient harbour city of Tarsus has lost its function as a result of rapid progradation. But this belief needs some correction: in fact, Tarsus did not stand on the coast of the

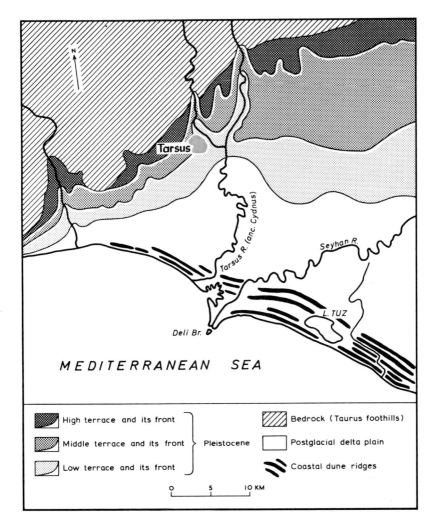

Fig. 3: The deltaic plain of Çukurova.

deltaic plain, but was founded on a slightly dissected terrace of the Tarsus River, and its decline as a port cannot therefore be directly ascribed to an advancing coastline which left the city stranded inland. The decline was the result rather of the rapid siltation of the Tarsus River.

Similar progradational processes have been operating in western Anatolia since the end of last Glacial. In the deltaic plain of the Küçük

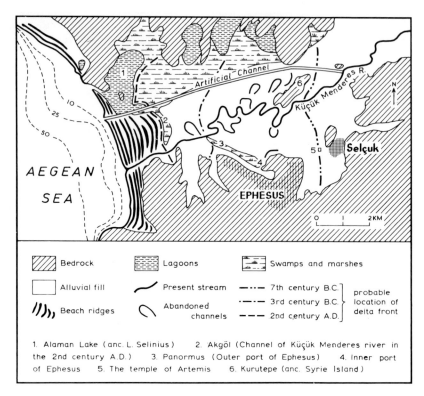

Fig. 4: The deltaic plain of the Küçük Menderes.

Menderes (Lesser Meander) (Fig. 4) the advance of the coastline through river action seems to have been much slower at the beginning. Indeed, during the period of more than 6000 years which elapsed between the time of the last preceding stand of sea-level and the seventh century B.C., the delta front could have reached only a line connecting Syrie island and the Artemision of Ephesus (Grund, 1906a and Erinç 1955), leaving the western part of the present plain occupied by extensive and deep lagoons. Subsequently, progradation was accelerated, as a result of which Syrie island became landlocked, and it seems to have become necessary to shift the site of Ephesus (in 286 B.C.) and to undertake dredging operations in the harbour as well as in the channel of Lesser Meander, and later to divert the river into an artificial channel. But as the rapid progradation reached a rate of 300 m in a century, with accompanying heavy siltation, all these and later efforts could not prevent the decline of Ephesus as a port, the site of which lies at present 7 km inland.

Coastal changes in the post-Glacial epoch followed essentially the same pattern in the Meander plain (Fig. 5). The initial shoreline was situated 30 km inland near the present town of Söke (Grund, 1906b and Göney, 1973). As a result of rapid progradation, the coastline reached the ancient harbour city of Myus in the fifth century B.C., and Priene was lying inland at the beginning of the first century A.D. Around A.D. 300, the front of the delta was in the vicinity of Miletus, and Latmos Bay (the present Bafa Lake) was being transformed into a lagoon. As the progradation continued, Miletus gradually lost its importance as a port. Nevertheless, even in the fourteenth century the port of Miletus (its name in the meantime having been changed to Balat) was deep enough to be visited by small vessels. But

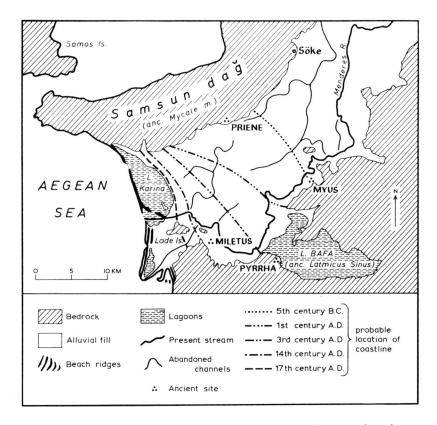

Fig. 5: Coastal changes in the post-Glacial epoch in the Meander plain.

in the succeeding centuries silting and progradation brought about the final ruin of the port and the city. By the seventeenth century the place was already lying 2 km inland, and at present the distance between the ruins of Miletus and the coast exceeds 5 km.

Another interesting progradational feature in western Anatolia is the delta of the Gediz River, which occupies about 400 km^2 in the Gulf of İzmir (Erinç, 1955). The river has shifted its course several times, and was eventually diverted to the south. The subsequent southward advance of the delta became a serious menace for the sea passage connecting the port of İzmir to the open sea, and the river was therefore diverted in 1886 into an artificial channel leading to the deeper and broader outer part of the Gulf of İzmir.

The deltaic plain of Troy (Fig. 6) is another post-Glacial aggradational feature covering an area of 70 km^2 (Bilgin, 1969). Here the shoreline ran 1·5 km west of Troy at the time of the Trojan War, and has since then advanced therefore by about 4 km during some 3000 years.

In a survey of changes in the natural environment brought about by exogenous forces since the end of the Last Glacial, the effects of mass movements, karst processes and wind action should also be considered. In this respect, Turkey may be divided into fairly clearly defined morphogenetic regions. Indeed, *mass movements*, particularly landslides, are a very effective factor in shaping and changing the landforms in the northern part of Turkey, where they are favoured by the coincidence of high precipitation, steep and dissected topography, and clayey geological formations. Lake Tortum owes its origin to a huge landslide in the more distant part, while Lake Sera to the west of Trabzon was formed as a result of similar mass movements in 1950.

Karstification, on the other hand, is a process confined to the limestone areas of the country, mainly in the Taurus Mountains and in some parts of central Anatolia. Karstic processes were most active during Glacial epochs, but undoubtedly continued to operate during the post-Glacial as well. They provided several sheltered caves which were used as habitations by prehistoric man. Karst processes account also for considerable changes in drainage during prehistoric and historical times. It is evident that, in such regions, man has been an eye-witness to strange changes, leading on the one hand to the gradual conversion of a fertile plain, which he once ploughed, into a lake, or, on the other, to the transformation of a lake, where he used to fish, into an alluvial plain. The best known example of such changes during historic times is the Suğla Lake with the prehistoric site of Süberde.

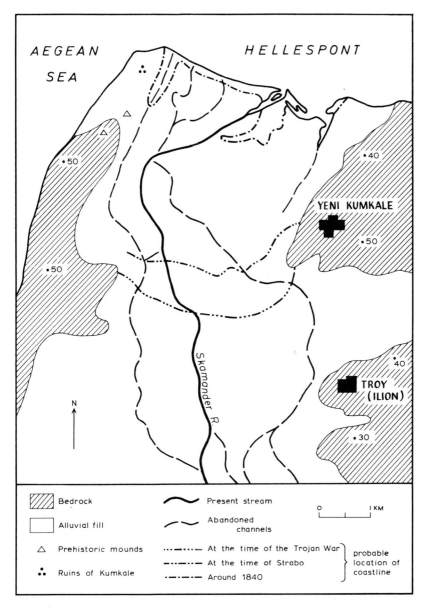

Fig. 6: The deltaic plain of Troy.

As to the changes in landscape caused by wind action, they have been restricted either to some coastal areas (particularly along the Mediterranean), or to the floors of arid and semi-arid depressions which were formerly occupied by pluvial lakes. The best known examples of inland dunes and blown sand relief which formed during the post-Glacial epoch lie between Karapınar and Karaman in the heart of central Anatolia (Erinç, 1962).

Changes in the Physical Environment due to Endogenous Processes

Turkey is located on a very active belt of the earth's crust, and owes its general shape as an upwarped area to neotectonic deformations during the Late Pliocene and Pleistocene. The country is crossed by several fault lines along which are aligned fresh volcanic features and zones of destructive earthquakes. Geological and geomorphological evidence indicates that tectonic movements have continued up to the present time. Indeed, even the youngest marine terraces of Pleistocene age have been deformed, at least locally. Several formations of deposited beach rock containing antique débris are found at present below or above their original level of formation. The considerable difference between the morphologically determined (2600 m) and the climatically expected (2200 m; see pp. 88, 92) elevations of the snow line during the last Glacial in the humid Pontic Mountains has been interpreted as a possible consequence of tectonic uplift in the post-Glacial epoch (Erinç, 1949; Planhol and Bilgin, 1964), whereas negative crustal movements seem to have been responsible for the abnormally low elevation of the Last Glacial snow line in the south-west (Planhol, 1953). Along the north Anatolian transcurrent fault line, stream courses have been offset laterally at a rate of 2·5 cm per century since the Upper Pliocene, and in the same zone recent earthquakes have caused displacements of 1 m vertically and 4 m horizontally (Ketin, 1969; Erinç, 1973). Flemming (1973) notes vertical shifts of south-west coastal sites.

Seismic activity occurs very frequently, and during historic times severe earthquakes have resulted in the complete destruction of several towns, and led to the formation of faults and landslides (İlhan, 1971). It is, therefore, certain that tectonic forces have been active also throughout the post-Glacial epoch and that they have caused some appreciable changes in the physical environment.

Volcanic activity, another manifestation of endogenous forces, has played an important role in shaping the country during the Pleistocene. A considerable part of Turkey is covered by volcanoes and lava-fields of Pleistocene age. Obsidian ejected by some volcanoes was used in prehistoric times as an excellent material for artefacts. Volcanic activity continued into the post-Glacial epoch, though its intensity has decreased. Volcanic structures of post-Glacial age, consisting mainly of pyroclastic cones, maars and lava streams, are widespread around Kula in western Anatolia, in several parts of central and south-eastern Anatolia, and around Lake Van. The Kula volcanic region—the ancient Katakekaumene of Strabo (13, 4, 1)—merits particular attention because of the 60 or more pyroclastic cones grouped in a relatively small area, the extensive lava sheets, the long lava streams (*coulées*) covering recent valleys and alluvium, and the remarkably well-preserved fossil footprints of prehistoric man in the tufa (Ozansoy, 1969). At present, Turkey has no active volcano, with the exception of some volcanic edifices which are in a stage of post-volcanic exhalations (Ağrı, Tendürek, Nemrut). However, Strabo's description (12, 1, 7) clearly indicates that at least some of the lateral cones located along fissures on the slopes of Mt Erciyeş, the outstanding landmark of central Anatolia, were still active at the beginning of our era. The last recorded volcanic explosions in Turkey were those of Mt Nemrut in A.D. 1441 and 1443.

Changes in the Physical Environment due to Human Activities

Some changes in the physical environment within Turkey are associated with several forms of human activity, though their degree evidently depends on the length of settlement on the one hand, and on the type of economy and the level of technology on the other. Turkey, with its long history of continuous settlement, must therefore be counted among those countries where man has played a significant part in changing the natural environment. Some human intervention has been beneficial but, in general, occupation of the land in former centuries has been associated with a reckless exploitation of natural wealth. This has been the case particularly in historic times because of the increased demands of a growing population and a rising level of technology. One of the main results of this destructive economy has been the devastation of natural forests, as described above. Former woodlands were converted either to grazing ground or fields; while, on the other hand, natural pastures suffered from overgrazing. It appears that the reckless use of land since early Classical times has led to soil erosion on an increasingly intensive scale. At present, the annual loss of soil within Turkey is estimated at between 400 and 450 million cubic tons. Wherever the protective cover of natural vegetation has been substantially removed by man over a number of centuries, soil erosion has been aggravated by conditions of steep slopes, extremely dissected landforms, great altitudinal differences and high intensities of rainfall. The chief results of heavy loss of soil have been a sacrifice of good agricultural land, a general fall in agricultural yields and potentials, and an increased rate of siltation, which has been one of the main factors leading to the decline of so many flourishing harbour cities in the past.

Postscript

As to the Quaternary Lake Van, its changes of level are reflected in fill-terraces or wave-cut benches of relative heights of 80, 55, 30 and 12 metres (Schweizer, 1975). The youngest high stand is obviously of post-glacial age according to C^{14} determinations (personal communication).

References

Ardel, A. and Kurter, A. 1973. The Sea of Marmara. İst. Univ. Coğ. Enst. Dergisi 10, 67–70 (in Turkish).
Aytuğ, B. 1967. Etude de la flore de l'age néolithique dans la région de Süberde, sud-ouest de l'Anatolie. Rev. Fac. Sci. Forestières, Univ. Istanbul 17, 1–13.
Bener, M. 1970. Beach rock formations in the coastal strip Antalya–Gazipasa. Publ. Geogr. Inst. Univ. Istanbul.
Bilgin, T. 1969. 'Biga Yarımadası güneybatı kısmının Jeomorfolojisi. İst. Univ. Coğrafya Enstitüsü Yayini. 55.
Bilgin, T. 1972. Munzur Dağlarının glasiyal ve periglasiyal morfolojisi. Publ. Geogr. Inst. Univ. Istanbul 69.
Brice, W. C. 1966. South-West Asia. London: University of London Press.
Cohen, H. R. and Erol, O. 1969. Aspects of the Palaeogeography of Central Anatolia. Geog. Journ. 135, 388–398.
Darkot, B. 1936. Quelques observations sur l'evolution des basins fermés en relation avec la variation du climat. C. R. Congr. Intern. de Geogr., Warshau 2, 209–215.

Degens, E. T. 1971. Sedimentological history of the Black Sea over 25,000 years, *In: Geology and History of Turkey*, (Campbell, A. S. ed.), pp. 407–429. Tripoli (Libya): Petr. Expl. soc. Libya.

Erinç, S. 1949. Eiszeitliche Formen und gegenwärtige Vergletscherung im nordostanatolischen Randgebirge. *Geologische Rundschau* 37.

Erinç, S. 1950. Climatic types and the variation of moisture regions in Turkey. *Geogr. Review* 40, 224–235.

Erinç, S. 1952a. The present glaciation in Turkey. *Proceed., 17th Intern. Geogr. Congress, Washington* 326–330.

Erinç, S. 1952b. Glacial evidences of climatic variation in Turkey. *Geog. Annal.* 1–2, 89–98.

Erinç, S. 1953. Geography of Eastern Anatolia. *Public. Geogr. Inst. Univ. Istanbul* 15. (in Turkish).

Erinç, S. 1954. The Pleistocene history of the Black Sea and the adjacent countries with special references to the climatic changes. *Review Geogr. Inst. Univ. Istanbul* 1, 3–51.

Erinç, S. 1955. The Geomorphology of deltas of Gediz and Küçükmenderes rivers. *9. Meslek Haftasi, Türk Coğr. Kurumu* 1, 33–66.

Erinç, S. 1960. On the Pleistocene terraces of Çukurova (Cilician Plain). *VI. Intern. INQUA Congress*.

Erinç, S. and Bener, M. 1961. Analysis of two long precipitation records in Turkey: Istanbul and Tarsus. *İst. Univ. Coğr. Enist. Derg.* 12 (in Turkish).

Erinç, S. 1962. On the relief features of blown sand at the Karapınar surroundings in Interior Anatolia. *Rev. Geogr. Inst. Univ. of Istanbul* 8, 113–130.

Erinç, S. 1973. Geomorphological evidence of neotectonics in Turkey. *Abstracts, Ninth INQUA Congress, Christchurch, New Zealand* 87–88.

Erol, O. 1963. Die Geomorphologie des Orontes Deltas und der anschliessenden pleistozänen Strand und Flussterrassen. *Publi. Univ. Ankara, Dil ve Tarih-Coğrafya Fak.* 148.

Erol, O. 1971. Geomorphological evidence of the recessional phases of the pluvial lakes in the Konya, Tuzgölü and Burdur basins in Anatolia. *Ann. Geogr. Res. Inst. Univ. Ankara* 3–4, 13–52.

Flemming, N. C. *et al.* 1973. Archaeological evidence for eustatic and tectonic components of relative sea-level changes in the South Aegean. *In: Marine Archaeology* (Blackman, ed.) London.

Flint, R. F. 1957. *Glacial and Pleistocene Geology* pp. 419–421.

Gall, H. 1966. Gletscherkundliche Beobachtungen im Hochgebirge von Lasistan, *Mitt. Österr. Geogr. Ges.* 108, 2/3.

Gassner, G. and Christiansen-Weniger, F. 1948. Dendroclimatological studies on the annual growth rings of Anatolian pines. *Orman Genel Müdürlüğü Yayınları* 58 (in Turkish).

E

Göçmen, K. 1976. Alluvial Geomorphology of Lower Meriç (Maritza) river and its delta. Unpublished Ph.D. thesis, Geogr. Inst. Univ. Istanbul.

Göney, S. 1973. Büyük Menderes deltası. *Ist. Univ. Coğ. Enst. Dergisi* **18–19**, 339–354.

Grund, A. 1906a. Vorläufiger Bericht über physiographische Untersuchungen im Delta—Gebiet des Kleinen Meander bei Ajasoluk (Ephesus). *Sitz. math.-naturwiss. Klasse K. Akad. Wissen.* **115**, 241–262.

Grund, A. 1906b. Vorläufiger Bericht über physiographische Untersuchungen im den Deltagebieten des Grossen und Kleinen Meanders. *Sitz. math.-naturwiss. Klasse K. Akad. Wissen.* **115**, 1757–1769.

İlhan, E. 1971. Earthquakes in Turkey. In: *Geology and History of Turkey* (Campbell, A. S. ed.), pp. 431–442, Tripoli (Libya): Petr. Expl. Soc. Libya.

Kayacık, H. and Aytuğ, B. 1968. A study on the wooden materials of the Gordion royal tombs with special reference to forestry. *Rev. Fac. Sci. Forestières, Univ. Istanbul* **18**, 1–18.

Ketin, I. 1969. Über die nordanatolische Horizontalverschiebung. *Bulletin of the Mineral Research and Exploration Institute of Turkey*; Foreign edition, no. 72.

Klaer, W. 1962. Untersuchungen zum Klimagenetischen Geomorphologie in den Hochgebirgen Vorderasiens. *Heidelberger Geogr. Arbeiten* **11**.

Louis, H. 1938. Eiszeitliche Seen in Anatolien. *Z. Ges. Erdkunde z Berlin.*

Louis, H. 1944. Die Spuren der eiszeitlicher Vergletscherung in Anatolien. *Geol. Rundschau* **34**.

Ozansoy, F. 1969. Pleistocene fossil human footprints in Turkey. *Bull. of Min. Res. Explorat. Inst. Turkey* **72**.

Planhol, X. de 1953. Les formes glaciaires du Sandrasdağ et la limite des neiges éternelles dans le SW de l'Anatolie. *C.R.S. Soc. Géol. France* no. 13.

Planhol, X. de and Bilgin, T. 1964. Glaciaire et périglaciaire quaternaires et actuels dans le massif du Karagöl (Chaînes pontiques-Turquie). *Rev. Géog. Alpine*, 497–512.

Schweizer, G. 1975. Untersuchungen zur Physiogeographie von Östanatolien und Nordwestiran. *Tübinger Geographische Studien* **60**.

Sungur, K. 1967. Geomorphological studies in the Konya-Ereğli basin. Unpublished Ph.D. thesis. Geog. Inst. Univ. Istanbul.

Sungur, K. 1978. *Physical Geography of Burdur and its Surroundings*.

Uslu, S. 1960. Untersuchungen zum anthropogenen Charakter der zentralanatolischen Steppe. *Geiss. Abh. zur Agrar-und Wirtschaft. europäischen Ostens*.

8
The Quaternary History of the Lake Basins of Central and Southern Anatolia

Oğuz Erol

Introduction

The geologists of the last century who first mentioned the lake basins of Anatolia drew attention to the lacustrine deposits, but Louis, writing in 1938, was the first to give descriptions of the traces of abandoned Pleistocene coastal features, including cliffs, around the edges of these basins. Recent investigation has been concerned both with the detailed geology of particular basins, and with their general history.

The prevalent opinion is that the vestiges of large lakes should all be dated to the Last or Würm Pluvial period, but since 1969 I have been convinced that some of the high lake levels and Quaternary deposits in the Tuzgölü Basin must date from times earlier than the Würm Pluvial, and in 1973 I announced the discovery of pre-Würm coastal formations in the Burdur Basin. Moreover, recently, Atalay (1973a, b) has concluded that the terraces and deposits in the Akşehir-Eber lake basin belong to the older Pluvials and Klear has correlated the higher terraces of Lake Van with a pre-Würm, possibly Riss, moraine-wall in the mountains (1965, p. 353; Schweizer, 1975).

Not all of the lake basins of Anatolia show evidence of former Pluvial phases (Map 1), and it is generally considered that the closed lakes in basins without fluvial or karstic outlets would have been most sensitive to Pluvial changes (Penck, 1918; Lahn, 1946, p. 94). Some early writers (de Tchihatcheff, 1867; Bukowski, 1890–2) believed that the Quaternary lakes were simply the relics of the Neogene lakes, but Lahn (1948, p. 77) has suggested that the Quaternary lakes were formed principally in the small secondary basins which resulted from subsidence within the larger primary Neogene basins, and I share this opinion.

In fact, the situation is more complex than many authorities have supposed. For example, in a partly karstic basin, like that of Konya, subterranean drainage will have little effect when the level of the lake is low, but would have become more operative as the level rose during a Pluvial phase: for in such circumstances the karstic cavities act as emergency outlets. Or again, if there is a subsidence in the central part of a basin, a step-like descending succession of terraces may be formed, as in the case of Tuzgölü: while in the absence of such a subsidence, or if sedimentation keeps pace with subsidence, then the lake bed would keep its level, and the younger terraces might rework the older, or the younger sediments cover the older, as in the Konya Basin. In addition, the lowering of the outflow thresholds and other local changes might cause accidental interruptions in the development of a basin. High water levels should not therefore be automatically attributed to climatic causes, and, in their study, the tectonic, hydrographic and geomorphic history of the basins and their surrounding mountains must also be taken into account.

The Lake Basins of Eastern, Northern and South-eastern Anatolia

The Pluvial coastlines of Lake Van have recently been studied systematically by Schweizer (1975), and it seems that the maximum level of the lake was 80 m above that of the present (1726 m above sea-level), and there are terraces too at 55, 30 and 12 m. The high terrace at 70—65 m, which in some earlier works was considered to be of Pliocene age is dated by Klear (1965, p. 353; cf. Vita-Finzi, 1969, p. 616)* and Schweizer (1975) to the Riss, and the lower, at 55 and 30 m, to the Würm.

In the small Hazar Basin to the south of Elazığ, at 100 m above the lake, there has been found an elevated fossiliferous level of probable Pliocene or Pleistocene age (Erol, 1969, pp. 187–8).*

Lahn (1948, p. 43) noticed that the Amık Lake in the district of Hatay was once more extensive. It was later lowered naturally by the Orontes River, and is now artificially drained (Erol, 1969, p. 188).

---

*The later work when it incorporates the older ones, is cited in the References.

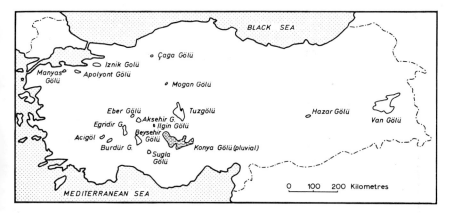

Fig. 1: The lake basins of eastern, northern and south-eastern Anatolia.

In the Mogan Basin to the south of Ankara there are two small lakes which were dammed by dejection cones during the Holocene. They are of too recent origin to have been influenced by Pluvial episodes, and the origin of the 10 m terrace is problematic.

The Çaga Lake in north-west Anatolia, according to Inandık (1965, p. 82) was once larger, and was drained through a recent capture by a river (Erol, 1969, p. 188).

The İznik lake basin of north-west Anatolia contains fairly clear traces of Pluvial coastlines (Ardel, 1954, p. 229; Bilgin, 1967, p. 135). The recent lake surface is at 85 m above sea-level, and elevated terraces can be observed, especially on the northern side of the basin, at the following heights above the lake: 15, 20, 25, 30, and, according to some observers, 75–80 m. These terraces are generally attributed to the Last (or Würm) Pluvial (Morrison, 1968, p. 879).

South of the Marmara Sea, the Manyas, Apolyont and Simav Lakes once covered larger areas and have been drained by captures in the Holocene (Erol, 1969, p. 188).

The Lake Basins of South-central Anatolia and the West Taurus Lake District

From the above review it will be apparent that records of Pluvial terraces in the lake basins of eastern, northern and south-eastern Anatolia are few and of obscure significance. This may be partly due to the lack of research.

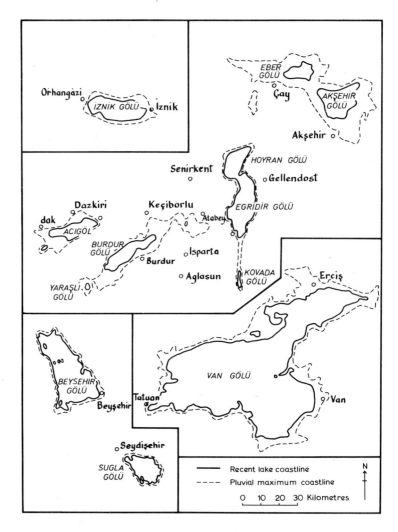

Fig. 2a: The former extent of some Anatolian lakes.

But there is, in my opinion, a more fundamental explanation. In the cases detailed above, and especially in the Van area, summers are relatively cool and the distinction between Pluvial and Interpluvial conditions would not be very pronounced; while, in south-central Anatolia and the Lake District, the relatively warm summers would result in more marked and effective Interpluvial "dry" regimes. It is for this reason that I have concentrated my researches on three lake basins in this region, those of

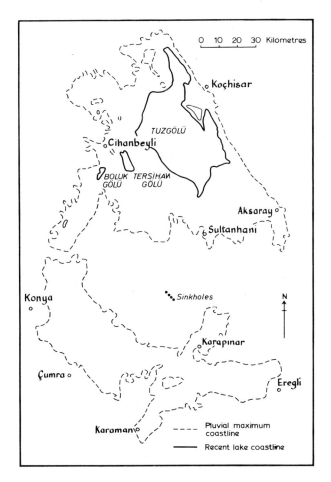

Fig. 2b: The maximum extent of Tuzgölü and Lake Konya.

Tuzgölü, Konya and Burdur. Before examining these in detail, however, I will review the evidence from the other lakes in this area.

In the large lake basin of Akşehir-Eber-Karamuk at the western margin of south-central Anatolia, Atalay has observed seven terraces at the following heights above the present water level of Lake Akşehir (960 m above sea-level): 5, 10, 13, 15, 18, 20 and 50 m. The maximum level was, in the Eber Lake, 35 m higher than its present stand and 24 m higher in the case of Karamuk. Although other authorities attribute the lake terraces to the Last (the Würm) Pluvial, Atalay (1973a, pp. 19–20) and Yalçinlar (with Atalay, 1973, pp. 281–8) have remarked that the terraces contain

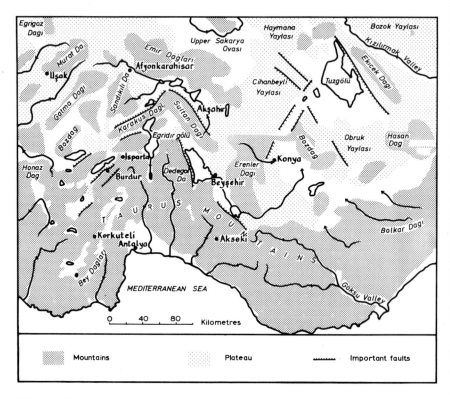

Fig. 3: The lake basins of south-central Anatolia and the west Taurus lake district.

deposits of different type, the higher ones having a red-coloured, thick (1 m) soil-cover, while on the lower ones there are only 40–50 cm of soil. It follows that the higher terraces might have been formed during the earlier Pluvials. According to Atalay, the 50-m terrace may date from the Günz-Mindel period, the 20-m from the Riss, the 15-m from the Würm, and those at 5–10 m above Lake Akşehir from the Holocene.

The small lake basin of Ilgin lies between those of Akşehir and Konya. Chaput (1936, pp. 85–92) observed that the surface of this lake rose during the Pleistocene, when it had an outlet through Akgöl towards the Sakarya river system.

The large Lake Beyşehir occupies the northern basin of the Beyşehir–Suğla depression. This was formed as a result of down-faulting, especially along its south-western border, and the basins display karstic characteristics along their south-west margins. The shallow Lake Suğla in the southern depression is now artificially drained dry, but all around the bottom of the basin there are at 2–5 m traces of coastlines which are obviously recent, for they have eroded the edges of the older *hüyüks* or settlement mounds. Similar very young coastal traces at 2 m are seen around Lake Beyşehir also, and these too have eaten into the edges of the old *hüyüks* (Farrand and Solecki, 1963, pp. 8–11; Cohen, 1967, pp. 37–8). It is evident that the levels of these two lakes rose, almost certainly on several occasions, during late prehistoric and historic times, i.e. during the Holocene; but further, I have found Dreissensia fossils, which in the Burdur and Konya Basins are indications of Pluvial conditions, in the spit sediments at an elevation of 1095–1100 m above sea-level at the head of the outlet of the old Lake Suğla towards the Carşamba river gorge, that is towards the Konya Basin. These, it is suggested, are a clear indication that, at some time during the Pleistocene, Lake Suğla rose 5–10 m above its present level. I have observed similar Quaternary fossils, found by Lahn (1948, p. 35), near the outlet of Lake Beyşehir. Evidently during the Pleistocene Pluvials these two lakes only rose to the level of the outflow channels and karstic seepages which are abundant along the south-west edges of their basins (Alagöz, 1944; Acatay, 1966; Aygen, 1959).

The higher terraces around these lakes observed by Farrand and Solecki (1963, p. 8) at 60–70 m, and by myself at 10 and 25 m (in the summer of 1974) should doubtless be attributed to river erosion during a phase of the Pleistocene (Farrand and Solecki, 1963, pp. 8–9).

As for conditions during the Interpluvials, it is generally accepted that the lake basins were dried out and even dissected from time to time during the Pleistocene (Lahn, 1946, pp. 97–8; 1948, p. 35; Farrand and Solecki, 1963, p. 10). I can add my observations made in the Çarşamba river gorge on the outlet of the lake basins, the incised meanders of which are cut in places over 100 m deep in very hard Mesozoic limestones. There are at least two shoulders or narrow terraces along the slopes of the gorge, the bottom of which is filled with a red-coloured alluvium consisting of mainly fine sands and clays. It appears that the gorge was incised over a very long time, embracing perhaps all the Pleistocene and stretching back into the Upper Pliocene. This down cutting obviously occurred in oscillations, and during the last stage at least the gorge was deeper than it is today, for its bed has been raised by a deposit of fine alluvium washed down from the basins.

Moreover, it seems from a first examination of the bore-hole logs of the D.S.I. (State Water Division) by Cohen, Franks and myself (Erol, 1969, p. 190) that there are at least three peat levels beneath the present Lake

Fig. 4: The large swallow-cave of Lake Suğla which is dried out today. The traces of the high water levels are visible on the limestone cliff.

Fig. 5: The coastal spit belonging to the older Pluvial levels of Lake Suğla and the erosional notches of the recent lake at its edge. This recent lake is also dried out today.

Beyşehir and, on these peat deposits, traces of subaerial erosion which point to episodes when the lake became dry. Hopefully, the palynological investigations of Dr J. Franks will make it possible to put dates to these times of desiccation. Similar results may also be obtained from the bore-cores of the lignite programme of the M.T.A. (Mining Research and Exploration Institute of Turkey), though these are taken mainly from Pliocene formations (Lebküchner, 1960; Bering, 1971a, b, p. 85).

In conclusion, in the double basin of the Beyşehir-Suğla depression there are clear traces of Holocene terraces at 2–5 m, and in the Suğla Basin some indications of earlier rises during the Pleistocene, limited by the outflows to 10–15 m. Under opposite conditions, it seems fairly clear that the basins were drained and even dissected during the Interpluvials. In brief, traces of Interpluvials are here more marked than those of Pluvials, but since they lie under the cover of younger sediments they can only be observed through drilling. This is a typical high intermontane basin with an outlet.

The Eğridir-Kovada lake basin shows fairly strong karstic conditions, especially in its southern section, but is partly of tectonic origin (Bering, 1971b, pp. 64–72). The general opinion in the literature is that there is no clear evidence for a higher Pluvial lake level in this basin, but on air-photographs I have noticed possible terraces and coastal traces, to the south-west of the lake, at 39, 14, 9 and 4 m and have confirmed through field observation the lacustrine origin of the three lowermost. So far, there is no evidence of Interpluvials of the sort noticed at Beyşehir.

The Acıgöl lake basin, to the north-west of the Lake District, is of tectonic origin (Erinç, 1967, pp. 140–3; Bering, 1971b, pp. 23–33) and contained a Pleistocene Pluvial lake of which clear traces remain. Erinç (1967, pp. 140–3) dates the 34-m rise to the Last (the Würm) Pluvial: he does not give notice of any older Pluvial traces, but remarks that the old lake appears to have been drained to the west by an ancient channel near the Bozkurt railway station. This may explain why there is only one high coastline. The Acıgöl basin may, therefore, in respect of its general character, be compared with the Pluvial lakes of Konya.

The other small basins of the Lake District, being of markedly karstic character, show fewer Pluvial traces. Around the Pınarbaşı and Karataş Lakes in the Tefenni Basin to the south-west of Burdur some high-level Pluvial traces were reported by de Planhol (1956, pp. 48–9; cf. Ardel, 1957, p. 10), but not by Bering (1971b, p. 44). At the Gebrem Ovası and the Salda Lake in the same area, de Planhol (1956) did not see any Pluvial traces, though Ardel did (1952, pp. 80–2; 1957, p. 10) observe clear coastal traces (sandpits, cliffs) and deposits at approximately 4, 7, 15, 25 and 40 m around the Salda Lake, of which those at the higher three levels evidently derive from Pluvial phases.

The small Yaraşlı Basin just south-west of the Burdur Basin contains very clear coastal traces and cliffs; and in the Atabey Ovasi north-east of Burdur, I have observed coastal traces and Pluvial deposits with fossils.

On air photographs, 5–10 m terraces, probably reflecting climatic oscillations during the Holocene, show up at the margin of the crater lake of Gölcük near İsparta, and around Lake Ovacik, north-west of Burdur, within the Söğüt Mountains.

To conclude this general review, the Pluvial episodes are generally attributed to lowered temperature and slightly increased rainfall, resulting in an increase of fluvial and karstic activity, glaciation, and the expansion of lakes (Pfannenstiel, 1944, 1954; de Planhol, 1956; Güldali, 1970, p. 67; Erinç, 1970, p. 14; Klear, 1965; Erol, 1969): but some assume only a lowering of temperature (Louis, 1938b, p. 44). In general, the Pluvials are taken as synchronous with the glacial epochs of higher latitudes.

The Tectonic History of the Turkish Lake District and South-central Anatolia

The three lake basins chosen for special study, those of Tuzgölü, Konya and Burdur, lie in an area which experiences a climatic regime transitional between the Mediterranean type and the Continental and which is therefore particularly sensitive to climatic fluctuations. These basins have been carefully selected because of their differences in respect of structure and topography, which follow from the complex tectonic history of the entire Lake District. This district falls within the zone of the "West Taurus Scharung" where the south-east/north-west ranges meet those trending south-west/north-east and includes four series of lakes, in order from south to north as follows:

1. the small and irregularly distributed depressions of the high calcareous inner Taurus Mountains;
2. the chain of larger tectonic depressions from Beyşehir through Eğridir to Burdur, whose southern margins are marked by step-faults in limestone;
3. beyond the main northern boundary faults of the Taurus, a line of depressions including those of Bor, Ereğli, Konya, İlgin, Akşehir and

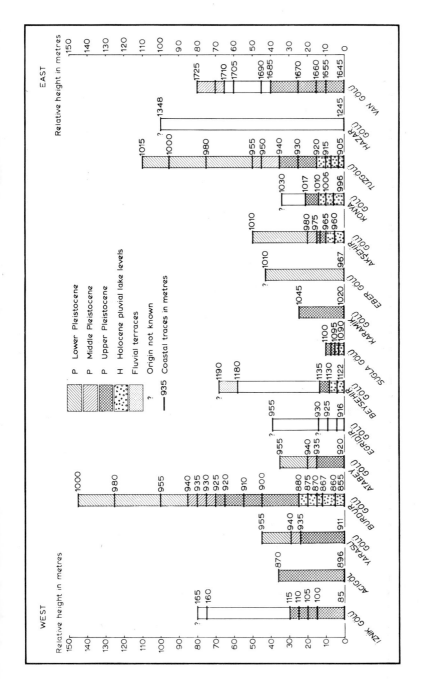

Fig. 6: Comparison of heights and ages of the terraces of the Anatolian lakes.

Acıgöl, in a zone transitional between mountains and plateau, the "Lykaonische Senken-zone" of Wenzel and Bering;

4. north of the Boz and Emir Mountains, the wide and shallow basins of Tuzgölü and the Upper Sakarya, on the plateau proper.

Bering and others, arguing from their observation that there was only one period of glaciation in the Taurus, considered that the main uplift of Anatolia occurred in the Middle Pleistocene, just before the Würm Glaciation, after a long period of sedimentation throughout the Pliocene and Lower Pleistocene; but from my work in the Tuzgölü Basin, I believe that there were four phases of uplift, marked by erosion surfaces datable to the Upper Miocene, Middle Pliocene, Upper Pliocene, and Early Pleistocene. Of these, only the earliest or Upper Miocene surface was the outcome of a complete cycle of erosion, for in the other three cases the cycles were incomplete. Post-Villafranchian or Basal Pleistocene tectonic movements, continued in central places into the Holocene, have resulted in the formation, through down-faulting, of smaller basins within the wider Neogene depressions, and it is in these smaller basins that the Holocene lakes accumulated, fed by water from the surrounding mountains.

The Tuzgölü Basin

The geosyncline was occupied here by a sea in Upper Cretaceous–Lower Tertiary times, but in consequence of tectonic movements during the Oligocene this gave place to lagoons and finally, in the Miocene, to a lake. The following erosional surfaces can be traced:

DI   at 1400–1500 m, formed in the Upper Miocene;

DII at 1250–1300 m, Middle Pliocene;

DIII at 1100–1150 m, Upper Pliocene, associated with a red fluvial deposit;

DIV   at 1050 m, developed during the Basal Pleistocene (Villafranchian) on red fluvial deposits different in constitution from those of DIII. These red deposits and the associated erosional surface were formed over a fairly long period between the end of the Pliocene and the Pluvial phases of the Pleistocene.

The post-Villafranchian tectonic movements produced subsided troughs in the central part of the basin, in which accumulated the Late Pleistocene and Holocene lake sediments. The sinking depression was filled with 1500 m of sediments, which now overlie the Lower Tertiary

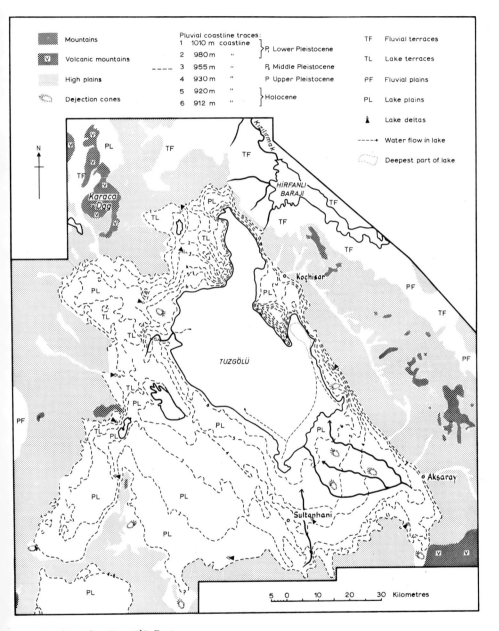

Fig. 7: The Tuzgölü Basin.

formations (Diker, 1958), while the surface of the lake fell in height after each successive rise of the pluvial lake, leaving a stepped sequence of terraces.

The older literature makes no mention of terraces older than the Würm Pluvial. I have, however, traced above the present lake surface (905 m above sea-level) terraces at the following heights, of which the two highest series appear to date to the Günz, Mindel and possible Donau Pluvials of the Lower Pleistocene:

1. 110 m (with a parallel series at 95 m)—marked by deltaic sediments and freshwater lacustrine fossils (*Amphocyprus fl. marginata*, etc.) covered with thin (10–12 cm) brackish gypsum layers;

2. 75 m—seen in the deltas at Kırkışla and Hoydos. This level is associated with a red soil, like that of the higher terrace. Until this stage, water had filled the entire basin; but in the subsequent phases only the smaller inner basin was occupied by the lake;

3. 50 m—this lake drowned some valleys which had been cut, presumably, during a phase of recession between stages 2 and 3. Its shoreline is marked by grey clayey soils. The waters had now receded from the border mountains, the alluvium from which was deposited as individual deltas in the valleys opening into the lake. This stage is tentatively dated to the Riss Pluvial.

4. 35 m and 25 m—much clearer than the higher levels: with grey, clayey and salty deposits, rather different from the more limey grey soils of level 3, and probably Würm in age, like the equivalent sediments of the Konya and Burdur Basins.

5. 15 m and 10 m—mainly depositional, and, to judge from their relations with the *hüyüks*, of Early Holocene age.

6. 7 m and 3 m, associated with erosion on the East coast and with a deltaic plain at the mouth of the İnsuyu (Cihanbeyli), evidently formed, to judge from the direction of spits, by dominant Northerly winds (Fig. 5). From their relations to the *hüyüks*, it is evident that these coastlines were formed during Late Holocene and Recent times, that is to say within the last 6000 years.

The Tuzgölü and nearby Boluk and Tersihan Lakes were united during the Last Würm Pluvial, but have since become separated and taken on differing chemical constitutions, according to the nature of the waters of the fault-springs from which they are, in large measure, supplied. Boluk is predominantly potash, Tuzgölü common salt (Irion, 1970). In fact, a 30–40 cm crust of salt coats the bottom of Tuzgölü, and a specimen from it has been dated as 1–1·5 million years old (Bagge and Willkomm, 1966).

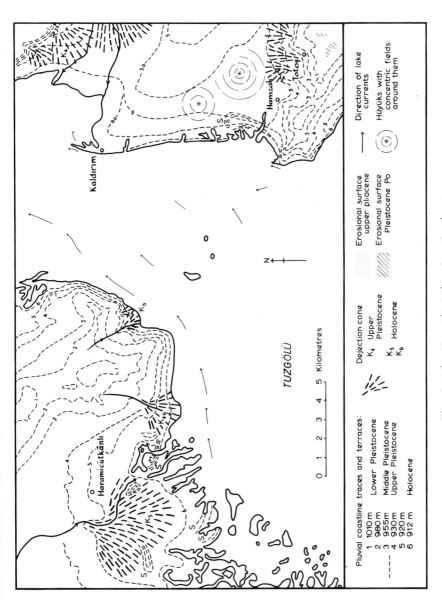

Fig. 8: The Tuzgölü Lake. S = Sand spits.

The salt probably therefore began to accumulate from Lower Pleistocene times onwards, during the dry interpluvials when the lake became parched and saline, and after being buried under the Pluvial lake sediments would be brought from beneath to the surface by recent fault-springs.

These saline interludes appear to have wiped out the freshwater fauna of the lake, for freshwater fossils are only found in the higher and older Pluvial remains. The present saline phase of the lake only dates back some 5–7000 years, for there is evidence that the lake was composed of fresh water during the Würm Pluvial.

The Konya–Ereğli Basin

This comprises two depressions, of Konya in the west and Ereğli in the

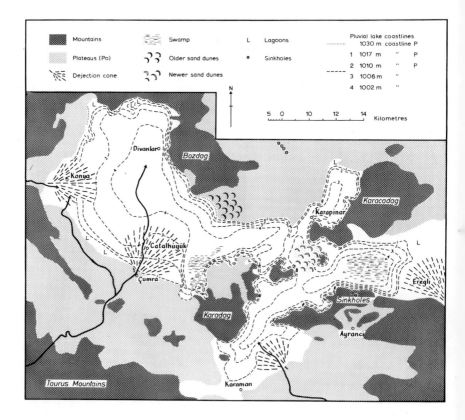

Fig. 9: The Konya–Ereğli Basin.

east. In the Konya depression, as in that of Tuzgölü, there can be traced an undulating surface of Basal Pleistocene (Villafranchian) age. It stands there at 1050 m above sea-level, and within it an inner and narrower basin, formed through down-faulting, was occupied by the Pleistocene Pluvial lake. This lake has left coastal traces at 1017 and 1010 m, from the Würm Pluvial, and at 1006, 1002 and 1000 m, marking the Holocene recession with re-advances. (Fig.11).

This dating is based on the following observation. Between two spit deposits near Dervişinhani, formed at the 1010 and 1006 m stadials, were found five Mesolithic stone tools (Cohen, 1969; Cohen and Erol, 1969), which indicate that men were searching for food on the lower spit between the eleventh and ninth millennia B.C. The seventh millennium B.C. site of Çatalhüyük stands on flats at approximately 1004 m, that is to

Fig. 10: The pediment-like footplains consisting of red Plioquaternary (Villafranchian) continental sediments at about 1050 m, at the foot of Bozdağlar in the north-west of the Konya lake basin. The edge of these sediments were eroded by the Pluvial Konya lake. Photograph is taken from the Konya–Aksaray road.

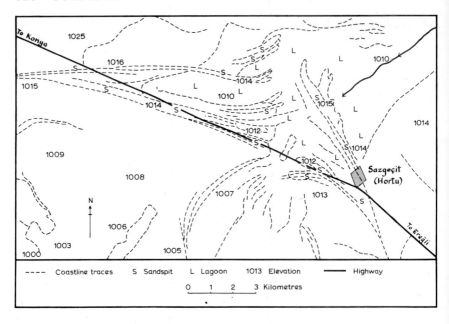

Fig. 11: The inner basin of Konya.

say contemporary with the 1002 m lake level. Taken together, these observations date the 1006 m and lower lake levels to the Holocene.

There is significant evidence on the cliffs of the old shoreline in the north-east of the basin of a marked change in the direction of the prevailing wind at the time of transition from the Pleistocene to the Holocene. East of Divanlar (Fig. 12) the coastal traces at 1017, 1010 and 1006 m were formed by longshore currents which ran from north to south and transported pebbles which were large at the two higher levels, but smaller when the lake stood at 1006 m. By contrast, on the Zülfüönü promontory, which is associated with the 1002 m stage of the lake, a flat sand-spit was built up from south to north. We may therefore conclude that the 1017 and 1010 m levels were established under Pluvial conditions brought about by dominant and strong north and north-east winds. To judge from the smaller pebbles of the 1006 m level, these winds became less strong and were impelling weaker currents at the time of transition from Pluvial Pleistocene to post-Pluvial Holocene conditions. By the time of the 1002 m level, milder and drier conditions were established, with longer summers under the influence of predominantly southerly winds, and the receding lake left for occupation flats of good farmland.

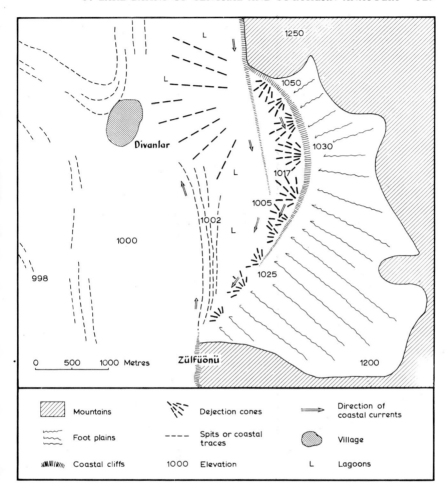

Fig. 12: Coastal traces east of Dinvanlar.

Indeed, there is evidence that in this Early Holocene period the lake dried out completely, under conditions of marked aridity. For Sungur (1970) and Erinç (1970) have observed to the south of Karapınar some older parabolic dunes built up on the dried lake bed by strong south-west winds. During a subsequent fairly wet period, these dunes became covered with vegetation, and later still smaller dunes accumulated on top of them.

This view runs counter to that of de Meester (1971, p. 19), who believes that the lake dried out finally and completely at the beginning of post-

Pluvial times (*c.* 16,000 B.C.), although his conclusion is hard to reconcile with the observation of fossil-shells of *c.* 12,010 and 10,950 B.C. It is here suggested, rather, that a marked dry period during the Early Holocene, just preceding the time of the Aceramic Neolithic settlements, that is *c.* 8–7000 B.C., was followed by a limited transgression of the lake during the Climatic Optimum of *c.* 5–3000 B.C., that is during the Later Neolithic and Bronze Ages. The increased rainfall of this phase would, of course, favour the expansion of agriculture.

As indications of the alternation of Pluvial and Interpluvial conditions in pre-Würm times, one may point first to some traces of crescent-shaped topographic lines at 1030 m in the west of the basin (though there is as yet no proof that these features were associated with coastal formations); second, to the fossil dunes observed by de Meester in the north of the Merdinevli Yayla, which evidently date from a pre-Würm Pleistocene Interpluvial (as in the Burdur Basin, these dunes are at the north-east margin of the depression and were apparently piled up by southerly winds); and, thirdly, the karstic sink-holes between Karapınar and Sultanhanı which are too large and numerous to have been formed entirely during the Würm Pluvial, and of which the older types, with flattened profiles, doubtless date to earlier Pluvial phases.

Evidently in places the younger Pluvial deposits cover the older and extend beyond them: at Kayacık about 10 km north-east of Konya, for instance, recent lagoon deposits overlie older coastal spits, and there is a thick cover of sediment, clearly of great age, under the bottom of the Würm-age lagoon.

All in all, the sedimentary history of the Konya Basin, with the covering of older deposits by newer as the lake re-advanced, is more complex than that of Tuzgölü where the steps of successive Pluvial phases of the lake were more regular and uninterrupted.

The Burdur Basin

The Quaternary basin was formed here through down-faulting within the Pliocene fluvio-lacustrine deposits (Fig. 13), a process which occurred, according to Ardel, at the transition from the Pliocene to the Early Quaternary: or, according to Bering, in the Middle Pleistocene; or again, in the opinion of de Planhol, based on a dating of the travertine deposits of Kurnaköy, after the Würm (in the Finiglacial). But the Kurnaköy travertines are only the latest of a series deposited from Upper Pliocene

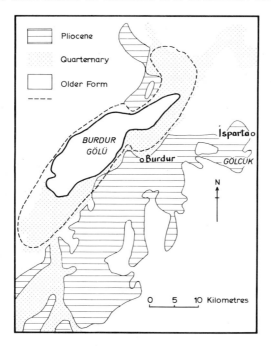

Fig. 13: The Burdur Basin.

times onwards, especially under Pluvial conditions, so that such a late date as that put forward by de Planhol for the Burdur Quaternary lake basin is hardly likely. There is a late Pliocene erosion surface at 1150–1250 m to the south of Burdur, and another of Basal Pleistocene or Villafranchian age, can be observed at 1050–1100 m above sea-level around İğdeli in the Tefenni Basin: it corresponds with surface DIV of Tuzgölü and Konya. These erosion surfaces record the pre-Pluvial history of the area (p. 122).

The author began by following the general view, that the high coastal traces around the Quaternary Burdur Basin were formed during the Last or Würm Pluvial, but in consequence of his fieldwork he now believes some of them to be older, and to be evidence of a composite overlapped structure formed through a series of advances and retreats of the lake.

The problem of dating the terraces is complicated by the continuing subsidence of the basin, as shown by recent earthquakes; by unconformities between the terrace surfaces and the underlying deposits; and by the lack of absolute laboratory datings.

The main Quaternary formations are as follows:

1. a series of surfaces, at *c.* 1000 m and 980 m above sea-level, of

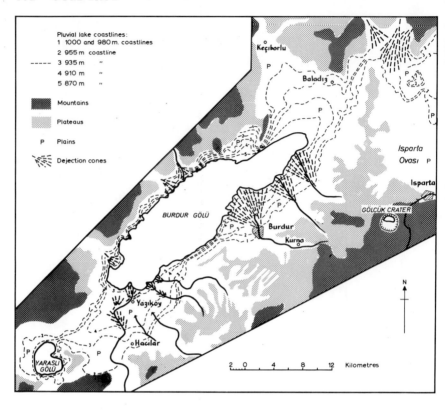

Fig. 14: The Burdur Basin morphology.

sandstone conglomerates, which lack any Dreissensia fossils and therefore date probably to the Lower Pleistocene (Lower PI) (Fig. 15);
2. lightly cemented conglomerates between 955 and 910 m,
containing Dreissensia fossils typical of fluvial conditions, and
doubtless formed during several advances and retreats of the lake
during pre-Würm times (Fig. 16). Within these sediments, the author
suggests drawing a distinction between

    i. the Lower Pleistocene (Upper P1) greenish-grey deltaic con-
glomerates, associated with the highest or 955 m pluvial level and
    ii. the mainly yellow sandstones, left by the next transgression at
935–940 m, and attributable to the Middle Pleistocene (P2-Riss).
Associated with these deposits, and therefore dating to a pre-
Würm Interpluvial, the author believes, are the sand dunes found
at 935–940 m some 4–5 km east of Baradız village;

3. between 910 m and the recent 855 m level, loose, red, firm-grained deposits, of Upper Pleistocene or Würm Pluvial (P3) age. There are traces of similar loose deposits as high as 925 or even 930 m, which may mark an exceptional rise of the lake during this period.

Very recent and fresh traces, observable at 880, 875, 870, 867 and 860 m, are doubtless to be attributed to the Holocene (H). A piece of pottery,

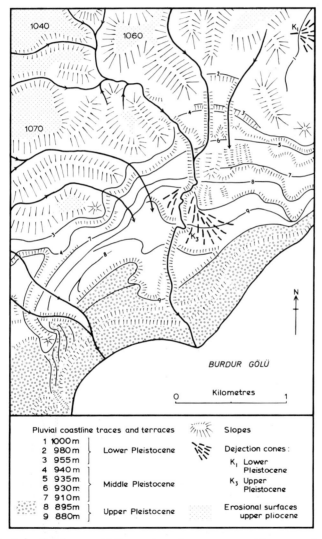

Fig. 15: Lake Burdur—middle section of west coast. (Alternatively, terraces 7 and 8 may be classified as Upper Pleistocene, and terrace 9 as Holocene.)

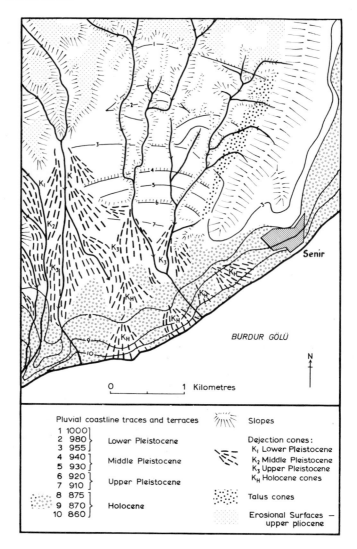

Fig. 16: Lake Burdur—west coast near northern extremity.

found below 6–7 m of alluvium in the dry bed of the Suludere River, points to increased deposition of alluvium after Aceramic–Neolithic times.

A find of microliths, probably of Mesolithic age, on a sand-dune east of Baradız (Louis, 1938a, b; Kansu, 1945, p. 278), gives no significant aid to dating if, as I believe, these dunes are relics of an early Interpluvial, much older than the Mesolithic.

The Aceramic Neolithic site of Hacılar was established near a karstic spring on a 925–930 m terrace plain, after the Würm Pluvial, some 3–4 km south of the contemporary coastline.

The Yaraşli lake was joined with that of Burdur to its south-west during the Lower and Middle Pleistocene, but during the Upper Pleistocene (P3) the water fell below the level of the col at 935–940 m to the north of Düver. The Atabey Basin to the north-east likewise was directly connected with that of Burdur until the Upper Pleistocene when the link was broken by the dejection core of the Gönen River. Above the present water level at 918–920 m the author has traced on air-photographs signs of coastlines or terraces at 955, 940, and 935 m. The 955 m terrace can be followed southwards towards the Aliköy-Diyedin vineyards, and here it seems that the dejection cone of İsparta has buried it possibly during the Upper Pleistocene (P3). I have observed clear coastal features (cliffs and deltaic deposits with dreissensia fossils) up to 935–940 m. Underground karstic drainage, which today keeps dry the Atabey Basin, may have played a part in its progressive desiccation in the Late Pleistocene.

In this same Atabey Basin, to the north of Bozanönü railway station, in the cave of Kapali in at the foot of a lake cliff, Ş.A. Kansu found Aurignacian artefacts of Late Würm age. Since the cave stands at about 935–940 m above sea-level, and the lake surface must then have been below this, it follows that the 955 m stadion was pre-Würm.

A Comparison of the Tuzgölü, Konya and Burdur Basins

In conclusion, the three basins differ in the following respects:

1. the Tuzgölü Basin, wide and shallow, received a low influx of water and sediments in proportion to its size. The infilling of the basin therefore could not keep pace with the subsidence of its central parts, and so its successive Pluvial terraces are arranged in a simple step-like series;

2. the fairly narrow and shallow Konya-Ereğli Basin received much water and sediment from the Taurus, and the younger terraces covered the older, so that only traces of the Last or Würm Pluvial survive;

3. into the deep and narrow intermontane trough of Burdur, much water flowed and sediment was washed, but, since the rate of subsidence exceeded that of sedimentation, the Pluvial terraces are

arranged in a stepped series as in Tuzgölü; though in Burdur the sediments are thicker and more conspicuous.

As for the dating of these Pluvial basins, the usual view is that all the pluvial traces in Anatolia belong to the Last (Würm) Pluvial, which was contemporary with the Last or Würm Glaciation, the only one which has left its mark on Anatolia, for the country was not uplifted to "Glacial" elevations until immediately pre-Würm times. As will be evident from the observations set out above, I take another view: that this lack of evidence of early glaciation in the mountains gives no grounds for assuming that there were no Pluvial phases in the lake basins of Anatolia in the Early and Middle Pleistocene. On the contrary, there is abundant evidence of pre-Würm fluvial terraces and Pluvial phases. I believe that glaciation did not leave traces in Anatolia in the Early Pleistocene because the climate of the country was then predominantly of warm Mediterranean type, as indicated by the red sediments, with short intervals of cool and rainy conditions which produced the Lower Pleistocene fluvial and Pluvial episodes in the lake basins. The earlier glaciations of the mountains, which probably occurred during these cool and wet intervals, would therefore be weak, and their traces would be obliterated by the stronger penultimate and eventual ultimate glaciations.

In the Middle and Upper Pleistocene, warm and dry Interpluvials certainly occurred, but, by contrast with what happened in the Lower Pleistocene, they were of shorter duration than the periods when cold and wet conditions prevailed and produced more marked glacial conditions in the mountains and more prolonged Pluvial phases in the basins.

In Holocene and Recent times, the cold/wet and warm/dry epochs and seasons appear to have been more evenly balanced.

References

Acatay, T. 1966. The relation between Beyşehir Lake and Manavgat River. *D.S.I. Teknik Bült.* **9**, 1–24. In Turkish.

Alagöz, C. 1944. Une etude sur les phénomènes karstiques en Turquie. *Publ. Turkish Geogr. Soc.* No 1. In Turkish. French summary.

Ardel, A. 1951. Morphologie de la région des lacs (Turquie) I. *Istanbul Üniv. Coğrafys Enst. Derg.* **1**, 1–19. In Turkish. French summary.

Ardel, A. 1952. Morphological observations in the Lake District II. *Istanbul Üniv. Coğrafya Enst. Derg.* **2**, 65–77. In Turkish.

Ardel, A. 1954a. Au sujet des variations de niveau du lac d'Iznik pendant le Quaternaire. *Rev. Geogr. Inst. Univ. Istanbul* **1**, 177–178.

Ardel, A. 1954b. Partie occidentale de la région des lacs, Turquie. *Rev. Geogr. Inst. Istanbul.* 1, 66–84.

Ardel, A. 1957. Geomorphology of the marginal plains of Western Taurus (Acc. to X. de Planhol). *Istanbul Üniv. Coğr. Enst. Derg.* 4, 1–15. In Turkish.

Atalay, I. 1973a. A study of the structure, geomorphology and soil erosion in the Akşehir–Eber lake basin. Unpublished doctoral thesis. Istanbul University. In Turkish.

Atalay, I. 1973b. Quaternary deposits and geomorphology of the Akşehir–Eber–Karamuk basin. *Abstracts of the papers. Congr. of Earth Sc. on the Occasion of the 50th Anniv. of Turkish Republic.*

Aygen, T. 1959. Speleology. *Publ. of D.S.I. No 88.* In Turkish.

Bagge, E. and Willkomm, H. 1966. Geologische Altersbestimmung mit 36 Cl. *Atomkernenergie* 11, 176–184.

Bering, D. 1971a. The development of the Neogene and Quaternary intermontane basins within the Pisidian Lake District in S. Anatolia *Newsl. Stratigraphy* 1, 27–32.

Bering, D. 1971b. Lithostratigraphie, tektonische Entwicklung und Seengeschichte der neogenen und quartaeren intramontanen Becken der Pisidischen Seenregion (Südanatolien). *Beihefte Geol. Jahrbuch.* 101.

Bilgin, T. 1959. Researches on the pluvial conditions in Turkey. *Revue Géogr. Turque.* 18–19, 179–181. In Turkish.

Bilgin, T. 1961. On the geomorphic evolution of the Iznik lake depression and the origin of the Garsak Gorge. *Rev. Geogr. Inst. Istanbul.* 7, 75–86.

Bilgin, T. 1967. Samanli Mountains. *Publ. Geogr. Inst. Istanbul.* No 50. In Turkish.

Bukowski, G. von 1890–92. Geologische Forschungen im westlichen Kleinasien. *Verh. Kais. K. Geol. Reichsanst.* 5, 134–141.

Butzer, K. W. 1958. Quaternary stratigraphy and Climate in the Near East. *Bonner Geogr. Abh.* 24.

Chaput, E. 1963. Voyages d'études géologiques et géomorphogeniques en Turquie. *Mem. Inst. Fr. Archeol. Stamboul* II, VIII.

Cohen, H. R. 1967. The neolithic cultures of Anatolia in relation to their natural environment. Unpublished thesis. University of Manchester.

Cohen, H. R. 1969. Environment of the Early Neolithic Settlements in South Central Anatolia. Unpublished text of Research seminar on Archaeology and related subjects. Institute of Archaeology, London.

Cohen, H. R. and Erol, O. 1969. Aspects of the Palaeogeography of Central Anatolia. *Geogr. Journ.* 135, 388–398.

Darkot, B. 1938. Quelques observations morphologiques en relation avec les variations récentes du climat en Turquie. *Publ. Inst. Géogr. Univ. Istanbul* No 4, 89–93.

Diker, S. 1958. Report on the gravimetric and magnetometric researches in Central Anatolia. Unpublished report of M.T.A. No 2660. In Turkish.

Erinç, S. 1967. On the Pleistocene high level of Acıgöl. *Istanbul Üniv. Coğr. Enst. Derg.* **8**, 140–143. In Turkish.

Erinç, S. 1970. The Quaternary of Turkey and the contribution of geomorphology on it. *Jeomorofoloji Derg.* **2**, 12–35.

Erinç, S. 1972. Turkey: Outlines of a Cultural Geography. *Int. Jahrb. Ges. Geographie–Unterricht.* **13**, 125–149.

Erol, O. 1963. Zur Frage der Rumpfflaechen in Anatolien, unter besonderer Berücksichtigung des Gebietes um Ankara. *Mitt. Geogr. Gesell. München.* **48**, 173–191.

Erol, O. 1966. The geomorphological importance of the remains of fossil mammals found between Üçbaş and Akdogan villages in the northwest of Ankara. *Annals Geogr. Res. Inst. Univ. Ankara.***1**, 109–120. In Turkish. English summary.

Erol, O. 1968. The travertine cones of Boluk Lake, in the south of Cihanbeyli, Tuzgölü Area, Central Anatolia. *Revue Turque Geogr.* 20–21, 64–98. In Turkish. English summary.

Erol, O. 1969. The geology and geomorphology of the Tuzgölü basin. A research from the viewpoint of neotectonics, pluvial lake terraces and potash-salt formation. Unpublished report of T.B.T.A.K. In Turkish.

Erol, O. 1970. Les haut niveaux pléistocènes du Tuzgölü (lac Salé) en Anatolie centrale (Turquie). *Ann. Géogr.* **79**, 39–50.

Erol, O. 1973. Quaternary deposits of the Burdur Lake Basin. *Abstracts of Papers. Congress of Earth Sciences on the occasion of the 50th Anniversary of Turkish Republic.*

Farrand, W. M. and Solecki, R. S. 1963. An archeological reconnaissance in the Beyşehir–Suğla Area of Southwestern Turkey. *Report of the Columbia University Archeological Exp. to Turkey.*

Farrand, W. R. 1965. Geology and physiography of the Beyşehir–Suğla depression, Western Taurus Lake District, Turkey. *Türk Arkeol. Derg.* **13**, 149–154.

Güldalı, N. 1970. Karstmorphologische Studien im Gebiet des Poljesystems von Kestel (Westlicher Taurus, Türkei). *Tübinger Geogr. Stud.* **40**.

Inandık, H. 1965. The lakes of Turkey. *Publ. Geogr. Inst. Istanbul Univ.* No. 44.

Irion, G. 1970. Mineralogisch Sedimentpetrographische und geochemische Untersuchungen am Tuzgölü (Salzsee), Türkei. *Chemie Erde.* **29**, 167–225.

Kansu, Ş. A. 1945. Preliminary report of the prehistoric investigations in the region of Isparta and Burdur, carried out in June 1944. *Belleten* **9**, 213–62.

Klear, W. 1965. Geomorphologische Untersuchungen in den Randgebirgen des Van–See (Ostanatolien). *Zeitschr. Geom.* **9**, 246–256.

Lahn, E. 1946. Les dépôts pliocenes et quaternaires de la région de Konya–Burdur. *Rev. Fac. Sci. Univ. Istanbul* **B11**, 85–106.

Lahn, E. 1948. Contribution a l'Etude Géologique et Géomorphologique des Lacs de la Turquie. *Publ. of M.T.A.* Series B. No 12.

Lebküchner, R. F. 1960. Bericht über das Ergebniss der Bohrkampagnen der

Jahre 1957 und 1959 im Braunkohlengebiet von Beyşehir–Konya. Unpublished report of M.T.A. No. 2924.

Louis, H. 1938a. Über alte Hochstaende Anatolischer Seen. *C. R. Congr. Int. Geogr. Amsterdam 1938* **2**, 325–335.

Louis, H. 1938b. Eiszeitliche Seen in Anatolien. *Zeitschr. Ges. Erdk. Berlin* 268 279.

Meester, T. de 1971. *Highly calcareous lacustrine soils in the Great Konya Basin, Turkey.* Centre for Agricultural Publ. and Documentation.

Morrison, R. B. 1968. Pluvial lakes. *Encyc. Geom.* 873–883.

Penck, W. 1918. *Die tektonischen Grundzüge westkleinasiens.*

Pfannenstiel, M. 1944. Die diluvialen Entwicklungsstadien und die Urgeschichte von Dardanellen, Marmarameer und Bosporus. *Geolog. Rundschau.* **34**, 342–434.

Planhol, X. de 1956. Contribution à l'Etude Géomorphologique du Taurus occidental et de ses plaines bordières. *Revue Géogr. Alpine* **44**, 1–86.

Schweizer, G. 1975. Untersuchungen zur Physiogeographie von Ostanatolien und Nordwestiran. Geomorphologische, klima- und hydrogeographische Studien in Vansee- und Rezaiyehsee-Gebiet. *Tübinger Geographische Studien,* **60**, (9).

Sungur, K. 1967. Geomorphological researches in the Konya–Ereğli basin. Unpublished doctoral Thesis, Istanbul University.

Sungur, K. 1970. Volcanic activities and volcanic landforms in the Konya–Ereğli basin. *Istanbul Üniv. Coğr. Enst. Derg.* **9**, 103–110. In Turkish.

Tchihatcheff, P. de 1867. *Asie Mineure.* **4**, *Géologie.*

Vita-Finzi, C. 1969. Late Quaternary continental deposits of central and western Turkey. *Man* **4**, 605–619.

Wenzel, H. 1932. *Sultan–Dagh und Akschehir–Ova.*

Wenzel, H. 1935. *Aufbau, formen und abflussverhaeltnisse Mittelanatoliens.*

Yalçınlar, I. and Atalay, I. 1973. Geological and geomorphological observations in the Sultandağları, Eber and Akşehir lake basins. *Istanbul Univ. Coğr. Enst. Derg.* **10**, 281–290. In Turkish.

9
The Desiccation of Anatolia

William C. Brice

Degeneration of the Flora and Fauna since Classical Times

It is evident from what is said on the subject by Classical authors that the forests of Anatolia were much more extensive two millennia ago than they are now. Strabo refers (XII, ii, 7) to the forest around Mount Argaeus (the modern Erciyes above Kayseri), a source of timber, which has now gone; and elsewhere (XIII, i, 65) he mentions a former wooded region at Thebe in the Troad which had already lost its trees by his time. Again, the large forest, eighty stadia in circumference, at Daphne near Antioch, which contained the sacred grove of Apollo (Strabo XIV, ii, 6) has now disappeared, save only for a few laurels and cypresses near the springs of Harbiye; and little trace remains of the "royal forests" mentioned by Livy (I, 54, 36) between Mysia and Lydia, or of the forests seen by Xenophon (*Katabasis* I, iv 4) near Muş, at the southern fort of Bingöl Dağ.

At the same time as the forests have receded, so too has their fauna. The lion was widespread throughout the Near East in antiquity: Ammianus, for example (XVIII, 7) describes how the Emperor Julian flushed them from burning grass in the district of North Syria around Nisibin, Urfa and Harran; and, even in the early part of the last century, Colonel Chesney (I, 442) saw some in the Taurus and Amanus Mountains and near Aleppo. The species is now extinct in all this region, as are the wild cattle known to Varro (*De re rust.* II, i) in the Troad and elsewhere.

Possible Natural Causes thereof

Now we know of no natural change of climate which would be enough to explain this widespread reduction in the forests, or the associated loss of soil and silting of valleys and harbours, which is chronicled elsewhere in this volume (Chapters 6 and 7). Probably the best indication of recent changes of climate is afforded by the terminal moraines of the high mountain glaciers of the Cilo district in eastern Pontus, for example, or on Uludağ, the Bithynian Olympus. Professor Erinç has used these to chart the changing extent of the glaciers, and the shifts of climate which effected them. In an earlier study (1952) he concluded that, in the latter half of the first millennium B.C., coincidentally with the "Sub-Atlantic" epoch in Europe, there was a noticeable extension of the Anatolian glaciers. In his contribution to this volume (p. 90) he refers to glacial advances in the spell A.D. 1600–1680 and at two subsequent times about 1720 and 1850— all of which three episodes would fall inside the time of the "Little Ice Age" of the Alps of Europe (A.D. 1430–1850). Now by analogy with the reaction of vegetation to climate during the major Glacials and Interglacials, it would be expected that a cooling of the plateaux would lead to an extension of steppe at the expense of woodland. It is unlikely that these colder spells would be sufficiently long or emphatic to have any marked effect on vegetation; though the possible cumulative effects of the droughts of the eighteenth and nineteenth centuries listed by Professor Erinç (pp. 98, 99) should be kept in mind.

Human Causes

On the other hand, there is abundant evidence of economic changes in Graeco-Roman times and subsequently which would have affected drastically the natural vegetation and fauna of the peninsula. In sequence of time these may be enumerated broadly as:

1. The wholesale exploitation of timber by contractors in Imperial times. Strabo's remarks (XIV, vi, 5) about how this was carried out in Cyprus summarize the motives and spirit of this exploitation:

> Eratosthenes says, that anciently the plains abounded with timber, and were covered with forests, which prevented cultivation; the mines were of some service towards clearing the surface, for trees were cut down to smelt the copper and silver. Besides this, timber was required for the construction of fleets, as the sea was now navigated with security and by a large naval force; but when even these means were insufficient to check the growth of timber in the forests, permission was given, to such as were able and inclined, to cut down the trees and to hold the land thus cleared as their own property, free from all payments.

2. The cutting and burning of trees by nomadic tribes in order to clear land for pasture, and in the case of pines to tap their turpentine. Theophrastus (IX, ii, 7) described already in Classical times the reckless system by which

turpentine was collected about Mount Ida, after which "the tree, being decayed, falls in consequence of the undercutting, by the force of the winds"; and Sir Charles Fellows in 1838 saw an identical method of tapping and destroying trees employed by the Tahtaci or "Woodmen" in the Lycian alps (*Asia Minor and Lycia*, 1852, p. 191).

3. In the present century, and particularly since the foundation of the Turkish Republic, the number of inhabitants has increased markedly, and woodland has been cleared to make way for farms to support them. Much of this new reclamation is on slopes too steep to hold the soil once the trees have gone, and the consequent erosion has been carefully charted, and often checked, through the advice of the Istanbul Faculty of Forestry (Yamanlar, 1962).

Changes of Vegetation through the Holocene

General Evidence

We may then safely attribute these recent dramatic changes of vegetation to human causes, but, on a longer scale of time, the changes during the Holocene seem to have been largely the consequence of shifts of climate. De Tchihatcheff, the talented and industrious Russian traveller and naturalist, made some perceptive generalizations about the flora of Anatolia which may still be considered a good basis for studying the nature and cause of these changes (de Tchihatcheff, 1853).

1. There is a very limited range of Arctic and Alpine species on the mountains of Anatolia; the *Ranunculus glacialis*, willow grass and dwarf birch, for example, are not found there, though they are common on the high alps of Central Europe. The reason is that, during the Last Ice Age, Anatolia did not experience extensive glaciation by ice-sheets, and was not colonized by these Arctic species which invaded Europe on the fringe of the ice, and after the general melting found homes on the mountain summits.

2. In marked contrast, the surviving forests of Anatolia, which in the central plateau are found as isolated patches on the slopes of widely separated mountains, such as Erciyes and Hasan Dağ, are exceptionally rich in species. The Lebanese oak, the chestnut-leaved oak, the Oriental pine, the Cilician fir, Lebanese cedar, Oriental plane and Pontic azalea are widely found in these rich assemblages, built up partly from Tertiary relicts which took refuge here during the rigours of the Ice Age, and partly from Oriental

species which mixed with them when they spread back to Europe from the Caucasus and Himalayas after the ice sheets had melted. The disconnected "outliers" of forest on the plateau must have been connected at an earlier stage when the cover was more continuous.

3. There are several indications, in respect of the composition and elevation of the surviving forests of Anatolia, that they have become adapted to dry conditions. The snow-line is very high for the latitude—between 3400 and 3500 m for example in Mount Erciyes—and certain mountain species which are common at high levels in Europe, such as the birch, the larch and the fir, are rare or absent because of the scarcity of snow. On the other hand, some species which thrive under dry conditions in autumn and winter—the vine for example—are found at unusually high altitudes. The beech grows up to around 2250 m above sea-level in the Pontic ranges, and cedars, hornbeams and the Cilician pine to at least 2000 m in the Taurus.

Sequence of Changes

The stages by which the vegetation of Anatolia has evolved since the Last Ice Age may be summarized as follows:

1. At the time of greatest cold, there were mountain glaciers but no extensive ice-sheets or areas of tundra, such as characterized north and central Europe. The plateau basins were occupied by extensive lakes of fresh water, around which the rest of the plateau and the lower slopes of the mountains were covered with steppe vegetation of grass and bushes. The forests would be restricted to a relatively narrow zone between the steppe and the snow-line, and consist largely of hardy species of pine, birch and juniper. The dry and cold climate with protracted winters, and the associated cold steppe, would recall conditions now prevailing in Siberia or northern Mongolia.

2. As the climate became progressively warmer, even though the precipitation was no less than before, the great lakes receded throughout the Late Glacial period, leaving by post-Glacial times expanses of alluvium with reeds and thickets where wild cattle could thrive. This terrain could be easily cleared by burning and would make good farm-land; and it is evident from what we know of such Neolithic establishments as Çatal Hüyük and Hacılar that the earliest permanent settlers on the plateau chose localities of this sort where they could practise a mixed economy of hunting, fishing, farming and herding. As in previous major Interglacials, and to a lesser extent during minor interstadials within the Würm Glaciation, forests would become more extensive as the timber belt widened both upwards and downwards,

and the milder conditions would encourage colonization by species from further south and east, which had formerly been deterred by the long severe winters—cedar, oak, hazel, plane, beech and the like.

3. There is in the northern plateau belt in the early Holocene no evidence of a "fluvial" phase such as was experienced at this time in North Africa and Arabia. Ganji deduces a continuing phase of desiccation which reached a climax about 6000 B.P.: Erol sees evidence of a change of prevalence of winds in Central Anatolia from north-east to south-west, which protracted the arid phase of the early post-Glacial: while Erinç points specifically to the period of 7000–5000 B.P. (the time of the "Climatic Optimum" of northern Europe) as the stage of maximum aridity on the Anatolian plateau, when the dunes of the Konya Basin were accumulated. All three authorities notice a somewhat moister phase when the lakes rose slightly in the later Holocene—though they differ as to its exact timing—but it was only a minor interruption in the general process of desiccation.

So by about 4000–3000 B.P. the inland lakes of the plateaux of Anatolia and Iran had shrunk and been replaced in many cases by mud flats and salt sumps. With the disappearence of these bodies of water, which must formerly have kept local humidity high, the precipitation would become less and the air drier both over the plateau basins and on the ranges. The thickets of the alluvial flats would give way to the now familiar dry steppe or camel-thorn scrub, while the levels and composition of the mountain forests would become adjusted, as explained above, to circumstances of dry air, high snow-line, and winters warm for the height.

4. With the Graeco-Roman colonization and wholesale exploitation of the forests and pastures, hillsides were denuded, valleys and harbours became silted, and winds piled dunes over the more heavily grazed parts of the plateau. At this stage, human rather than natural causes must be held to account for the changes.

5. Although the methodical and organized spoliation of the forests and bulk export from the rural estates and ranches ceased with the overrunning of the outer Byzantine themes by the Turkish tribes in the eleventh century A.D., the "nomadization" of the countryside which followed would ensure that the central plateau and the high alps of the border ranges (the *yaylas* or summer pastures) would not grow anything higher than close-cropped grass or scrub. To Livy the central plateau was already *axylon* or "treeless", and Strabo refers to the immense flocks which formed the wealth of Amyntas, the last king of Lycaonia; but from contemporary accounts of the overrunning of cities by the nomads (Brice, 1955) there seems little doubt that the range of pastoralism extended vastly following the irruption of the tribes.

Recent Experiments in Restoration

After the first shock of the invasions, there was some rebuilding of towns, though rarely on the old sites. But the central plateau and its verges have remained one of the largest and most specialized stretches of sheep country in southern Asia. An experimental enclosure controlled by the Turkish Government Soil and Water Undertakings near Karapınar in the dry heart of the plateau has shown how vigorously the grass and scrub will rise and thicken naturally when grazing animals are excluded. Upstream of İsparta in the Lake Region of the south-west, an entire mountain has been replanted with spruce and larch, while on the opposite side of the valley the soft tufa has been shielded here and there from wind erosion by tiers of grass clumps, and the spates of the intervening stream retarded by series of check dams. Experiments of this kind demonstrate how easily and quickly a lost vegetation can be restored if the rural economy is modified. The urgent need is to retard the alarming loss of soil in the catchments of the great new high dams, otherwise their artificial lakes will become simply expensively reclaimed new alluvial plains, perhaps in about half a century.

In this context these experiments are of interest as a confirmation of the view that the changes in the vegetation of Anatolia, at least over the past two thousand years or so, though mimicking the effects of rapid desiccation, are largely to be explained through economic causes: likewise in the case of coastal silting and the prograding of deltas, automatic consequences of the deterioration of the vegetation cover; for the immense quantities of silt which are now entering the lakes behind the barrages would in natural circumstances find their way to the lower valleys and the sea. At the same time, the evidence for the cooling of temperatures over the plateaux between the seventeenth and nineteenth centuries A.D. and the possibly associated series of droughts pointed out by Professor Erinç (see pp. 98, 99) should be recalled; for we may have here an instance of a moderate decline of temperature combined with a run of dry seasons which would at least weaken the hold of the natural vegetation and render it more vulnerable to damage through over-grazing.

References

Brice, W. C. 1955. The Turkish colonization of Anatolia. *Bull. John Rylands Lib.* **38**, 18–44.

Erinç, S. 1952, Glacial evidences of the climatic variations in Turkey. *Geograf. Annaler (Stockholm)*, **34**, 89–97.

de Tchihatcheff, P. 1853–69. *Asie Mineure, description physique, statistique et archéologique de cette contrée*. 4 Volumes, Paris.

Yamanlar, O. 1962. Turkiye Şartharina uygun yeni bir erozyon Klasifikasyonu. *Ist. Univ. Orman Fakult. Dergisi* **11**, 53–66.

10
Post-Glacial Climatic Changes on the Iranian Plateau

M. H. Ganji

Introduction

There is an increasing need for information about past climatic variations. This need stems, on the one hand, from endeavours to reconstruct the environment in which man began his life on our planet; and, on the other hand, from a growing concern that man's activities may influence climate and a feeling that a better understanding of the behaviour of the atmosphere may make it possible to anticipate and even to avert adverse climatic changes, whether these spring from natural or artificial causes. Since meteorological records extend back over only a relatively short period, they may not reveal the range of natural climatic conditions that have existed in the geologically recent past and that may recur fairly soon. For this reason, a variety of natural and cultural phenomena, linked in some fashion to climate, have been investigated, in the fields of geology, geomorphology, pedology, botany, zoology, ecology, palaeontology, archaeology, ancient history, historical geography, folklore, place names, and the like.

The question of post-Glacial climatic changes with which this chapter is concerned has received exhaustive attention in North America and Europe, where, apart from the prevailing scientific atmosphere, topographical features and evidences of glaciation have greatly facilitated field research and scientific study. The amount of work done and published about the areas with which we are concerned, however, is by no means comparable to the vast amounts of research undertaken in the West. In the monumental work of J. K. Charlesworth (*The Quaternary Era*, London 1966), out of thousands of references only a very small fraction relate to this part of the world.

Nevertheless, in Iran there have been some studies and observations by professional geographers and geologists as well as by ordinary travellers who were impressed by the anomaly that wide-spread ruined settlements and archaeological sites are found within hydrological basins and former river beds with now no sign of water. Huntington (1905) and Hedin (1910) both attributed the present dryness and sparse population of the country to the gradual desiccation of the Iranian Plateau during the Pleistocene period.

Leaving aside the pioneering work of the above writers and that of Desio, who in 1934 published an article on the geology of Zardeh-Kuh and dealt with certain glacial features of that region, one can consider the veteran and eminent geographer Hans Bobek of Berlin and Vienna Universities as the first and foremost professional geographer to dedicate himself to this field. As early as 1937 he published his first scientific paper on the role of glaciation in north-western Iran, and during the next thirty years or so has made six trips to Iran and published six papers which have aroused both interest and controversy, and inspired others to follow where he has led. (I have had the good fortune of knowing Hans Bobek since 1938 and have accompanied him on some of his excursions in Iran.)

In 1957 two papers by Gabriel and Stratil Sauer added to our knowledge of the desert landforms of Iran and of their relations with climatic processes. In 1958 Butzer published his paper, and three years later Wright wrote on Pleistocene glaciation in Kurdistan. During the sixties he and his colleagues J. H. McAndrews and W. van Zeist (1967) as well as Hutchinson and Cowgill (1963) drew useful conclusions from the analysis of pollen from lake Zeribar. In 1969 Ehlers published his studies of terraces in the Chalus Valley and their relations with the level of the Caspian and the vagaries of Pleistocene climate of the Iranian Plateau. In 1970 Krinsley, who for years had worked on playas and internal drainage patterns in various parts of the world, published his valuable report on the playas of Iran. In 1973 an Iranian scholar, Siahpoosh, who for years has undertaken serious research in matters relating to early settlement and civilization in the Iranian Plateau, published a book in Persian which brought together practically all the previous work done in this field.

I propose to review the whole question briefly and to arrange in chronological order the work previous to Krinsley's latest study, in an attempt to trace the gradual development of ideas on the subject. Interest will be focussed on the material that relates to the past 20,000 years.

At this point it is salutary to quote Hans Bobek:

> Here we are still far from a satisfactory knowledge of the most fundamental facts. This implies that the establishment of any ambitious detailed sequences of Quaternary events is still far ahead of sound research. (Bobek, 1963, p. 403).

Geographical Background

Throughout this paper, the term "Iranian Plateau" will be applied, as by Fisher and Bobek, to Iran only, although any opinion expressed about climatic changes in Iran may reasonably be applied to Afghanistan also.

The Iranian Plateau, thus defined, has an average altitude of roughly 1500 m with high mountains extending along its western and northern margins. In the north the Elburz mountains, varying in width from 64 to 128 km with many summits from 3600 to 4800 m in altitude, culminate in Mt Damavand (5678 m) which lies approximately in the centre of the mountains belt.

To the west and south-west, the Zagros Mountains extend from the Turkish border south-eastward for 1600 km to the vicinity of Bandar Abbas, from where they are continued by the low Makran Mountains to the western

Fig. 1:   Map of Iran showing places named in this chapter.

border of Pakistan. They rise from the north-west and south-east to culminate in Zardeh-Kuh which has an altitude of 4548 m.

In the east, a series of broken hills and ranges form what is generally termed the Eastern Mountains, which provide a link between the northern and southern arcs of the Alpine system. Near Meshed in the north-east, the mountains bend abruptly away from their east–west orientation to their junction with the southern arc east of Iranshahr. In this section the mountain crests do not exceed 2000 m, but occasional summits reach 3000 m, which means that they may be as much as 2000 m above the local desert flats along the Afghan border.

Lesser mountains below 2000 m, and lower divides, further separate the internal basins of the Plateau. Collectively, the interior basins occupy nearly two-thirds of the country and contain playas, dune-fields, broad alluvial fans and isolated mountains.

The Nature of the Problem

The Pleistocene and Recent epochs, which together constitute the Quaternary period, are abnormal from the standpoint of paleoclimatology, being a time of marked cyclic change. The entire history of the genus Homo has been confined to this period. It follows that no true man has ever experienced the normal geological climatic pattern, and that the human race has always had to cope with changes of condition that result from swings of the delicate balance, first towards the advance, and later towards the retreat of the ice. This is why the study of post-Glacial climatology is so important for human history.

During the Pleistocene epoch there were four or five main periods of ice advance, separated by marked stages of retreat, which in turn experienced numerous lesser swings.

During each Glacial stage the polar ice-cap would extend southward in a sheet up to 6 km thick to cover thousands of square kilometres of territory. Concurrently, continental ice-caps from mountain masses in middle latitudes would move northward with the result that they would sometimes approach or even join the polar ice. At such times the moisture-laden cold air over the ice would engender widespread storms and cyclonic depressions, that would bring heavy rains to the warmer country on its southern borders. On the other hand, the retreat and shrinkage of ice would weaken such circulations, and in consequence the ice-free southern borderlands would experience long periods of drought and wind-erosion which led to the formation of deserts. In general, the Iranian plateau has been experiencing, with fluctuations, these interglacial conditions ever since the end of the Würm glaciation, and this observation has led many to believe in the gradual desiccation of the area (Huntington and Wadia)—a theory which has been doubted recently by Bobek (1963, p. 403).

In fact, many episodes of Pleistocene history appear more clearly in the records of regions never covered by ice than in those of deglaciated regions. Even the Tropics, which throughout geological times have shared only to a minor degree in climatic changes, furnish valuable clues concerning Pleistocene conditions, such as atoll and reef developments and changes of sea-level. Similarly, inland lakes and salt lakes of arid regions like Iran often bear witness to the climatic changes caused by the glaciation.

Climatological Evidence

This is of four kinds:

1. Geological climatology or true paleoclimatology; is based on evidence from rocks from the oldest pre-Cambrian to the Quaternary. Evidently "normal" climates have characterized most of the earth's history, interrupted occasionally by glacial conditions.

2. Geochronological climatology, from approximately the start of the Recent Epoch to the appearance of historic records, during which time there has been an amelioration of glacial conditions and various fluctuations or possible cyclic changes.

3. Documented climatology which gives evidence of possible cyclic changes.

4. Instrumental climatology since the middle of the last century, a period too short to enable climatologists to arrive at conclusive results.

Of the above four basic divisions 1 and 4 are not of interest here, the first falling outside the terms of reference and the fourth being too short-lived (Ganji, 1968, p. 212). We will therefore limit ourselves to the evidence regarding the second and the third, with special reference to Iran.

Geochronological and Documentary Evidence

Varves

These are annual layers of clay and silt deposited in quiet waters subject to freezing during winter and thawing in summer. This technique is not applicable in Iran, except possibly in some mountain lakes.

Glaciation and Snow-line

The end of the most recent (Würm) Major Glacial period of the Pleistocene Epoch is usually placed at approximately 8500 B.P. when, in Europe at least, climatic conditions had returned essentially to those of today. The ice, however, had begun to withdraw many thousand years before then, probably about 20,000 B.P. Evidently withdrawal and eventual disappearance of the ice has been a gradual process that has taken place parallel with the warming of the climate. Vestiges of former ice-fields, and in particular glacial moraines, have therefore been used by geographers as clues to the former climatic conditions. In Iran, Bobek has recognized six major centres of former, obviously Würm, Glaciations. They are the central Elburz, Savalan (Sabalan) Kuh, the Irano-Turkish and adjoining Irano-Iraqi border ranges, Ushturan Kuh, Zard Kuh and Kuh Dinar. The most important single group is the Takht-e-Sulaiman in the central Elburz. On the basis of prolonged studies, Bobek concludes that the climatic snowline of the post-Glacial period was about 600 to 800 m below the present level, and he assumes an overall pattern of zones of temperature as at present, but about 4·5°C lower (Bobek, 1963, p. 406).

Desert Evolution and Desiccation

During Late Pleistocene post-Glacial times on the continent of Asia, many million square kilometres of land became desert or semi-desert. Such terrain extends almost continually from the western Sahara across Syria and Arabia into the Iranian Plateau and on to Turkestan and Mongolia, with a branch from Iran towards Baluchistan and the Thar area of Rajputana. It has been contended that this great arid zone was a counter-effect of the Pleistocene Ice Age of the Northern Hemisphere, and that this widespread desiccation at the end of the Pleistocene was the natural consequence of the Pleistocene Glaciation in Asia and Europe (Seth, 1963, p. 449). Although the Plateau of Iran, a part of this wide arid belt, has been undergoing general desiccation, it is evident that there have been fluctuations, as indicated by the advance and withdrawal of deserts in prehistoric times and the occupation and abandonment of settlements in later stages.

Erosional Features

Apart from the desert proper, there are many physical features that provide evidence of climatic change—dry river-beds, river plains, valleys, river terraces, alluvial fans, fan-like gravel plains, pediments, dissected hills, bad lands, as well as sand dunes, loess and other aeoline deposits. Bobek, Krinsley and Ehlers in particular have given much weight to these features in their studies, whether carried out actually on the ground or with the help of air photographs.

Lakes and Playas

Water bodies of the arid zones have been aptly named ''Nature's rain-gauges''. In and around the Iranian Plateau, permanent lakes like the Caspian Sea, Lake Rezaieh (Urmia), and the Hamun of Sistan, have long attracted attention, and the Caspian in particular has received much attention from Russian geographers and scholars.

Playas or Kavirs as they are locally called (defined by Krinsley as ''Flat area that may be underlain by lacustrine sediments deposited during periods of higher precipitation/evaporation ratio than prevail today'') have been variously explained on climatic grounds. Bobek has made extensive study of almost the entire playa area of Iran, while Ahmad Mostofi and his colleagues at the Geographical Institute of Tehran University have undertaken useful research which is embodied in their scientific publications (in Persian).

Biological Evidence

Tree-ring studies began in America in the early years of this century when Douglas and Huntington demonstrated a close relationship between annual rainfall and the width of rings in certain long-lived trees. Lately a chronology of over 8200 years has been developed (LaMarche, 1974, p. 1044).

Unfortunately, no work has been done in this field in Iran where there are very few long-lived trees; though there are a few historical trees like the well-known cypress trees of Kashmar and Abarghoo, reputed to be more than 2000 years old, which may be used for this purpose in future. For like reasons, peat deposits have not been used for dating in Iran. However, certain pollen studies have contributed to our knowledge of the post-Glacial climates of Iran (see next section under 1963 and 1966).

Archaeological Evidence

This includes the abandonment of settlements in the arid interior of the Iranian Plateau, usually through shortage of water. At one time men lived by rivers and springs or lakes; and later at the foot of hills where there was a reliable permanent flow of water.

A period of increased precipitation would result in agricultural prosperity, abundance of food, increase of population and expansion of settlements: whereas a period of aridity would lead to crop failure, famine, disease and death, the abandonment of settlement and migration to higher and moister areas.

Anau has undergone the following sequence according to Brooks (1926, pp. 318–9): occupation about 9000 B.C. and again in 6000 B.C.; a short abandonment about 3000 B.C.; complete abandonment in 2200 B.C.; and a final re-occupation about the year 750 B.C.

Since Brooks wrote, hundreds of archaeological excavations have been made on the Iranian Plateau, all of which bear witness to climatic changes which led to alternate occupation and abandonment of sites. Unfortunately there has been no systematic study of this evidence which is potentially so rich. As an example one can quote the most recent work done under the directorship of E. Nagabhan, Professor of Archaeology at Tehran University in Dasht-i Qazvin, some 150 km to the West of Tehran.

Documentary Climatology

There is ample scope for research, as there are hundreds of relevant Persian manuscripts. Siahpoush is the only Iranian writer who so far has brought together a few examples, in his book already referred to (pp. 3, 29, 30, 31, 34, 38, 55, 56, 64, 65, 81 and 82).

Chronology of Contributions

Exactly 100 years have elapsed since Blandford, a member of Goldsmith's mission to Iran, circulated his first systematic geological paper on the central parts of Iran, in which he expressed for the first time an opinion about the probable origin of the central deserts of Iran. Since then there has been a proliferation of observation and theory (Krinsley, 1970, p. 4). The chronological ordering of this work, it is hoped, may assist future students better to plan their work.

    1873 W. T. Blandford indicated on a map of south-west Asia, several areas which he considered to have been previously occupied by extensive lakes. Prominent among these were the Great Kavir, the Lut Desert and the Seistan Basin.

    1892 F. A. Buhse, while crossing the Great Kavir near Khur, uncovered a 70 cm layer of salt, from which he concluded that the Kavir was the site of a Tertiary sea, under climatic conditions different from those of the present.

    1905 E. Huntington explored exhaustively stratigraphic evidence as well as historical data (especially with regard to Alexander the

Great's march across the southern Lut Desert). He concluded that the more recent history of Iran probably began with an arid climate at the end of the Tertiary, after which there ensued a fluvial period composed of some fifteen epochs of expanded rivers and lakes. These wet times were separated by "interfluvial" phases, marked by shortened rivers and diminished lakes, possibly as a result of the alternation between Glacial and Interglacial episodes. He concluded that south-eastern Iran has experienced a change from a more humid climate during Classical times to its present arid state.

1910   S. A. Hedin traversed the deserts of central Iran about which he wrote admirable descriptions. He was the first to comment on the rise of ground-water in the desert sections. He indicated clearly that the bases of sand dunes adjacent to the Great Kavir were getting "wet feet", which implied a rise in the water table following increased precipitation.

1923   K. Kaehne first studied the terraces of Lake Urmia (Rezaiyeh) and mapped at least three of them at 75, 160 and 270 m above the level of the lake.

1927   B. Asklund discovered terraces at different places within or not far from the Great Kavir.

1935   H. Rieben, in his important study of the geology of Azarbaijan, delineated terraces between 50 and 200 m, 200 and 300 m, and above 500 m in the Lake Urmia basin, evidence of former pluvial periods with heavier precipitation and river-flow.

1937   H. Bobek published the first result of his geological studies in the north-western parts of Iran. Amongst other achievements he mapped two raised beaches at 45 and 55 m above the waters of Lake Urmia. He further calculated that the lake could have been maintained at its maximum level by a 5°C depression of mean annual temperature. He also mapped the Würm Glacial moraines in the Elburz mountains and supplied some information on the level of the Caspian Sea.

1943   A. Desia looked into the glaciations of Zard-Kuh and parts of the Elburz mountains, and came up with some climatic inferences.

1955   E. K. Ralph published his radiocarbon dating to 12,320 B.C. of certain finds in the loess area of north-eastern Iran.

1957   A. Gabriel wrote of the inner deserts of central Iran, and reported that old high-water marks were repeatedly encountered in the Kavir. He further considered the Great Kavir to be the product of two Late Glacial periods of greater precipitation followed by post-Glacial climatic variations between wet and dry, manifested by alternations of salt and silt layers.

1957   G. Stratil-Sauer recognized two pluvial periods in the Lut, evidenced by two thin superimposed layers of sediments. He considered that these were of Riss and Würm origin, and that the Würm pluvial was followed by a post-Glacial arid period.

1959   H. Bobek, after some time in Iran, published a booklet on the features and formation of the Great Kavir and Massileh. He now claimed that the extensive erosion surfaces within the Great Kavir, formed subaerially, required a considerable length of time, and presupposed substantially lower levels of water and sediment-fill in the separate basins of the Kavir. These levels rose as the fill material spread across the fans and erosion surfaces. Bobek also noted a rise in the ground water into the base of the sand dunes adjacent to the Kavir.

1960   In connection with oil surveys, H. Huber made a new approach to the problem of climatic changes through the study of seismic soundings and drillings in the Qom playa. He recognized two distinct layers of deposit; one, 350 m in thickness, consisting mostly of medium or coarse grained sand and gypsum; the other, upper and younger, 46 m thick, of five salt beds with intercalated layers of brown or green clay and silt and two sand horizons. He concluded that the lower section was deposited under perennial fresh water, whereas the upper, composed of alternating true evaporites and temporary lake sediments, was formed under climatic conditions comparable with those of the present.

1961   H. Bobek, commenting on Huber's work, maintained that the upper section was too thick for the Holocene but reflected a sequence of climatic changes comparable with those of the Pleistocene. He placed the lower section in the Plio-Pleistocene. The salt beds would then represent the warm and dry Interglacial times, and the clay members the cold glacial periods with a permanent water-cover.

1963   H. Bobek, on reconsidering the above case, argued that, since the Qom playa basin was shallow and subsiding, only a slight increase in its water would be sufficient to produce the change from a seasonal to a permanent lake. Such an increase could, according to him, have been effected by the decreased rate of evaporation during the Glacial period without any additional precipitation. Admittedly, the lower section implied a slightly increased precipitation, but on the evidence of the later sections of the Great Kavir, the fill of the separate playa basins within it never reached a higher level than the present. The climate during this long period of erosion must have been essentially arid, to judge from the surrounding pediments with their mainly angular gravel. Bobek doubted strongly that a lake ever covered the entire area of the Kavir, and added that the reported beachlines and terraces could be easily explained as erosional features due to certain tectonic effects or to the grain of the Miocene outcrops.

1963   W. van Zeist and H. E. Wright jointly made a preliminary pollen study at Lake Zeribar.

1963   G. E. Hutchinson and U. M. Cowgill undertook the chemical examination of a core from Lake Zeribar. According to Krinsley (1970) the converging evidence of pollen, fauna and chemistry, supported by radiocarbon dates, led to the following inferred climatic sequence. At the time of Würm III (20,000 B.P.) in Europe, Lake Zeribar had a cool, dry climate resembling that of the higher parts of the Iranian Plateau today. The lake was deep between 22,500 and 14,000 B.P. and the cool temperate species disappeared soon after. The lake fluctuated considerably between 14,000 and 6000 B.P. (Krinsley, 1970, p. 7).

1966–
68   H. E. Wright, continuing his pollen analysis and radiocarbon dating at another site, Lake Mirabad, 300 km to the south-east of Lake Zeribar, found a similar sequence at least down to 10,400 years, and concluded that the area and its neighbourhood were probably treeless before 14,000 B.P. Around 5500 B.P., there became common another species which implies a deeper lake. The striking change from warm savanna to forest at 5500 B.P. reflects a distinct increase in precipitation or a decrease in temperature.

1968   M. J. Dresch (accompanied by the present writer and a group of professors from Tehran University) made a reconnaisance flight to the Lut Desert. On that occasion, he concluded that the basin fill was a lake deposit subsequently eroded by wind during dry periods. The rising base-level would inhibit such erosion during moister periods.

1969   Vita-Finzi, discussing the quaternary chronology of the alluvials of Iran, recognized two major phases of deposition: one began more than 50,000 years ago (from archaeological evidence) and had probably ended around 4500 B.C.; the other took place, after a long erosional hiatus, during the Middle Ages. He tentatively correlated these two depositional phases with the Würm Glacial and with the Neoglacial (late phase). He speculated that the annual precipitation totals may have remained unchanged, since a reduction in the present proportion of cyclonic rains to convectional downpours would be sufficient to result in the deposition of the sort of coarse material which he observed. So he agrees with Bobek in seeing no evidence of pluvial conditions in Iran during the Pleistocene.

1969 E. Ehlers, working along the southern shores of the Caspian, demonstrated the synchroneity of glacial advances with high lake levels in this area. He traced a 48 m beachline to its confluence with a dominant 40–60 m terrace level of the Chalus River. The river terrace was followed by Ehlers into the mountains and apparently to the moraines, of the end of Würm, from the Takht-i Sulaiman glaciation. Ehlers further recognized a three-fold division of the Würm Glaciation in the Central Elburz Mountains.

1969 H. Bobek, on pursuing his studies and reconsidering his previous ideas, emphasized the compatibility of the uppermost salt layers (7 m thick) with the present climate (slightly moister than in the past). Reconsidering the Qom playa sequence, he concluded that the salt layers were deposited during "wet interglacials" and that the clay layers represent deposits laid down in a cold dry climate. However, the thickness of the uppermost salt layer suggests that it spans the entire post-Würm period including the Hypsithermal phase (Würm), the Neoglacial (cold), and the Recent (moister). He considered the post-Würm depositional environment to have been generally similar to that of present, that is warm and arid in spite of the possibly slightly higher precipitation.

1970 M. T. Siahpoush summed up the above story in Persian for the benefit of Iranian readers.

Conclusion

As indicated in an earlier section, much remains to be done before one can express a definite opinion about post-Glacial climatic changes in the Iranian

Plateau. Bringing all the various theories together, one can recognize two different schools of thought, the old and the new. According to the first, the post-Würm climate of the Iranian Plateau has been characterized by a steady and gradual desiccation; according to the second, in spite of fluctuations in the amount of precipitation and temperature, the post-Glacial climate has been, in the main, not very different from that of the present.

The morphological, stratigraphic and chronological evidence indicates that during the Würm Maximum (20,000 B.P.) the outward slopes of the Zagros and Elburz had mean annual temperatures 5 to 8°C less than the present (Krinsley, 1970, p. 244). The snow line was depressed by as much as 1800 m (see page 88, above) and the whole area received heavy snowfalls during the winter months. The Caspian Sea and the Urmia Lake were both considerably expanded, with water levels of 78 m and 55 m, respectively, above the present (Ehlers, 1969 and Bobek, 1937). Further south, in the Zaribar region, radiocarbon-dated stratigraphy suggests that the climate was cool and relatively dry, not unlike that of the present. Precipitation appears to have been on the whole less than now (van Zeist, 1967), but lower temperatures resulted in less evaporation and consequently more runoff, which filled the intermontane lakes as well as some of the interior basins nearer the pediments. During the summer months, water evaporated from the shallow lakes and intense winds from the northern quadrants eroded the dry superficial lake sediments, transporting the material to the site of the present sand-dune fields in the south-east. The general direction of the dunes suggests that the prevailing winds of the time were from the north and north-west, as they are now.

Immediately after the Last Major Glacial advance, under the climatic conditions described above, there followed a period of decreased precipitation along the outer flanks of the northern mountains, with probably more rainfall in the interior sections (Bobek, 1937). Temperatures seem to have risen concurrently, with the result that excessive evaporation created greater aridity. According to Krinsley (1970, p. 247), the aridity thus produced must have reached its climax around 6000 B.P. after which a change in climate occurred about 5500 B.P. when most of the lakes within or around the mountains began to rise; which change may have resulted from either an increase in precipitation or a decrease in temperature (van Zeist and Wright, 1963, p. 67).

After this near-Pluvial period there seems to have set in a fairly long period (4400 to 2850 B.P., Siahpoosh, 1973, p. 26) of less rainfall and higher temperatures which, although broken up by periodic fluctuations, has resulted in considerable aridity. As far as precipitation is concerned, all the

evidence indicates that this has been the driest phase in the climate of the
Middle East since 8800 B.P. (Siahpoosh, 1973, p. 27).

Between 2850 and 1300 B.P. climate has been moister on the whole, as
evidenced by the great prosperity of Persian empires before the advent of
Islam. After the latter date one can say that climate has been more-or-less
similar to that of the present with the usual fluctuations both in temperature
and precipitation.

To sum up, the climatic fluctuations of the past 4000 years in the Iranian
Plateau have been too short and insignificant to result in morphologic
changes, but since this period coincides with the development of agriculture
and civilization on the Iranian Plateau its understanding requires a separate
investigation of the archaeological and historical climatology of the region.

References

Asklund, B. 1927. Zur Geologie Ostpersiens auf Grund der von Sven Hedin
    gesammelten Gesteinproben. In: Eine Routenaufnahme durch Ostpersien II
    (Hedin, S. A., ed.) pp. 381–533, Stockholm.
Bobek, H. 1937, Die Rolle der Eiszeit in Nordwestiran: Zeitschr. Gleds cherk. 25,
    130–183.
Bobek, H. 1959. Features and Formation of the Great Kavir and Masileh, Vol. 2. Arid
    zone Research Center, Tehran.
Bobek, H. 1961. Die Salzwusten Irans als Klimazeugen, Oesterr. Akad. wiss. Anz. der
    phil. hist. Kl. 3, 7–19.
Bobek, H. 1963. Nature and implications of Quaternary climatic changes in Iran,
    UNESCO–WMO Symposium on Changes of Climate, Rome Oct. 1961, pp. 403–413.
Bobek, H. 1968. Vegetation. In: The Cambridge History of Iran I, The Land of Iran,
    (Fisher, W. B., ed.), pp. 280–293. Cambridge: University Press.
Bobek, H. 1969. Zur Kenntnis der Sudlichen Lut, Osterr. Geogr. Gesell. Mitt. 3,
    155–192.
Brooks, C. E. P. 1926. Climate through the Ages. London: Benn.
Butzer, K. W. 1958. Quaternary stratigraphy and climate in the Near East, Bonner
    Geogr. Abh. 24, 157.
Desio, A. 1934. Appunti geografici e geologici sulla catena dello Zardeh Kuh in
    Persia, Geol. e Geogr. di Dainelli Mem. 4 (13), 141–167.
Dresch, M. J. 1968. Reconnaissance dans le Lut (Iran), Assoc. Géogr. Fr. Bull.
    143–153.
Ehlers, E. 1969. Das Chalus-Tal und seine Terrassen Erdkunde. 23, 215–229.
Farrand, William R. 1971. Late Quaternary paleoclimates of the Eastern
    Mediterranean Area. In: Late Cenozoic Glacial Ages, (Turekian, Karl K., ed.),
    pp. 529–564. New Haven.

Gabriel, A. 1957. Ein Beitrag zur Gliederung und Landschaft skunde des innerpersischen Wustengurtels. *Gesell Wien. Festschrift Z. Hundertj.* 265–298.

Ganji, M. H. 1968. *In: The Cambridge History of Iran*, I. *The Land of Iran*, (Fisher, W. B., ed.), pp. 212–245. Cambridge: University Press.

Hedin, S. A. 1910. Zu Land nach Indien durch Persien, Seistan, Belutschistan, Leipzig: Brochaus.

Hubert, H. 1960. The Quaternary deposits of the Darya-i-Namak, Central Iran, *Oil Co., Geol. Note* **51**, App. 4, *Strat. Sect.*

Huntington, E. 1905. The Basin of eastern Persia and Sistan. *In: Explorations in Turkestan 1904*, pp. 199–324. Washington: Carnegie Inst.

Hutchinson, G. E. and Cowgill, U. M. 1963. Chemical examination of a core from Lake Zeribar, Iran. *Science* **140**, 67–69.

Kaehne, K. 1923. Beitrage Zur Physischen Geographie des Urmiabeckens. *Gesell. Erdkunde Berlin, Zeitschr.* 104–132.

Krinsley, Daniel B. 1970. *A Geomorphological and Paleoclimatological Study of the Playas of Iran*, U.S. Dept. of Interior, Geological Survey, Washington, D.C.

La Marche Jr., Valmore C. 1974. Paleoclimatic inferences from long tree-ring records. *Science* **183**, 1040–1083.

Negahban, E. O. 1973. Preliminary Report of the Excavation of Sagzabad, Marlik, *J. Inst. Depart. Archeol. Tehran Univ.* **I**, 1–11.

Rieben, H. 1935. Contribution à la geologie de l'Azerbeidgan Persan. *Soc. Neuchateloise Sci. Nat.* **59**, 19–145.

Seth, S. K. 1963. A review of evidence concerning changes of climate in India, *UNESCO–WMO Symposium on Changes of Climate*, Rome, Oct 1961, pp. 443–454.

Sia-poosh, M. T. 1973. *On the Palaeoclimatology of the Iranian Plateau* (in Persian). Tehran: Ibn–Sina Publishing Co.

Vita–Finzi, C. 1969. Late Quaternary alluvial chronology of Iran. *Geol. Rundschau* **58**, 951–973.

Wright, H. E. Jr., McAndrews, J. H. and van Zeist, W. 1967. Modern pollen rain and its relation to plant geography and Quaternary vegetational History. *J. Ecol.* **55**, 415–443.

van Zeist, W. 1967. Late Quaternary vegetation history of Western Iran. *Rev. Palaeobot. Palynol.* **2**, 301–311.

van Zeist, W. and Wright, H. E. Jr. 1963. Preliminary pollen studies at Lake Zeribar, Zagros Mountains, Southwestern Iran. *Science* **140**, 65–67.

11
The Environment of Southern Sistan in the Third Millennium B.C., and its Exploitation by the Proto-urban Hilmand Civilization[1]

Lorenzo Costantini and Maurizio Tosi

The Hilmand Culture

The remains of the proto-urban ("Hilmand") civilization of Sistan have been investigated by the Italian Archaeological Mission during six seasons of work, beginning in 1967 (Tosi, 1968, 1969, 1973). This civilization, which took shape in the third millennium B.C., flourished around two main nuclei: one near the confluence of the Hilmand and Arghandab Rivers to the west of Kandahar, where the main site is Mundigak; the other in the delta of the Hilmand River, where it enters the inland lake or Hamun of Sistan, the chief excavation here being at Shahr-i Sokhta. At the beginning of the third millennium B.C., there was a comparable culture in the Valley of Quetta (Casal, 1964; Dupree, 1963; Shaffer, 1971).

Although the Hilmand civilization was involved in the production and exchange of stones and metals, notably for export to Mesopotamia, it was essentially self-supporting, and in view of its geographical isolation it provides an excellent opportunity to study the balance between population and environment in this region of south-west Asia at this stage of technology.

In particular, there is at Shahr-i Sokhta a chance to study how and why in Period III of its sequence (*c.* 2500–2200 B.C.) the population increased to its maximum, and thereafter declined. Evidently, during these three centuries of its *floruit*, the Hilmand culture made the most intense and successful use of its local resources, and various possibilities in the realms of economic and demographic evolution may be considered to account for

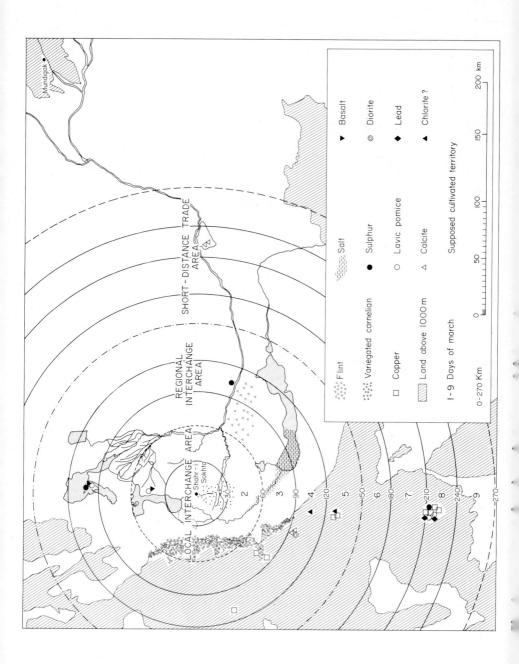

Mundigak

SHORT-DISTANCE TRADE AREA

REGIONAL INTERCHANGE AREA

LOCAL INTERCHANGE AREA
Shahr-i Sokhta

30
60
90

2
3
4
120
5
150
6
180
7
210
8
240
9
270

Flint

Variegated carnelian

Copper

Land above 1000m

1-9 Days of march

0-270 Km

Salt

Sulphur

Lavic pomice

Calcite

Supposed cultivated territory

Basalt

Diorite

Lead

Chlorite ?

0   50   100   150   200 km

why this should have happened then. In this context, however, it will be sufficient to consider what was the physical environment of the Hilmand delta in the third millennium B.C., and how far it differed from that of now in the same region.

Sistan: Position and Geographic Characteristics [2]

The large basin which feeds the Hamun-i Hilmand covers an area of about 350,000 km[2] and forms the easternmost portion of the Iranian plateau. It is oval in shape with a south-east/north-west axis. The highest areas— more than 5000 m above sea-level—are to be found to the north-east and compose the first western buttresses of the Hindu Kush; while the deepest depressions, as low as 470 m in the Gaud-i Zirrah, lie to the south-west.

The Iranian part of Sistan, the main home of the Hilmand Civilization, occupies the central and southern portions of the terminal lake basin, at the south-west end of the Plio-Pleistocene sediments; here the Hamun-i Puzak to the north-east and the Gaud-i Zirrah to the south-east are entirely in Afghan territory. Because of the great distance, 600 km, from the sea, and the barrier formed by the coastal ridges of the Makran, the climate is extremely continental with hot dry summers and cold damp winters (Sacco, 1964, pp. 53–88; Fairservis, 1961, pp. 14–16).

In an eccentric, almost peripheral, position inside the basin, at the western end of the ellipse, running north and south, lies the irrigable area of the Iranian Sistan. Here the terminal branches of the delta coming from the south-east are met by the very strong north-westerly winds of summer. As can be seen in the ERTS satellite photographs (Fig. 2) this circumstance gives rise to an alternating and interpenetrating series of sand-dune and clayey strips which determine the pattern of the outlying arable land and related settlements. This effect is particularly apparent in the area between the two terminal lakes.

The catchment of the river is ten times larger than the terminal-lake zone of Sistan. This entire zone is not flat, but irregular, in consequence mainly of wind action on the exposed alluvial sediments and, to a lesser extent, of the construction of embankments and canals. The resulting slight variations of altitude, though usually only in the order of a few metres, are sufficient to effect biological differences. Thus, the whole Hilmand delta may be divided into two main zones: the *alluvial plain* with the present or subfossil river beds where, during the Holocene, alluvial deposition has prevailed; and the *dasht*, an irregular complex of Plio-Pleistocene sediments some 15–20 m higher than the alluvium. Over these higher sediments wind action prevails, water is lacking, and

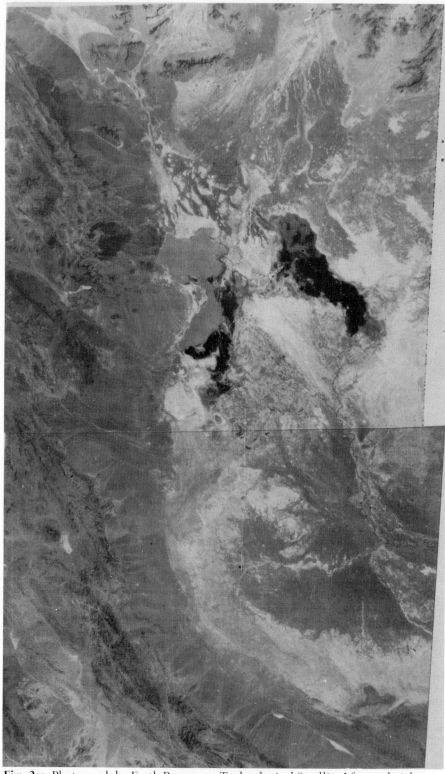

Fig. 2a: Photograph by Earth Resources Technological Satellite I from a height of 569 miles, covering approximately 115 miles square; provided by the US Geological Survey, EROS Data Center of Sioux Falls (South Dakota).

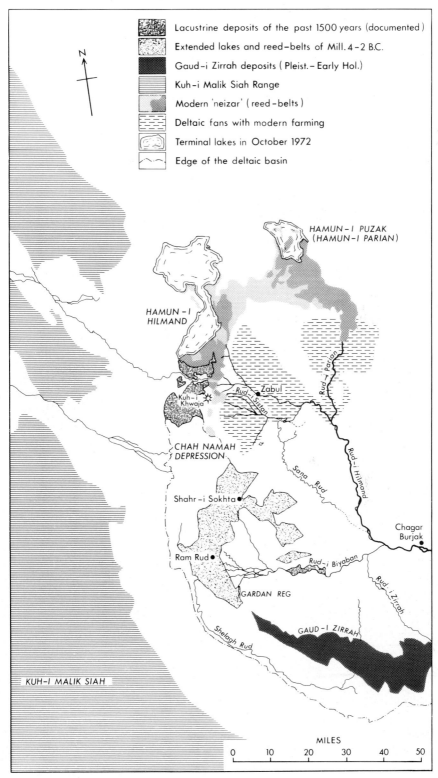

Fig. 2b: Guide-trace to accompany Fig. 2a.

conditions are bad for farming. Besides, the gravel surface sustains no vegetation and is thus unsuitable even for grazing sheep and goats.

The interlocking of these different kinds of terrain is more marked in Sistan than in the other landlocked basins of Central Asia, and has affected the rural economy of the region. Inside the oval of the Sistan delta, the Plio-Pleistocene terrace strips occupy about 18% of the territory, about the same proportion as the terminal-lakes (15%). The remaining 67%, except for the strips of unstable dunes, where the north-west wind action is strongest,[3] is open to economic exploitation and human settlement.

Gradual degradation of soil combined with wind erosion has given rise to vast sandy spaces and dunes, of which there are three main strings, all aligned with the north-west wind. The first is on the left bank of the Hilmand between the Hasan Khan and Niatak canals; the second a little further south in the western portion of the Chah Nahma depression or roughly the end portion of the Sana Rud, into which, for a short time at the beginning of the Christian era, flowed the main branch of the delta; the third near Ram Rud, at the southern end of the Rud-i Biyaban, mostly in Afghan territory. This last is probably of recent origin, as it covers most of the historical sites of the southernmost settled area of Sistan, today known as Gardan Reg. This constant overlapping of sand dunes and human settlements is the most direct evidence we have of the instability of human occupation in Sistan. It is indeed a peculiar feature of the historical geography of all the central Asian basins that dunes are common in terrain which evidently has a high economic value—for instance on a larger scale in the Soghdian Basin along the lower courses of the Amu-Darya and the Syr Darya (Kynin et al., 1955, pp. 18–39; Ostrovskÿ, 1960; Tolstov, 1948, pp. 25–36).

The mountains surrounding the Sistan Basin are formed of a variety of rocks, mainly of Cretaceous and Eocene age. On the north-west border are seen the remains of volcanic activity with often massive lava infiltrations, lying partly within the present bounds of the terminal lakes (Jux and Kempf, forthcoming, App. I). One of these is the basalt *mesa* of the Kuh-i Khwaja which, with its maximum height of 609 m above sea-level, is clearly visible from afar over the flat territory of Sistan.

To a depth of several hundred metres, the depressions are filled with formations of débris dating back to the Plio-Pleistocene period, with three main stratigraphic series: Pliocene formations, heavily affected by tectonic movements, that are more pronounced towards the edges of the depression; thereafter, Pleistocene alluvial pebbles and clays; which are in turn covered by more recent clay deposits (Italconsult, 1959, pp. 6–47). As stated earlier, in the local economy only the more recent of these deposits are productive, and they were formed through a marked fall of water level in the basin which led to the terracing of the Pleistocene deposits, which today stand at 15–20 m above the alluvial plain. Isolated strips of these terraces which extend into the flooded zones were favoured for settlement since they afforded protection from exceptional floods and saved arable land, and Shahr-i Sokhta itself is situated on one of these strips.

The recent deposits inside the present basin consist of large detrital cones at the ends of the terminal arms of the delta, which discharge about 8 g of mud per litre. These distal deposits of the river, which are gradually filling-in the terminal lakes, support the important strips of lake-side vegetation. On the ERTS photograph (Fig. 2), the *Typha*, *Phragmites* and *Scirpus* lakeside vegetation is concentrated into large patches at the ends of the detrital cones of the main delta distributaries of the Rud-i Sistan to the west and the Rud-i Parian to the north, and stretches out round the contiguous lake sides.

The western side of the lake is more exposed to the north-westerly winds, receives no water from the torrential piedmont watercourses, and is completely bare. Suffering as it does from wind erosion, from calcareous deposits on the eastern banks as a result of inundation (Italconsult, 1959, pp. 46–7; Jux and Kempf, in press), from soil loss due to torrential flooding, and from prolonged periods of drought, this is the most inhospitable part of Sistan.

Salt, diorite, copper, flint, sulphur etc. were quarried (Fig. 1; Bartolucci, 1959, Pl. II; Tipper, 1921, pp. 51–79), but the success of the Hilmand Civilization depended on the high potential for agriculture of the territory during the initial phase of settlement, when the biological conditions were still in climax balance. These conditions will now be described.

Climate

The climate of Sistan is distinguished by extreme aridity and strong, continuous winds. The two seasons are a hot summer between May and October, and a cold, damp winter between November and April (Fig. 3). Rainfall is very low and varies from year to year (Fig. 4), the annual average being 50–100 mm. The rains are violent when they do come, and they fall throughout the winter (Sacco 1964, pp. 46–7; Snead, 1972, p. 6; Jux and Kempf, in press). [4]

These conditions are favourable for grain, which requires snow and cold during the winter period and a gradual rise in temperature from January to June (Fig. 3). Cereals are the only crop that flourishes in present-day Sistan, and the climate is such that production could be increased

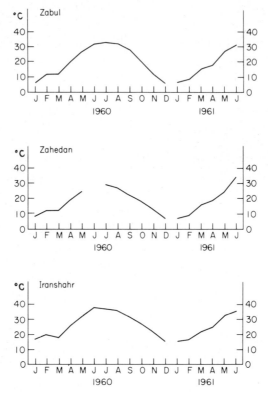

Fig. 3: Mean monthly temperatures at three places in Sistan.

(Italconsult, 1959, pp. 66–70). On the other hand, rainfall should be more evenly distributed through the year for general agriculture. The river floods from March to June, through the melting of the snows on the Hindu Kush, and about 75% of the flooding occurs in the three-month period between March and May (Fig. 5).

Humidity is affected by the mass of water enclosed in the lake basin of the Hamun, near which the maximum humidity exceeds 50%, about double the average recorded in Shahr-i Sokhta in 1971–72. This alone is sufficient to account for the heavy concentration of plant and animal species in the lakeside strips where cattle-raising could be carried on under ideal conditions (Annandale, 1919/21, pp. 10–14; Gnoli, 1967, pp. 100–1; Scerrato, 1974, pp. 101–12).

The whole region is exposed to the destructive action of the prevailing north and north-west winds which cause considerable damage to agriculture through erosion of the soil surface, formation of dunes, burial of vegetation, bending and defoliation of trees and plants, and damage to fruit trees. Furthermore, the intense evaporation of water from the soil

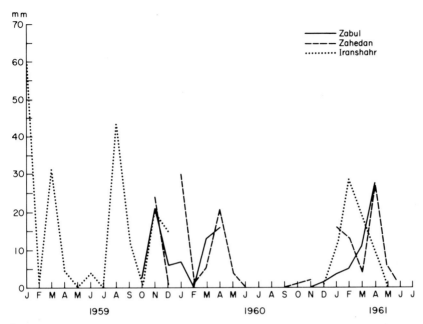

Fig. 4: Monthly rainfall totals at three places in Sistan.

increases the salinity of the surface. Fruit trees cannot be grown without protection in orchards.

It is probable that climatic conditions in protohistoric Sistan were much the same, although the riparian forest with its tall, woody trees, which was then more extensive (see p. 175), may have mitigated considerably the detrimental effect of the heat and winds.

Hydrography

The lakes are fed exclusively by the watercourses which enter from the north and east slopes (Hilmand, Kash), as those from the west and south

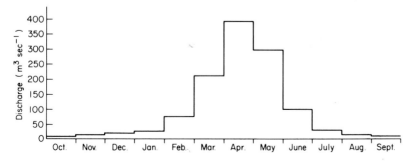

Fig. 5: Average total monthly discharge of the lower Hilmand River.

are merely steep torrential channels from regions of low rainfall. In brief, the essential elements of the hydrographic system are the terminal lakes and the Hilmand, on both of which the settlement of the territory depends (Italconsult, 1959, pp. 48–60; Snead, 1972, pp. 25–62; Jux and Kempf, in press; Raikes, in press). These form a closed cycle where the water supplied to the delta distributaries beyond Chahgar Burjak is distributed over a wide area along two main courses (the Rud-i Sistan and Rud-i Parian) which form the terminal lakes. An auxiliary catchment system is assured by the Shelagh Rud on the south edge of the Hamun, where the excess waters, under the influence of a 20 m drop in altitude, flow for 110 m along the course of the Shelagh and empty into the Gaud-i Zirrah depression.

The terminal lakes cover an area of about 1930 km^2 in the dry season (July–January), and expand to a maximum of 3900 km^2 in the period of flood water (February–June). The lakes then cover about 14% of the total surface of Iranian Sistan, including the area of most of the protohistoric settlement. This region of maximum flood lies within the 472 m contour line which encloses a zone about 200 km long and 20 km wide. According to Italconsult figures (Italconsult, 1959, p. 48), this seasonal increase of 2000 km^2 seems to be usual: however, the lakes have dried up completely five times in the last 100 years (Annandale, 1919/21, p. 10; Jux and Kempf, in press), thus causing not only a drastic reduction in the biomass but also a serious crisis in the economic system. In normal times, however, the lake water is fresh, drinkable and densely populated with fish, shellfish, insects and amphibians (Annandale, 1919/21, pp. 241–3).

The Hilmand, 1400 km long, and with a drainage basin extending over 150,000–170,000 km^2, is the largest tributary of the Hamun and the most important river in the entire territory lying between Mesopotamia and the Indus. Beyond the junction with the Arghandab it suffers a 25–30% loss through evaporation in the stretch between Qal'ah Bust and Chahgar Burjak, where for 225 km it flows in a narrow bed between steep terraces in a region with an arid climate. Figure 5 shows the average monthly discharge. This represents a considerable amount of water, enough to support a large farming population.

In order to appreciate the circumstances of the settlement of the territory during the third millennium B.C., one must study the behaviour of the river over the last 5000 years. It has been known for some time that its course has undergone a deviation of about 90° in a clockwise direction (Fairservis, 1961, pp. 17–21, Fig. 4, pp. 97–102, Fig. 49; Snead, 1972, pp. 53–62; Jux and Kempf, in press; Raikes, in press). The distribution of the protohistoric settlements leaves no doubt that at that time the main branch of the delta coincided closely with the present Rud-i Biyaban to the west of Chahgar Burjak. The river ran in an east-west direction for about 70 km, fanning out in the last 25 km which lay in what is now entirely Iranian territory. In this way the final section irrigated an area of about 400 km ^{2}, as is clearly visible in the ERTS satellite photograph (Fig. 2). The protohistoric settlements lie within the deltaic fan in this area except for a separate cluster situated on the Gardan Reg about 30 km further to the south of the subfossil course of the river (Fairservis, 1961, pp. 59–76).

The satellite photograph provides us with the following additional information:

1. the northernmost branch of the Rud-i Biyaban runs north-north-west until it reaches two depressions characterized by a pure, white microcrystalline clay deposit; we believe we have here identified the boundaries of two terminal lakes or marshes which are today completely dried up. These deposits are contiguous with the raised plane of the Pleistocene *dasht*, and if we accept their lacustrine origin—which remains to be confirmed by the sedimentological analyses now in progress—we must suppose that Shahr-i Sokhta lay between two marshy zones, in a situation not unlike that of present-day Zabul between the Hamun-i Hilmand and the Hamun-i Parian;

2. the main arms of the delta have gradually shifted. Three branches can be seen to leave the Chahgar Burjak node: the Rud-i Zirrah towards the south; the Rud-i Biyaban towards the west; and the present course of the Hilmand towards the north. The combined sections of the Hilmand and the Rud-i Zirrah delimit the extension of the Holocene river deposits, on the outer (western) edge of which lie the terminal lakes and the Shelagh Rud, through which the excess waters flow towards the Gaud-i Zirrah.

Briefly, four main shifts of the main river have been hypothesized, of which only the last three are thought to concern human occupation. Put simply, the shift has involved a regular clockwise deviation of the bed, the main possible causes being the force of the earth's rotation (the Coriolis effect—Raikes, in press) or the combined action of tectonic phenomena at the level of the continental platform, associated with vulcanism on the western side of the depression (Jux and Kempf, in press). Without of course going into any specialized hydro-geological analysis, it seems worth mentioning the evidence of the terminal branches of the present Rud-i Sistan and Rud-i Parian with respect to the layout of the subfossil courses visible in the ERTS photograph. The Rud-i Hilmand seems to run in a constant northerly direction, while shifts may have taken place in the various left-hand branches (the Rud-i Zirrah, Rud-i Biyaban and Sana Rud, progressively) until the fan was closed by the present-day Rud-i Sistan which irrigates the lower portion of northern Sistan. At the same time, the terminal lakes were set up, fed by the successive left-hand branches. They are visible as a lighter strip, 15 km wide on the average, along the entire western periphery.

In such complex and changeable conditions of drainage, habitation was bound to be unstable. The earliest settlements found so far, which include Shahr-i Sokhta, may all be placed around the terminal stretches of the Rud-i Biyaban. The Sana Rud, on the other hand, supplied water to settlements of the Achaemenid period, about the mid-first millennium B.C. (Scerrato, 1962, 1966). The Sana Rud clay deposit is so thin that this arm may be assumed to have had a short life and to have been immediately re-absorbed by the main river which since Parthian times has certainly followed more-or-less the present line. What is surprising, however, is the extraordinary parallelism between the course of the present-day Rud-i Sistan and that of the protohistoric Rud-i Biyaban, which seem to correspond even as regards their bends. Shahr-i Sokhta and the lesser third-millennium settlements were thus closely linked with a complex hydrographic network which distributed the water in a capillary fashion. The terminal lakes thus appear to have functioned as permanent reservoirs of water and food.

Three separate biological areas may therefore be distinguished in both modern and protohistoric Sistan: the *pre-desertic steppe depression*, south of the Rud-i Biyaban, delimited by the Gaud-i Zirrah and the Shelagh Rud; the *delta* proper, with the irrigable areas; and the *lake zone* along the entire north perimeter. This distinction, with corresponding strips of different vegetation, is found today 60 km further north, where the present delta lies.

Flora and Fauna

In the districts not irrigated by the river, vegetation is completely absent, except for small areas in which the winter rains are collected, for the gravelly soil and the strong and persistent wind make it hard for any plant association to survive. At most, between these arid Plio-Pleistocene terraces and the zones irrigated today, there are fairly broad strips of land where xerophile Gramineae prevail. These are the arid-zone grazing areas where the vegetation must stand up to long periods of drought: they may occasionally be flooded, but their water requirements are mainly satisfied by the scanty rainfall.

The aquifer, found here at an average depth of 5 m below the surface, makes a contribution to the water balance of this intermediate zone, although it has no effect on the surface of the Plio-Pleistocene terraces, some of which are 10 m higher. The plant associations covering the intermediate areas, which are characterized also by high concentrations of surface salt, are of the halophile type. The dominant species, capable of forming a fairly good coverage immediately after the first rains, are *Aeluropus*, *Phalaris*, *Lamarchia* and *Schismus*, and these provide a forage of which sheep and goats in particular are very fond (Sacco, 1964, p. 69). In this area are found semi-permanent camps of nomadic herdsmen who graze camels as well as sheep and goats. The halophile vegetation certainly favours the raising of goats, which are partial to the presence of salt and are more adaptable to the arid conditions of these soils, and which account for up to 56% of the total flocks (Fig. 6).

Evidently animal husbandry was supplemented by hunting, for at Shahr-i Sokhta the bones of gazelles (*Gazella subgutturosa seistanica*) made up 0·9% of the total fauna finds. Low though it may seem, this percentage is the highest among those of the wild species, and the state of the bones shows clearly that the animal had been eaten. The *Equus hemionus* (0·07%) was also used for food. These are animals of the dry steppe, adapted to the climate and typical of the Iranian plateau, even though today they are close to extinction. However, it seems unlikely that the animals attested at Shahr-i Sokhta were captured in the vicinity of the city, which was surrounded by intensively cultivated or marshy zones. Being shy, they

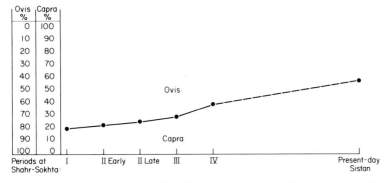

Fig. 6: Changes through time in the relative proportion of sheep (*Ovis*) and goats (*Capra*) in Sistan. (Courtesy of L. Caloi and B. Compagnoni.)

probably ranged on the outskirts of the basin and the irrigated zone, but within reach of the sheep- and goat-herds. They doubtless provided a supplementary source of food and were taken to the town to be bartered. Soviet research in southern Turkmenia has revealed a similar situation in the period Namazga IV–V. There, the bones of *Equus hemionus* and *Gazella subgutturosa* represent 20·1% of the osteological finds made in the craft quarter of the proto-urban centre of Altyn tepe, situated in the small irrigated valley of Meana-Čaača, while they account for 50·6% at Šor-Kepe, a village on the pre-desertic edge of the Dara Kum, where they are evenly distributed throughout the settlement (Ermolova, 1970). It is probable that in Sistan very similar conditions prevailed. In addition, the pre-desertic bird species found at Shahr-i Sokhta, such as the rock-partridge (*Alectoris graeca*) and the grey partridge (*Perdix perdix*), could be hunted in the autumn.

As we approach the terminal branches of the delta, the vegetation becomes thicker and the first trees and shrubs appear, in conditions of almost constant humidity from the river water and the shallower aquifers. Both the shrubs and trees belong to the Tamaricaceae family, and of particular importance is *Tamarix articulata* which may be transplanted by means of cuttings (Mobajen and Tregubov, 1970, p. 15).

The tamarisk, adapted to salty soils, can be used to make windbreaks to protect the tilled areas, and grows spontaneously near canals where it has the useful effect of reducing evaporation under its shadow. In the vicinity of the less-used peripheral canals, tamarisk is sparser, and willows of semi-spontaneous origin become more frequent.

The predominance of tamarisk over willow in the more densely settled areas follows from the different vegetative cycle of the two species, for the tamarisk grows faster and dominates wherever the thick riparian forests are regularly cleared. Sheltered behind tamarisk windbreaks, the more easily irrigable areas between the branches of the Hilmand delta are intensively cultivated, though some districts suffer from very cold winters, spring floods and difficult water supplies.

At the present time, the productive surface area in the terminal lake zone comes to about 100,000 hectares, half given over to extensive farming, half to perennially irrigated pasture.

The aerial photographs indicate:

    47,410 ha = winter crops
    40,650 ha = fallow
  126,830 ha = uncultivated
      950 ha = orchards

Today wheat is the main crop, followed by barley, legumes and lucern and clover forage. From our data we deduce that wheat and barley were widely grown in early times, together with grapes (*Vitis vinifera*), Cucurbitaceae, flax and some leguminous crops.

Ecosystems

The vegetation of the whole lake area may be divided into that of the interior and that of the perimeter. The main association of the inner strip comprises *Typha angustifolia*, *Phragmites communis* and *Ph. communis stenophylla*, which prevail over small isolated clumps of *Juncus maritimus* and *Ciperus rotundus*. As the water level changes, large areas are often completely exposed without, however, any serious damage being done to the vegetation. Both *Phragmites* and *Typha* are in fact very simple plants which reproduce by dissemination and by radical budding, and thus have a powerful capacity for survival. This very lake area was constantly occupied throughout the complex history of Sistan, as here the environment was least likely to deteriorate. The territory is known as *naizar*, and the inhabitants as *gaudars*, or cattle herdsmen (Scerrato, 1974). The abundant *Typha* and *Phragmites* vegetation is an excellent source of forage for the beef cattle, a local variety of *Bos indicus*, with small body, high powers of resistance, and relatively underdeveloped horns. [5] The whole year round the herds graze directly in the lake, sometimes standing shoulder-deep in the water to feed off young shoots and other tender parts of the plants (Sacco, 1964, pp. 76–8).

Further out is a transitional zone of *Scirpus mucronatus*, *Cynodon dactylon*, and *Aeluropus repens*, associated here and there with *Tamarix* thickets, in which graze cattle, sheep and goats, while the herdsmen grow sporadic autumn cereal crops and *Cucurbitaceae*.

The lake-water is fresh and drinkable, and supports a fish fauna of mountain type, rich in numbers but with few species, as is usually the case in abnormal environmental conditions (Annandale, 1919/21, p. 236). It is a mountain association which has adapted to the conditions of a marshy depression.

Among the fish are *Discognatus*, *Scophiodon* and *Schizothorax*, but the lake also teems with numerous species of molluscs, crustaceans, amphibians and insects of no direct economic value.

The bird life of the lake, permanent and migratory, is rich and varied. Today there are about 65 species, 29 of which have been identified among the bone finds from Shahr-i Sokhta.⁶ Among these the coot and the pochard predominate. There are also a number of domesticable species such as the goose (*Anser anser*) the duck (*Aythya niroca*), or fishing birds, such as the cormorant (*Phalacrocorax*) and the pelican (*Pelecanus crispus*). There are also a few birds of prey such as the kite (*Milvus migrans*) and an occasional white-tailed eagle (*Haliäetus albicilla*), which today is no longer found in the region.

The only predatory mammal which has adapted perfectly to lake conditions is the otter (*Lutra lutra seistanica*), which has a wide range of fish and bird fauna at its disposal for food and appears to be common in most inland waters of Iran (Lay, 1967). The remains of at least two specimens are included among the Shahr-i Sokhta finds.

Evidently the lake and lake-margins offered a variety of opportunities. First, there was the herding of cattle which requires vast areas, as these animals are not very partial to the lake species and merely crop the shoots; second may be considered fishing and hunting, and the gathering of the eggs of migratory birds during the brooding period (between November and January). Hunting is amply documented by the Shahr-i Sokhta finds, where too large quantities of eggshell fragments have been found all over the settlement, mainly of wild species.⁷

Thirdly there would be scope for cottage industries, linked to the cutting of reeds for weaving into mats, baskets and trelliswork, an activity which is also widely documented in the settlement and among the grave goods in the protohistoric graveyard.

The satellite photograph (Fig. 2) shows that Shahr-i Sokhta lay between two terminal swamps. This does not mean that the town was a swamp settlement; indeed, the scanty use made of reeds in building indicates that wood was readily available. But it is quite possible that the houses in the surrounding villages were not unlike those of the present-day *gaudar* villages, where the residence and cattleyard are combined in single cells entirely built of reeds and situated on the islands and peninsulas surrounded by the swamp, and communicate and make contact with the mainland by means of rafts built of bundles of *Typha* and *Scirpus*. Here man and his material culture appear to be as completely adapted as the plant and animal species, both wild and domestic.

The ancient town made use of these three separate zones, not counting the surrounding mountain desert area with its mineral resources, and operated in this setting. It may have been developed as a specialized manufacturing centre for the international trade in lapis lazuli, turquoise and shells, and for processing local resources like alabaster and copper.

However, its main function would have been as a local market, where the resources of the surrounding district could be re-distributed (Fig. 1).

Notes

1. This chapter is the outcome of a long co-operation between the authors and the Italian Archaeological Mission to Iran, sponsored by the Istituto Italiano per il Medio ed Estremo Oriente (IsMEO). It is an assembly of the preliminary results of our environmental and archaeological researches, and the proposal of Mr Brice appeared to us to offer an apt opportunity to present it. The manuscript was composed, between May 20th and June 23rd 1974, jointly by the authors, who had independently selected the data connected with their specialities.

2. The geography of Sistan has been treated over the last 75 years in numerous studies, some of them specific, which together provide a collection of data unique in the Near East. The first detailed survey was connected with the work of the Afghano-Persian Border Commission (McMahon, 1906). During the First World War, the first archaeological survey was carried out (Stein, 1928, pp. 906–56), and an expedition investigated the aquatic fauna (Annandale, 1919/21; Annandale and Prashad, 1919/21). Before the Second World War, Clapp (1940) added a geological description to that of Huntington (1905) who had done pioneer work while operating with the Border Commission of 1899–1902. The first to apply the geographical data to the archaeological evidence was Fairservis (1961), who visited the region in 1949/50. Since 1960, ecological studies have been carried out in association with the American, German and Italian archaeological expeditions which have been operating in both the Iranian and the Afghan parts of the region.

3. These sand dunes, produced through the erosion by wind of clay topsoil, cover several thousand hectares and each year lead to the abandonment of villages and cultivated fields.

4. The annual mean rainfall varies between 51 mm (Zabol, at the centre of the basin), 110 mm (Qal'ah Bust, to the west), and 116 mm (Zahedan, to the south).

5. Information kindly provided by Dr Bruno Compagnoni and confirmed on the present-day zoological data gathered in the region by N. Corti for Italconsult.

6. P. Cassoli has listed the following species of birds from the osteological material of the 1967–72 campaigns:

Very abundant:	Coot	*Fulica atra* L.
	Pochard	*Aythya ferina* L.
Abundant:	Bean Goose	*Anser fabalis* Latham
	Cormorant	*Phalacrocorax carbo* L.
	Ferrugineous Duck	*Aythya nyroca* Gülg.
	Greylag Goose	*Anser anser* L.
	Harlequin Duck	*Histrionicus histrionicus* L.

Present:	Black Vulture	*Aegypius monachus* L.
	Black Kite	*Milvus migrans* Bodd.
	Dalmatian Pelican	*Pelecanus Crispus* Bruch.
	Grey Heron	*Ardea cinerea* L.
	Mallard	*Ana platyrincos* L.
	Mute Swan	*Cygnus olor* Gmelin
	Crane	*Grus grus* L.
	Allen's Gallinule	*Porphyrio porphyrio* L.
	Partridge	*Perdix perdix* L.
	Red-crested Pochard	*Netta rufina* Pallas
	Tufted Duck	*Aythya fuligola* L.
	White-fronted Goose	*Anser albifrons* Scop.
	White-tailed Eagle	*Haliaetus albicilla* L.
Rare:	Black-pecked Grebe	*Podicipes nigricolli* Brehm.
	Egyptian Goose	*Alophocen aegyptiacus* L.
	Great-crested Grebe	*Podicipes cristatus* L.
	Little Grebe	*Podicipes ruficolli* Pallas
	Raven	*Corvus corax* L.
	Rock Partridge	*Alectoris graeca* Meian.
	Shag	*Phalacrocorax aristotelis* L.
	Stock Dove	*Columba oenas* L.

7. Preliminary information kindly provided by Professor F. Sauer.

References

Annandale, N. 1919/21. The aquatic fauna of Seistan—a summary. *Rec. Indian Mus.* Calcutta **18**, 3–16; 235–53.

Annandale, N. and Prashad, B. 1919/21. The mollusca of the inland waters of Baluchistan and of Seistan. *Rec. Indian Mus.* Calcutta **18**, 17–63.

Bartolucci, G. 1959. Preliminary report, geo-mining survey. In: *Socio-Economic Development Plan for the South Eastern Region, Plan Organisation of Iran*, Rome: Italconsult.

Casal, J. M. 1964. *Fouilles de Mundigak (MDAFA* **17**), Paris.

Clapp, F. G. 1940. Geology of Eastern Iran. *Bull. Geol. Soc. America* **51**, 1–101.

Dupree, L. 1963. Deh Morasi Ghundai, a Chalcolithic Site in South Central Afghanistan. *Anthrop. Papers Am. Mus. Nat. Hist. N.Y.* **50**.

Ermolova, N. M. 1970. Novye Materialy po izuceniju ostatkov mlekopitajnscih iz drevnih poselenij Turkmenii. *Karakumskie Drevnosti* **3**, 205–232.

Fairservis, W. A. 1961. Archaeological Studies in the Seistan Basin of South-Western Afghanistan and Eastern Iran. *Anthrop. Papers Am. Mus. Nat. Hist. N.Y.* **58**, 1–128.

Gnoli, G. 1967. Ricerche stroriche sul Sistan antico. *IsMEO Rep. Mem. Rome.* **10**.

Huntington, E. 1905. *The Basins of Eastern Persia and Seistan. Publ. Carnegie Inst. Washington* **26**, 219–317.

Italconsult 1959. *Preliminary Report-Agricultural Survey (Socio-Economic Development Plan for the S.E. Region, Plan Organisation of Iran)*, Rome: Italconsult.

Jux, U. and Kempf, K. E. in press. Regional geology of Afghan Sistan. *In: Prehistoric Sistan* I (Tosi, M. Ed.). Rome: IsMEO Dep. Mem. **18.**

Kynin, V. N., Murzaev, M. and Rodin, L. E. 1955. Rel'ef, nastitel'nosti poěvi. *In: Očerki prirody Kara-Kumov.* Moskva.

Lay, D. M. 1967. *A Study of the Mammals of Iran.* Field Mus. Nat. Hist. Zool. Papers 54, Chicago.

McMahon, H. 1906. Recent survey and exploration in Sistan, *J. Roy. Geog. Soc.* **28,** 209–228; 333–352.

Mobajen, S. and Tregubov, V. 1970. *Guide pour la carte de la vegetation naturelle de l'Iran* (UNDR-FAO no. IRA 7, Bulletin 14), Teheran.

Ostrovskÿ, I. M. 1960. *Rel'ef peskov zapadnoj casti nizmennyh Karakumov,* Moskva: Akademiya Nauk (Acad. Sci.) U.S.S.R. Inst. Geog.

Radermacher, J. 1974. Historische und gegenwartige Bewasserungssysteme. *In: Nimruz Archäologische Landesaufnahme in Süd-West Afghanistan.* (Fischer, K. Ed.), Bonn.

Raikes, R. L. in press. Environmental Studies at Shahr-i Sokhta. *In: Prehistoric Sistan* I (Tosi, M. Ed.). Rome: IsMEO Dep. Mem. **18.**

Sacco, T. 1964. Contributo allo studio della flora pabulare di alcune zone del Baluchistan e Sistan Iraniano. *Allionia.*

Scerrato, U. 1962. A probable Achaemenid Zone in Persian Sistan. *East and West* **13,** 186–197.

Scerrato, U. 1966. Excavations at Dahan-i Ghulaman (Seistan-Iran), First Prelim. Report, *East and West* **16,** 9–30.

Scerrato, U. 1974. A proposito dell' 'Airyana Vaejah'. Notizie sulle possibilita 'di allevamento del bovino nella Drangiana come attivita autonoma. *In: Gururajamanjarika,* Napoli.

Shaffer, J. G. 1971. Preliminary Field Report on Excavations at Said Kala Tepe. *Afghanistan* **24,** 89–126.

Snead, R. E. 1972. *Physiography of the Seistan Basin* (Progressive Mimeographed Paper).

Stein, A. 1928. *Innermost Asia. Detailed Report of Explorations in Central Asia, Kan-su and Eastern Iran,* Oxford.

Tate, G. P. 1910–12. Seistan. *A Memoir on the History, Topography, Ruins and People.* Calcutta: Superintendent Govt. Printing.

Tipper, G. H. 1921. The geology and mineral resources of Eastern Persia *Indian Geol. Surv. Records* **53.**

Tolstov, S. P. 1948. *Po sledam drevne Horezmijskoj civilizacii,* Moskva-Leningrad.

Tosi, M. 1968. Excavations at Shahr-i Sokhta, a Chalcolithic Settlement in the Iranian Sistan, Preliminary Report on the First Campaign, Oct.–Dec. 1967. *East and West* **17,** 9–66.

Tosi, M. 1969. Excavations at Shahr-i Sokhta. Preliminary Report on the Second Campaign, Sept.–Dec. 1968. *East and West* **19,** 283–386.

Tosi, M. 1973. The Cultural Sequence at Shahr-i Sokhta. *Bull. Asia Inst. Pahlavi Univ.* 3, 64–80.

12
Studies in Historical Seismicity and Tectonics*

N. N. Ambraseys

Scope of Studies

One of the most important advancements of recent years in tectonics has been the recognition, not so much of an orderly global distribution of seismicity—which was already known and commonly accepted as early as 1858—but of its relation with an equally orderly system of tectonics. It is precisely the recognition of this relationship that has contributed to the concept of the new global tectonics which, although still a hypothesis, do account remarkably well for the observations of seismology, of geomagnetism and of other branches of science. Today, in one form or another, the new global tectonics have been notably successful in explaining many gross features of the earth's surface and in allowing an assessmant of the rate and direction of movement of its crust.

However, very little is still known in detail, on any scale less than global, about motions taking place at plate margins, particularly at converging continental plates where apparently there are tectonic processes which are complicated. Along most of these margins seismicity in the last few decades has been comparatively moderate and its pattern diffused, features perhaps typical of a crust with a strong memory of its past deformation history. Some of these continental plate-margins may be broad zones, so broad that they may in fact constitute non-rigid plates or plates of a very fine mosaic structure, in which distinctive tectonic features are not easily resolved from seismic data covering a few decades or from cursory field studies of the local tectonics.

The systematic study of boundary zones of converging or diverging continental plates and of strike-slip faults that trend along arc structures,

---

*This chapter reflects the interpretation of material available in 1973.

as well as the identification of the relative rigidity of these zones, is of considerable importance not only because of its significance in global tectonics *per se*, but also because it is precisely in these zones that destructive earthquakes occur with great loss of life and property. The special interest here is the insight into the question of eventual earthquake prediction to which a coherent answer, other than grossly empirical, requires first of all a thorough understanding of the processes involved in the generic cause of earthquakes.

For such a study, however, we need more seismic information and more field evidence of recent tectonics. In particular we need more high-quality mechanism solutions and a better documentation of local tectonics and of the nature of the strain changes that may lead to earthquakes. But especially, we need a significantly more extensive sample of seismicity, particularly of the larger events, covering much more than a period of the last few decades for which data are available today but which is a negligibly short length of time when compared with the time scale that is involved in tectonic processes. Obviously, large earthquakes which are important events are far less numerous than small earthquakes, and as such are not easily counted unless the period of observation is sufficiently long. It is possible, therefore, that the present seismic distribution may not accurately reflect the distribution after a much longer period of time, particularly in areas of complex interaction of continental plates. Equally, the present diffused and erratic pattern of seismic activity, for instance in the Alpide belt, may be shown to be due to a scanty sample of data.

Thus, in spite of the considerable volume of data for earthquakes in the present century, a much longer period of observation seems to be needed, a requisite that can only be achieved by resorting to macroseismic data for earthquakes prior to this century, and by choosing for study seismic regions which have a long and well documented history.

It is the purpose of this chapter to review the progress of historical seismicity since 1970 and to see how the accumulation of fresh evidence and re-examination of old has led to a better picture of the seismicity and tectonics of the Middle East.

Development of Studies

The region selected for study comprises the eastern part of the Alpide belt and extends from Greece to Afghanistan. The object of the study so far has been to extract information about earthquakes in this region which could throw some light on recent seismotectonics. In the event this initially cursory search has proved rewarding, not only because it has disclosed useful information about local seismicity and tectonics, but also because it has provided considerable experience which may be used in further work in this field.

In retrieving and assessing the value of historical data prior to 1800, we resorted to original sources of information and we avoided using modern works (Ambraseys, 1962a). This involved the assistance of historians in reading through published and unpublished documents, local histories and inscriptions in different languages, a rather slow process (Ambraseys, 1961). Our scheme has been to make an absolutely fresh collection of data on contemporary evidence alone, in which earthquake events are set forth in an account of local history. In such a study, factors such as population density, uniformity and concordance of source material, natural exaggerations implicit in the description of early events, archaeological evidence (Ambraseys, 1973), and the attitude of early and more recent authors as to the importance of what they are recording and their approach towards phenomena such as earthquakes, are important and whenever possible have been taken into consideration.

Population density and its changes over a period of time have considerable bearing on the extent of recorded material available on early earthquakes, from which to make an assessment. For instance, not all desert areas in the Middle and Near East have always been sparsely populated, nor do desert areas totally lack, in one form or another, a recorded history; chronicles written in isolated monasteries do give on occasion detailed information about local events, covering many centuries. However, there are certainly some regions which are unlikely to produce much literary or physical evidence of early or recent macroseismic history. These regions are the core of the Syrian Desert, the whole of the Great Nafud, the central zone of the Dasht-i-Kavir and Dasht-i-Lut and the whole of the central Kara Kum. For these regions the information found so far is fragmentary, lacking in detail and dealing only with a few places situated on the main caravan routes. Yet, this apparent lack of evidence for early earthquakes in the Dasht-i-Kavir and the Dasht-i-Lut cannot and should not be interpreted to mean that these areas have been free from large earthquakes. Strong shocks, felt simultaneously in settlements and towns bordering these deserts on more than two sides, and situated hundreds of kilometres apart, suggest that large-magnitude earthquakes are not uncommon in the *kavirs* of Iran. It is interesting to note perhaps that so far we have not come across similar evidence for the Syrian Desert and the Great Nafud.

Given sufficient information, it is not difficult to assess a measure of relative magnitude for early earthquakes. This can be achieved by comparing factors such as the size of the area over which different shocks were felt, the duration of their aftershock sequence, and the degree of damage caused in epicentral areas. Large magnitude, intermediate earthquakes in the Eastern Mediterranean Basin may be identified by the huge area over which they are felt and by the comparatively minor but otherwise widespread damage they cause. Large shallow events originating in the Red Sea and in the Dasht-i-Lut are equally well identifiable, and macroseismic data from large shocks in the twentieth century may be used to "calibrate" earlier events.

Equally important is the historical seismicity of the first few decades of this century, for which macroseismic data may be used to minimize bias in the instrumental epicentres of the larger events. Examination of instrumental data prior to 1953 revealed deficiencies in ISS determination of epicentres, and differences between macroseismic and instrumental positions of more than one degree were the rule rather than the exception (Ambraseys, 1977). It is not surprising, therefore, that in many instances seismicity in the Middle and Near East on a scale less than global is incompatible with local tectonics (Berberian, 1973; Heuckroth and Karim, 1970; Nowroozi, 1971).

Perhaps one of the most interesting aspects of the study of historical seismicity has been the identification of areas of intense tectonic activity and of very recent faulting associated with early events. A careful survey of the long-term historical records proved useful in guiding field studies to surface geological features representative of recent tectonic activity. For instance, in describing the earthquake of 1035 A.D. in the Anatolian zone, twelfth century chroniclers give sufficient details to guide one today to the site where nine centuries ago major faulting occurred and where fault-creep is still in progress (Ambraseys, 1970a). Similarly, a sixteenth century account of the destructive earthquake of 1493 in Iran, east of Birjand, gives all the information one needs to discover the remains of an interesting thrust fault-break on the ground. The extensive ground deformations associated with the 1648 earthquake in the Hayotojor Valley are vividly described by an unknown monk of an Armenian monastery near Van in Turkey. A search in consular archives and depositories of local documents begins to reveal a wealth of unpublished and very little known information about historical earthquakes which, unless it is retrieved and published, will soon perish. A remarkable example is the 28-page long manuscript field-report of the Russian consul in Kermanshah, the first draft of which was recently found, giving minute details about the little-known Silakhor earthquake of 1909 in Iran. The report, which is accompanied by six photographs and a detailed list of damage for 118 villages along the Dorud fault-break, is a fine example of the information that can be retrieved about important and unknown earthquakes in the Near and Middle East (Ambraseys and Moinfar, 1973). Documents of a similar nature describing the Tursaq earthquake and faulting of 1917 are another striking example of an almost totally unknown earthquake being disclosed by the retrieval of unpublished information. The same can be said about the Salmas earthquake of 1930 and the earthquakes of the first decades of this century which occurred between Lakes Van and Urmia. Here, unpublished and published, but very little-known documents in Armenian, Turkish and Russian reveal details of great importance.

Scores of similar case histories of probable faulting have now been found, and some of them have already been checked out from the ground. Faulting in the Near and Middle East is not a phenomenon as rare as it was thought to be. In fact, there is considerable evidence to show not only large, but also relatively small earthquakes being associated with surface faulting that have never been documented, even for earthquakes of this century. This is understandable, since observation of the presence or absence of surface faulting, which in some cases can be very small, depends amongst other things upon the effort and detail put into field work, which until recently was minimal. Field studies and re-examination of available data suggest that it would be a mistake to suppose any longer that only a small proportion of shallow earthquakes in the Near East is accompanied by significant surface faulting. With the assistance of historical information, man-made lineaments on the earth's surface, such as early roads in Anatolia or surface and underground water supply and irrigation canals in Iran and Mesopotamia, may provide ideal markers that can be used to detect recent faulting or creep and rapid vertical movements of the ground. Discontinuities produced by faulting or creep on man-made lineaments are still visible on aerial photographs and on the ground itself. In places, surface and underground canals have excavated into their old beds, off-setting the slow rise of the ground; elsewhere, bottom erosion could not keep pace with the rise of the canal bed and the water supply system was abandoned, today showing a reversed gradient. Long lines of underground canals, having at some time during their life-time been sheared off by fault movements, either during earthquakes or through

I

creep, have fallen into disuse. Some of them have been repaired with new, short alignments which cross fault-breaks. Today, these alignments are off-set again by a few metres. The evidence of movement is most noticeable along sea coasts where raised beaches and sunken coast lines testify to recent vertical movement of the land relative to sea-level (Flemming, 1969, 1972; Flemming et al., 1971).

Many authors have recently summed up our accumulative knowledge of active tectonics in the Near and Middle East, but few convincingly break fresh ground. One exception is perhaps McKenzie's extended synthesis of the many factors, both instrumental and macroseismic, which not only lead to a better understanding of the advantages and limitations of plate tectonics in continental regions, but also show quite clearly the excellent agreement that may be obtained between calculated source parameters and observed faulting (McKenzie, 1972). However, even more important than the scrutiny of recent faulting, for resolving ambiguities in the choice of the true source parameters, and in particular for resolving the pattern of recent tectonic activity, is the information that can be gleaned from evidence for the mechanism of earthquakes that occurred long before the advent of modern seismology. It is precisely for this reason that the study of historical tectonics should be encouraged.

Seismic Activity

Examination of historical data for the first seventeen centuries A.D. has revealed an interesting pattern of regional seismicity, the distribution of which is shown by the shaded areas in Fig. 1. The map was constructed by superimposing only epicentral areas of historical earthquakes so that epicentres of individual events do lie within the shaded areas shown. Areas not shaded, although they might have suffered some damage, particularly from large distant shocks, have not been intimately connected with important earthquake sources. The data used are far from being homogeneous for all magnitudes. However, it is believed that for the larger shocks homogeneity is quite well represented; but continuing regional studies are required to establish more accurately the seismicity of the whole area and the time sequence of important events, as well as the interaction of contiguous tectonic units.

Figure 1 shows quite clearly not only that historical seismicity follows a well defined pattern, but also that this pattern fits surprisingly well the seismicity of the past seventy years, following as it does boundaries of well

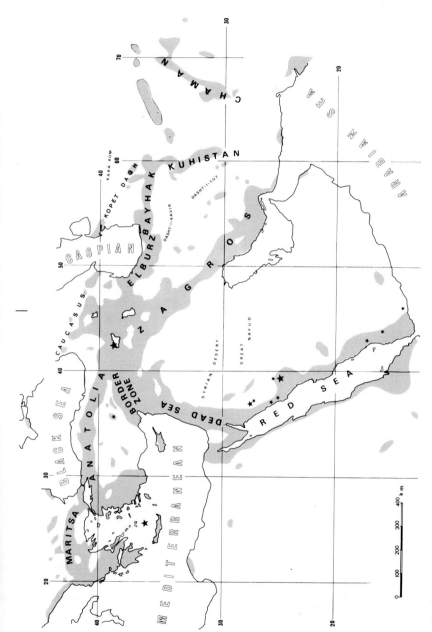

Fig. 1: Regional seismicity—first to seventeenth centuries A.D. Points of volcanic activity are marked by stars.

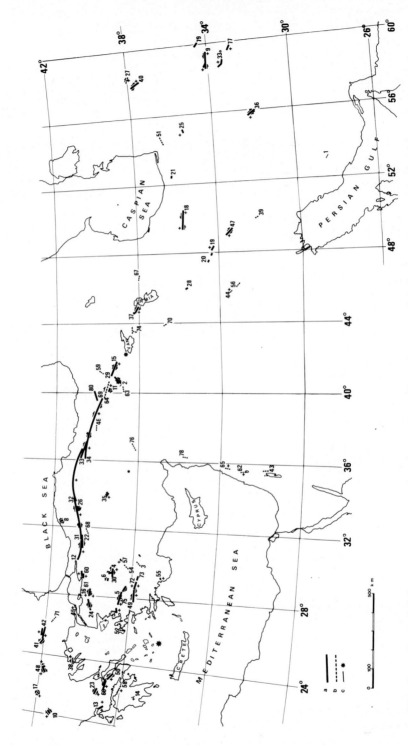

Fig. 2: a. Ground deformations associated with tectonic effects. b. Ground deformations in need of authentication. c. Ground deformations of secondary nature, and volcanic eruptions.

established major tectonic units. It also brings out new seismic zones, hitherto unknown, which, having been quiescent during the present century, have escaped notice. These zones are the Maritza zone in the Balkans, the Border and the Dead Sea in the Near East and the Bayhak and Kuhistan zones in Iran. Further east the Chaman zone begins to emerge and another region north-east of Herat for which there are still insufficient data. As a matter of fact, these newly noticed seismic zones seem to fit the negative image of the seismicity of this century.

A cursory survey of the data for the past seven centuries and a series of field studies of some of the sites of historical earthquakes have so far revealed more than eighty cases of earthquakes being associated with significant ground deformations. A list of these cases is given in Table I and Fig. 2 shows their location. Not all cases listed in Table I are necessarily of tectonic origin, and some of them should certainly be investigated further. The significance of these unproven cases of faulting lies in the fact that ground deformations have been identified in the vicinity of, or aligned with, pronounced structural trends and with recent faulting. They are listed in Table I solely for the purpose of giving the local geologist an opportunity of checking them.

With very few exceptions, observational data of faulting for the last twenty years agree surprisingly well with results from high-quality mechanism solutions. For earlier events mechanism studies are rather poor, and short-period solutions and inconsistencies should be expected.

Historical Seismicity and Tectonics in the Middle East

So far there is no evidence that the seismic activity in Greece, in the Aegean Sea and in Asia Minor (Western Anatolia) has been discontinuous, with significant periods of quiescence. These regions have been affected by small and large earthquakes, both shallow and of intermediate depth, and by occasional eruptions of the Santorin volcano (Fig. 3). Seismic sea-waves, some of them locally destructive and associated with submarine slumping, volcanic eruptions and tectonic sources, are known to have occurred on the Greek and Turkish coasts (Ambraseys, 1962b). In Greece as well as in Asia Minor surface faulting seems to be taking place along relatively short lengths of pre-existing faults and structural discontinuities, perhaps created initially by a different stress pattern which predisposes the region to react today in a seemingly irregular and complex fashion (Ambraseys and Tchalenko, 1972; McKenzie, 1972).

Table I: Summary of evidence of ground deformations associated with earthquakes of the past seven centuries

No	Date	Time GMT	Epicentre	M	h	Q	L	Az	V_m	V_a	H_m	H_a	
1	1972 Apr. 10	020653	28.5–52.8	6.9	30	ABddk	20	120	z	z	10	zR	IR–Ghir
2	1971 May 22	184358	38.8–40.5	6.7	n	BCd	20+	48	z	z	20	zL	TR–Bingöl
3	1971 May 12	082608	37.5–29.9	6.2	n	D	4+	45	?	–	?	–	TR–Burdur
4	1970 Mar. 28	210223	39.2–29.5	7.1	20	AB	23U22	160U90	220	54U40N	30	25L–25R	TR–Gediz
5	1969 Mar. 28	014830	38.6–28.4	6.1	10	CDd	32/18	115	80	40N/80S	20	zL	TR–Alaşehir
6	1969 Mar. 23	210843	39.2–28.5	5.7	15	Cdk	5+	100	25	zN	10	zL	TR–Demirci
7	1968 Sept. 24	041954	39.2–40.2	5.1	15	D	6+	150	25	15N	z	zR	TR–Kigi
8	1968 Sept. 3	081952	41.8–32.3	5.8	5	Ddk	3+	155	20	10W	30	10L	TR–Bartim
9a	1968 Sept. 1	072728	34.0–58.2	6.2	15	Ad	20	125	10	zNE	40	10L	IR–Dasht-e-Bayaz 2
9	1968 Aug. 31	104739	33.9–58.9	7.2	13	AE	80+	95	255	100N–S	450	210L	IR–Dasht-e-Bayaz 1
10	1967 Nov. 30	072349	41.4–20.5	6.4	30	B	15U1+	40U145	50	20SE	z	zR–z	AL–Debar
11	1967 Jul. 26	185301	39.5–40.4	5.6	30	D	4+	118	10	zN	20	10R	TR–Tunceli
12a	1967 Jul. 30	013100	40.7–30.4	5.7	16	Add	15	120	40	zNE	20	zR	TR–Mudurnu 2
12	1967 Jul. 22	165653	40.6–31.0	7.1	5	A	80+	90	180	55N	190	70R	TR–Mudurnu 1
13	1966 Oct. 29	023925	38.8–21.0	5.7	20	CEd	4+/2+	150/160	40	10E/ZW	–	–	GR–Acarnania
14	1966 Sept. 1	142254	37.4–22.1	5.5	n	Addk	2+	155	z	zSW	–	–	GR–Megalopolis
15a	1966 Aug. 20	115909	39.4–40.9	5.2	15	Addk	4+	110	20	zNE	–	–	TR–Varto 2
15	1966 Aug. 19	122210	39.2–41.7	6.6	30	Ad	7/15	115	25	10NE	30	zR	TR–Varto 1
16	1964 Oct. 6	143119	40.3–28.2	6.9	10	Bd	40	100	z	zN–S	10	zR	TR–Manyas
17	1963 Jul. 26	041712	42.1–21.4	6.1	5	ABddT	6+	115	10	zN	z	zL	YG–Skopje
18	1962 Sept. 1	192039	35.6–49.9	7.2	25	A	100	103	75	23N–S	60	17L	IR–Buyin
19	1958 Aug. 16	191344	34.4–47.9	6.6	5	AEdd	20	132	150	30SW	z	zR?	IR–Firuzabad
20	1957 Dec. 13	014504	34.4–47.7	7.1	40	AEddk	20/10	135	z	zSE	–	–	IR–Farsinaj
21	1957 Jul. 2	004223	36.1–52.7	7.3	10	AEddk	3+	120	z	zN–S	z	z	IR–Elburz
22	1957 May 26	063330	40.6–31.2	7.1	0	CDd	40	78	45	zN	160	50R	TR–Abant
23	1954 Apr. 30	130236	39.3–22.2	7.0	0	Cd	12+	125	20	zN	20	zL	GR–Sophades
24	1953 Mar. 18	190613	40.0–27.3	7.2	0	BCd	58+	60	–	–	430	210R	TR–Gönen
25	1953 Feb. 12	081530	35.4–55.1	6.4	0	CEd	8+	65	160	zN	z	z	IR–Torud

26	1951 Aug. 13	183330	40.8-33.2	6.5	0	CD	18/8+	80	30	zN	40	zR	TR-Kursunlu
27	1948 Oct. 5	201209	37.8-58.3	7.2	5	BddkT	10+	115?	z	zN	z	zR	SV-Ashkhabad
28	1946 Aug. 17	233740	35.5-46.0	5.5	n	Dk	2+	45	z	z?	80	z?	IQ-Penjween
29	1946 May 31	031241	39.3-41.2	6.0	n	CDd	30+	120	z	zN	z	10R	TR-Ustukran
30	1944 Jun. 25	041619	38.9-29.3	6.0	n	Ad	25U10	160U120	40	zE	z	zL	TR-Muhipler
31	1944 Feb. 1	032230	41.0-33.0	7.5	n	BC	190	75	100	64N	350	170R	TR-Gerede
32	1943 Nov. 26	222036	41.0-34.0	7.6	n	B	265	95	150	57N	z	zR	TR-Ladik
33	1942 Dec. 20	140303	40.7-36.6	7.3	n	B	47+	118	100	10N	175	65T	TR-Erban
33a	1941 Feb. 16	163903	33.3-58.9	6.3	n	AE	5+/10+	110U/160	160	30SUW	?	—	IR-Muhammatabad
34	1939 Dec. 26	235716	39.7-39.7	7.9	n	B	350	112	200	95NE	370	160R	TR-Erzincan
35	1938 Apr. 19	105915	39.5-33.7	6.7	n	B	15+	125	60	35NE	100	65R	TR-Kırşehir
36	1933 Nov. 28	110924	32.1-56.0	6.3	n	Cd	12+	150	100	zNE	z	zR?	IR-Buhabad
37	1930 May 6	223427	38.2-44.7	7.2	n	BC	30	120	500	120NE	410	60R	IR-Salmas
38	1932 Sep. 26	192042	40.4-23.8	6.9	n	CDdk	12+	95	400	180S	25	zL	GR-Chalkidiki
39	1929 Jul. 15	074414	32.3-49.7	6.3	n	Ck	1+	150	z	zE?	z		IR-Londeh
40	1929 May 1	153736	37.8-57.8	7.1	n	BC	50+	150	210	60SW	z	zR?	IR-Kopet Dagh
41	1928 Apr. 18	192237	42.0-24.7	6.9	n	B	46	125	350	140NE	z	zL	BL-Plovdiv 2
42	1928 Apr. 14	085943	42.0-24.6	6.8	n	BC	37/64	110/105	50	30S/N	z		BL-Plovdiv 1
43	1927 Jul. 11	130355	32.0-35.5	7.0	n	Ddk	10	170	200	10E	z		IS-Jordan
44	1917 Jul. 15	175840	33.5-46.5	6.1	n	Dk	2+	135	20	zSW	z		IQ-Tursaq
45	1912 Aug. 9	012900	40.5-27.0	7.6	n	Ddk	20	40	180	zSE	z		TR-Marmara
46	1909 Feb. 9	(1129)	(40.1-38.0)	—		DF	8+	95	z	z	z		TR-Enderes
47	1909 Jan. 23	0248	33.6-48.9	7.4	—	AE	40+	135	250	100NE	z	zR?	IR-Silakhor
48	1904 Apr. 4	102559	41.9-23.1	7.5	n	D	30U10	55U160	300	zSW	z	zR-L	BL-Krupnik
49	1899 Sep. 20	(1030)	(37.8-28.1)	—		CDFd	50+	90	150	80N	30	10R	TR-Aydin
50	1894 Apr. 27	(1942)	(38.7-23.1)	—		CDF	62	123	150	60NE	60	10L	GR-Locris
51	1890 Jul. 11	(0055)	(36.5-54.6)	—		CFdk	5	60	z	zS?	z	zL?	IR-Tash
52	1881 Apr. 3	(1125)	(38.3-26.1)	—		CFddk	4	20	50	zE	z		GR-Chios
53	1880 Jul. 29	(0453)	(38.6-27.2)	—		CFd	10+	75	60	zN	z		TR-Emiralan
54	1875 May 3	(09—)	(38.3-29.7)	—		Fd	20	40	110	30SE	z		TR Çivril
55	1870 Feb. 22	—	(36.6-29.0)	—		Gk	2	90	30	zN	z		TR Fethiye

continued

No	Date	Time GMT	Epicentre	M	h	Q	L	Az	V_m	V_a	H_m	H_a	
56	1864 Dec. 20	—	(33·0-46·0)	—	—	Gk	2+	140	50	zSW	—	—	IQ-Zorbat
57	1862 Nov. 3	(03—)	(38·6-30·1)	—	—	CGk	3+	45	50	zSE	—	—	TR-Çukur
58	1861 Dec. 26	(0649)	(38·4-22·1)	—	—	CFk	18	105	220	130N	—	—	GR-Vostiza
59	1859 Jun. 2	(1030)	(39·9-41·3)	—	—	F	1+	35	100	—	—	—	TR-Erzerum
60	1855 Apr. 11	(0733)	(40·3-29·1)	—	—	CFd	20	90	50	zN/S	—	—	TR-Gemlik
61	1855 Feb. 28	(0350)	(40·0-28·5)	—	—	Fdd	8	100	50	zN	—	—	TR-Kirmasti
62	1837 Jan. 1	(1633)	(32·9-35·5)	—	—	Gdk	15	170	30	zE	—	—	IS-Zfat
63	1790 May	—	(38·6-40·0)	—	—	Gd	20	80	20	zSE	—	—	TR-Bingöl
64	1784 Jul. 19	—	(39·4-40·2)	—	—	Gd	90	115	100	zN	—	—	TR-Pulumur
65	1759 Nov. 25	(04—)	(33·7-35·6)	—	—	Gdk	5	10	50	—	—	—	LB-Niha
66	1740 Jul. 22	(22—)	(38·8-33·7)	—	—	CF	30+	115	120	zN	—	—	GR-Kallidromo
67	1721 Apr. 26	—	(38·0-46·5)	—	—	Gdk	2	—	—	—	—	—	IR-Sahend
68	1668 Aug. 2	(15—)	(40·3-31·5)	—	—	Fd	10+	60	50	zN	—	—	TR-Beypazi
69	1668 Aug. 7	(16—)	(40·2-38·0)	—	—	F	380	110	400	zN	—	—	TR-Tokat
70	1666 Nov.	—	(36·7-43·9)	—	—	Gk	2	125	z	z	z	z	IQ-Zibar
71	1661 Mar. 15	—	(41·9-25·9)	—	—	G	10+	130	160	z	z	—	BL-Maritsa
72	1653 Feb. 23	—	(37·9-28·2)	—	—	CFd	50	200	80	zN/S	—	—	TR-Gevcek
73	1651 Jun. 9	(04—)	(37·8-29·3)	—	—	CF	10	50	40	zN	—	—	TR-Honaz
74	1648 Mar. 31	(05—)	(38·3-43·7)	—	—	CFd	30	80U180	100	—	—	—	TR-Hayotojor
75	1592 Sep.	—	(38·5-27·9)	—	—	CFd	10	90	100	zN?	—	—	TR-Ahmatli
76	1544 Jan. 22	—	(38·2-36·8)	—	—	Gd	20+	60?	—	—	—	—	TR-Elbistan
77	1493 Jan. 10	(18—)	(33·0-59·8)	—	—	CEGd	6+	120	—	—	—	—	IR-Muminabad
78	1404 Feb. 22	—	(35·9-36·3)	—	—	Gk	20	10	—	—	—	—	SY-Shughr
79	1336 Oct. 20	(10—)	(34·5-59·5)	—	—	G	15?	150?	—	—	—	—	IR-Khwaf
80	1254 Oct. 11	—	(40·0-40·0)	—	—	G	50	60?	500	—	—	—	TR-Sadagh

M   magnitude of surface waves

h   focal depth in kilometres

Q   Quality of field evidence of faulting or of the nature of ground deformations.

     A   detailed field studies carried out by the Author

     B   detailed field reports, published and unpublished

     C   cursory field surveys of the whole or part of the fracture zone

     D   summary field reports and incomplete surveys in need of authentication

     E   field studies currently in progress

     F   detailed historical data

     G   incomplete and fragmentary historical data

     d   trace discontinuous

     dd   trace very discontinuous, not accessible in places, or eroded; total length of ruptures deduced from few and widely spaced features.

     k   all or most of observed or reported ground deformations probably not of tectonic origin

     T   overall sense of motion deduced from triangulation and levelling

L   length of ground deformations or faulting in kilometres

     +   values of actual L likely to be larger than those shown in Table 1.

     /   parallel or sub-parallel fault-breaks

     U   arcuate or complex fault-break

Az   azimuth of general trend of ground ruptures in degrees; strikes taken between 0° and 180°E.

V_m maximum observed or reported vertical displacement in centimetres

V_a average observed or reported vertical displacement along L, in centimetres, followed by indication of downthrown block

     z   ground deformations of small amplitude or of imperceptible sense of motion.

H_m maximum observed or reported relative horizontal displacement in centimetres

H_a average observed or reported relative horizontal displacement in centimetres taken along length L, followed by designation of sense of motion

     R   right lateral (dextral)

     L   left lateral (sinistral)

( )   macroseismic data

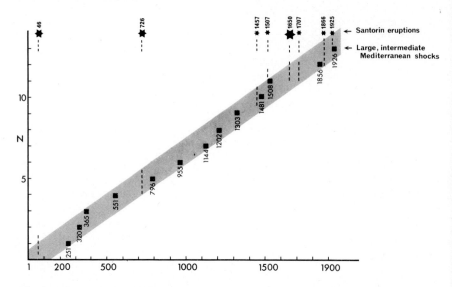

Fig. 3: The eruptions of the Santorin volcano related to the paroxysmal seismicity of the Eastern Mediterranean basin.

In Greece, with the exception of cases 13 and 23 (Table I and Fig. 2), all known instances of ground deformation are of ambiguous origin. In the vicinity of cases 13, 23 and 50 there are many faults visible on aerial photographs, but none of them go through major features, and on the ground every type of faulting is present. Ground deformations associated with cases 14 and 38 seem to be the result of reactivation of secondary structures, while those associated with case 58 are most probably the result of large-scale slumping of the steeply-sloping submerged cones of the Gulf of Corinth, where subaerial and submarine slumping has occurred without the assistance of a local earthquake (Ambraseys, 1963, 1967).

In Asia Minor faulting seems to be associated with almost all large shallow earthquakes, but its pattern is equally discontinuous and seismicity is less erratic than in Greece. For instance, in cases 5 and 49 faulting does extend far beyond that reported in literature for these earthquakes, and the same can be said about cases 16, 24 and 60. The agreement between mechanism solutions and observational data is excellent (McKenzie, 1972). It is questionable, however, whether there is sufficient evidence for a through-going extension of the Anatolian Fault across Asia Minor and the northern part of the Aegean to the Ionian Sea. West of the 30th meridian features of recent faulting abound, but they lack

Fig. 4: Fault-break associated with event no. 47 (Table 1) passing near Dorud.

Fig. 5: Fault-break near Dasht-e-Bayaz (Iran) associated with event no. 9 (Table I).

Fig. 6: Faulting associated with event no. 4 (Gediz) (Table I).

the continuity of the Anatolian zone. It is very probable that in Western Anatolia crustal deformations are the consequence of the interference of a new direction of motion with old structural trends which has reactivated pre-existing faults in a complicated manner to accommodate the new motion; case 4 is an example of the response of a block structure to such a motion (Ambraseys and Tchalenko, 1972).

The overall seismicity of the Central Balkans is defined by the Maritsa zone which is characterized by occasional large shocks, less frequent than elsewhere in the region. These shocks, although locally destructive, are not felt very widely, but they are associated with strong aftershocks and with occasional faulting (Ambraseys, 1970b). Field evidence of surface faulting for cases 41, 42 and 48 indicates conclusively normal motion. However, further west in the Maritsa zone a series of retriangulation and levelling in the meizoseismal region of case 17 shows significant left-lateral motions and creep rates of 15 mm year—across a WNW–ESE trending fault (Lilienberg and Mescherikov, 1965). Ground deformations, however, associated with the Skopje earthquake proper were almost imperceptible, showing no preferential sense of lateral motion, and only small vertical displacements were conspicuous down to the north (Arsovski, 1970). Case 10 in Albania is well documented and field evidence shows again normal motion with a small and rather inconclusive right lateral displacement (Sulstarova and Kociaj, 1969). This sense of movement is not in very good agreement with the fault-plane solution of this event. It is not improbable, however, that the motion was taken by a major conjugate structure bearing 145°E, on the other side of the border in Yugoslavia, on which there was evidence of some left-lateral motion (Arsovski, 1970). Two more cases between 10 and 17, not listed in Table I, suggest large block structures undergoing extension (Ambraseys, 1970b).

The seismicity in the Anatolian zone has been discussed briefly elsewhere (Ambraseys, 1970a, 1971) and no special comment is needed except perhaps to note that large shallow earthquakes have occurred in this zone, perhaps the largest in the Near East. An interesting feature of these large events is the great distance to which they are felt to the south of the zone. Most of these events seem to originate from the eastern half of the zone, roughly between 35°E and 40°E, and to be associated with long aftershock sequences. Seismicity alternates between the Anatolian zone and the Border zone to the south, with very long periods of relative inactivity (Ambraseys, 1971). Seismicity within the Border zone itself, however, is not uniformly distributed. The evidence available now suggests that it is along the two boundaries of the zone, to the north-west and south-east, that most of the larger events take place. Earthquakes seem to be more numerous but rather local along the north-west boundary; swarms of earthquakes are also known to have occurred there. The south-east boundary of the Border zone, although it has a much more discontinuous activity, has shown very large shocks, perhaps as large as those that occur in eastern Anatolia, followed by aftershock sequences of abnormally long duration. These shocks are concentrated near the southernmost end of the boundary, and it is difficult to say whether they belong to the arbitrarily defined Border zone or to the Dead Sea zone. In the former, relatively few cases of faulting have been found so far, but there is some evidence there of vertical ground movements and rapid growth of anticlines.

Further to the south, the Dead Sea System is equally active, but large earthquakes there do not seem to be connected directly with the rift proper. In the north, much of the activity and the larger events have occurred east of the axis of the system, while in the south the activity is diffused on either side of the rift. Between the Border zone as a whole and the Dead Sea system seismicity does alternate with time, but with longer periods of overlapping activity than exist between the Border and the Anatolian zone. However, as one would expect, a meaningful interpretation of interaction patterns between contiguous tectonic units requires the knowledge of the boundaries of such units in advance, a requisite which at this stage we cannot satisfy on any scale smaller than regional. There is no evidence of very large shocks in the Dead Sea system, and the cases of faulting found are few and inconclusive. One interesting point may be mentioned here; the absence of any evidence for creep of the Khirbet Kumran fault-break near the north end of the Dead Sea, after it moved by thirty centimetres—shearing off man-made structures, during the earthquake of 31 b.c. (Zeuner, 1954). Also on the east bank of the Jordan River, much earlier but less well preserved fault-breaks show no evidence of subsequent movements. There is also evidence for at least two large earthquakes in this region which were associated with destructive seismic sea-waves in the Dead Sea.

Further south in the Red Sea, there is evidence of large earthquakes occurring between relatively short periods of inactivity. Earthquake swarms and locally destructive earthquakes, as well as a considerable number of minor volcanic eruptions, are known to have occurred on the western coastline and in the interior of the Arabian Peninsula. However, data are insufficient at present to allow a more detailed study of this area and of the western coasts of the Red Sea. There is some evidence, nevertheless, that in Eritrea and Northern Ethiopia seismicity of rather local nature has been almost continuous throughout the period between the sixteenth and seventeenth centuries.

In the Eastern Mediterranean Basin proper, large intermediate earthquakes seem to occur almost continuously with a remarkable regularity. A study of all major events of the last twenty centuries in the Basin shows that on the average a major earthquake of intermediate depth occurs once every 150 years. Using as calibration events the earthquakes of 12 October 1856 and 26 June 1926 which showed M $\gg$ 8+, the earthquakes shown on Figure 3 were selected on the basis of the size of the area over which the shocks caused concern, i.e. a felt area corresponding to about 5 $\times$ 10^{6}km^2. Figure 3 also shows the time sequence of major and minor eruptions of the Santorin volcano, and their relationship with the paroxysmal seismicity of the Basin. The location in time of the 1650 eruption with respect to the subdued seismicity of the Basin in the seventeenth century is interesting. Only four of these major shocks were associated with widely felt seismic sea-waves, and only two of these occurrences were of catastrophic magnitude.

The boundary area between the Anatolian and Border zones and the Zagros exhibits a well-established almost continuous seismicity of rather low magnitude with a few larger shocks which in some cases are associated with ground deformations. Prolonged sequences of small earthquakes, with no principal or major shock and lasting for months, are also known to occur to the south-west of Urmia and to the south of Lake Van. As a rule the larger shocks in this region are not felt very far and, although historical evidence suggests ground deformations associated with almost all these large shocks, it is only cases 70 and 74 that seem to be reasonably well established. It is of interest perhaps that lineaments along which surface faulting is suggested by the historical data, which so far have, with very few exceptions, not been checked, are visible on aerial photographs.

In the Zagros proper, most earthquakes occur to the south-west and south of the main thrust, and they are accompanied by rather short after-shock sequences. In the southern part of the Zagros seismicity seems to be more uniformly distributed in time than in the north with a noticeable absence of large shocks. In the north the zone becomes broader and exhibits occasional larger shocks which seem to occur at intervals of time which we have so far been unable to assess. From this part of the zone large shocks are felt at much greater distances to the north and north-east than to the south and west. An interesting feature of the north-west part of the Zagros is the occurrence of earthquake swarms of damaging magnitude. At least one of these sequences resulted in significant ground deformations and widespread damage in south-west Kurdistan. However, very few cases of faulting have so far been found, all of them being minor with no evidence of lateral motion. Vertical movements and rapid growth of anticlines have been identified mainly on the south-west flanks of the Zagros. The evidence for this type of movement is most noticeable in north-eastern Iraq and in Khuzistan.

Earthquakes in the Elburz seem to occur along a line which traverses the mountain range obliquely in a north-west/south-east direction. Large shocks, perhaps larger than those in the Zagros, are known to have occurred in this zone, most of them probably shallow to judge from the comparatively small area over which they were felt. Smaller shocks are known to occur almost continuously, particularly near the western coasts of the Caspian. The evidence regarding the seismicity of the southern borders of the Elburz with Central Iran is less explicit. Archaeological evidence alludes to an earthquake which in the third millennium B.C. devastated Sagziabad, a site near case 18. Historical data also indicate a number of earthquakes which since the fourth century B.C. have caused the ruin of the region of Shahr-rey. This information seems to suggest the existence of an important structure between the Elburz and Central Iran. It also suggests, however, that these major historical events might have occurred within the sparsely populated massif of the Elburz proper, for instance in the Taliqan Valley or in Ruyan; in which case one can visualize a whole sequence of earthquakes in the Elburz, not necessarily catastrophic from the point of view of damage to the city of Shahr-rey itself, but certainly catastrophic in the eventual result to the district of Shahr-rey as a whole, which in early times extended deep into the Elburz. Questions like this, however, have to await the retrieval and study of additional data. It is very probable that, as with the Zagros and the Border zone as a whole, deformations are being taken up within a very broad zone of "incompetent" crustal material in which only a relatively small proportion of the total strain energy is stored and eventually released by earthquakes. The absence of any long-term evidence of large magnitude shocks and the relatively low seismicity, particularly of the Zagros, preclude the possibility of the build-up of unreleased energy. They rather suggest that energy is being spent latently at a slow rate, causing the zone material to flow rather than fracture; evidence of this may be found in the rapid growth of anticlines and in slowly creeping faults. In such zones not

K

only is the return period of the larger events likely to be long, but the short-term distribution of smaller shocks would be diffused and seemingly erratic. Also, local tectonics are likely to be complex, particularly where crustal material has been affected by pre-existing geological structures which left residual features to buttress or deflect local motions, thus predisposing the material to react in irregular and complex fashion to otherwise simple regional patterns of deformation.

Further east of the Elburz, historical data begin to point to a hitherto unknown zone of very high seismicity which neither present seismic activity nor tectonics seems to reflect. This zone, which for the sake of convenience we have called the Bayhak, extends from north-central Mazanderan all the way to the Herat region. It is characterized by occasional earthquakes of exceptionally large magnitude, to judge from the data which are available, much larger than anywhere else in Iran, followed by long aftershock sequences and major ground deformations. Unfortunately we cannot say much at present with regard to the exact location of these deformations, except perhaps that they were responsible on some occasions for drastic change in surface and underground water supply and for the eventual abandonment of many sites.

Another hitherto unsuspected zone of apparently very high seismicity, which begins to emerge from the study of historical data, runs almost north-south along the borders between Iran and Afghanistan, and has shown exceptionally large earthquakes which were associated with faulting. This zone, which for the sake of brevity we have named after the region most seriously affected in early times, i.e. Kuhistan, is not as yet well defined. It seems to extend in places further to the west, and there is some evidence that eventually it may cover the whole of the Qayn-Birjand highlands and part of the Lut as well as the rapidly sinking Hilmand and eastern Sistan. In the Kuhistan zone opportunities are available for identifying and establishing on the ground evidence for early and more recent cases of faulting. Cases 33a, 36, 77 and 79 were found and checked on the ground within a very short period of time, while good evidence of the location and features of other suspected historical fault-breaks awaits verification in the field.

Further east, the data available for Afghanistan and western Pakistan are insufficient to provide a reliable pattern of seismicity. Large-magnitude shocks are known to have occurred along the Chaman zone with at least two cases of major faulting. Similar evidence points to major events having occurred along the borders of Turkmenistan and Afghanistan between the Murgab and the Amu-Darya.

Speculations

There is no denying that there is at present a lack of knowledge of basic facts bearing on long-term observations of seismicity and tectonics, and that it is through the study of historical seismicity that such facts may become known.

Returning to the map shown in Fig. 1, it is possible to say unequivically that a seventeenth-century man of science did have all the information he needed to produce such a map and that he would most certainly have produced it had he been motivated to do so. Today, to any one familiar with tectonics, such a map, or for that matter Mallet's 1858 map of world seismicity (Mallet, 1858), or Fig. 1, would look suspiciously similar to that compiled quite recently from ESSA data for the period 1961 to 1967 (Barazangi and Dorman, 1969).

In constructing the map shown in Fig. 1 no data were rejected, and no theories to fit the data were tried. It may be true that certain zones of seismicity, such as the Dead Sea and Kuhistan, stand out prominently because they lie between regions which because of their physiography are lacking in macroseismic data. It may be equally true that within these semi-desert regions further study may eventually disclose and define internal zones of activity. Yet the importance of the agreement of much of the spatial distribution of seismicity shown in Fig. 1 with tectonic units deduced from other microseismic or geological evidence is that it gives confidence to the assumption that the rest of the distribution is significant also.

The results of the present study, which is far from complete, have been considerably to extend the period of usable observations. On all counts the evidence emerging from these studies points to incompatibilities with some hastily adopted models of continental plate tectonics in northern Iraq, in Turkey, and particularly in Iran (Nowroozi, 1972; Takin, 1971). For instance, it is difficult to accept the Zagros ranges as being a plate boundary in the conventional sense of the term. There, long-term seismicity as well as the seismicity of the last few well-documented decades have been significantly lower than one could expect to find in a boundary zone that has undergone recent deformations and shortening, allegedly of many hundreds of kilometres. The idea of the Zagros being part of a circum-Arabian ophiolitic crescent is interesting (Ricou, 1971), but that the Zagros is the consequence of a crustal slab dipping north or north-east under central Iran is at present rather untenable seismically; the low precision with which focal depth in the Zagros can be determined, and the paucity of large shocks, make it almost impossible to resolve crustal behaviour unambiguously. With the data available at the moment it is equally difficult to presume that the Lut is a rigid plate. All evidence points to intense internal deformation with occasional faulting and to a very wide zone of historical seismicity which follows the flysch zone along the Iran-Afghanistan border (Stöcklin *et al.*, 1972). It is very probable that little of Iran, of the Border Zone, and of the region west of Asia Minor may be considered to consist of individual plates. It is more likely that here we are dealing with "non-rigid plates" or with zones of a fine mosaic structure, capable of undergoing large deformations aseismically, or in more general terms with an abnormally low seismic energy-release, too small to account by itself for the rate of opening or closing of neighbouring units.

The study of historical seismicity is not of value to the seismologist alone. Apart from the obvious usefulness of acquiring knowledge intimately connected with the local geographical history of all areas of the Near and Middle East and with their ruling dynasties, natural phenomena such as earthquakes have a powerful effect on man and information concerning their occurrence is clearly of interest to the social historian. Particularly in such countries as Turkey and Iran, which have been affected by earthquakes throughout their history, the effect of these upheavals on the population gives a further dimension to our knowledge of such subjects as the rise and decay of cities; the shifting of populations; the behaviour of those involved in an earthquake and their attitude towards it; their subsequent capacity for economic recovery; and their ability or desire to benefit from the experience to try to guard against its repetition, as, for instance, in the improvement of building materials and methods of construction or the adaptation of some features of their way of life. It is interesting to note, for example, that the site of a large city prone to severe earthquakes is seldom changed because of the vested interests involved in the maintenance of the place on a site originally chosen for the advantages of its position. In the countryside, however, where water supply is of overriding importance, the breaking of a line of qanats or the blockage of a natural spring by earthquake activity will bring a hasty death to a village. On a less local scale, the occurrence of an earthquake is a useful point of reference with which to cross-check events in different regions and also to compare the local calendars used to date them. Even the most obscure case can be of use in fixing the date of a political event more accurately, in particular where it is mentioned, as is often the case, along with notices of eclipses or other terrestial and celestial occurrences.

By comparing the way in which an earthquake is described with accounts of the disasters inflicted on man by his fellows, an adequate perspective of the latter can be obtained; although the adjectives used are usually rather similar, the atrocity of man on man is invariably regarded as the more fearful. Nowhere is the destruction of a city recorded with the same horrified shock as the devastations wrought upon the cities of the Middle East by the Mongols, for example. Clearly, there are other associated advantages in historical study of this nature—these are common to all historical research, embarked upon in any field.

References

Ambraseys, N. N. 1961. Data from a XV-century Arabic MS on the seismicity of South-west Asia. *Revue pour l'Etude des Calamités*, No. 37, p. 18, Geneva.

Ambraseys, N. N. 1962a. On the chronology of Willis' earthquakes in Palestine and Syria. *Bull. Seism. Soc. Amer.* **52**, 77.

Ambraseys, N. N. 1962b. Data for the investigation of the seismic sea-waves in the Eastern Mediterranean. *Bull. Seism. Soc. Amer.* **52**, 895.

Ambraseys, N. N. 1963. Seismic sea-wave in the Gulf of Corinth. *Bull. Seism. Soc. Amer.* **53** (4), 849.

Ambraseys, N. N. 1967. The earthquakes of 1965–6 in the Peloponnesus; a field report. *Bull. Seism. Soc. Amer.* **57** (5), 1044.

Ambraseys, N. N. 1970a. Some characteristics of the Anatolian Fault Zone. *Tectonophysics* **9**, 159.

Ambraseys, N. N. 1970b. An early earthquake in Macedonia. *Proc. Bulgarian Acad. Sci., 3ESEE*, 73.

Ambraseys, N. N. 1971. Value of historical records of earthquakes. *Nature* **232**, 375.

Ambraseys, N. N. 1973. Earth sciences in archaeology and history. *Antiquity* **47**, 229.

Ambraseys, N. N. 1974. The historical seismicity of North-Central Iran. *Publ. Geolog. Survey of Iran*. Tehran.

Ambraseys, N. N. 1977. The seismicity of Iran during the first half of the 20th century (in preparation).

Ambraseys, N. N. and Moinfar, A. 1973. The Silakhor earthquake of 23rd January 1909. *Annali di Geofisica* **26**, no. 4.

Ambraseys, N. N. and Tchalenko, J. 1972. Seismotectonic aspects of the Gediz, Turkey earthquake of March 1970. *Geophys. Journ. Royal Astr. Soc.* **30**, 242.

Arsovski, M. 1970. Contemporary tectonic properties of some active zones in Jugoslavia. *Bulgarian Acad. Sci.* **1**, 184.

Barazangi, M. and Dorman, J. 1969. World seismicity map compiled from ESSA

Coast and Geodetic Survey epicenter data 1961–1967. *Bull. Seism. Soc. Amer.* **59**, 369.

Berberian, M. 1973. The Seismicity of Iran; preliminary map of epicentres and focal depths. *Geol. Survey of Iran*, scale 1:2,500,000, Tehran.

Flemming, N. 1969. Archaeological evidence for eustatic change of sea level and earth movements in the Western Mediterranean during the last 2,000 Y. *Special Paper* no. 109, Geol. Soc. America.

Flemming, N. 1972. Eustatic and tectonic factors in the relative vertical displacement of the Aegean Coast. *In: The Mediterranean Sea,* (D. J. Stanley), p. 189.

Flemming, N., Czartoryska, N. and Hunter, P. 1971. Archaeological evidence for eustatic and tectonic components of relative sea level change in the South Aegean. *Colston Papers* **23**, 1.

Heuckroth, L. and Karim, R. 1970. Earthquake History, seismicity and tectonics of the regions of Afghanistan. *Publ. Seismological Centre*, Kab. University, Kabul.

Lilienberg, D. and Mescherikov, Y. 1965. Morphostructural characteristics and contemporary movements of region affected by the Skopje earthquake. *Sovremennis Dvijenie Zemnoi Kori*, no. 2, Tartuz.

Mallet, R. 1858. On the facts and theory of earthquake phenomena. *Report of the British Assoc. for the Adv. Sci.*

McKenzie, D. 1972. Active tectonics of the Mediterranean region. *Geoph. Journ. Royal Astro. Soc.* **30**, 109–185.

Nowroozi, A. A. 1971. Seismo-tectonics of the Persian Plateau, Eastern Turkey, Caucasus and Hindu-Kush regions. *Bull. Seism. Soc. Amer.* **61**, 317.

Nowroozi, A. A. 1972. Focal mechanism of earthquakes in Persia, Turkey, West Pakistan and Afghanistan and plate tectonics of the Middle East. *Bull. Seism. Soc. Amer.* **62**, 823.

Ricou, L. E. 1971. Le croissant ophiolitique peri-Arabe. Revue Geol. Phys. Geol. Dynam. **13**, 327.

Stöcklin, J., Eftekhar-nezhad, J. and Hushmand-zadeh, A. 1972. Central Lut reconnaissance East Iran. *Geological Survey of Iran*, Report No. 22, Tehran.

Sulstarova, E. and Kociaj, S. 1969. Tërmeti i 30 nëndorit 1967 dhe brezi sizmogjen Vlorë-Dibër. *Buletin Univ. Shtetëror Tiranës, Ser. Shkencat Natyrore* **2**, 65–94.

Takin, M. 1971. Iranian geology and continental drift in the Middle East. *Nature* **235**, 147.

Zeuner, F. 1954. Recent movement on the western fault of the Dead Sea rift. *Geol. Rundsch.* **43**, II.

Synopsis of Part III

There is general agreement that in the plateau basins water accumulated during the Glacial Periods of the Pleistocene, and dried out during the Interglacials. In sub-tropical Africa, exactly the opposite appears to have happened. Thus, during the Late Glacial and Early Holocene the African lakes were expanding, while those of Anatolia and Iran were becoming progressively reduced.

The milder climate of post-Glacial times on the Northern Plateaux was tolerable for settlers who could build shelters and food stores well enough to weather the winters; and the newly exposed alluvial flats around the receding lakes seem to have been just right for these colonists. They could find there many kinds of food, through fishing, hunting and snaring as well as farming and herding, while reeds and timber were easily come by for building. Tosi and Constantini (Chapter 11) have revealed how life was led near the shore of such a lake, the Hamun of Sistan, at a time, just after the mid-Holocene, when the climate may have been slightly moister than now.

Since then, the effects on flora and fauna of the minor fluctuations of climate have been obscured by the more extreme effects brought about by closer settlement and exploitation.

The nature and extent of the effects of changes of climate on the inhabitants in historic times are debatable; but the effects of seismic changes and especially the calamities of earth-movements are indisputable and often well chronicled, as Ambraseys has shown (Chapter 12). Mr Norman Falcon has kindly drawn my attention to a remarkable example, the great Saidmarreh Rockfall of prehistoric times, probably triggered by an earthquake, which dammed the Saidmarreh River (see Oberlander (1965) *The Zagros Streams*, Syracuse Geog. Series No. 1). This, the greatest recorded rockfall in the world, was directly responsible for the deposition of about 100 m depth of alluvium up-stream of the blockage. It seems likely too that earth movements and consequent disturbance to the flow of the lower Orontes were responsible for the accumulation of the six metres of alluvium which have buried the lower-lying suburbs of the ancient city of Antioch.

Evidently the effects of earthquakes are too local to warrant the distant cross-datings on which Schaeffer built his comparative stratigraphy of Western Asia; but over limited areas, as in the waters of the Southern Aegean following the eruptions of Thera, archaeological correlations can fairly be made, on the analogy of episodes recorded in more recent times.

IV

Mesopotamia and the Gulf

The archaeologists of the early years of the present century, notably de Morgan and Sidney Smith, argued from the evidence of texts, of excavations, and of the current deposition of alluvium that the composite delta of Lower Mesopotamia had been advancing steadily into the head of the Gulf throughout historic times. In the last generation a wealth of new evidence bearing on this thesis has been accumulated through archaeological work upstream and along the western shores of the Gulf in eastern Arabia; and above all through intense geological exploration in the course of the quest for oil in southern Iraq and on the bed and margins of the Gulf. It is now clear that the Gulf was dry in the Later Würm, and was being flooded throughout Late Glacial and Early Holocene times. Moreover, there is good reason to think that the land itself is unstable, especially along the western and northern margins of the Gulf. In addition to all this new light on topographic changes from seismic and marine effects, the cyclic shifts of deposition and erosion, following climatic alterations in Arabia, are at last becoming fairly clear.

13
Erosion and Sedimentation Along the Euphrates Valley in Northern Syria

T. J. Wilkinson

Introduction

In a study of the relations between ancient Middle Eastern settlements and their physical environment two types of change in the landscape must be envisaged. First, the natural environment will have altered, due to shifts of rivers, the acceleration of erosion or the impoverishment of vegetation; second, much evidence of human occupation will have been lost through wholesale erosion or sedimentation. An appreciation of the first type of change will affect our views of the economic capability and potential of the area in the past (Higgs and Vita-Finzi, 1972), whilst the second process must be kept constantly in mind during archaeological reconnaissance. This chapter presents the results of a preliminary study of changes in the landscape around the site of Dibsi Faraj in Syria which was occupied during the Late Roman, Byzantine and Islamic periods. Particular attention has been given to processes of erosion and sedimentation along the south bank of the Euphrates and within its tributary wadis (Fig. 1), but occasional reference will also be made to areas up, down or across the river which were examined in less detail. I propose to describe first the processes which are at present shaping the landscape as well as the geomorphological features that are associated with them; then the stages in the evolution of the landscape during the Late Quaternary; finally, these two studies will be combined in an attempt to outline the past alterations of erosion and deposition in the area.

Present Fluvial Activity

The Euphrates is a swift, turbid river which rises in the highlands of Anatolia and in Syria, and thereafter flows through a series of gorges which alternate with broader, but still entrenched, reaches of valley. The area studied lies just to the east of the major bend in the Euphrates (Fig. 1) where the valley, here 5–10 km wide, is flanked by gentle northern but steep or truncated southern slopes. The river flows some 60–80 m below the steppeland surface of the adjacent plateau, which is composed of soft, white Paleogene limestone capped by a coarse chert conglomerate thought by Van Liere (1960) to be of Neogene age.

The annual regime of the Euphrates ranges over 1–6 m, from low water in September/October to high in April or May after the melting in spring of the Anatolian snows (Ionides, 1937). Under normal conditions of flow, water is conducted along the main course, a steep, slightly sinuous[1] channel floored with gravel, but during floods it fills a more extensive zone fringed by bluffs of the flood plain. The flood plain is complex and contains, in addition to the flood channel, relict channels and minor terraces; levees are rare near Dibsi. The flood plain terraces consist of low spreads of silt about 5–7 m above the lowest level of the stream and, being subject to only sporadic floods, they are the parts most favoured today for permanent settlement. It appears from exposed sections that the flood plain has risen in level through lateral accretion within the channel and through vertical accretion outside its banks, as described by Wolman and Leopold (1957); the latter process appears to have been predominant higher than about 4 m above the autumn river-level.[2] This implies that the low terraces of the flood plain are formed not so much by slight incision as by gradual accretion, associated with channel levels which are essentially stable. Periodically, lateral and downslope movements of the channel rework most of the sediments, but leave others as residuals destined to be obscured by later deposition.

Complications also arise through accessions of sediments from short tributary wadis of ephemeral flow. In the south and south-west of the Dibsi watershed (Fig. 2) these form wide, shallow valleys with valley side-slopes covered in calcareous reddish-brown steppe soils leading down to only sparsely alluviated or bare wadi floors. In the north-west (to the north of the line x–y) these give way to incised wadis with steep side-slopes of rapidly weathering limestone. Here the wadi floors are characterized by head-reaches of bare rock which lead in the middle reaches to scrolls and point-bar deposits on meander bends. Nearer the Euphrates, these merge

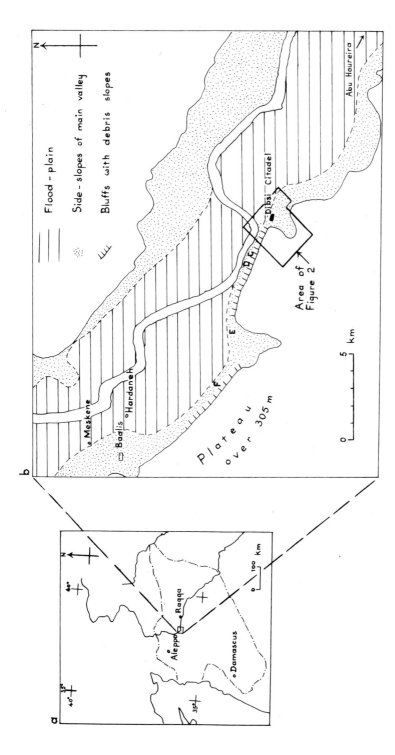

Fig. 1: Location of Dibsi Faraj.

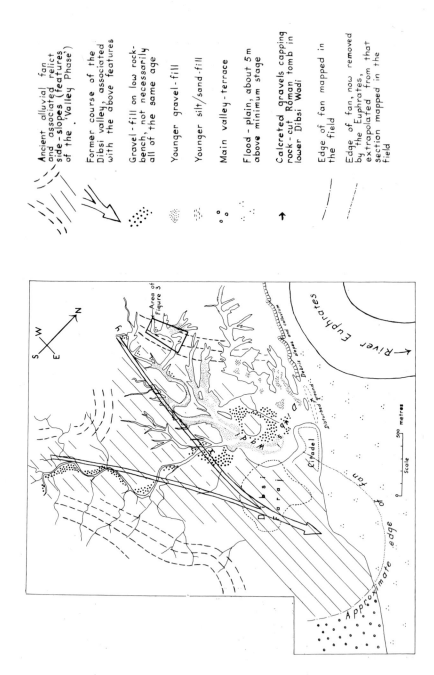

Fig. 2: The geomorphology of the Dibsi Basin.

Ancient alluvial fan and associated relict side-slopes (features of the 'Valley Phase')

Former course of the Dibsi valley, associated with the above features

Gravel-fill on low rock-bench, not necessarily all of the same age

Younger gravel-fill

Younger silt/sand-fill

Main valley-terrace

Flood-plain, about 5 m above minimum stage

Calcreted gravels capping rock-cut Roman tomb in lower Dibsi Wadi

Edge of fan mapped in the field

Edge of fan, now removed by the Euphrates, extrapolated from that section mapped in the field

Area of Figure 3

River Euphrates

Debris slopes and colluvium

Disturbed ground

Citadel

Approximate edge of fan

Scale

0   500 metres

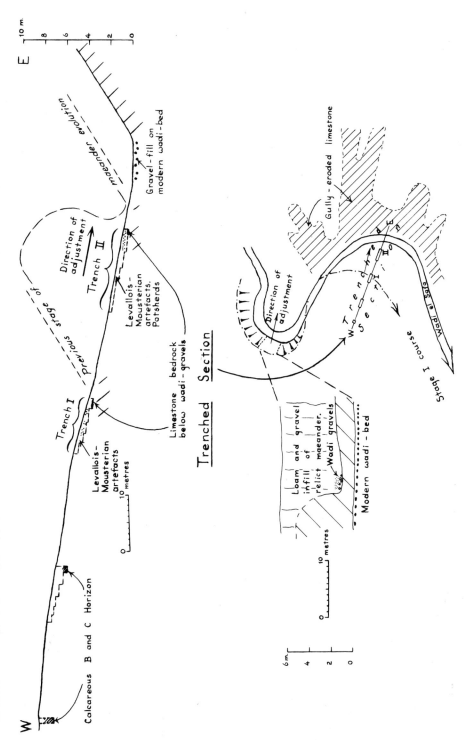

Fig. 3: The course of incision in Wadi el Safa.

Fig. 4: The Euphrates Valley, viewed from between E and F (Fig. 1): (a) Looking north-west. Recent aggrading fill overlapping on to higher flood-plain terrace and accumulating between remnants of earlier fan. R = relict valley side-slopes. (b) The river has recently reworked the flood-plain and debris-slopes in this area. R = Relict wadi side-slope.

into a continuous fill of moderately bedded gravels or well bedded silts, depending on the prevailing conditions of deposition. Figure 2 illustrates how this fill, shown by a light stipple, penetrates the incised wadis, in certain cases almost up to the head-reaches; and it appears that, given a sufficiently high sediment yield from the side-slopes and interfluves, aggradation, which began in the lower parts of the wadis, can alluviate almost the entire length of the wadi.

The fill normally encroaches into the main valley as an alluvial fan, which builds up and interdigitates with the flood plain as it rises; aggradation of the wadi floor is thus further encouraged. This situation continues while the flood plain remains free from attack; but, if the fan is truncated by meanders sweeping downstream, the wadi becomes rejuvenated, incisions are made in the fill, and much of this material is evacuated (Miller, 1883; Wright, 1960). This interaction between the sedimentation of the main river and that of its tributaries further complicates the chronological record, and today the 15 km strip of land between Dibsi Faraj and Hardaneh (Fig. 1) shows examples of both aggrading and incised wadi-fills, according to the recent alluvial history of the flood plain (Fig. 3).

Along the south bank further interactions are indicated by the talus-fringed limestone bluffs which skirt the plateau (Fig. 4). These slopes have gradients of up to 35°, but are locally steepened where the trimming of their bases by the Euphrates has accelerated the removal of debris. There is additional evidence of truncation along most of this same bank, where bluffs, truncated wadi-fans and relict valley-side slopes contrast with the gentle, more mature profiles of the north bank.

Clearly, in this area, local geomorphic interactions are of considerable importance, and, when considered over a relatively short span of time, such as the Holocene, they will tend to blur the boundaries of any chronology that assumes distinct episodes of erosion and alluviation.

Stages in the Evolution of the Landscape

In the Dibsi area three distinct alluvial facies could be distinguished.
(a) Beds, 2–3 m thick, of coarse chert conglomerates.
(b) Alluvial sediments resembling those of the modern Euphrates.
(c) Debris and alluvial fans of local materials including gravels derived from facies (a) and (b).
Facies (a) are considered by Van Liere (1960) to be of Neogene age, and

together with sediments of type (b) constitute a capping over the local plateau some 70 m above the river level. Facies (b), at their maximum altitude, form complex sequences of partly indurated gravels, sands and silts. They are thought by Van Liere to be representatives of an early Quarternary course of the Euphrates; whilst de Heinzelin (1967) combines both (a) and (b) into one formation: the "Dibsi formation", and he suggests that they represent a stage when the valley was absent and instead the river flowed in a braided manner to the south-west to debouch into a closed basin, the Sabkhat Jabbour, situated south-east of modern Aleppo.

On a descent from the level of the plateau, gravels of facies (b) are not encountered until one reaches the vicinity of the modern valley floor. Here they form the "Main valley terrace" of Van Liere or the "Mureibit formation" of de Heinzelin, and their surface stands some 2–4 m above the surface of the adjacent 5 m flood-plain terrace. The 5–8 m capping of stratified silts encountered by Van Liere around Raqqa is only represented by rare residuals of silty soil near Dibsi. Although he considers the Raqqa silts to be the product of a final stage of valley-floor alluviation, it may be wiser to view them as the finer products of lateral and vertical accretion and to include them in the same period of accumulation as the gravels of that terrace.

Associated with this terrace are broad, shallow valleys which converge on the modern village of Dibsi and debouch as an ancient alluvial fan of facies (c) to the east. Upstream also, slope facets resembling those of this phase are to be found as relict features in wadis C and E (Fig. 1) as well as in the main valley near Hardaneh (Fig. 4).

Without *in situ* Palaeolithic sites or radiometric dates for the terrrace and fan/valley sequence, the geological succession can only be outlined. We may reasonably suppose that remnants of this phase are approximately contemporary and their morphology suggests a slow evolution associated with wadi-incision less pronounced than that of today. This development was protracted, continuing into the Middle Palaeolithic,[3] and was probably related to river levels approximating to those of the main gravel-terrace. The overlap of the fan-gravels at Dibsi Faraj implies that the final period at least of the valley phase post-dated the main valley-terrace, but, in view of the interactions mentioned above, it is likely that a considerable period elapsed during which fans were built and truncated and earlier stratigraphic features removed.

Within this setting, during a period when wadis cut back into the plateau, the head waters of this valley phase at Dibsi were captured and the citadel rock was isolated. Incision of these wadis was localized, however, and their characteristic deeply incised valleys are manifest today in the vicinity of the Euphrates.

In the course of investigations a series of trial-trenches was dug on a meander spur, and these revealed the trend of incision on one of these wadis, the Wadi el Safa (Fig. 3b). Two earlier wadi-beds were encountered, consisting of loose, fluvially worked fine and medium gravels resting on limestone. These occurred approximately 4 m (marked I) and 0·5 m (II) above the present wadi-bed, and, although both contained a derived assemblage of Levalloisian/Mousterian flint artefacts, the lower gravels in addition contained several potsherds [4] which testified to incision of at least 0·5 m during the last 5000 years. A single phase of wadi incision and head-cutting would fit this evidence, but this hypothesis was confounded by the discovery of what appeared to be several portions of an exhumed valley, sections of which occurred on several concave meander-scar-faces upstream. Aerial views of this excavated area demonstrated, however, that the fills of loam and gravel exposed in the scar-faces were not the remains of an ancient valley-fill removed by a later cycle of headcutting: instead, they were seen to be infills of old meander-scars isolated by the constant adjustment of the wadi bed to lateral movements of the channel elsewhere. This process is depicted in Fig. 3a, which shows that, if a meander is to maintain its geometry, a lateral shift in one direction must be balanced by compensatory movements elsewhere.

In the lower Dibsi wadi, amongst the complex of sediments, is a set of loose gravels resting on bedrock some 2–3 m above the present wadi bed. There is no continuous sequence of terraces along the wadi, and it is unjustifiable to attempt a simple bench-for-bench correlation of these with the high stages at Wadi el Safa, since deposits I and II are probably merely the remnants of a previous continuum of wadi-beds interrupted by later adjustments of channel.

A second deposit, this time a poorly bedded set of calcreted ferruginous gravels, situated around the level of the present valley floor, formed the capping to a tomb of probable Late Roman date which had been cut in the bedrock. The site is indicated by a small arrow on Fig. 2. This "wadi-bed conglomerate" (Butzer and Hansen, 1968) also occurred in the lower reaches of wadi E upstream (Fig. 1), where it lies a little above a present-day seepage of ground-water. It is likely that both conglomerates were formed relatively late in the Pleistocene during periods when the ground-water tables were high, and that, since their formation, [5] incision of the wadi beds has been minimal.

With regard to the youngest wadi-fills, sections dateable by archaeological evidence showed that aggradation had continued in different wadis from pre-Roman times to the present. When it is considered that such fills grade to flood plain terraces of different ages, and show varying stages of incision, it is evident that, in such a dynamic area, there have been many deviations from the general pattern of events suggested by Vita-Finzi (1969). In fact, at C in Fig. 1, it was possible to distinguish at least two phases of fan-truncation which fell within the last 2000 years, and a third phase is imminent today. Conversely, more substantial fans, remains of which are found at C, D, E and F (Figs 1 and 4), were able to form in pre-Roman times, possibly during a period when the truncation of fans was inhibited, either because the Euphrates was confined to midstream, or because it was less powerful than it is today. This suggestion is only tentative, but it illustrates how important it is to take into account interactions between fans and the trunk river when reconstructing the past geography of the flood plain.

Discussion and Conclusions

In the Dibsi area, during the Late Quaternary, the cross-profile of the Euphrates Valley evolved from a gentle symmetrical shape to the markedly assymetric section which it shows today. The earlier form still remains along the gently sloping northern edge of the valley, which is eroded by only slightly incised wadis whose fill grades, with no sign of frequent truncation, into the modern flood plain. Here, the flood plain, not having been reworked by the Euphrates, appears to have had sufficient time to build up around sites: whereas, in marked contrast, along the southern edge of the valley, archaeological sites as well as fans, debris-slopes and flood plains have frequently been truncated or removed.

An examination of processes now operating has shown that the constant reworking of slope debris and fans has kept both slope-profiles and wadis rejuvenated. Judging from the remains of archaeological sites, this process has prevailed throughout the last 2000 years and, by inference, must have continued, with occasional lapses, through the late Pleistocene, during which time it has enabled the south-bank wadis to maintain their incision and head-cutting. The examples of cut and fill associated with these periodic rejuvenations are not synchronous in different wadis, but depend upon the shifting course of the river, and consequently, as Wright (1960) suggests for smaller gullies, these cycles are not controlled by climate. In fact, indices of palaeohydrology are limited to specific deposits such as the "wadi-bed conglomerate", which demonstrate changes from time to time in the water table.

It is apparent from the geomorphic record that large gaps occur in the alluvial sequence of both the wadis and the main valley, but, judging from the present position of the river, the past alluvial heritage, and the general morphology of the terrain, it appears that the present southward bias in erosion by the Euphrates prevailed for much of the Late Quaternary. This is only conspicuous, however, between Meskene and Abu Houreira and it is suggested here that such long-term trends in the movements of rivers may have influenced the distribution of ancient sites, for example those mapped by Van Loon (1967) *et al.*, as well as the location and subsequent removal of water supply systems and ancient cultivated land.

Acknowledgements

I would like to warmly thank: R. P. Harper (Director of Dibsi Faraj excavations, and Dumbarton Oaks, Washington) for giving me the opportunity to perform this study; David Williams (Institute of Archaeology, London) who excavated the Wadi el Safa site; Richard and Vivienne Anderson who took kite-photographs of the same site; as well as: Peter Furley and Rafik Zouzou (Department of Geography, University of Edinburgh), Andrew Moore (Director) and Neil Roberts (excavator), both of Abu Houreira excavations and Claudio Vita-Finzi (Department of Geography, University College, London) who all commented and gave encouragement during the process of writing this chapter.

Notes

1. Flood-plain gradients were around 1:2000–1:3000 whilst channel sinuosity (Leopold *et al.*, 1964) varied from 1·2–1·4.

2. According to Wolman and Leopold (1957) ". . . A flood plain becomes a terrace when the channel incises itself to the point where the former active flood plain is no longer over topped by that annual flood which on average occurs less than once every two years".

In this case, although sedimentation, not incision, has put these surfaces out of reach they are still terraces within the above definition.

3. The surface within this old valley system possessed a "rain" of flint artefacts including many of the Levalloisian/Mousterian industry.

4. These were well rolled and have eluded exact diagnosis, but appear to be late pre-historic or early historic.

5. No artefacts were found.

References

Allen, J. R. J. 1965. A review of the origin and characteristics of recent alluvial sediments. *Sedimentology* **5**, 89–191.

Butzer, K. W. 1959. Recent Nile deposits. *G.J.* **125**.

Butzer, K. W. and Hansen, C. L. 1968. *Desert and River in Nubia.* Wisconsin: University of Wisconsin Press.

de Heinzelin, J. 1967. Investigations on the terraces of the middle Euphrates. *In* (Van Loon, 1967). See below.

Higgs, E. S. and Vita-Finzi, C. 1972. Prehistoric economies: a territorial approach. *In: Papers in Economic Prehistory* (E. S. Higgs, Ed.), pp. 27–36, Cambridge.

Ionides, M. G. 1937. *The Regime of the Rivers Euphrates and Tigris.* London: Spon Ltd.

Leopold, L. B., Wolman, M. G. and Miller, J. P. 1964. *Fluvial Processes in Geomorphology.* London: Freeman and Co.

Miller, H. 1883. Methods and results of river terracing. *Proc. Phys. Soc. Edin.* **7**; also 1970. *In: Rivers and River Terraces* (G. H. Dury, Ed.), pp. 19–36, London: Macmillan.

Van Liere, W. J. 1960. Observations on the Quaternary of Syria. *In: Berichten van de Rijksdienst voor het Oudheidkundig bodemonderzoek,* 10–11.

Van Loon, M. 1967. The Tabqa reservoir survey, 1964. *Annales Archaeol. Arabes Syriennes.* Damascus.

Wolman, M. G. and Leopold, L. B. 1957. *Flood plains.* U.S. Geol. Surv., Prof. Paper 282–C.; also 1970. *In: Rivers and River Terraces* (G. H. Dury, Ed.) pp. 166–197. London: Macmillan.

Wright, H. E. 1960. Climate and prehistoric man in the eastern Mediterranean. *In: Prehistoric Investigations in Iraqi Kurdistan* (Braidwood, R. T. and Howe, B.), pp. 71–97. Chicago: University of Chicago Press.

14
The Holocene Geological History of the Tigris-Euphrates-Karun Delta

Curtis E. Larsen and Graham Evans

Introduction

The geomorphology, Quaternary stratigraphy and Holocene development of the Tigris–Euphrates–Karun delta are very poorly known. It is often surprising for the modern research worker to discover that much more is known about these aspects of many other deltas in the world which lack the detailed historical record available for this region.

The delta certainly attracted attention in the early nineteenth century. The appearance of Lyell's *Elements of Geology* (1839) led to some early studies. Petroleum exploration in the Mesopotamian plain produced new data during the 1940s and 1950s. But, other than a few suggestive reports about changes in the form of the delta very little was learned about the importance of the various processes that produced its present form.

This paper is an attempt to summarize research on the Tigris–Euphrates–Karun delta during the last century and to present an up-to-date view of its Holocene history. Although the geology of the area is poorly known, research in the adjacent Persian Gulf and a re-examination of the older data make it necessary to attempt a fresh interpretation of the existing information.

Early Studies

Classical research opened the question of the growth of the delta in Holocene times. Charles Beke presented a series of articles between 1834 and 1839 which claimed that the front of the delta had prograded from a point 640 km inland to its present position (Beke, 1834a, b; 1835a, b; 1836; 1839). These changes were thought to have taken place in the period following the "Deluge". The amount of progradation since 325 B.C. was calculated by accepting the validity of Pliny's accounts of Nearchus's voyage northward through the Persian Gulf to rendezvous with Alexander (Plinius Secundus, translation by P. Holland (1634)). (Recorded distances used for this estimate had been originally measured in *stadia*.) Beke argued that, if the delta had grown a known amount since the time of Nearchus, the position of the shoreline before the "Deluge" could also be calculated by extrapolation, and concluded that it had then lain north of Baghdad. This view did not go unchallenged: Carter (1834a, b; 1835a, b) was quick to note that there was a potential error in determining a modern length for the Greek *stadion*. On the basis of other interpretations, he argued that there had been little if any change in the position of the shoreline since Nearchus's time.

Neither of these earlier writers had first-hand knowledge of the Mesopotamian region, and it was not until 1838 when Ainsworth (1838) presented reports of geologic reconnaissance in southern Mesopotamia that this became available. He too discussed the accounts of Nearchus's voyage, but he produced some geomorphological observations to substantiate his views. He claimed that deltaic progradation had occurred, but to an amount far less than that claimed by Beke, and suggested that there had been as much as 112 km of growth since the time of the "Deluge" (judged to be at the beginnings of recorded history, between 4000 and 5000 years ago). These early studies had thus started an argument which was to continue and which is revived in this short article.

Following these earlier suggestions, little was written on the development of the delta until De Morgan (1900) discussed the accounts of Nearchus and to these added some geographical evidence from reports of Sennacharib's expedition against Elam in 696 B.C.: De Morgan also presented a map showing the supposed position of the earlier shorelines of the delta (Fig. 1). Once again, however, there had been neither detailed geomorphological nor geological research on the deposits of the area to substantiate the conclusions.

In the period following World War II the topic of delta progradation appeared once again: a map was included in a popular archaeological book showing a 6000–7000 B.P. shoreline for the Persian Gulf which was located in the vicinity of Baghdad and Samarra (Lloyd, 1947). The original ideas of Beke had obviously not been challenged seriously enough during

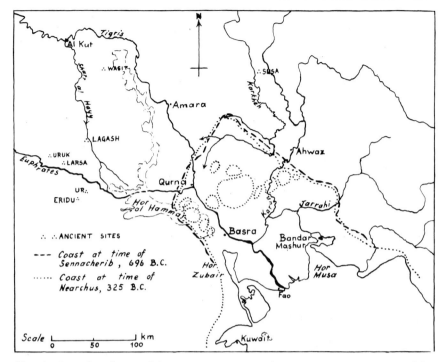

Fig. 1: Past shorelines of the Mesopotamian Delta Region as reconstructed by De Morgan (1900).

the preceding century to produce any marked divergence from his earlier assertions.

Such a challenge, however, came eventually from Lees and Falcon (1952) who broke with tradition and presented a new (and subsequently widely accepted) interpretation of the evolution of the area, based primarily on modern geomorphological and geological evidence; these authors stressed particularly the evidence of recent tectonic activity. They claimed correctly that changes in the delta had been far more complex than had been assumed by earlier workers, and moreover they made the important assertion that the idea of a simple delta which had accumulated Samarra to the present shoreline was untenable. In addition, they directed criticism at Woolley's (1938) evidence for the "Deluge" at Ur, which had been based on evidence for the deposition of 2·7 to 3·7 m of clay and silt at c. 1 m above sea-level between a lower archaeological horizon of Ubaid age (7000–5400 B.P.) and an upper of the Uruk period (5400–5100 B.P.).

They described the Mesopotamian alluvial plain as a tectonically active synclinorium undergoing subsidence coupled with simultaneous minor uplift along small, superimposed anticlinal areas. The high gravel terraces in the Zagros Mountains and along the coastal plain of the Persian Gulf were considered to be the result of major orogenic episodes recorded in the Iranian Mountains. These terrace systems were seen as evidence of periodic uplift.

Similar events were thought to account for special features of the observed landforms in the delta region. The first of these was the apparent longevity of marsh areas south of Amara. Lees and Falcon (1952) contended that sedimentation from the Tigris–Euphrates would have filled these areas were it not for this continued subsidence. Woolley's Deluge deposit and alluvium of similar age near Dar-i-Khazineh in Khuzistan were also considered to provide stratigraphic evidence for recent subsidence. Lees and Falcon also noted that ancient Sassanian (A.D. 220–640) or Abbasid (A.D. 758–1258) irrigation canals had been inundated by the waters of the adjacent Gulf in the estuaries of Khor Musa and Khor Zubair. Again these features were explained as the result of subsidence due to tectonic activity. They reported sediments containing marine and estuarine faunas which were found beneath the surface of the delta region as far inland as Amara. These were considered to represent a local marine inundation produced by tectonic downwarping. Lees and Falcon then went on to add, on the basis of undated lacustrine silts underlying alluvium located further inland, that there was no evidence of a marine transgression into the region of the Mesopotamian plains since the Pliocene. In addition, they claimed that there was no evidence for appreciable progradation of the delta. Instead they thought that there had been a delicately balanced system of subsidence and sedimentation.

Recent tectonism in the Mesopotamian plain continued to be discussed by later researchers: Mitchell (1958) for example, in a description of some of the structural features of the Mesopotamian plain noted deposits containing other recent marine faunas as far inland as Najaf. However, whilst he considered tectonic activity, he also called attention to the possibility that Pleistocene sea-levels higher than the present could have been responsible for the Recent marine faunas. Deposits containing possibly related faunas were also reported by Voûte (1957) from even further inland in the Abu Dibbis depression at approximately 25 m above sea-level. Lees and Falcon had been aware of these faunas, but had considered them to be relict forms living in a brackish lake. The theory of continual subsidence also affected the archaeological interpretations; thus Raikes (1966) suggested that the Deluge deposits at Ur indicated a marine incursion induced by subsidence.

Environmental Background

Subsidence due to regional tectonics is only one of the environmental variables that affect deltaic landforms (Thom, 1975). Eustatic fluctuations of sea-level, climatic and subsequent hydrologic changes, as well as cultural interference with the natural processes, are some of the factors that may have been as important, or even more important, in some areas. The geographical features observed in the Mesopotamian plains and the Tigris—Euphrates—Karun delta are undoubtedly the result of an interplay of a variety of such factors.

Subsidence and Regional Tectonics

The alluvial plains of Iraq occupy a structural trough, the origin of which is related to active orogenic processes in the Zagros Mountains of Iran. Compressional forces, resulting from crustal spreading along the Red Sea rift system, have brought about both the formation of the trough and the development of the folded and faulted areas of the Zagros (Haynes and McQuillan, 1974). During its development, this down-warped area has received the erosion products of the bordering mountain ranges. Folding has continued since the Late Tertiary and may still be active, as suggested by the persistence and frequency of seismic events in Iran (Al-Naquib, 1967; Nowroozi, 1972; McQuillan, 1973). The Persian Gulf occupies the seaward extension of the same down-warped area. However, the Arabian shore of the Gulf, although possibly an area of minor local movement, is now regarded as a relatively stable shelf (Sarnthein, 1972; Kassler, 1973).

Evidence for Quaternary Eustatic Sea-levels

Studies from the Mediterranean have furnished evidence for multiple interglacial sea-levels during the Pleistocene as high as 30–100 m above the present. Fairbridge (1961) presented alternative compilations of data for the Pleistocene, which involved three extended periods of higher sea-level. The first alternative presented a correlation with the three supposed major Interglacial periods of the Pleistocene, so that these postulated high sea-levels were shown to decrease in elevation from the "Günz/Mindel" (+ 100 m), through the "Mindel/Riss" (+ 30–40 m), to the "Riss/Würm" (+ 2–12 m). The second alternative presented the same three major high sea-levels on a compressed time scale. More precise dating of Pleistocene events since 1961 has led to the revision of both of these possibilities. Butzer, for example, showed an at least fivefold division of high sea-levels at similar elevations, but related to events which have occurred since 400,000 B.P. (Butzer, 1974).

Although any world-wide correlation of sea-level is hazardous, the possible occurrence of highs similar to those in the Mediterranean would have vastly influenced the Mesopotamian plains. In Qatar, on the east coast of the Arabian peninsula, marine deposits collected from sites above present sea-level indicate higher Quaternary sea-levels (Vita-Finzi, in press). Raised beaches have been reported from adjacent coastlines as well as from the Arabian and Iranian shores of the Gulf (Snead, 1969; Powers et al., 1963). These, in conjunction with the deposits containing marine fossils from Najaf (Mitchell, 1958) and Abu Dibbis (Voûte, 1957), make it extremely likely that major marine transgressions extended into the Mesopotamian plains during the Pleistocene.

A low sea-level has been proven for the Late Pleistocene by both Sarnthein (1972) and Kassler (1973): the former discussed submerged aeolian dunes on the floor of the Gulf at depths up to -100 m; and the latter has noted submerged erosional terraces from depths of -5 m to -125 m. In addition, Kassler has collected oolitic sand samples from the entrance of the Persian Gulf which indicate sea-levels around 73–83 m below present between 21,000–18,000 B.P. A marine transgression, dated from relict shallow water carbonate sediments, appears to have begun at approximately 18,000 B.P. and continued to rise rapidly until 7000 B.P. Sea-level then began to stabilize near -10 m.

A dated stratigraphic sequence for the Trucial Coast of Arabia has demonstrated that a rise of sea-level occurred from 7000 B.P. to 4000 B.P., during which time the sea transgressed over aeolian sands which were reworked by wave action and were then covered with marine calcareous sediments as the transgression continued inland (Evans et al., 1969) to terminate in a shelly beach ridge. This ridge marks the attainment of the near present stand, although several authors have argued from evidence elsewhere that present sea-level was not attained until 1000 to 2000 B.P. (Shepard, 1963; Scholl et al., 1969). The height of this ridge indicates that sea-level may have been approximately $+1$ m above that of today. The possibility exists, of course, that this slightly varied feature may have been due to greater exposure of the coast before the build-up of the barrier islands which protect it. However, unpublished work by one of the writers and colleagues has shown similar but still undated deposits, at similar levels in Bahrain; so that a slightly higher relative sea-level in the Holocene now seems very probable.

Climate

Iraq lies within the Saharo-Arabian desert belt, which, modified by topography, extends across Arabia and into the alluvial plains of the lower Tigris and Euphrates, the lower Iranian coastal plain, and the deserts of northwestern India (Rumney, 1968). The catchments of the Tigris and Euphrates, however, are located in the eastern extension of the Mediterranean scrub woodland zone. These differences are significant in interpreting changes in the delta region. This is best shown in Table I which displays conspicuous gradients for both temperature and precipitation along the section from Erzurum to Basra. The statistics evidently imply substantial evaporation in lowland Mesopotamia.

Table I: Temperature and precipitation

Averages of maximum daily temperature		Average monthly precipitation	
Annual	Warmest month (August)	Wettest month	Driest month
		inches	
Erzurum 53°F	80°F	3·1	0·9
Mosul 82°F	110°F	3·1	<0·1
Baghdad 87°F	110°F	1·1	<0·1
Basra 87°F	105°F	1·4	<0·1

In summer, dust storms become severe; they are most common in southern Iraq and at the head of the Persian Gulf and are apparently due to semi-permanent low pressure over the Gulf which draws hot, dry winds across the alluvial plains. Vast quantities of aeolian sediment are brought into the region and also further south into the areas covered by the Persian Gulf (Kukal and Saadallah, 1973). This material must have made and undoubtedly still makes a substantial contribution to sedimentation in both areas, although at present it is not possible to measure how much. The variability of climate throughout the Holocene is unfortunately not known for this area, although it obviously has been of considerable importance, not least for the availability and supply of sediment and the rate of evaporation.

Hydrological Influences

Three rivers are largely responsible for the accumulation of the alluvial plains of Iraq: the Tigris, Euphrates and Karun. They unite near Basra to form the Shatt al-Arab which is their combined outlet to the Persian Gulf. The Euphrates is the westernmost river and has headwaters in western Turkey; the Tigris has its headwaters in eastern Turkey, but many of its tributaries originate from the mountain country of Iran just to the east. The Karun is the shortest of the three, with a drainage network entirely in the Zagros Mountains of Iran.

The Tigris and Euphrates at present carry a high concentration of dissolved salts as well as detrital sediment. (See Phillip, 1968; Berry *et al.*, 1970 for details of the detrital load.) These salts appear as evaporites in the sediments in this arid region. In combination with the deposition of sediment due to evaporation of the river waters the Tigris discharges water and detrital sediment into marsh areas and irrigation networks between Baghdad and Amara and these areas receive some 85% of the mean annual discharge noted below the Diyala River. Of a discharge of 27 km^3 into the Gulf through the Shatt al-Arab, 22 km^3 are supplied by the Karun and only 5 km^3 can be attributed to the Tigris and Euphrates. The original water-supply from precipitation totals 325 km^3, but much of this is lost through evaporation and irrigation before the delta region below Amara is reached (Cressey, 1958; Ubell, 1971).

Geological Evidence from the Delta Region

The Recent marine and estuarine faunas discovered at five localities between Amara and Faó provide a rudimentary basis for the reconstruction of Pleistocene and post-Pleistocene changes in the area. The sediments and their associate faunas from these five localities were cited by Lees and Falcon (1952), but the details did not appear until later (Hudson *et al.*, 1957).

At Amara, at the most landward of the sites, marine foraminifera *Buliminella* sp., *Strebulus* sp., and *Triloculina* sp., were found in borings in deposits at 1–11 m below the present bed of the Tigris (MacFayden, unpublished; cited in Lees and Falcon, 1952). Regrettably, no information is recorded regarding the sediments in which this fauna was found. Furthermore, the Recent time range noted presents difficulties in interpretation.

To the southeast, two petroleum wells near the shore of the Hor al-Hammar show other Recent faunas from as much as 12 m below sea level. One of these borings, Zubair No. 31, yielded a more detailed and complete sedimentary record and has been used as the type section for the marine Hammar Formation (Hudson *et al.*, 1957; Al-Naquib, 1967) which has been considered to be Holocene in age.

The above site, Zubair No. 31, is located on the axis of the Zubair Anticline, about 16 km northwest of Zubair, at a surface elevation of 2 m above sea-level. At this locality the upper 6 m of the sequence are composed of buff and reddish silts with the uppermost 1 m containing a high concentration of halite and gypsum. These silts contain ostracods (*Cyprideis littoralis* and *Limnocythere* sp.) from depths of 3–4 m and were thought probably to represent an estuarine environment, whereas the remainder of the deposits, both above and below, were thought to be fluvial or lacustrine in origin (Hudson *et al.*, 1957). At depths of 6–8 m marine clays of the Hammar Formation were found with an echinoid and crab fauna, whilst further below there were 4 m of coarse to very coarse, well sorted, marine sand which has been also included in the Hammar Formation. Some sand samples suggest an aeolian contribution to this deposit. The fossils which are common in the Hammar Formation are the lamellibranchs *Pitar belcheri*, *Brachidontes variabilis*, *Corbula sulculosa*, and *Abra cadabra*; the gastropods *Miniolia edyma* and *Hindia idyllis* are also present.

Below the Hammar Formation lie 6 m of sand and gravel, with silty interbeds, described as the Miocene Dibdibba Formation by Hudson *et al.* (1957). (These are at present dated as Miocene–Pleistocene.) The uppermost 0·5 m of this unit is a buff clay with halite and gypsum which was thought to represent a former land surface.

A second site which provided deposits containing a good fauna is located at Nahr Umr No. 2, due north of Zubair No. 31 on the north shore of the Hor al-Hammar. At this location 26 m of Recent sediments were encountered before the Dibdibba Formation was reached. The top 11 m consist of alluvium and aeolian sands with selenite crystals and below this are 10 m of a marine marl with a fauna similar to that of the Hammar Formation which suggests correlation with that unit. The deposits between 11–15 m are of doubtful origin although Hudson *et al.* (1957) seem to have thought them to be of freshwater origin. The lowest unit described consists of 6 m of siltstone and gravelly sandstone which was identified as being the Dibdibba Formation.

In addition, MacFayden (in Lees and Falcon, 1952) reported both estuarine and marine faunas from a boring at Qarmat Ali, near Basra: here a mixture of freshwater and marine faunas was present at 1 m and 5 m below ground level. Distinctly marine faunas were identified in sediments from 3, 17 and 20 m.

A few water wells drilled to depths of 9 m, in the vicinity of Fao, revealed up to 6 m of estuarine silt and as much as 9 m of marine silt, overlying 3 m of a more consolidated silt with freshwater gastropods together with some marine forms which resembled those found in the Hammar Formation.

In addition to these records a sedimentary sequence (60 m in thickness) was reported by Thomas for the Bandar Mashur area (quoted in Lees and Falcon, 1952). This showed 6 m of estuarine silt at the surface, marine and estuarine sediments between 18 and 24 m, and marine sediments at 37 m. A profile showing these borings is given in Fig. 2. The lack of detailed stratigraphic relationships and a general shortage of information makes anything other than a general correlation difficult.

Discussion

Hudson et al. (1957) considered that the marine sediments found beneath the present delta indicated local subsidence rather than a regional change in sea-level. Yet it does not appear necessary to invoke recent subsidence to account for the sequences found in these stratigraphic profiles. Instead, the near subsurface stratigraphy shown in Fig. 2 may reasonably be taken to be a marine transgressional sequence formed during the Flandrian Transgression, succeeded by a regressive sequence developed since the sea has attained its approximate present level. As sea-level rose to near present levels or above, it clearly displaced the shoreline inland to the vicinity of or perhaps even further inland than Hor al-Hammar. The coarse marine sand underlying marine clays in Zubair No. 31 most likely represents a nearshore littoral deposit formed by reworking of the Dibdibba Formation on the Zubair Anticline, though they may possibly be due to the encroachment of aeolian sands into marine waters (see for example Shinn, 1973). These, together with the alluvial deposits overlying the Hammar Formation and those seaward of the Hor al-Hammar, can most reasonably be interpreted as having been produced by deltaic progradation to the southeast following the attainment of a sea-level close to the present (c. 4000–5000 B.P.). If this interpretation is correct, it suggests at least 150–180 km of progradation during the last 5000 years.

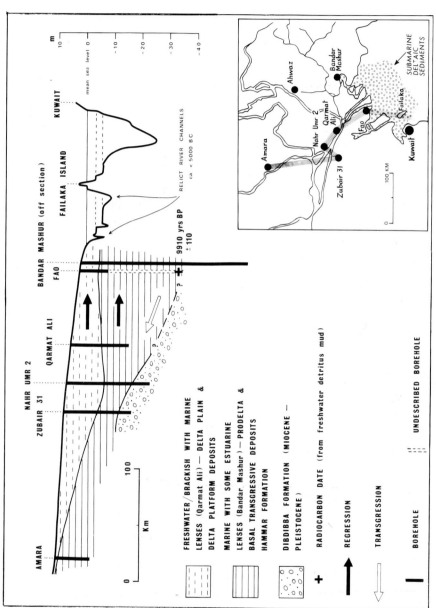

Fig. 2: The stratigraphy of Lower Iraq, from borings.

In any case, new evidence which has appeared since the studies by Lees and Falcon and by Hudson *et al.* makes the claims of rapid tectonic subsidence in the delta unlikely: Kassler (1973), using unpublished oil company reports by V. S. Colter, has noted that deltaic sediments near Kuwait have apparently been deposited on a more or less horizontal surface 35 m below sea-level (Kassler, 1973). This surface is of a similar depth to a − 34 m to − 36 m marine platform that can be traced from Abu Dhabi to Kuwait and which has been tentatively dated as 9000 to 11,000 B.P. (See the date quoted below from Godwin *et al.*, 1958, on the age of a freshwater detritus mud from approximately this level.) The regional continuity of this surface indicates that only limited or minor post-Pleistocene crustal movement has occurred below the delta. A similar interpretation has been advanced by Sarnthein (1972). The profile in Fig. 2 shows bathymetry, based on US Naval Oceanographic Office Chart 62340 (scale 1:350,000), and points to the presence of two shallow, potentially younger submerged platforms at − 3 m and − 5 m. Both could be features cut into marine and estuarine sediments of the Hammar Formation, if they are not merely depositional surfaces. A platform at a similar level of − 5 m can be traced all the way from Abu Dhabi to Kuwait (Kassler, 1973). Using Kassler's dating criteria (based on the sea-level curve of Fairbridge, 1961), these two platforms could be younger than 7000 B.P. What is more important, their apparent continuity indicates no major tectonic movement in the delta during the Holocene. Some apparent contradictory evidence was presented by Colter (Kassler, 1973) in the form of radiocarbon dates obtained from oyster shells in a marine mud at − 37 m offshore from Kuwait which vary in age from 5080 to 5980 B.P.; these were claimed to indicate shallow-water conditions, but Kassler has disputed this interpretation because of the lack of shallow-water sedimentary structures in the associated sediment and has consequently argued that this evidence is inconclusive.

But perhaps the single most important evidence that the Tigris–Euphrates–Karun delta has not been a site of Holocene tectonic subsidence is that a freshwater detritus mud, which is thought to have formed in a freshwater marsh area close to contemporary sea-level, collected from − 32 m at Fao, has yielded an age of 9910 (± 110) years B.P. When the depth of this sample is plotted against age it falls almost exactly on the curve derived from dates from the Southern Baltic and the Gulf of Mexico which is thought to give the eustatic rise in sea-level (Godwin *et al.*, 1958; Godwin and Willis, 1959). In contrast, the data from other areas of known tectonic downwarp such as the Netherlands, or other deltaic regions such as the Niger (Allen and Wells, 1962), give values which fall below this curve, i.e. they are anomalously deep for their age.

Conclusion

This essay has reviewed two basic ideas which have been alternately in favour—of substantial growth as against insignificant growth of the Tigris–Euphrates–Karun delta during the Holocene. More detailed appreciation of the geological conditions during the Holocene is not possible at present due partly to incomplete investigation, partly to delay in the publication of work that has been done, but perhaps most of all to our inadequate understanding of recent tectonism, sea-level change, and the development of deltas.

The independent works of Sarnthein (1972) and Kassler (1973) from both the Iranian and Arabian portions of the adjacent Persian Gulf have noted the absence of any evidence of major tectonic movements during the Late Pleistocene and Holocene; although, of course, local subsidence due to compaction has undoubtedly occurred. Further, these and other researchers, as we have seen, have documented the history of the Flandrian Transgression in the Gulf. In view of the apparent absence of major tectonic movements, shifts of sea-level must evidently have played a paramount rôle in the shaping of the coastal landforms of the area.

Since the attainment of a near-modern sea-level approximately 5000 years ago, 150 to 200 km of progradation have almost certainly taken place. The exact area covered by the original transgression is unknown. It remains for future researchers to collect and describe subsurface information in order to ascertain the extent of the Hammar Formation and related deposits. What is perhaps more important, it will be necessary to obtain precise chronological control through radiocarbon dating of stratigraphic sequences. A detailed sedimentological study of the character and history of this interesting area is long overdue.

There is nevertheless still much to be gained by a re-examination of historic records. The Sumerians for example, have left ample accounts that portray themselves as a people living on or near the sea (Jacobsen, 1960; Falkenstein, 1951). The cities of Ur and Eridu (Fig. 1) are historically linked with the sea, yet now lie as much as 100 km from the present shoreline. The position of the various archaeological sites of this period may provide extremely useful evidence in delimiting the extent of alluviation since 5000 B.P.

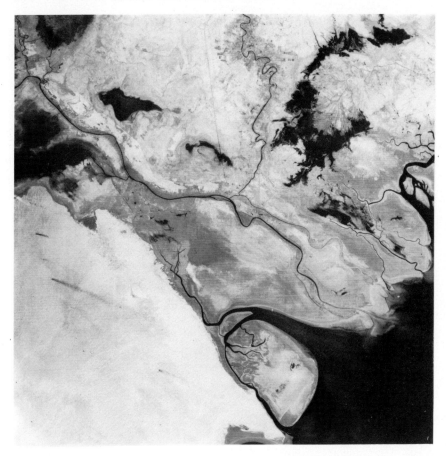

Fig. 3a: Satellite picture of the head of the Gulf taken on 23 December 1972. Depressions are waterlogged and show up well at this season, especially around the outer margins of the "bird's foot" delta of the Jarrāhi River. This delta seems to have been built out into a former extension of the Gulf.

The detailed understanding of the development of the Holocene Tigris–Euphrates–Karun delta will be difficult. The present deltaic landforms are the results of the interplay of many processes. Erosional and depositional events have been established by Lees and Falcon (1952) and these can be compared with the historic record of possible swamp encroachment in southern Iraq (Adams and Nissen, 1972).

Each of these variables can be expected to have affected significantly the morphology of the delta. Climatic changes have undoubtedly produced fluctuations in sediment-load brought to the delta through varying runoff.

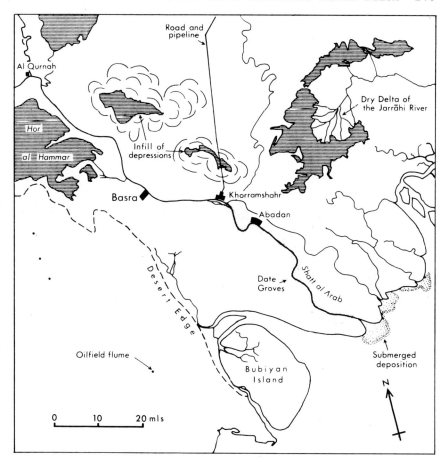

Fig. 3b: Guide-trace to accompany Fig. 3a.

Thus Melguen (1973) showed a marked growth of a small Iranian delta during the Holocene in response to changing climatic conditions. Any fluctuation of sea-level will have affected the régimes of the various rivers, albeit near their mouths, and have caused local incision or alluviation. In addition, the local compaction of deltaic sediments should be considered as a possible factor in any observed subsidence. Local transgressions produced by shifts of river mouths, accompanied by continued compaction, are well known from deltaic areas that have been intensively studied (see Evans, 1973, for review). Also, the effects of cultural changes along the various river systems are of obvious importance. It is known that present irrigation projects in Iraq have influenced severely both runoff and sedimentation (Ubell, 1971). At the same time, Mesopotamia is known to have a 5000-year history of irrigation through projects of various magnitudes, and these must certainly be considered as a factor in the interpretation of delta morphology.

Information on the importance of these several factors is only beginning to be collected from the Gulf region. A detailed knowledge of local palaeoclimates, for example, does not exist, although Holocene sea-levels are better understood. There is still much to be learned from the archaeological and historical records of Mesopotamia. The extent of compaction also is unknown. Finally, the effects of tectonic movements must be re-examined to ascertain their real role in the delta region. Multidisciplinary efforts by geologists, archaeologists and engineers must be directed toward this end if this region, which is of such great importance in historical studies, is ever to be completely understood. It is hoped that this brief review and reassessment will act as a catalyst for more work in this region.

References

Adams, R. McC. and Nissen, H. J. 1972. *The Uruk Countryside*. Chicago: University of Chicago Press.

Ainsworth, W. 1838. *Researches in Assyria, Babylonia, and Chaldea*. London: John W. Parker.

Allen, J. R. L. and Wells, J. W. 1962. *J. Geol.* **70**, 381–397.

Al-Naquib, K, M. 1967. *Geology of the Arabian Peninsula—South western Iraq*, U.S. Geol. Surv. Prof. Paper 560–G, Washington.

Beke, C. T. 1834a. *London and Edinburgh Phil. Mag. and J. Sci.* Ser. 3, 4, 107–112.

Beke, C. T. 1834b. *London and Edinburgh Phil. Mag. and J. Sci.* Ser. 3, 7, 280–282.

Beke, C. T. 1835a. *London and Edinburgh Phil. Mag. and J. Sci.* Ser. 3, 6, 401–408.

Beke, C. T. 1835b. *London and Edinburgh Phil. Mag. and J. Sci.* Ser. 3, 7, 40–46.

Beke, C. T. 1836. *London and Edinburgh Phil. Mag. and J. Sci.* Ser. 3, 8, 506–515.

Beke, C. T. 1839. *London and Edinburgh Phil. Mag. and J. Sci.* Ser. 3, 14, 426–432.

Berry, R. W., Brophy, G. P. and Naqash, A. 1970. *J. Sedim. Petrol.* **40**, 131–139.

Butzer, K. W. 1974. In: *After the Australopithecines: Time, Ecology, and Culture in the Middle Pleistocene* (K. W. Butzer and G. Isaac, Eds), The Hague: Mouton.

Butzer, K. W. and Hansen, C. L. 1968. *Desert and River in Nubia*. Madison: University of Wisconsin Press.

Carter, W. G. 1834a. *London and Edinburgh Phil. Mag. and J. Sci.* Ser. 3, 4, 178–182.

Carter, W. G. 1834b. *London and Edinburgh Phil. Mag. and J. Sci.* Ser. 3, 5, 244–252.

Carter, W. G. 1835. *London and Edinburgh Phil. Mag. and J. Sci.* Ser. 3, 7, 192–202.

Carter, W. G. 1835b. *London and Edinburgh Phil. Mag. and J. Sci.* Ser. 3, 7, 250–256.

Cressey, G. B. 1958. *Middle East J.* **12**, 448–460.

De Morgan, J. 1900. *Délégation en Perse* **I**, 1–32.

Evans, G. 1973. In: *Marine Archaeology Proc. of 23rd Colston Research Society.* (D. J. Blackman, Ed.) pp. 89–114. London: Butterworth.

Evans, G., Schmidt, V., Bush, P. and Nelson, H. 1969. *Sedimentology* **12**, 145–159.

Falkenstein, A. 1951. *Sumer.* **7**, 121–122.

Fairbridge, R. W. 1961. In: *Physics and Chemistry of the Earth.* (L. Ahrens, Ed.), Vol. 4, pp. 99–185.

Godwin, H. and Willis, E. H. 1959. *Am. J. Sci. Radiocarbon Suppl.* **1**, 63–75.

Godwin, H., Suggate, R. P. and Willis, E. H. 1958. *Nature* **181**, 1518–1519.

Haynes, S. J. and McQuillan, H. 1974. *Bull. Geol. Soc. Am.* **85**, 739–744.

Hudson, R. G. S., Eames, F. E. and Wilkins, G. L. 1957. *Geol. Mag.* **94**, 395–398.

Jacobsen, T. 1960. *Iraq* **22**, 184–185.

Kapel, H. 1969. *Atlas of the Stone Age Cultures of Qatar.* Aarhus University Press.

Kassler, P. 1973. In: *The Persian Gulf.* (B. H. Purser, Ed.), pp. 11–32. Berlin: Springer.

Kukal, Z. and Saadallah. 1973. In: *The Persian Gulf.* (B. H. Purser, Ed.), pp. 179–122. Berlin: Springer.

Larsen, C. E. 1975. *J. Am. Ori. Soc.* **95**, 43–57.

Lees, G. M. and Falcon, N. L. 1952. *Geog. J.* **118**, 24–39.

Lloyd, S. 1947. *Foundations in the Dust.* London: Penguin.

Lyell, C. 1839. *Elements of Geology.* Philadelphia: Kay.

McQuillan, H. 1973. *Geol. Mag.* **110**, 243–248.

Melguen, M. 1973. In: *The Persian Gulf.* (B. H. Purser, Ed.), pp. 99–113. Berlin: Springer.

Mitchell, R. 1958. *Bull. Soc. Geog. Egypte* **3**, 127–139.

Nowroozi, A. A. 1972. *Seismol. Soc. Am. Bull.* **62**, 823–850.

Phillip, G. 1968. *J. Sedim. Petrol.* **38**, 35–44.

Plinius Secundus, C. 1634. *The Historie of the World.* (Trans. by P. Holland). London: A. Islip.

Powers, R. W., Ramirez, C. D., Redmond, C. D. and Elsberg, E. L. 1963. *Geology of the Arabian Peninsula: Sedimentary Geology of Saudi Arabia.* U.S. Geol. Surv. Prof. Paper 560–D, Washington.

Raikes, R. L. 1966. *Iraq* **28**, 52–63.

Rumney, G. R. 1968. *Climatology and the World's Climates.* New York: MacMillan.

Sarnthein, M. 1972. *Marine Geol.* **12**, 245–266.

Scholl, D. W., Stuiver, M. and Craighead, F. C. 1969. *Florida Submergence Curve Revisted:* its relation to coastal sedimentation rates, *Science* **163**, 562–564.

Shepard, F. P. 1963. *Submarine Geology.* New York: Harper.

Shinn, E. 1973. *In: The Persian Gulf.* (B. H. Purser, Ed.), pp. 199–211. Berlin: Springer.

Snead, R. 1969. *Physical Geography Reconnaissance: West Pakistan Coastal Zone,* Univ. of New Mexico Pub. in Geog. 1, Albuquerque.

Thom, B. G. 1975. *Zeit. Geomorph.* **22**, 144–170.

Ubell, K. 1971. *Nature and Resources* **7**, 3–9.

Vita-Finzi, C. (in press). *In: Archaeological Survey of Qatar* (B. de Cardi, Ed.).

Voûte, C. 1957. *Sumer.* **33**, 1–14.

Woolley, C. L. 1938. *Ur of the Chaldees,* pp. 18–21. London: Pelican Books.

15
The Marine Terraces of the Bay of Kuwait

Taiba Al-Asfour

The Field-Work

Sea-level changes along the north coast of Kuwait Bay have been investigated with reference to the coastal terraces in the areas of Kathma, Ghidhai, Mudairah and Al-Bahra (Figs 1, 2). "Staircase" topography has been observed everywhere between the Jal az-Zor escarpment and the present coastline. In some cases, the terraces are clearly continuous for long distances, while in others they are represented by isolated fragments.

Three methods of investigation were adopted:

a. levelling

b. radiocarbon dating of shells

c. sediment analysis, including particle-size measurement and electron-scanning microscopy.

It emerged from the programme of levelling that the area as a whole has been considerably affected by structural deformation since the terraces were formed, and that this has resulted in a general tilting downwards from west to east (Fig. 3).

The C^{14} dating results fall into two main groups. The first, from the higher terraces (1–5), ranges between > 42,950 years B.P. and 23,300 ± 600 years B.P. The highest sample in Ghidhai, from an elevation of 63 m above sea-level, gave a date of 28,350 ± 1150 years B.P. The second group of samples, from the lowest terraces in the Mudairah and Al-Bahra areas, has a maximum age of 4570 ± 70 years B.P. and a minimum of 3,250 ± 80 years B.P.

In general, the conclusion of the work on sediment analysis is that the fluvial environment is represented mainly on the top of the escarpment, and on the First, Second and parts of the Third terrace. The aeolian environment is the most difficult one to separate from the other two and is represented everywhere, especially in the middle zone. The marine-beach environment is mainly represented on the present beach as well as on the Fourth terrace, especially in Kathma, Ghidhai and Mudairah. It is represented also by material on the Sixth, Fifth and Fourth terraces in Al-Bahra.

The combined results of the three methods of investigation indicate that all the terraces were formed by sea-level changes, and that the First, Second and probably the Third terraces also experienced freshwater action.

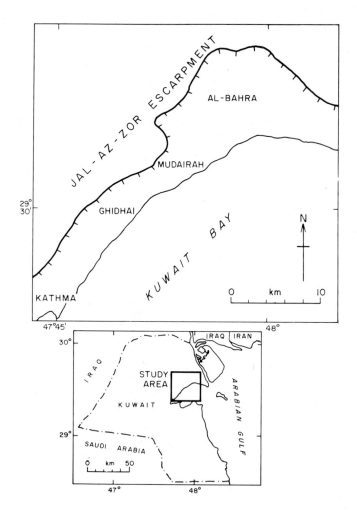

Fig. 1: Location map, Kuwait

Fig. 2: The marine terraces along the north side of the Bay of Kuwait.

	W						E
Location / Terrace Number	*Kathma I*	*Kathma II*	*Ghidhai*	*Mudairah*	*Al-Bahra I*	*Al-Bahra II*	*Al-Bahra III*
1	91	82	93	71	80		
2	78	70	79	60	56	64	
3	67		65*	52	40	48	
4	51	41	53	31	32 ?	39	33
5			34		22 ?	30	19
6		11	13	12†	16	14†	12/6

* *Dated* 28,350 ± 1150 B.P.   † *Dated* 4,570 ± 70 — 3,250 ± 60 B.P.

Fig. 3: Bay of Kuwait. Terrace heights (in metres), showing the general fall in elevation from West to East. (The correlation is tentative, and editorial. The author suggests that the 11-metre terrace at Kathma 2 may accord with No. 5, and the 33-, 19- and 12-metre levels at Al-Bahra 3 with Nos. 2, 3 and 4 respectively.)

Interpretation and Comparisons

The Gulf is a tectonic basin, formed in Late Pliocene to Pleistocene times, the Iranian coast being aligned by the Zagros orogeny. It is possible that the uplift of the Oman Mountains, which are structurally related to the Zagros, continued well into the Quaternary. Recent investigation has shown that the Musandam Peninsula of Oman is undergoing subsidence, which has amounted during the last 10,000 years to more than 60 metres (Vita-Finzi, 1973).

It has been remarked above that the top three terraces date from the Pleistocene period, and show signs of fluvial action. During the Glacial period, several wadis in the Arabian Peninsula flowed into the sea. Holm (1960) referred to two main rivers, the Nisah-Sahbah which flowed towards the south-east of Qatar, and the Rimah-Wadi al-Batin which extended from Najd and followed the western border of Kuwait until it reached the Tigris-Euphrates Valley. These water-flows were active during the Pluvial periods of the Pleistocene and carried gravels, cobbles and pebbles which were deposited as deltiac material.

The present area of research includes several wadi systems, and although these seem to be smaller in size than those described by other authors in the surrounding area, a general similarity is implied. The west and north of Kuwait, as well as the upper part of the Jal az-Zor escarpment, are covered by fluvial deposits laid down by running water. The remnants of these main channels, represented for example by the Wadi al-Batin, were referred to by Holm (1960) as being active during the Pluvial periods of the Pleistocene; another wadi channel on a smaller scale is the al-Musannat in the south-west of the country. As well as these, several wadi drainage-areas in a variety of shapes cover the north and west of the country, and these river channels and wadis have responded to both climatic and sea-level changes in the area.

How far can the exposed terraces of Kuwait be correlated with other topographical features in the Gulf area which took shape when the sea-level was higher than now? According to Fairbridge (1961), at the end of the Pliocene the level of the sea was about 150 m higher than at present, and Holm (1960) has indicated that inland sabkhas on the coast of Saudi Arabia are found at the same height. The retreat of the sea to its present level left its mark on the coast of the Arabian Gulf in the form of marine terraces, high deltas and inland sabkhas.

Mitchell (1958) described recent marine fauna near Najaf in Iraq at a height of between 40 and 41 m, pointing to possible higher sea-levels during the Pleistocene. Voute (1957) also referred to recent marine fauna in the Abu Dibbis depression, and according to Larsen (1975) a high sea-level of about +25 m would have been necessary in order to connect Abu Dibbis with the sea. These levels are similar to those found for the Fifth terrace in Kuwait; and these heights also fit well with those of the Qatar raised beaches at +25–30 m which were reported by Kapel (1967) to have an age of > 39,800 years. Raised beaches at similar elevation (30 m and higher than 80–90 m) on the Makran coast of Iran were reported by Falcon (1947), who attributed them to uplift. Butzer (1958) later suggested that eustatic changes of sea-level have played a part in the formation of those beaches. He added a 60 m level, and suggested that the whole sequence, including the raised beach of 30 m at Kharag Island, Qishm, and Bushire, corresponded to the altimetric sequence from Sicilian to Monastirian.

The 60-m raised beaches can be followed on the Makran coast as well as on Kharag Island (Butzer, 1958). Glennie's (1970) inland sabkha of Umm as-Samin in Oman suggests a relic of an arm of the sea at a height of less than 70 m, and evidence of similar heights has been reported by Kassler (1973).

So much for the higher exposed terraces. Let us turn now to the post-Pleiocene history of the Gulf, which involves the long process of the Flandrian transgression (Fig. 4). During the Late Würm Glaciation, the sea reached its minimum level of − 100 or − 120 m, and as the maximum depth of the Gulf does not exceed 100 or 110 m near the Strait of Hormuz, it would have then remained a dry basin, except for the flow of the water of the Tigris and Euphrates Rivers. Sarnthein (1972) believes that the Shatt al-Arab at that time reached the shelf margin in the Gulf of Oman, which at present stands at − 110 m. He observes that, during the post-Glacial transgression, aragonitic sediments, deposited under dry conditions, dominated the north-east area of the Gulf, where they are now covered by calcareous, clayey, terrigenous sediment deposited by Zagros rivers. This suggests that the climate of the Zagros mountains must have been much drier during the transgression than it is today, and the Zagros rivers in consequence less active.

The maximum retreat of sea-level to about − 120 m is recorded by Kassler (1973) from the evidence of an eroded submarine platform in the Gulf of Oman and the Strait of Hormuz, formed while the Gulf floor stayed above the level of the sea. As the sea rose eustatically to a higher level of − 100 m, the Main Würm position according to Fairbridge (1961), it formed (Kassler, 1973) at a depth of − 100 m a submarine platform which extends along the Gulf of Oman as well as inside the

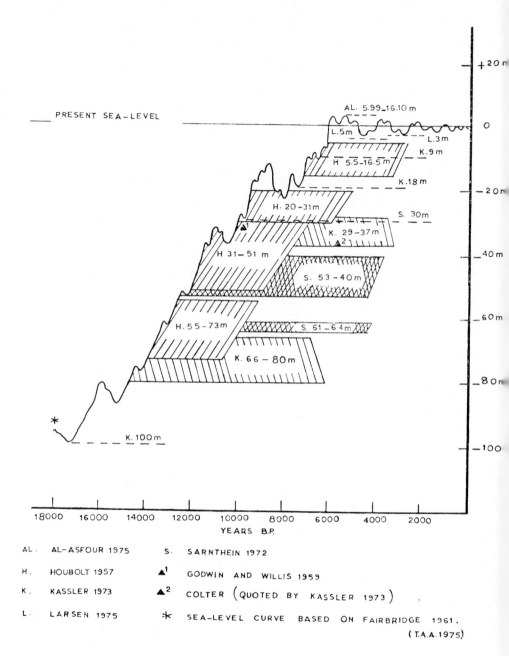

Fig. 4: Tentative correlation of Late Pleistocene and Holocene sea-level changes in the Arabian Gulf.

Arabian Gulf. A rapid rise of sea-level began about 17,000 years B.P., and is marked by the formation of several wide submarine platforms, such as that at −65 m described by Carrigy and Fairbridge (1954) on the stable west coast of Australia. In the Gulf area, it is possible that this coincides with the formation of Kassler's −66 to −80 m platform, and Sarnthein (1972) presented depositional evidence to show transgression still-stands in the Gulf at −64 to −61 m, and −53 to −40 m. This stage in the transgression is indicated by the frosted quartz and ooid concentrations embedded in lithified aragonitic mud, which are interpreted by Sarnthein to be components of drowned sand dunes associated with a fossil ridge-and-trough system of dunes. He correlated his results with those of Van Andel et al. (1967), who described similar formations at the same depths on the Sahul Shelf of Australia. Meanwhile, Sarnthein (1972) believed that at that time the entire Arabian Gulf coastal region attained a morphological maturity, as indicated by the break of slope along the longitudinal profile at a water-depth of approximately 50 m. This corresponds to the "Second offshore terrace" of Houbolt (1957), which occurs at −31 to −51 m.

Houbolt (1957) referred to a submarine terrace, the "First offshore terrace", at −20 to −31 m, which is broadly developed east and north of Qatar, while Kassler (1973) recognized a submarine platform at −29 to −37 m, which he dated from Fairbridge's curve to 11,000–9000 B.P. Kassler would place on this platform the deltaic deposits which Colter observed off Kuwait at a depth of −35 m and took as evidence of a subsidence of 37 m over the past 5000 years. Moreover, the freshwater detrital mud noted by Godwin et al. (1958) and Godwin and Willis (1959) from an organic layer at a depth of about −32 m with an age of 9910 ± 100 years B.P. fits within the depth range of −29 to −37 m to which belongs Kassler's submarine platform. Evidently this organic deposit was inundated by the advance of the sea in the Gulf.

About 11,000 years B.P., at the commencement of the Holocene period, the sea began to rise rapidly, with short pauses, at a rate of about 20 to 30 mm a year, to within 15 m of its present level. Marine platforms associated with this period are universally recorded between −15 to −24 m, while within the Gulf area evidence for this period is provided by the work of Houbolt (1957), whose submarine terrace, or, as he called it, the "near-shore terrace" lies at a depth of −5·5 to −16·5 m. Kassler (1973) also points to a submarine platform at −18 m.

During the last 6000 years, sea-level has fluctuated above and below the present datum. According to Fairbridge (1961), the highest recorded level in most places has been about 3–5 m above the present (e.g. the older Peron Terrace, Australia), although he indicates that a higher figure could be obtained as a result of isostatic rebound, geodetic, tidal and other effects. It is possible that the lowest terraces in our research area, which extend between Mudairah and Al-Bahra, and have ages between 4570 ± 70 and 3560 ± 60 years B.P., corresponded to this high stage of sea-level. The difference in heights, which range from a maximum of 14 m in the middle of Al-Bahra to a minimum level of 6 m further east, is presumably related to tectonic movements in and around the area investigated.

Other dated evidence from the gulf comes from Abu Dhabi, where a detailed stratigraphic sequence indicates marine transgression from 7000 to 4000 B.P. (Evans et al. 1969), while Taylor and Illing (1969) reported that the age of the strandlines in Qatar, which have heights between 1·5 and 2·5 m, range between 3930 ± 130 and 4340 ± 180 years B.P.

Evidence of undated marine transgression in the Gulf can be related to the lowest terraces in the research area, or to more recent stages, ranging in height from between 1·5 to 6 m above sea-level. These features extend along the Arabian coast of the Gulf from Kuwait as far as Oman. Along the coast of Kuwait, recent marine deposits containing shell fragments similar to those on the present beach have been found by the author in the Al-Sha'aib and Al-Dhba'iyyah areas on the southern coast. A sample of shells which came from Al-Dhba'iyyah at a height of c. 5 m above sea-level gave an age of 940 ± 80 B.P., but further investigation is necessary due to the possibility of contamination. Milton (1967) referred to these marine terrace deposits, as did Khalaf (1969) who has identified a recent marine terrace with a thickness of up to 4 m at Ras Ashairij and at Al-Khiran. Perry and Al-Refai (1958) indicate that oolitic sandstone, found at Ras al-Jlay'ah at a height of about 6 m above sea-level, extends into the coast of Saudi Arabia. Evidence of sea-level recession of 1·5–3 m on the coast of Al-Hasa in Saudi Arabia was mentioned by Cornwall (1946), and included the abandonment of old settlements for new sites on the Gulf coast. In 1960 Holm reported undisturbed shell beds, at heights of 1·5–2 m above sea level, which extend from Ras al-Mish'ab to Salwah and along the Trucial coast. This level may also, as Holm (1960) suggested, correspond to the level which Cornwall (1946) had in mind when he referred to the 1·5 to 2 m recession of sea-level.

Evidence of lower sea-levels in the Gulf during the last 6000 years, which can be correlated with Fairbridge's scale of 1961, may be found in the recent data provided by Larsen (1975). According to Fairbridge (1961) a fall of sea-level to −4 m (the Bahama emergence) occurred between 4600 and 4000 B.P., and left buried peat, drowned forests, and submarine platforms. Larsen (1975) referred to two submarine platforms, at − 5 and − 3 m, in the deltaic area north of the Gulf, both cut into marine and perhaps estuarine clay or silt of the Hammar formation. The − 3 m submarine platform has also been observed by Larsen off Bahrain.

References

Butzer, K. W. 1958. Quaternary stratigraphy and climate in the Near East. *Bonner Geog. Abhandl.* **24**, 1–57.

Carrigy, M. A. and Fairbridge, R. W. 1954. Recent sedimentation physiography and structure of the continental shelves of Western Australia. *J. Roy. Soc. W. Australia* **38**, 65–95.

Cornwall, P. B. 1946. Ancient Arabia: explorations in Hasa, 1940–41. *Geogr. J.* **107**, 28–50.

Evans, G., Schmidt, V., Bush, P. and Nelson, H. 1969. Stratigraphy and geologic history of the Sabkha, Abu Dhabi, Persian Gulf. *Sedimentology* **12**, 145–159.

Fairbridge, R. W. 1961. Eustatic changes in sea-level. *In: Physics and Chemistry of the Earth,* (L. H. Ahrens *et al.*, Eds) Vol. 4, pp. 99–185. Oxford: Pergamon Press.

Falcon, N. L. 1947. Raised beaches and terraces of the Iranian Makran coast. *Geogr. J.* **109**, 149–151.

Glennie, K. W. 1970. *Desert Sedimentary Environment.* Amsterdam: Elsevier Publishing Co.

Godwin, H. and Willis, E. H. 1959. Cambridge University natural radiocarbon measurements I. Radiocarbon 1: 63–75. *Am. J. Sci. Radiocarbon Suppl.*

Godwin, H., Suggate, R. P. and Willis, E. H. 1958. Radiocarbon dating of eustatic rise in ocean-level. Nature **181**, 1518–1519.

Holm, D. A. 1960. Desert geomorphology in the Arabian Peninsula. *Science* **132**, 1369–1379.

Holmes, A. 1944. *Principles of Physical Geology.* London: Thomas Nelson.

Houbolt, J. J. H. C. 1957. *Surface Sediments of the Persian Gulf near the Qatar Peninsula.* The Hague: Mouton and Co.

Kapel, H. 1967. *Atlas of the Stone-Age Cultures of Qatar.* Denmark: Aarhus, University Press.

Kassler, P. 1973. The structural and geomorphic evaluation of the Persian Gulf. *In: The Persian Gulf: Holocene Carbonate Sedimentation and Diagenesis in a Shallow Epicontinental Sea.* (B. H. Purser, Ed.), pp. 11–32. Berlin: Springer-Verlag.

Khalaf, F. I. 1969. *Geology and Mineralogy of the Beach Sediments of Kuwait.* M.Sc. Thesis, University of Kuwait.

M

Larsen, C. E. 1975. The Mesopotamian Delta Region: a reconsideration of Lees and Falcon. *J. Am. Oriental Soc.* **95**, 43–57.

Milton, D. I. 1967. Geology of the Arabian Peninsula, Kuwait. *U.S. Geol. Surv. Prof. Paper* 560–F, 1–8.

Mitchell, R. C. 1958. Instability of the Mesopotamian Plains. *Bull. Soc. Géog. Egypt* **31**, 127–140.

Perry, J. T. O'B and Al-Refai, B. H. 1958. *Notes on the Geology of the Coastline North-West of Ras Al-Jilai'a, South-East Kuwait.* Kuwait Oil Company (Unpublished report).

Sarnthein, M. 1972. Sediments and History of the Postglacial Transgression in the Persian Gulf and North-West Gulf of Oman. *Mar. Geol.* **12**, 245–266.

Taylor, J. C. M. and Illing, L. V. 1969. Holocene intertidal calcium carbonate-cementation, Qatar, Persian Gulf. *Sedimentology* **12**, 69–107.

Van Andel, Tj. H., Heath, G. R., Moore, T. C. and McGeary, D. F. R. 1967. Late Quaternary history, climate and oceanography of the Timor Sea, Northwestern Australia. *Am. J. Sci.* **265**, 737–758.

Vita-Finzi, C. 1973. Late Quaternary Subsidence. *In:* The Musandam Expedition 1971–72: Scientific Results, Part I. *Geogr. J.* **139**, 414–421.

Voute, C. 1957. A prehistoric find near Razzaza (Karbala Liwa): its significance for the morphological and geological history of the Abu Dibbis depression and surrounding area. *Sumer* **33**, 1–14.

16
Recent Alluvial History in the Catchment of the Arabo-Persian Gulf

Claudio Vita-Finzi

In this chapter an attempt is made to provide archaeologists and historians with an alluvial chronology spanning the last 20,000 years which owes nothing to palaeoclimatic conjecture and can therefore make an independent contribution to the analysis of former patterns and modes of occupation.

The Alluvial Record

As can be seen from Fig. 1, the catchment of the Arabo-Persian Gulf is dominated by the Tigris and Euphrates. Its Iranian sector is well endowed with streams; in contrast, much of the Arabian shore is wholly lacking in clearly defined watercourses, although widespread gravel deposits testify to the presence of extensive wadi networks earlier in the Quaternary (Holm, 1960; Powers *et al.*, 1966).

Information on the recent fluvial history of the area is patchy and poor in dates, most of these being maxima derived from archaeological remains found within or beneath river-laid deposits. Nevertheless, two widely separated parts of the catchment have yielded Late Quaternary sequences which have much in common. In the basin of the Saidmarreh (a tributary of the Karkheh), as in other parts of northern and central Iran, the modern channels have cut through two successive alluvial fills. The older (Tehran Alluvium) consists of lime-rich alluvial fan material and, to judge from archaeological evidence, it was laid down between 36,000 and 7000 years ago. The younger (Khorramabad Alluvium) is a well stratified channel deposit whose accumulation after the sixteenth century A.D. is attested by

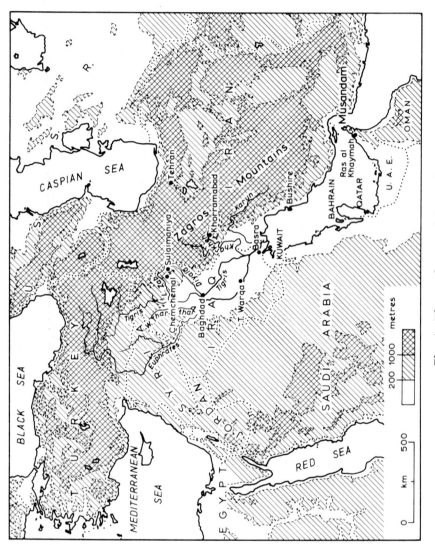

Fig. 1: The catchment of the Gulf.

radiocarbon and archaeological dating (Vita-Finzi, 1969a). In the Musandam Peninsula of northern Oman, at the mouth of the Gulf, the wadis are floored by the calcrete-capped alluvial and colluvial fills of the Makhus Formation, whose relationship to coastal aeolianites indicates deposition during the last major marine regression. About 10,000 years ago incision supervened, and, outside those areas that are affected by subsidence, has persisted until the present day, barring a brief depositional episode (represented by the Khasab Alluvium) which has been dated archaeologically to the fifteenth to nineteenth centuries A.D. (Vita-Finzi, 1973).

Let us now see how far other parts of the catchment conform to this pattern. Alluvial fans closely comparable with the Makhus deposits of Musandam have been traced as far south as Ras al Khaymah. Beyond this point the south-eastern shores of the Gulf are composed largely of recent marine deposits, although work now being conducted in Qatar suggests that the sequence proposed for Musandam is also applicable to parts of this peninsula. Various Quaternary alluvial deposits and duricrusts have been reported from eastern Saudi Arabia (Powers et al., 1966; Chapman, 1971), but their ages are still uncertain.

The alluvial record in some of the eastern tributaries of the Tigris is better documented. In the Chemchemal Plain, for example, Wright (1952, 1960) identified a predominantly fluvial deposit up to 60 m thick which was laid down after the occupation of the Middle Palaeolithic site of Barda Balka. Its incision, largely accomplished by about 8700 years ago, was followed by the deposition of a second alluvial unit some 9 m thick which contains potsherds dating to about 750–600 B.C. and which has since been trenched by the streams. In the Sulaimaniya Valley, two post-Tertiary alluvial deposits are represented, the older composed largely of gravels, and the younger of fine-grained deposits (Voûte and Wedman, 1963). The Lesser Zab near Sungassar is also bordered by two Pleistocene terraces, the older encrusted with secondary lime (Buringh, 1960, quoted by Voûte and Wedman, 1963. p. 398).

The Euphrates rises in Turkey, in whose western and central portions two Late Quaternary fills have already been recognized, the older (Sinop Alluvium) associated with Middle Palaeolithic artefacts and the younger (Meander Alluvium) with Roman potsherds (Vita-Finzi, 1969b). In the river's Syrian reaches, van Liere (1960–61) has identified a valley fill (the Main Gravel Terrace) up to 25 m thick which yields Palaeolithic artefacts, and a lower silty fill which was incised after the Middle Ages. Van Liere believes the latter is "prehistoric, up to Byzantine" in age, although he does not supply the evidence on which this belief is based; on the other hand, de Heinzelin (1965), whose generalized sequence for the middle Euphrates is not easily reconciled with van Liere's, describes an alluvial deposit 10 m thick at Shash which contains Islamic sherds and which is now being trenched. Wadi Tharthar, which flows into the depression of that name, has also cut through two fills, of which the older is exposed to a depth of 50 m and the younger is 6–8 m thick (Dorrell, 1972); I have found potsherds, some of them possibly Islamic, near Tell al Rimah in a 3 m deposit which corresponds to the latter fill.

Many workers, including some of those cited above, are understandably suspicious of attempts to force widely scattered observations on alluvial fills into a regional sequence (cf. Schumm and Parker, 1973). It is accepted that recent local tectonic events have influenced the timing of alluvial deposition and dissection in some parts of the mountain belt, but the fact remains that, as in the Mediterranean catchment (Vita-Finzi, 1969c), the data to hand can be accommodated by two Late Quaternary aggradational episodes, of which the earlier drew to a close some 10,000–7000 years ago and the later took place during historical times. As we are here concerned with the physiographic effects, rather than the origins, of the Gulf record, it is sufficient to observe that only a climatic explanation (as distinct from one stressing tectonic or anthropogenic factors) would seem capable of accounting for the observed parallels.

Discussion

The Gulf became dry land during the marine regression that brought sea level to −130 m between 20,000 and 15,000 years ago (Bloom, 1971; Shackleton and Opdyke, 1973). As already indicated by the aeolianites of the Makhus Formation of Musandam, dune-development on the Gulf floor (Sarnthein, 1972; Kassler, 1973) coincided with the older of the two aggradational episodes in its borderlands; the terrestrial evidence for piedmont alluvial deposition by short-lived flows (Vita-Finzi, 1969a, b; 1973; Beaumont, 1972) is corroborated by the paucity of fluvial sediment on the bed of the Gulf and the absence of a true delta at its mouth (Sarnthein, 1972). In short, the Gulf and its Mesopotamian extension appear to have formed a generally waterless depression containing a few swampy tracts, rather than a "fertile plain, floored with alluvium from the united waters of the Tigris and Euphrates" (Holmes, 1944, p. 417).

The ensuing marine transgression was at its most rapid between 12,000 and 8000 years ago, and within a further 3000 years brought sea-level close to its present position (Bloom, 1971). As aggradation gave way to incision of the older fill, sediment began to be exported beyond the piedmont zone. This mechanism helps to account for the evidence of a general increase in terrigenous sedimentation off the Iranian coast during the last 9000 years (Diester-Haass, 1973; Seibold et al., 1973) and more specifically in the submerged delta of the Rud Hilla, near Bushire, during the last 6000 (Melguen, 1973); and it may also explain the burial of sites of the 5th–3rd millennia B.C. in various parts of the lower Mesopotamian plain (Harris and Adams, 1957; Adams and Nissen, 1972).

The trend towards a reduction in longitudinal channel-gradients was temporarily reversed by renewed aggradation, though this time throughout the length of each river basin. To judge from the form and composition of the younger fill, it was laid down by streams characterized by lower flood peaks and more equable regimes than their modern counterparts. Incision during the last two or three centuries has again promoted sedimentation downvalley (Berry et al., 1970) as well as offshore, and is associated with marked channel instability (Ionides, 1937). One corollary of this thesis is that the high sediment loads of the modern Tigris and Euphrates are typical only of periods during which active erosion is taking place in their upper reaches, and consequently that active delta growth at the head of the Gulf has prevailed only during 8000 of the last 20,000 years, that is to say, between about 10,000 and 2000 years B.P. and over the last 300 years or so. Although the tectonic instability of the area is beyond dispute (Lees and Falcon, 1952; Mitchell, 1957; Raikes, 1966), the subsidence required to accommodate the silt brought down by the great rivers may thus be far less than has been supposed.

The contribution of the events postulated in this chapter to the history of land-use must await further surveys of the kind pioneered by Adams (1965) in the Diyala Plains. It is, nevertheless, worth observing that, whereas the economic potential of the older alluvial fill varied greatly according to where and when it was laid down, the younger phase of deposition appears to have been generally beneficial as regards not only the inherent fertility of the resulting alluvium but also the conditions of abundant soil-moisture and periodic silt-replenishment that accompanied it. In contrast, the periods of stream-incision resulted, among other effects, in the depression of local water-tables—a serious disadvantage in areas where plant growth was heavily dependent on groundwater, though doubtless of benefit where drainage was impeded—and the development of "slotted" streams (Fisher, 1961, p. 366) requiring barrages and weirs if they were to be used for irrigation.

References

Adams, R. M. 1965. *Land behind Baghdad*. 187 pp. Chicago: University of Chicago Press.

Adams, R. M. and Nissen, H. J. 1972. *The Uruk countryside*. 241 pp. Chicago: University of Chicago Press.

Beaumont, P. 1972. Alluvial fans along the foothills of the Elburz Mountains, Iran. *Palaeogeog. Palaeoclimatol. Palaeoecol.* **12**, 251–273.

Berry, R. W., Brophy, G. P. and Naqash, A. 1970. Mineralogy of the suspended sediment in the Tigris, Euphrates and Shatt-al-Arab rivers of Iraq, and the recent history of the Mesopotamian Plain. *J. Sedim. Petrol.* **40**, 131–139.

Bloom, A. L. 1971. Glacial-eustatic and isostatic controls of sea level since the last glaciation. *In The Late Cenozoic Glacial Ages* (K. K. Turekian, Ed.), pp. 355–379. New Haven: Yale University Press.

Chapman, R. W. 1971. Climatic changes and the evolution of landforms in the Eastern Province of Saudi Arabia. *Bull. Geol. Soc. Am.* **82**, 2713–2728.

De Heinzelin, J. 1965. Observations sur les terrasses du Moyen-Euphrate. *Bull. Soc. Géol. Fr.* **7**, 37–44.

Diester-Haass, L. 1973. Holocene climate in the Persian Gulf as deduced from grain-size and pteropod distribution. *Mar. Geol.* **14**, 207–223.

Dorrell, P. 1972. A note on the geomorphology of the country near Umm Dabaghiyah. *Iraq* **34**, 69–72.

Fisher, W. B. 1961. *The Middle East* (4th ed.). 557 pp. London: Methuen.

Harris, S. A. and Adams, R. M. 1957. A note on canal and marsh stratigraphy near Zubediyah. *Sumer* **13**, 157–163.

Holm, D. A. 1960. Desert geomorphology in the Arabian peninsula. *Science, N.Y.* **132**, 1369–1379.

Ionides, M. G. 1937. *The regime of the rivers Tigris and Euphrates*. 278 pp. London: Spon.

Kassler, P. 1973. The structural and geomorphic evolution of the Persian Gulf. *In: The Persian Gulf* (B. H. Purser, Ed.), pp. 11–32. Berlin: Springer-Verlag.

Lees, G. M. and Falcon, N. L. 1952. The geographical history of the Mesopotamian plains. *Geog. J.* **118**, 24–39.

Melguen, M. 1973. Correspondence analysis for recognition of facies in homogeneous sediments off an Iranian river mouth. *In: The Persian Gulf* (B. H. Purser, Ed.), pp. 99–113. Berlin: Springer-Verlag.

Mitchell, R. C. 1957. Recent tectonic movement in the Mesopotamian plains. *Geog. J.* **123**, 569–571.

Powers, R. W., Ramirez, L. F., Redmond, C. D. and Elberg, E. L., Jnr. 1966.

Geology of the Arabian Peninsula: Sedimentary Geology of Saudi Arabia *U.S. Geol. Surv., Prof. Pap.* **560–D**, 147 pp.

Purser, B. H. (Ed.) (1973). *The Persian Gulf.* 471 pp. Berlin: Springer-Verlag.

Raikes, R. L. 1966. The physical evidence for Noah's Flood. *Iraq* **28**, 52–63.

Sarnthein, M. 1972. Sediments and history of the Postglacial transgression in the Persian Gulf and northwest Gulf of Oman. *Mar. Geol.* **12**, 245–266.

Schumm, S. A. and Parker, R. S. 1973. Implications of complex drainage systems for Quaternary alluvial stratigraphy. *Nature, Lond.* **243**, 99–100.

Seibold, E., Diester, L., Fütterer, D., Lange, H., Müller, P. and Werner, F. 1973. Holocene sediments and sedimentary processes in the Iranian part of the Persian Gulf. *In:* Purser, 1973, 57–80. See below.

Shackleton, N. J. and Opdyke, N. D. 1973. Oxygen isotope and palaeomagnetic stratigraphy of Equatorial Pacific Core V28–238: oxygen isotope temperatures and ice volumes on a 10^5 year and 10^6 year scale. *Quaternary Res.* **3**, 39–55.

Van Liere, W. J. 1960–61. Observations on the Quaternary of Syria. *Rijksdienst oudheidk. Bodemonderz.* **10–11**, 7–69.

Vita-Finzi, C. 1969a. Late Quaternary alluvial chronology of Iran. *Geol. Rdsch.* **58**, 951–973.

Vita-Finzi, C. 1969b. Late Quaternary continental deposits of central and western Turkey. *Man* **4**, 605–619.

Vita-Finzi, C. 1969c. *The Mediterranean Valleys.* Cambridge University Press.

Vita-Finzi, C. 1973. Late Quaternary subsidence. *In:* The Musandam Expedition 1971–72: Scientific Results, Part I. *Geog. J.* **139**, 414–421.

Voûte, C. and Wedman, E. J. 1963. The Quaternary climate as a morphological agent in Iraq. *In: Changes of Climate*, pp. 395–402. Paris: UNESCO.

Wright, H. E., Jr. 1952. The geological setting of four prehistoric sites in northeastern Iraq. *Bull. Am. Sch. Or. Res.* **128**, 11–24.

Wright, H. E., Jr. 1960. Climate and prehistoric man in the eastern Mediterranean. *In: Prehistoric Investigations in Iraqi Kurdistan* (R. J. Braidwood and B. Howe, Eds), pp. 71–97. Chicago: University of Chicago Press.

17
Post-Pluvial Changes in the Soils of the Arabian Peninsula

John H. Stevens

The Palaeosols of Arabia

Soils are produced through the interaction over a period of time of a number of environmental factors—climatic, geological, topographical, biotic and human. The formation of soil involves not only the development of characteristic horizons within the profile, distinct from those of the parent material, but also the transformation of minerals. In effecting these changes, moisture is an agent of fundamental importance, but in most arid-zone profiles it is absent except during very restricted periods of the year, or where artificially introduced. Yet this has not always been the case, for climatic change has had pronounced effects on the amount of moisture in the soils, and consequently on the rate and type of soil formation. Many of the features of the present soils of the Arabian Peninsula took form during past moister periods, for soil development is now very restricted and localized.

Indications of Past Pluvial Episodes

Studies of cores from the Red Sea (Herman, 1968) suggest that, prior to the onset of the Last Glaciation in Europe, the climate of the Arabian Peninsula was more humid and cool than it is at present. These more humid conditions reached a climax in a pluvial period which was approximately contemporaneous with the Last Glacial period in Europe. During this period, in which there was an increased effective rainfall, a large quantity of detritus was removed from highland areas and deposited on the flanks of the mountain ranges as coalescing outwash fans or as flow-deposits. Good examples of both of these features are to be found in interior districts of Oman and of the United Arab Emirates (Fig. 1), where the extensive outwash plains could not have been formed under climatic conditions similar to those obtaining today; though it may well be that even older pluvial periods, possibly of Tertiary times, have made a substantial contribution to these features. The flow deposits rest on the outwash fans and may be up to 50 m in height and 200 m in width, and extend 20–30 km from the mountains, for instance in the vicinity of Bahla in Oman. Such formations may be the result of conditions during the Last Pluvial period, or during a subsequent sub-Pluvial period which has interrupted the general progression towards aridity. The most noticeable of these moister sub-Pluvial phases is recognized as having occurred in Neolithic times (Butzer, 1961).

Evidence from South-East Arabia

The Sequence of Soils in Oman

In 1969, I published a tentative paper on Quaternary events and their effect on the development of soil over the plains of outwash gravel in the Oman Mountain Ranges in the United Arab Emirates. Based on observations of soil-profile morphology, I suggested that the following sequence of events took place.

1. Deposition of the last major fans of alluvial outwash, including some flow-deposits.

2. Evaporation at, or near, the surface of a high water-table, resulting in the formation of gypsum crusts. Such areas are restricted to localities where natural sub-surface dams (formed by features of solid geology) have impeded the flow of drainage and raised the water-tables. On the Gharif Plain in the United Arab Emirates, long low unvegetated ridges, containing a large component of gravel, reflect the distribution of non-saline alkali and saline alkali soils. In some of these soils, the gypsic horizon may consist of crystals up to 8 cm in length and the horizon may contain over 15% of gypsum. Elsewhere over the outwash plains, gypsic horizons occur at depth and appear to be related to groundwater conditions: in these cases the amount of gypsum rarely exceeds 6%.

3. A wetter period caused erosion of the fans, so that they became deeply trenched with the fine material which was being redistributed further away from the mountains. In a number of instances this fine

outwash overlies a cemented horizon (caliche) of calcium carbonate, which is interpreted as being a further manifestation of the preceding dry period.

During this wetter period, which is probably to be correlated with the Neolithic sub-Pluvial, some of the previously mentioned flow-deposits may have been formed. In the Bahla area, the unstratified flow-deposits stand high and have been subjected to only limited erosion, while the gypsic horizon occurs at a depth of about 20–30 cm and contains only small crystals of gypsum. In the surrounding areas there is little evidence of deposition of eroded material from these flow-structures, and the soils contain little gypsum.

4. Aeolian activity returned, causing some infilling of erosion-gullies with fine material. During this period, some of the gullies on the western side of the Oman Mountain Ranges acquired red sand-grains blown in from the Rub-al-Khali and the Wahibah sands.

5. A period of limited erosion and further infilling of the gullies with material derived from the surfaces of the fans.

6. Aeolian activity with limited sheet-flow, the conditions prevailing today, resulted in a final smoothing of the landscape.

Such a sequence of events is broadly similar to that recorded by Chapman (1971) in studying the evolution of landforms in the Eastern Province of Saudi Arabia, notably in the areas of the Dammam Dome and Shedgum.

The soil-sequence which occurs on the outwash-plains of the Oman Mountain Ranges is shown in Fig. 2. The soil-profiles are characterized by a high content of gravel, particularly in close proximity to the mountains. It is only the yermosol and xerosol soils (Sierozems), as well as some halosols, that have significant gravel-free horizons, but even these soils display horizonation resulting from continued deposition and reworking of the original parent material. It would seem that at no period since the Last Pluvial has pedogenesis managed to keep pace with the modification of the parent material and, consequently, the characteristics of these soils are the outcome of an episodic rather than a continuous process of pedogenesis.

Reddened Soils

On both sides of the Oman Mountain Ranges occur isolated areas of reddish soils, of two types: first, palaeosols developed under different climatic conditions, which have remained relatively unaffected by

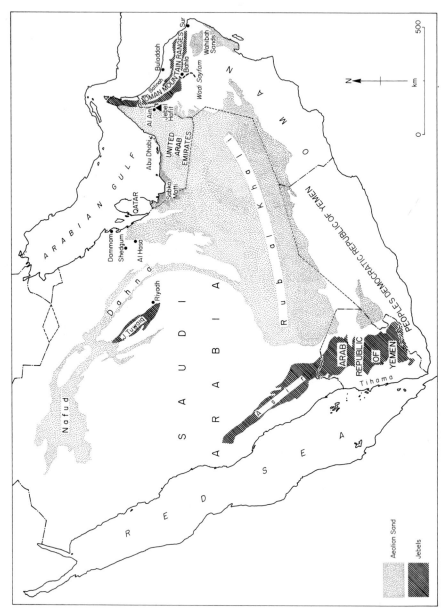

Fig. 1: The sand-seas and highlands of Arabia.

	DESERT FORELAND		GRAVEL OUTWASH PLAINS	OMAN MOUNTAINS
Sand dunes	Fine deposits overlying gravels		Coarse gravel outwash with some flow deposits and rock outcrops	Rock outcrops with debris accumulated in wadis and at base of slopes
Regosols	Vertisols Xerosols Halosols	Halosols Xerosols Yermosols / Yermosols Halosols Fluvisols	Yermosols, Halosols, Fluvisols, Rare Lithosols	Lithosols Fluvisols
Desert vegetation	Prosopis spicigera Acacia spp. Haloxylon salicornicum	Acacia spp. Calotropis procera Haloxylon salicornicum Perennial grasses	Rare Acacia spp. Perennial Grasses	

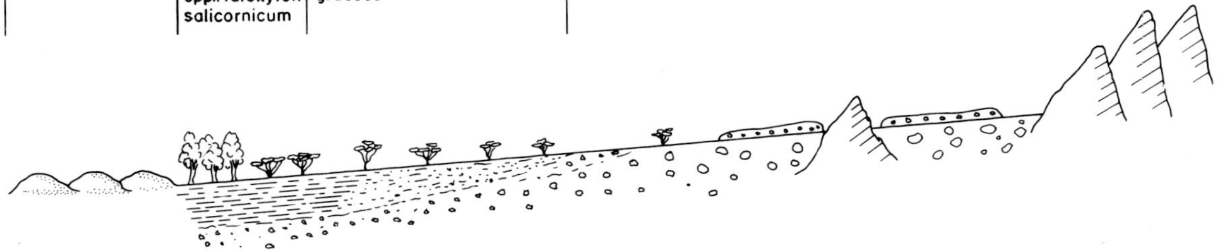

Fig. 2: Outwash deposits of the Oman Mountain Ranges.

subsequent erosion or deposition or even by pedogenesis; second, soils whose profiles reflect periods of pedogenesis under different environmental conditions, which have however been too short-lived to create a distinct type of soil. An example of this latter phenomenon is the rubefication (reddening) of outwash in certain localities on the higher terraces of the Batinah coast in Oman.

At Al Ain (Jebel Hafit)

A typical palaeosol is found near the oases of Al Ain on the western flank of Jebel Hafit. Here, a red limestone soil which has some similarities with a chromic luvisol (terra rossa) has developed on a conglomeratic limestone of Miocene age. The profile consists of 3 cm of fine aeolian sand overlying 12 cm of 5YR4/4* (reddish-brown) sandy clay loam which, in turn, rests on weathered limestone. It is this reddish-brown horizon, which is probably the remnant of a palaeosol; though it has undoubtedly been in part eroded since its formation. Table I gives some analytical data for this soil, as well as comparable data for a chromic luvisol in northern Jordan (Fisher et al., 1968) and for a xerosol at Al Ain. While the palaeosol is obviously very different from the xerosol, the full characteristics of a chromic luvisol have not developed completely. In particular, the pH and carbonate content of the palaeosol are higher than in the case of the chromic luvisol, while the content of free iron oxide—which remains relatively immobile in an arid environment and reflects past weathering— is lower. (The ratio of free iron oxide was determined by Deb's method, using sodium hydrosulphite and 0·05N hydrochloric acid to extract the iron.) The formation of free iron oxide and the redness of the horizon of sandy clay loam are most likely the outcome of climatic conditions in a pluvial period, a hypothesis which is confirmed by a coastal section at Wadi Haidha near Sur, Oman, where a similar horizon has been subsequently covered by about 0·75 m of gravel outwash.

Near Buladdah (Oman)

Rubefication, or the slight reddening of existing horizons, without major transformation of minerals, could take place over much shorter periods of time such as a sub-Pluvial period. The rubefication of horizons is a more frequent feature of soils of the Arabian Peninsula, particularly in the south, and may be enhanced by the moisture characteristics specific to particular horizons, especially gravel horizons containing a matrix of sand-

---

*Munsell notation given for moist soil.

Table I: Analytical data for a representative chromic luvisol (Jordan) a palaeosol (Al Ain, Abu Dhabi) and a xerosol (Al Jimi, Abu Dhabi)

PROFILE	Sample Depth	Texture International Limits			pH	Carbonates	Total C.E.C	Free Fe$_2$O$_3$	Conductivity
	cm	Sand %	Silt %	Clay %		%	mg/100g	%	mmhos/cm
CHROMIC LUVISOL									
Ajlun, Jordan	0–10	40	34	26	7·8	2	37·0	6·1	0·9
	10–32	31	25	44	7·7	4	32·6	8·3	0·4
PALAEOSOL									
Al Ain, Abu Dhabi	0–3	72	11	17	7·6	35	12·3	0·8	0·5
	3–15	36	22	42	8·3	6	28·2	3·9	0·3
XEROSOL									
Al Jimi, near	10–15	89	3	9	8·4	38	10·8	0·4	0·1
Al Ain, Abu	50–55	89	4	9	8·7	29	11·9	0·2	0·1
Dhabi	95–100	85	5	10	8·7	29	11·7	0·6	0·2

sized particles. A typical soil-profile showing evidence of rubefication occurs near Buladdah in Oman, under a sparse vegetation cover of *Cynomorium coccineum* and annual grass species, developed on outwash deposits:

0–10 cm   10YR 6/3 (light yellowish brown); loamy sand-sand, aeolian deposit, single grain structure with weak fine plates at the surface; frequent fine roots; dry; clear change.

10–18 cm   10YR 5/3 (brown); silty loam; weak angular structure with frequent pin-holes; frequent fine roots; rare fine carbonate mycelium; dry; clear change.

18–30 cm   5YR 5/6 (yellowish red)–7·5YR 5/6 (strong brown); sandy loam gravel; frequent fine roots; frequent small carbonate beads on gravel; redness associated with fine material; dry; sharp change.

30–80 cm   10YR 5/2 (greyish brown); loamy sand; single grain structure.

Some analytical data for this profile are given in Table II, and in the horizon which shows evidence of rubefication (18–30 cm) there is also a slight but significant increase in free iron oxide. There is also evidence of weak lessivage, for the upper surface of the larger gravels at the top of the rubefied horizon are coated with a veneer of fine silt and clay washed down from the overlying horizons, while there is also evidence of carbonate

Table II: Analytical data for Yermosol profile near Buladdah (Oman) showing limited rubefication

Sample Depth cm	Texture (International limits) Sand %	Silt %	Clay %	pH	Carbon-ates %	Total CEC me/100g	Free Fe$_2$O$_3$ %	Conduct-ivity mmhos/cm
3–8	86·5	10·1	3·4	8·1	33·5	4·4	0·1	0·12
12–18	69·5	15·5	15·0	8·1	34·5	13·5	0·5	0·19
20–25	79·0[a]	10·7	9·3	8·2	38·5	5·8	1·1	0·15
40–45	86·4	8·1	4·5	8·1	30·5	3·9	0·2	0·35

[a]33·5% of the sample was of gravel size—the analysis relates to the fine earth fraction (<2 mm)

accumulation. It could be argued that the rubefication is the consequence of the more humid conditions that prevail on the Batinah coast, but this seems unlikely since the horizon is covered by 18 cm of other deposits including one that is almost certainly water-lain.

On the Tihama of Yemen (at present)

However, on the coastal plains of the Arab Republic of Yemen, Asmaev (1968) has recognized that the slight accumulation of sesquioxides in the subsurface horizons of soils occurs as a result of present-day conditions of climate. The Tihama (coastal plain) has a climate characterized by a relatively humid spring and summer, during which as much as 350 mm of rain may fall. Under such conditions, Asmaev argues, there is perceptible liberation of iron and aluminium oxides, with a slight accumulation in an illuvial horizon. Furthermore, micromorphological examination of these soils indicates that there is some formation of clay minerals; but movement of these is very restricted. It would seem that under the prevailing conditions of climate pedogenesis is taking place more slowly than it did in the circumstances which caused the relic rubefication of some soils of the Batinah coast of Oman.

The Effects of Changes of Sea-level (especially in the *sabkhas*)

The coastlands of the Arabian Peninsula have been subject to fluctuating sea-levels over a considerable period of time, and Holm (1960), for instance, suggests that some of the *sabkhas*, or saline flats, in the vicinity of the oasis of Al Hasa in Saudi Arabia, at an elevation of 150 m above sea-level, reflect a higher level of the Arabian Gulf in the past. Around the coasts of the peninsula, though, the recent infilling of old lagoons has had a profound influence on soil-development. Associated with such areas are solonetz (saline-alkali) soils which have conductivities often in excess of 30 mmhos/cm at 25°C, while the exchangeable sodium percentage (ESP) may be as high as 60. These soils are usually of a heavy texture and of a low permeability, in consequence of their high content of sodium. They are also moist for much of the year, due to their low-lying situation and the resulting upward capillary movement of a saline soil solution, which leads to the formation of salt crystals at or very near the surface, giving a puffy appearance to these soils.

Sedimentation is an important process in the formation of these soils, notably along the Arabian coast of the Gulf. It has been investigated by a number of workers, including Bramkamp and Powers (1955) who studied carbonate and evaporitic sediments in Qatar; and Wells (1962) who discovered that dolomite was forming in some tidal sediments in Qatar; while Sugden (1963) examined aragonite formation in similar sediments, also in Qatar. Curtis et al. (1963) found that, in the sabkha near Abu Dhabi, anhydrite is present, and Kinsman (1966) and Butler (1969) made complete studies of the modern evaporite deposition there. While these deposits are not "soil" in the strict sense, the processes that contributed to their formation were responsible for the large areas of coastal and inland sabkha that now cover extensive areas of eastern Saudi Arabia and the United Arab Emirates—for instance, the Sabkha Matti which extends over 15,000 sq km. The sabkhas probably mark the infilling of coastal embayments by sedimentation on intertidal mudflats, the sedimentation being aided by a number of mechanisms including the deposition of aeolian material derived from the land, chemical precipitation as mentioned above, and the manufacture of calcareous mud by organisms, notably algae (Evans et al., 1964; Kendall et al., 1968, 1969).

Processes Elsewhere in Arabia

The Formation of Soils in the Humid Yemen

So far, the discussion has concentrated on the soils that have developed on the outwash-plains of the mountain areas and the coastal plains. Elsewhere over the peninsula, soil-formation since the last pluvial period has been mainly affected by aeolian processes and human activity. Only in the higher parts of Asir and the Arab Republic of Yemen have soils developed under natural vegetation-associations, namely woodlands of *Acacia-Commiphora*, *Olea-Tachonanthus* and montane *Juniperus*. These associations have been relatively unaffected by human activity, while aeolian influences too have been negligible. It is unfortunate that, to date, no studies have been made of the soils which occur under these vegetation-associations, for these areas are unique in the Arabian Peninsula, receiving as they do a relatively high precipitation, in excess of 500 mm annually.

Events in the Great Sand-seas

It is estimated that about 775,000 sq km of the peninsula are covered by aeolian sand. In such areas there is virtually no soil-profile morphology, since the parent material is constantly being subjected to movement and modification. Aeolian activity also exerts a profound influence on soil formation in areas immediately adjacent to the sand-seas, for in the interior of the peninsula it is a far more potent force in pedogenesis than the weathering of the sedimentary rocks. The products of fine weathering are rapidly removed before pedogenesis can commence, and on Jebel Tuwaiq, for instance, the surface is virtually devoid of any fine material except in small nooks and crannies where sheetflow has resulted in some accumulation. What is not removed by wind is transported by sporadic runoff from isolated rainstorms: in some instances there may be, at the base of slopes, up to 1·5 m of colluvial material capped by a surface of blocks and boulders—a circumstance which emphasises the point made above, that in the past there was far more effective moisture about. Thus, in the interior of the peninsula, agents of transportation of parent material exert a far greater influence on soil-profile morphology than the pedogenic processes, and most of the soils may be classified as lithosols, regosols or yermosols; with fluvisols occurring in association with the wadis.

Human Interference

Man has been the most potent agent in soil formation in specific areas of the peninsula. It only requires a very short period of time to alter completely the character of the weakly developed soils of the arid zone. Many of man's activities have been harmful, as overgrazing and the removal of trees for firewood and building have rendered the soils more prone to erosion. At the oasis of Al Hasa, excess irrigation water and saline drainage water which has been allowed to seep out of the cultivated area has formed swampy halosols with a dense *Phragmites* vegetation. These soils have now been reclaimed for cultivation, but, prior to reclamation, while being saline, they contained organic matter in excess of 12%.

Changes in technology can also have rapid effects on soil profiles. Wadi Sayfam, near Bahla in Oman, has for long been an important area for growing cereals with the aid of *falaj* water of good quality for irrigation. Within the last fifteen years, however, there has been a shift to pump-irrigation with the use of more saline water from directly beneath the cultivated area, and the result has been a dramatic increase in soil-salinity, with the likelihood that within the next twenty or thirty years many farms will become too saline for the cultivation of cereals. Human interference, though, does not necessarily harm the soils and one has only to cite the instance of the sand-stabilization scheme at the oasis of Al Hasa where saline top-soil is being used to reclaim for woodland 500 hectares of mobile sand-dunes (Stevens, 1974); or the forestry project along the main road from Abu Dhabi to Al Ain. As management of the range-lands becomes more scientific, here too the formation of soil will be artificially aided, and it seems likely that in the immediate future man will become an even more significant force in pedogenesis than he has been in the past.

Conclusion

Thus, post-Pluvial changes in the soils of the Arabian Peninsula are of two main types. First are changes induced by vagaries of climate. Due to the virtual absence of any detailed studies of soils over the peninsula, these effects must, to some extent, be speculative, but there can be no doubt that climatic change has been responsible for some quite marked modifications to the soils of the peninsula. Second are the changes induced by man, and here there is much firmer evidence. However, it must be remembered that the extent of soils which have undergone major modification through human agency is extremely small in comparison with the total area of the peninsula; though the area thus affected may be expected to expand in the future.

References

Asmaev, L. R. 1968. Data on the soils of the southwestern part of the Arabian Peninsula (Yemen). *In: Geography and Classification of Soils of Asia* (V. A. Kovda and E. V. Lobova, Eds), pp. 249–257. Jerusalem: Israel Program for Scientific Translations.

Bramkamp, R. A. and Powers, R. W. 1955. Two Persian Gulf Lagoons. *J. Sed. Petr.* **25**, 139–140.

Butler, G. P. 1969. Modern Evaporite deposition and geochemistry of co-existing brines, the Sabkha, Trucial Coast, Arabian Gulf. *J. Sed. Petr.* **39**, 70–89.

Butzer, K. W. 1961. Climatic change in arid regions since the Pliocene. *In: A history of land use in Arid Regions.* Proc. Arid Zone Research **17**, 31–56. UNESCO.

Chapman, R. W. 1971. Climatic changes and the evolution of landforms in the Eastern Province of Saudi Arabia. *Geol. Soc. America Bull.* **82**, 2713–2727.

Curtis, R. *et al.* 1963. Association of dolomite and anhydrites in the Recent sediments of the Persian Gulf. *Nature* **197** (4868), 679–680.

Evans, G., Kendall, C. G. St. C. and Shearman, D. J. 1964. Origin of the coastal flats, the Sabkha, of the Trucial Coast of the Persian Gulf. *Nature* **202** (4934), 759–761.

Fischer, W. B. *et al.* (1968). *Soil and Land Potential Survey of the Highlands of North West Jordan.* FAO/University of Durham. 50 pp.

Herman, Y. R. 1968. Evidence of climatic changes in Red Sea cores. *In: Means of Correlation of Quaternary Succession* (R. B. Morrison and H. E. Wright, Eds), Vol. 7, pp. 325–348. INQUA Congr.

Holm, D. A. 1960. Desert geomorphology of the Arabian Peninsula. *Science* **132** (2437), 1369–1379.

Kendall, C. G. St. C. and Skipwith, Sir P. A. d'E. 1968. Recent alga mats of a Persian Gulf lagoon. *J. Sed. Petr.* **38**, 1040–1058.

Kendall, C. G. St. C. and Skipwith, Sir P. A. d'E. 1969. Geomorphology of a Recent shallow-water carbonate province, Khor Al Baxam, Trucial Coast, S.W. Persian Gulf. *Geol. Soc. America Bull.* **80**, 865–892.

Kinsman, D. J. 1966. Gypsum and anhydrite of Recent Age, Trucial Coast, Persian Gulf. *2nd Symp. Salt. N. Ohio Geol. Soc.* **1**, 302–326.

Stevens, J. H. 1969. Quaternary events and their effect on Soil Development in an Arid Environment–the Trucial States. *Quaternaria* **10**, 73–81.

Stevens, J. H. 1974. Stabilisation of Aeolian Sands, Al Hasa oasis, Saudi Arabia. *J. Soil Water. Cons.*

Sugden, W. 1963. Some aspects of sedimentation in the Persian Gulf. *J. Sed. Petr.* **33**, 355–364.

Wells, A. J. 1962. Recent dolomite in the Persian Gulf. *Nature* **194** (4825), 274–275.

Synopsis of Part IV

There is broad agreement between Vita-Finzi and Stevens on the timing of the Late Glacial phase in Arabia when fans and outwash piled up below the mountains. In the wetter conditions of post-Glacial times these deposits were cleared further downstream, and thrown out as deltas into the rising waters of the Gulf. The main burden of Wilkinson's work on the terraces of the Middle Euphrates is to show how local circumstances can interrupt or obscure such broader cycles of erosion and deposit.

Larsen and Evans, through an examination of the deep topography of the Mesopotamian Delta, as revealed by a series of soundings, and especially by the crucial borehole off Fao, have advanced a powerful case for confirming the old hypothesis of de Morgan, that the land has encroached steadily on the sea over the last four or five thousand years.

Dr John Hansman, on the other hand, who has undertaken a detailed surface exploration of the Delta, has been good enough to point out in correspondence that he does not believe that the Gulf extended northwards as far as Ur in the third millennium B.C.; nor does he find evidence of any *substantial* advance of the Delta since the first millennium B.C. He believes that, as Lees and Falcon contended in 1953, the balance of alluviation and subsidence has preserved features like the Hor al-Hammar, low plains subject for millennia to periodic flooding, while at the same time the rivers have continued to build forward their flood terraces and deltas beyond these low areas.

Larsen and Evans argue strongly that eustatic changes of sea-level as opposed to local or isostatic movements were instrumental in controlling the recent geological history of the area of the Delta. Al-Asfour, however, has demonstrated the marked inclination of the marine terraces of the Bay of Kuwait, which must have been caused by local seismic shifts after the cutting of the lowest terraces, some four or five thousand years ago.

Norman Falcon too is convinced that crustal movements in the Delta region have continued to influence the topography through historic times. In correspondence he has kindly given his view that the Gulf Basin in front

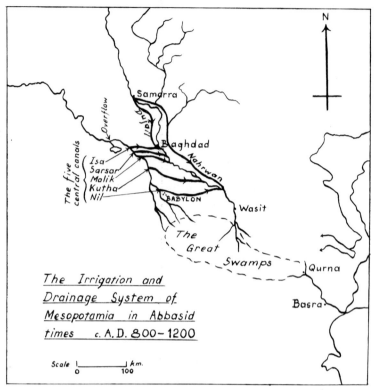

Fig. 1.

(that is to the south-west) of the Zagros Mountain range is one of the active basins of the world, and that geologists who know the area in the field and its geomorphology are convinced that tectonic activity is still going on. The direction of movement tends to be consistent in any one area, and those who have studied air photographs of the Gulf lowlands have little difficulty in picking out areas of "positive" from others of "negative" movement—which in theory could be as much as a centimetre a year. In these circumstances, he concludes, it would be rash to deny the possibility over the last few millennia of crustal movements substantial enough to affect the deposition of alluvium; and it is known that some salt plugs are still being extruded in such a way as to interfere with the drainage.

The drainage pattern of Mesopotamia in the Early Mediaeval (Abbasid) period is sketched in Fig. 1. The system of irrigation canals of that time was destroyed by the Mongol invasions of the early thirteenth century and since then the Great Swamps have been gradually, though still incompletely, filled in with alluvium.

V

The Deserts of the Indus and of Trans-Caspia

In his bid to conquer Asia, Alexander reached as far as the Oxus and the Indus, and it may be well to end our survey there too, at the fringe of Central and Monsoon Asia. In both of these great valleys the vagaries of the rivers, whether from seismic or climatic causes, have evidently much influenced local history. The Oxus-Jaxartes on the one hand, and the Indus and its Punjabi tributaries on the other, while flowing in opposite directions, take their origins in the same general area of the "Roof of the World", that is the plateau of the Pamirs and the western extremities of the ranges which spring eastwards therefrom. Now these mountains derive their snow partly from winter cyclones at the end of their run east from the Mediterranean; but mainly from the summer monsoon, again at its extremities. It could be therefore that climatic changes affect both river systems in parallel. And since South Arabia too falls just within the influence of the summer monsoon, there is good initial reason to compare climatic changes there with those in the regions now to be considered.

So before proceeding it may be apposite to date two fossil lakes in the Arabian peninsula. First, Lake Lisan is the name given to a former extension of the Dead Sea, and Mr M. E. Meadows of Cambridge has generously passed on his conclusions, that this began to accumulate possibly 60,000 years ago, reached its maximum *c.* 30,000 B.P., and survived until *c.* 15,000 B.P. (D. Need and K. O. Emery, *Bull. Geol. Surv. Israel* 41, 1967; Z. B. Begin *et. al.*, *ibid.* **63**, 1974). These dates correspond broadly with those established by Price-Williams (p. 83 above) for the climatic sequence in the nearby Wadi Gaza, where Phase I (*c.*60,000–40,000 B.P.), wetter than now, deteriorated into a more arid Phase II (*c.* 40,000–10,000 B.P.)

Second, Lake Mundafan, a vanished water-body in the western part of the Rub' al Khali, has been shown by H. A. McClure (*Nature* **263**, 1976, 755–6) to have built up during two phases, a) *c.* 36,000–17,000 B.P. and b) *c.* 9000–6000 B.P. Now phase a) was broadly contemporary with the Last Glacial "Pluvial" of South Arabia which Stevens has recognized (pp. 263–4 above) and with the Lower Khvalyn transgression of the Caspian (p. 338 below); and phase b) falls within roughly the same period as Price-Williams's rather damper Phase III in the Negev (p. 83 above), Stevens's South Arabian "Neolithic Pluvial" (pp. 264–5), the fresh-water lakes of the Thar Desert (pp. 287 and 309 below), and the Upper Khvalyn flooding of the Caspian (p. 339).

18
The Desiccation of the Thar Desert and its Environs during the Protohistorical and Historical Periods

S. K. Seth

Introduction

The Pleistocene and Holocene epochs are abnormal from the standpoint of palaeoclimatology, for they were times of marked revolutionary changes. The Pleistocene Ice Age was a compound affair with four or five main advances separated by stages of retreat, with many lesser swings. In fact it is an open question whether at present we are in an Interglacial or a post-Glacial period (Russell, 1941).

In the Indian subcontinent, there is some evidence of rainfall above normal in Baluchistan and upper Sind from approximately 4000 to 2500 B.C.—the remains, for example, of *gabarbands* or stone-built irrigation dams and terraces identified in the former region by Sir Aurel Stein (Piggott, 1950). Further, a dry period may have prevailed from 2000 to 300 B.C., when loessic deposits were laid down in Kashmir (De Terra and Hutchinson, 1936). Relatively coarse loess has also been identified in *Bhangar* deposits near Delhi, and this may have come from the Rajasthan desert in its earliest phases (Sen, 1952). Moreover, the stratification of a bore hole at Agra suggests that the uppermost 49 metres of the deposits in this region are largely composed of blown sand of aeolian origin (Oldham, 1893).

Relics of old extinct channels abound in the region, especially in the Ghaggar Plain and the Luni Basin. Since Rajasthan is supposed to have become dry only after the Last Glaciation, we should expect to find there evidence of an antecedent pluvial cycle. In fact, rounded hollows, potholes in granite hills (in the Abu-Idar region) with rounded sand particles, calcium segregated in the form of pans in deeper horizons, and accumulations of conglomerates all point to a more humid climate (Ghose, 1965). Some of this evidence comes from a period no earlier than 5000 B.C.; the lime concretions, however, are dated to about 28,000 B.C. (Abichandani, 1972), and their cores at least were deposited under warm, alternate dry and humid climates, during previous Interglacials.

Present Conditions

Physiography

The desert region can be divided into four distinct types (Fig. 1) (Pithawala, 1952).

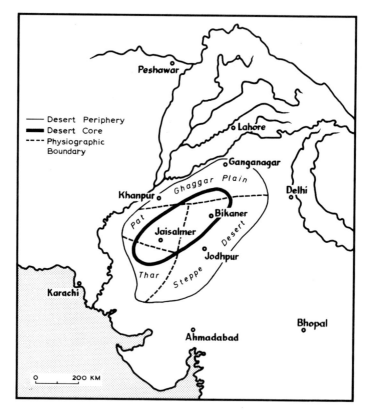

Fig. 1: The Thar Desert; four types of physiography.

Thar	Lies towards the south: completely covered with sand and sand hills up to 152 m high, higher in the west than in the east, trending north-east/south west or east-north-east/west-south-west, i.e. parallel to general course of monsoon; valleys silt-covered; salt incrustations common; western boundary formed by the lower eastern Nara river; average rainfall 102–254 mm.
Pat	Flat section extending northwards: covered with sand or sand hills running generally north/south and seldom rising over 91 m; flat sandy soil overlying impermeable clay; many salt and some fresh-water lakes in enclosed basins.
Ghaggar Plain	In the north: largely desert but showing remains of a gigantic drainage system of the past flanked by continuous ridges of sand, around which occur many archaeological sites; old alluvium fluviatile, with overlying sand and loess.
Steppe Desert	In the south-east: part of rocky uplands merging into the desert; peneplained, broken terrain covered with finer wind-borne debris; southern part drained by the Luni; transverse sand hills commoner.

The sand hills are of great antiquity and often show signs of denudation. Wells dug at Gadra Road encountered horizontal fine-grained sandstone to a depth of 103 m, which exactly resembles the wind-blown sand of the dunes. Some slight induration of the sand rock has occurred as a result of the periodical precipitation of carbonates, silica and iron oxide (Auden, 1950). The most sandy tracts are along the edges of the Indus Valley and of the depression marked by the Luni Valley. The present topography resembles a number of rocky islands jutting out of a vast sea of sand. This sea is not still, for denudation and aggradation are active. The Thar desert hollows and the direction of sand ridges, which lie parallel rather than at right angles to the prevailing winds, indicate that some areas were more deeply covered with sand in the past than at present (Medlicott and Blanford, 1879).

Climate

Aridity prevails in north-west India and south and south-west Pakistan over an area of roughly 384,000 km^2. As in similar districts elsewhere in the world, the arid region is enveloped by a semi-arid belt of varying width: 128,000 km² receive a rainfall of less than 254 mm, and there is even a small region which receives less than 102 mm per annum (Fig. 2).

An acceptable definition of aridity (Pramanik *et al.*, 1952) may be taken as follows: rainfall 254 mm or less, mean annual diurnal range 24°F or more; semi-arid: rainfall between 254 and 508 mm and an annual diurnal range of 18°F or more. In the region with which we are dealing, the arid and semi-arid areas may be generally assumed to be limited respectively by the annual isohyets of 254 and 508 mm.

Though the region concerned is indeed arid, it is considerably less so than some extreme deserts elsewhere. If, following Gorczynski, the percentage of aridity is defined as $K \times$ (latitude factor) $\times$ (temperature range) $\times$ (precipitation ratio), where $K = 5.4$ (in order to bring the index to 100 for the worst conditions)[1], then the aridity index for the following localities is:

Sahara (Colomb Bechar)	79%
California (Salton)	66%
West Rajasthan (Jacobabad)	40%

Any factor which brings about an increase in the precipitation ratio (e.g. difference between maximum and minimum larger, and average smaller, i.e. low precipitation with marked disparity from year to year) or in the temperature range (e.g. removal of the moderating influence of vegetation on the local climate) will tend to make the climate more arid.

The Indian desert occupies a small corner in a very extensive area of low rainfall from 50°W to 74°E Long., and is thus a continuation of the arid regions of North Africa, Arabia, Iran and Baluchistan. The semi-arid climate (dry hot steppe—BSh of Köppen) in Sind extends westward into the Arabian Sea, as it does into the Atlantic beyond the Sahara and into the Pacific beyond Mexico. As no human agency can interfere with the climate on the surface of the sea, it is obvious that man's activities have little to do with these *broad* macroclimatic divisions of the world (Banerji, 1952a).

The whole central Asian region is said to have been drying up for thousands of years (Manton, 1954) and the Indus Basin and Rajasthan fall within this general area. The Indian desert topography has evidently evolved within comparatively recent geological time, since the Pleistocene. There is no high range to intercept the moisture-bearing monsoon from the Arabian Sea, and intense solar action, drought, extremes of heat and cold and wind action lead to considerable mechanical disintegration. The sand and the loess deposits of north-west India are partly derived from this source, but a larger portion comes from the former sea shore and from the river channels, old and new (Wadia, 1926).

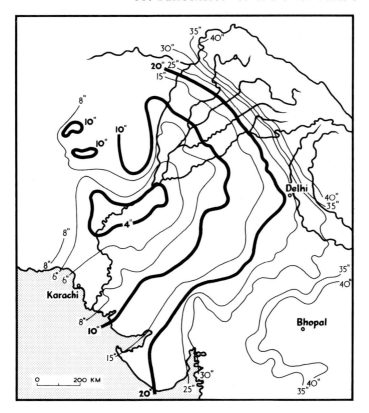

Fig. 2: The Thar Desert; annual rainfall

As these deposits accumulate, the desert conditions become accentuated; for the area is cut off from water circulation, except for occasional cloudbursts, and the internal drainage is too feeble to transport the blown sand to the sea.

Opinion is divided as to whether there has been any appreciable change in the rainfall regime during recent times. According to one view (Banerji, 1952b) the present (1886–1940) trend is towards warmer and drier conditions, with a decrease in rainfall in the arid and semi-arid areas, but with an increase in the Aravallis, which is confirmed by the channels dissected there in the alluvium. According to another view there has been no general decrease of rainfall during the last 70–80 years (Pramanik and Hariharan, 1952); the values of the coefficient of variation, however, show a marked correlation with dryness (Rao, 1958). Occasional deficiencies in precipitation may be attributed to larger movements in the upper air, but they usually have not lasted long enough to justify the conclusion that there has been a permanent change in climate (Walker, 1916). With regard to temperature, while there is no systematic trend, at some places there have been variations of an oscillatory character within a period of 30–40 years (Pramanik and Jagannathan, 1953). The amplitude is over 20°F in the extreme north-west (Jagannathan, 1957).

The dust in the atmosphere over the Rajasthan desert increases the mid-tropopheric subsidence rate by perhaps 50%. In the absence of dust, there would be less subsidence and a deeper monsoon layer, and, in turn, more rainfall. The desert would thus appear to be self-sustaining (Bryson et al., 1963).

Flora

The vegetation of Rajasthan, Punjab and Sind incorporates a number of Arabian and African elements which have gained entry and predominence where the indigenous vegetation has been cleared. In course of time these elements in the flora may increase still further (Sabnis, 1929). The desert flora is certainly by no means poor in content: over 500 species have been recorded. The plants are evidently related to the climate, as in Libya and Cyrenaica (Das and Sarup, 1951).

In the desert proper there is little permanent vegetation, but a lush ephemeral growth of herbs and grasses follows the rain. Bushes and trees subsist to some extent in the better-watered areas within the arid tracts, and more widely in the adjacent semi-arid portions.

On the Indian side, the main vegetational sub-type in the Punjab, Rajasthan and Gujarat is Desert Thorn Forest (Champion and Seth, 1968). Thorny *Mimosae*, including *Acacia* spp. *Tamarix, Prosopis cineraria, Prosopis juliflora* (introduced) occur throughout. *Calotropis* and other asclepiads are frequently seen. *Capparis decidua* is often conspicuous. Fleshy Chenopodiaceae occur on saline and *Calligonum* on sandy soils and dunes. *Lasiurus* and *Cenchrus* are the common grasses.

Edaphic, seral and degradational types are quite conspicuous— especially the last, which result from intensive biotic interference, mainly through pastoral nomadism. The scrub consists of *Zizyphs, Euphorbia, Salvadora, Calotropis, Crotolaria* and the like.

On the Pakistan side (Champion et al., 1970) the forest is again of Tropical Thorn type, with edaphic and seral variants. The degradational forms are as common as, or even more common than in India, and spring from the same causes. The common species are *Acacia senegal, Salvadora* (in saline areas) *Zizyphus, Capparis, Euphorpia, Tamarisk, Populus euphratica*, (on stream banks), *Calligonum polygonoides* (on sand hills), *Haloxylon ammodendron, Acacia nilotica* (in inundation areas) and *Prosopis juliflora* (introduced).

Fauna

The wild species are typical of the dry and desert habitat, with the lion confined to Gir in Saurashtra and the wild ass to the rann of Kutch. Tigers are recorded in the wetter portion of the semi-arid zone in the south-west, but there are no elephant or rhinoceros.

The domestic animals are also typically desert species, with the exception of the horse, which is doubtfully recorded from a late horizon of Rangpur in the Harappan period (Rao, 1973).

Past Conditions

Flora of the time of the Harappan Civilization (*c.* 3500–1500 B.C.)

Woody Remains.

The early use of timber and wood on a substantial scale is attested by the following observations:

Enormous embankments with burnt-brick revetments were raised around the metropolises of Harappa and Mohenjodaro. Kiln-fired bricks were also used for building purposes, but in general burnt brick was more common in the larger settlements (Piggott, 1950; Wheeler, 1953).

The use of kiln-fired bricks in stupendous quantities implies, first, that the fuel required for baking the bricks was available relatively easily and near; and, second, that the climate demanded something more durable than the sun-dried mud bricks which were used almost universally in the empires of the ancient East. From these arguments, and from the complementary evidence of elaborate systems of paved drains, it has been postulated that rainfall was more frequent as well as more substantial than at present, and the timber resources far more abundant (Piggott, 1950). This view is, however, not shared by all archaeologists. Childe, for example, argued that, in the region as a whole, rainfall was low and building timber scarce; but that the local Harappan environment was

N

distinguished by the extent and régime of the river flood, which gave rise to a scrubby vegetation, in which animals found shelter.

Constructional timber included: beams of deodar (*Cedrus deodar*); charred remains of pine rafters (*Pinus roxburghii*) and bamboo, in the uppermost Harappa strata on the citadel mound; and beams of sissu (*Dalbergia sissoo*) at Mohenjodaro (Piggott, 1950). Other uses of timber which have come to light (Chowdhury and Ghosh, 1951) are: shisham (*Dalbergia latifolia*) and deodar (*Cedrus deodara*) for the sides and top respectively of a coffin; ber (*Zizyphus* sp.) in the remains of a wooden mortar from the grain-pounding platforms; and elm (*Ulmus* sp. near *lancifolia*) from the surface deposits at the same site.

Excavations at the two later Harappan centres of Lothal and Rangpur have revealed dry deciduous and thorny species. At Lothal (Rao and Lal, in press) *Albizia, Acacia, Adina cordifolia, Tectona grandis* (teak) and *Soymida febrifuga*, together with an unknown member of Lauraceae have been identified; at Rangpur (Ghosh and Lal, 1963), much the same species, viz. *Albizia, Acacia, Soymida*, with the addition of *Tamarix, Melia* and *Pterocarpus santalinus*.

The remains of wood belong to two distinct classes—on the one hand, those species that were transported, among which should certainly be included pine, deodar and elm, and possibly also shisham; and, on the other, those which might be assumed to have been gathered locally, such as ber. The coniferous timbers were doubtless transported from the Himalayas by river. The shisham, the present range of which extends up to Marwara in Rajasthan, might either have been imported overland or have been cut on the southern fringes of the area of the Harappa culture about 3000 B.C., along the banks of the now dry Ghaggar River, for example, by the site of Kalibangan. The remains of elm match most closely the *Ulmus lancifolia*, which is now confined to the Eastern Himalayas, and it is likely that some allied species grew in this region in protohistoric times (cf. Puri, 1945). *Zizyphus*, a species typical of dry and arid tracts, occurs even now in the neighbourhood.

In short, the surviving specimens of wood do not support the theory that a moist forest flourished in the orbit of the Harappan civilization. A vegetation of scrub, bamboo and tall grass growing in pockets of marshy land, in a climate with a somewhat heavier rainfall for a few months in the year, would account adequately for the facts (Chowdhury and Ghosh, 1951). The pipal (Ficus religiosa), which some claim to recognize on the seals, also grows at the edge of riverine marshy tracts.

Pollen Remains

Few pollen-diagrams are available, and even these have to be evaluated with great caution, since the pollen-spectrum does not usually represent faithfully the adjacent forest flora. [2]

Within the arid region, two studies have been made in which inferences as to the climatic pattern have been derived on the basis of pollen preserved in lake sediments. Since no dates for the various strata and phases are given in the first study, only the later contribution by the same investigator is discussed here (Singh, 1971).

In the sediment deposits of the salt lakes of Sambhar (27°N, 75°E), Didwana (27°20'N, 74°35'E) and Lunkaransar (28°30'N, 73°45'E), and in those of the freshwater lake of Pushkar (26°29'N, 74°33'E), the following phases are recognized:

Date	Characteristics	Inference
Before 8000 B.C.	No pollen	Severe aridity
8000–7500 B.C.	High sedges; frequent *Artemisia*	Wetter
7500–3000 B.C.	Sedges decline—*Artemisia*, *Oldenlandia*; *Maytenus, Capparis, Mimosa rubicaulis*; Cerealia (carbonized wood remains)	Slightly drier
3000–1800 B.C.	Sudden rise in sedges, tree and scrub vegetation: *Sygygium*, *Mimosa rubicaulis, Acacia, Prosopis, Capparis, Tamarix*; *Calligonum, Zizyphus Maytenus*; *Typha*; Cerealia	Sudden increase
1800–1500 B.C.	Sedges decline; mesophytes (trees mentioned above) disappear; fresh water aquatics disappear	Short dry period
1500–1000 B.C.	—	Marginally wetter
1000 B.C.	—	Considerably more arid

The main argument for the climatic régime relies on the xerophytic or mesophytic character of the various types of pollen encountered. Thus, wet conditions or high rainfall are inferred from (i) the high value for sedges (ii) the high value of *Artemisia*, and the presence of *Mimosa rubicaulis* and Oldenlandia, and (iii) the presence of *Typha angustifolia*. It has been aptly contended (Mittre, 1971, 1972) that Cyperaceae and *Artemisia* are indicators not of high but of low rainfall, that grasses have no diagnostic value, that *Mimosa rubicaulis* indicates arid conditions, and that *Typha* is non-diagnostic as it is rare at Puskhar in the wetter zone, and in any case produces enormous quantities of pollen. It may also be mentioned that all the tree and shrub species identified (with the possible exception of *Syzygium*), namely *Acacia, Prosopis, Capparis* and *Tamarix*, are indicators of dry conditions. The pollen diagrams are also highly truncated. A critical review of the evidence cited in these papers suggests that dry rather than wet climatic conditions have to be postulated for the period of the Harappan civilization (Mittre, 1972). The popular theories of appreciable climatic change in the South Asian area during the past 4000–5000 years have thus to be discounted, and climate has been practically eliminated as a major factor in the environmental history of the Harappan civilization (Dales, 1966). The pollen diagrams for the last 10,000 years simply portray minor fluctuations within the prevailing dry or arid climate. The occurrence of Cerealia pollen may be discounted as it is not supported by other evidence of human activity (Mittre, 1971, 1972), except some carbonized wood remains which might indicate the introduction of Neolithic agriculture in the period 7500–3000 B.C. (Singh, 1971).

Cultivated Crops

The Harappans cultivated the following crops, which are more or less the same as those of their Sumerian colleagues; with the notable exception of cotton, three species of which still occur wild in the region: bread wheat (*Triticum compactum* and *sphaerococcum*), barley (*Hordeum vulgare* and *hexastichum* variety), *Setaria italica*, peas (*Pisum arvensis*), *Brassica* (perhaps *juncea*), sesamum, melons, and cotton (*Gossypium arboreum*). Rice (*Oryza*) has been recorded as husks from Lothal and Rangpur in late (c. 2000 B.C.) horizons, and these specimens may have been wild (Ghosh, 1961, 1963; Rao, 1973). Among the fruit trees were dates and bananas (Piggott, 1950; Wheeler, 1953). Although none of the other species mentioned above required a degree of irrigation as intense as that necessary for rice, a well developed irrigation system might be expected to have accompanied an organized agrarian economy; but in consequence of the periodic floods in the Indus system, and continuous aggrading of the valleys, no direct evidence of early irrigation is likely to be found.

Animal Remains in Harappan Times

Wild Animals

Remains of a great variety of wild animals have been recovered, but the main evidence is the many engravings on steatite seals from various sites. The delineation on these seals is of a surprising faithfulness, showing long familiarity with the animals depicted. It can thus be established that doves, parrots, hares, squirrels, mongoose, jackals, wolves, monkeys and bears must have existed in the territory. Suitable habitats must also have existed for tiger, rhinoceros, water-buffalo and elephant, bones of all of which, except in the case of the tiger, have been found at Mohenjodaro or Harappa. Rhinoceros bones have been discovered in association with microlithic tools and pottery of a chalcolithic period in the range 8000–12,000 B.C. in North Gujarat. The rhinoceros is also reported from Langhnaj, Kalibangan and Lothal, and there is in addition the old record from Amri. Horns of the Kashmir, spotted, sambhur, and hog deer too have been found (Piggott, 1950; Wheeler, 1953).

The tiger can thrive under quite dry conditions and is found even today in Rajasthan; but most of the higher mammals just listed could have thriven only in jungle or marsh, such as are no longer found, and could no longer flourish in the proximity of the chief archaeological sites. However, marshy land, suitable as a haunt for the rhinoceros, occurred in the Peshawar valley until 1850 (Holdich, 1909), and marshes are found even now in the Indus Valley proper. They are created by the confinement of the whole drainage of a mighty river to a narrow tract, along the western edge of the Indus Valley from near Jacobabad to Manchhar lake, and along the eastern edge from Khairpur to a place below Umarkot. The latter location, the eastern Nara, is the channel considered by some to be the ancient course of the Sutlej. Manchhar lake itself, lying between the Indus and the foothills of the Kirthar range near Johi, is normally between 12·8 and 16 km in length and equally as broad, but it swells to 512 km^2 in the inundation period. There are a number of prehistoric Harappan sites dotted around, or on islands near the edge of its maximum flooded extent. The thick reed growth of the waterlogged marshes in these areas must have harboured the elephant, buffalo and rhinoceros until comparatively late times.

Domesticated Animals

The Harappans possessed both zebu and humpless cattle (*Bos indicus*), buffalo (*Bubalus bubalus*), goat (*Capra hircus aegagrus* race *indicus*), sheep (*Ovis vignei* race *domesticus*), pigs (*Sus scrofa cristatus* var. *domesticus*), dogs, cats and fowls (Piggott, 1950; Wheeler, 1946).

In all probability the elephant, horse, ass and camel were also domesticated, although the bone evidence is not conclusive for the camel, which, it is claimed, was reared at Kalibangan. The horse was perhaps domesticated in Saurashtra (Rao, 1973).

Drainage

There have been profound changes in the drainage pattern of this arid and semi-arid region during the past five millennia. These changes will be briefly described before considering their causes, and their consequences for the bioclimate of the region.

The drainage may be conveniently considered under two broad heads: (i) the Indus system and (ii) the Saraswati–Yamuna system. The main shifts (designated as "northering" and "westering") result from processes which affect all rivers whose courses lie over alluvial plains, the building up of cones, and the widening and shallowing of channels.

(i) The Indus itself has only two fixed points in its course after it debouches into the plains, and is known to have changed its channel frequently. It has shifted in its lower reaches 160 km to the west, and no longer empties into the Rann of Kutch as it did during the time of Alexander. One major event which took place in late Harappan times (*c.* 2000 B.C.) was a tectonic disturbance at Sehwan, about 144 km downstream of Mohenjodaro, which dammed up the waters of the Indus and created a large lake extending several kilometres upstream of Mohenjodaro (Raikes, 1964). Lacustrine conditions may have lasted for over a hundred years. This event has left abundant traces in the form of deposits of lake silt as high as 9 m above ground-level in the upper reaches (Dales, 1966). In the lower reaches also, near Hyderabad, there are perched and bedded alluvial deposits at Jhirak (1·2 m deep), at Budh Thakar, and near Luka (Sahni, 1955) on the top of mounds 21 m high, containing freshwater shells (*Planorbis, Viviparus, Lymnaca* etc.) which point to prolonged lacustrine conditions.

In A.D. 862 the Indus had deserted its old course through the rocky gorge near Alore (or Aror) and begun to flow along the present channel between Sukkur and Rohri, upstream of Mohenjodaro. The Alore channel is in fact very narrow, and probably never carried the main current to the Khori creek. The city of Brahmanabad was destroyed by earthquake some time before A.D. 1020, and these two events may have been due to the same cause (Oldham, 1893). The channel through the rocky gorge beyond the Alore bund is occupied by the watercourse known as the Nara, which was once a major distributary of the Indus, but which now has no perennial connection with the main river; it has become reduced to a series of disconnected swamps which are united into a stream only during the monsoons. A more recent change of drainage occurred as a result of the 1819 earthquake, when 5120 km^2 was submerged for two years through the elevation of the so-called ''Allah bund'' which extends over 80 − 32 km and rises 3–8 m above the surrounding land. The mouth of the Khori creek was also depressed (Fig. 3). In 1826 the Indus burst every dam on its course and carved a passage through its old channel to discharge into Khori creek. On the way it overspread the Sind desert and cut its way through the Allah bund (Sahni, 1955).

There are signs of major floods too at the Harappan coastal site of Lothal. These must have occurred in the Sabarmati drainage, and possibly in the whole Indus system. Coastal uplifts or marine regression also took place along the northern margin of the Arabian sea during Harappan times, for several old ports now lie many miles inland.

On the major tributaries of the Indus, the greatest changes have occurred in the cases of the Ravi, Beas, and Sutlej. In the past the Ravi used to flow lower down the plain. The Ravi, Chenab and Jhelum had a confluence to the north-east of Multan about A.D. 1245. By the time of Timur's invasion in A.D. 1398, the Chenab had again changed its course and was flowing to the west of Multan. The confluence has now shifted about 48 km upstream. The Ravi continued to flow for some time to the east and south of Multan, until it too changed its course to the present one. Even now, in times of high flood, it reaches Multan by the older channel, which dates back to at least A.D. 800.

The Beas at one time did not join the Sutlej, but followed an independent course to the Indus. It now joins the Sutlej, due to the ''westering'' of this river. After the initial convergence of these streams, there were further changes in the course of the Beas, and its confluence with the Sutlej has now shifted by 240 km, from Bahawalpur to above Ferozepur (Medlicott and Blanford, 1879).

There is historical evidence that the Sutlej was not a Punjab river and did not join the Indus system until shortly before A.D. 1100, when it abandoned its southerly course and joined the Beas. The combined stream is still known locally as the Beas, not as the Sutlej, below the confluence. The oldest of the former southerly channels of the Sutlej is the Sirhind

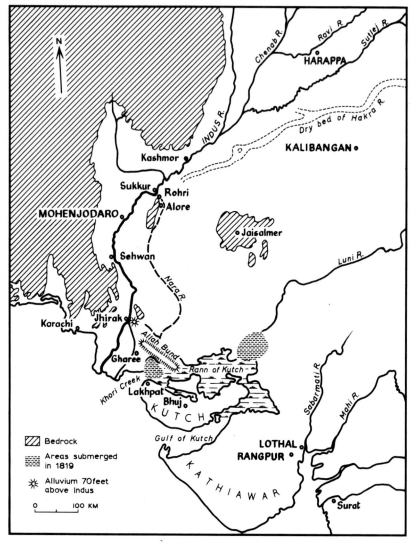

Fig. 3: Evidence of changes in the drainage of Sind.

between Sirsa and Hanumangarh, the three Naiwal courses being later. From Sirsa, the channel can be traced upstream to Tohana, and thence very indistinctly to Rupar near where the Sutlej now enters the plain (Krishnan, 1968). The Sutlej has been a mercurial river, and as late as 1790 it deserted its old bed under the fort of Ludhiana which is now 8 km from the stream and 3 m above it.

(ii) The most conspicuous changes have taken place in the Ghaggar plain

(Fig. 4). Many old abandoned courses can be traced by their flanking high banks and silted beds, but over considerable areas the former channels have been obliterated by moving sands. The chronology of stream movements is quite confused, but the main shifts have again followed from "northering" and "westering", with the further possibility of the diversion of considerable amounts of water to the Gangetic system, through the Yamuna.

The Saraswati is now a minor stream between the Sutlej and Yamuna, which subsequently joins the Ghaggar at Rasula in Patiala, the combined waters being engulfed in the sands at Hanumangarh in Bikaner (Pascoe, 1950). The Saraswati was definitely such a large stream in the Vedic period that it must have been snow-fed, and have derived its waters from the Sutlej or the Yamuna or both. Between Vedic and Mahabharat times, the Saraswati evidently suffered from the easterly diversion of drainage into the Yamuna.

The middle and lower reaches of the Saraswati are now known as the Naiwals, Hakra, Wahind, Sotar etc., and can be traced through Bahawalpur into the channel of the eastern Nara in Sind, which leads into the Rann of Kutch and is distinct from and to the east of the old channels of the Indus. This lower course in Bikaner, Bahawalpur and Sind continued to be well watered for a long period. In fact it is said (in Todd's *Annals of Rajasthan*) that the Hakra in Bikaner became dry for the first time about A.D. 1044 but was not completely dead until 1790. It is conjectured that in later periods the major part of the waters of the Saraswati (the Hakra, Sotar or Wahind) were derived from the Sutlej which, as the Sirhind, originally joined it between Hanumangarh and Sirsa (a name perhaps derived from Saraswati); and later, as one of the Naiwals, near Kurrulwala and Wullur (Krishnan, 1968).

Little is known about the geology of the Sirmur region of the Siwaliks in the area of the junction of the talus fans of the Sutlej in the west and the Yamuna in the east, from where the present Saraswati takes its rise. In view of Himalayan orogenies during the Pleistocene and even in recent times, it would be interesting to know if the subsequent rise of the Siwaliks, and resultant changes in the disposition of the talus fans, together with head erosion by the Yamuna (or Sutlej), had the effect of cutting off the original head waters of the Saraswati and allowing their diversion to the north-west or east. Tradition speaks of an eastern and a western branch; for example, in the Pehova inscription of Bhoj I of the Pratihara dynasty, the stream is called the eastern Saraswati (Ray Chowdhury, 1943).

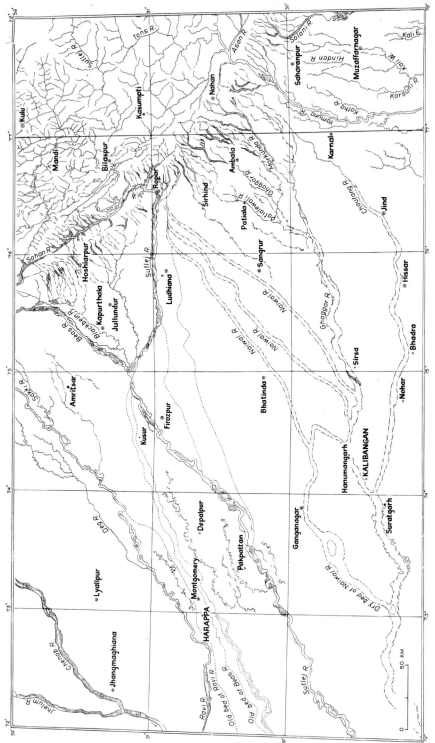

Fig. 4: Former drainage channels of the Punjab.

The highest elevation of the Sirhind watershed on the Delhi-Ambala ridge is only 282 m, and a trifling change in the surface topography might turn the affluents of one river into another (Krishnan, 1968). At just below 213 m, a string of seasonal brackish pools marks the shifting belt of the water-parting which, at Delhi, divides the Yamuna-Ganga drainage system from that of the Punjab. From Delhi the watershed declines in height towards the edge of the Thar, and the spreading waters of the Yamuna were at one time collected at the foot of the western extension of the plain in the Thar to flow mainly into the Indus and the lowlands of Sind (Geddes, 1960). The interchange of waters between the Indus and Ganges systems is confirmed through their sharing allied species of *Platanista* (freshwater porpoise) and other fauna (Medlicott and Blanford, 1879). It seems, then, that in Pleistocene times the drainage of the plain was more ambiguous than now. The shifting or temporary effacement of the watershed zone was perhaps due less to tectonic movements than to changes in alluvial deposition and erosion. In particular, the repeated fanning out of the distributary streams of the Yamuna over its cone often mixed the waters of the Ganga and the Indus, thus confusing their fauna too (Prasad, 1939).

Drainage from the Himalayas would be collected not at the base of the mountain but at the foot of the plain built of their detritus, that is at the edge of the plateau. The periodically shifting watershed was latterly the zone extending for 96 km west from the Delhi ridge (Geddes, 1960). It would thus appear that the Ganges captured the eastern branch of the Saraswati headwaters by means of the lower Yamuna, while the old Beas captured the western branch, which we now call the Sutlej. The Saraswati dwindled to a small stream, the greater part of the old combined channel remaining as the Ghaggar and Hakra. If such a capture took place in historic times, it would explain why the Yamuna is regarded as a tributary and not as the main stream of the Gangetic system, and why the Saraswati is still supposed, by subterranean flow, to meet the Ganges at Prayag (Allahabad). "Yamuna" means "one of a twin" and is usually applied to a new channel. So it seems that at one time the present Yamuna and Ghaggar formed one stream, which probably received the Sutlej also.

The entire disappearance of the Ghaggar–Hakra–Wahind system may have been due to the wholesale destruction of forests and intensive grazing in the Himalayan foothills, which would lead to severe erosion, and to wandering of the water channels as their beds were raised and their waters were diverted for irrigation, especially in the Ambala region. Other changes of drainage have followed the "northering" of the Sutlej and the drying up of that branch which fed the Ghaggar somewhere between

Binjor and Watar; the ''westering'' of the Sutlej and the dimunition of its flood waters in its lower reaches; the ''westering'' of the Indus and the diversion of its waters from the eastern Nara; [3] and the relative elevation of the Arabian coastline. We must take into account also the disruptive effect on the drainage of the deposition of blown sand of local origin, derived from the disintegration of rocks and from the sandy embankments of river channels, especially in the Indus basin, where coarser sand is deposited due to the greater gradient of the Punjab affluents, and to some extent from the rann of Kutch (Pithawala, 1952).

The Desert in History

In the Epics the southern bank of the Saraswati, which was a part of the Kurukshetra, was described as *not* arid, for trees and roads lined its banks. However, the Dvaitvana below the Kamyakvana was already a thorny forest on a level and arid plain, and stood at the head of a desert area (Marwar). The stream was described as at one point smothered and swallowed up in the sands close to the land of Sudras (Sodroi of Diodoros, Sogdoi of Arrian) and Abhirs (Abiria of Ptolemy) (Ray Chowdhury, 1943).

So, at the time of Alexander's invasion and retreat (327 B.C.), Sind (Mousikanos) was perhaps still a fertile tract, although by A.D. 712 the eastward penetration of Islam was thwarted by this bulwark of desert. Southern Baluchistan had certainly reached its present aridity in Alexander's time, for his retreating army was decimated in the cheerless wastes of Makran. The Upper Indus basin might, however, have sustained a somewhat moister climate till later times, and dense forests grew near Ohind, sufficient to enable Alexander to construct the first Indus flotilla.

Arrian, the chronicler of Alexander, has told how the Northern Punjab between the Jhelum and the Chenab was covered with dense forests with lofty trees, and numerous springs; but he describes the high plains and tableland west of the Ravi as already bare and desolate (Stebbing, 1922).

That the climate of Saurashtra during Ashoka's reign (*c*. 240 B.C.) was such that precipitation needed to be carefully stored is evident from the construction of the dam which created the Sudarshana lake near Junagadh in Girnar. Rudradaman's inscription of A.D. 150 mentions repairs to a break in the reservoir. This dam was again breached, and was repaired by Skanda Gupta's Governor in A.D. 457–58. It had, therefore, a useful life of at least 600 years. When it was finally breached is not known, but the Sudarshana lake exists no longer (Majumdar, 1960a, b).

For the early historic period, some indications regarding rainfall are available from Kautilya's *Arthashastra* (Shamasastry, 1929). Although supposedly composed in the third century B.C., it probably attained its present form three or four centuries later. In the 41st Section of the 24th Chapter, while dealing with amounts of rain sufficient for a good harvest in different regions, he says that 16 *dronas* are enough in dried-up areas, 23 such units in Malwa, and unspecified amounts in Western Rajasthan, implying that whatever rain falls in the last tract is helpful. This would indicate definite arid conditions and rain-fed agriculture of a precarious nature.

The accounts of the Chinese travellers, Hiuen-Tsang and I-Tsing, give some information about climate and vegetation during the middle years of the seventh century A.D. Hiuen-Tsang records in his diary that in general the plains below the western mountains were dry and saline (Ch. 2); there were dense and shady forests, and rice was cultivated, near Jullunder (a typically dry tract now); *Emblica officinalis* was grown on a large scale near Mathura (Ch. 4); Malwa was well forested; and, finally, at Broach, at Atali near Kutch, and in Saurashtra and south-western Rajasthan, the soil was saline or sandy, trees were few, and many dust storms occurred (Ch. 11). He had to cross a formidable stretch of desert to reach Sind from Gurjardesh (Barmer). On the other hand, the soil of Multan is described as good and fertile, and the climate as mild and pleasant. This indicates that, while desert conditions had settled on the Lower Indus Valley, the south-western part of Rajasthan around Barmer and the Punjab plains from Multan to Jullunder had not been desiccated to anything like their present condition. The onset of extreme aridity in many parts of Rajasthan (except for the core of the Thar) and in the Punjab plains is thus perhaps a comparatively recent phenomenon.

The Decline of the Harappan Civilization

Change of climate is frequently adduced as the main reason for the rapid decline and disappearance of the Harappa civilization between 2500 and 1500 B.C. As has been seen, a substantial change in climate can definitely be ruled out. A certain degree of desiccation (which would imply a higher rainfall previously) was certainly caused by the destruction of vegetation through improvident use of wood in the cities and through the practice of pastoral nomadism, but this cannot account completely for the decline.

So far as concerns those districts of the Harappan civilization that lay near sea-level, there is firm evidence that floods were the main cause of decline. Apart from the tectonic disturbance at Sehwan which led to a lake being formed, there is ample indication of the frequent deposition of silt throughout the span of the civilization. The perched alluvium at Budh Thakar, Jhirak and elsewhere has already been mentioned. At Mohenjodaro itself, the depth of the occupation deposits is 22·5 m, of which 10·6 m are above the surrounding plain and 7·3 m below the subsoil water-level; and here silt deposits are preserved as high as 9 m above the ground level. Multiple silt levels and repeated reconstruction suggest that the city was flooded no less than five times. It is impossible to estimate how long the cycles of the formation and disappearance of the lake lasted, but it is doubtful if the duration of any such episode would have exceeded a hundred years (Dales, 1966).

In Lothal also there is evidence of five major floods, with smaller ones in between. Noteworthy are those of c. 2350 B.C. (when a new dockyard was built and the township remodelled on a mound); 2200 B.C. (marked by damage to the embankments of the Acropolis); 2050 B.C.; 2000 B.C. (when the dock and warehouse were damaged, the river changed its course, and the dock was recommissioned by building an inlet channel); and 1900 B.C. (with the consequent destruction of all buildings and the virtual end of occupation). In Rangpur, also, there is evidence of this latest flood, which may be connected with the 70 ft of high silt deposits at Budh Thakar (Rao, 1973). At these lower riverine sites the brick embankments were obviously built as flood defences.

The decline of the city of Harappa, however, cannot be ascribed to flooding, and in general the northern settlements seem to have been abandoned abruptly, perhaps following an incursion of raiders: for there was no material decline before abandonment, contrary to what is seen at Mohenjodaro, Lothal, Rangpur and elsewhere (Dales, 1966).

In the Ghaggar plain, the Harappan phase is later in date. Kalibangan, for example, flourished between 1700 and 1500 B.C. The settlements here may have sheltered refugees from the northern and southern Harappan towns, and been themselves abandoned following a slow decline due to the movement of rivers away from the townships and to desiccation caused by the destruction of vegetation by nomadic pastoral groups, Scythians, Abhirs, Gurjars and the like.

Harappa and Mohenjodaro were large cities and must have produced food for their populations from the surrounding countryside. This, however, does not imply a more humid climate. Even now, without ploughing or manuring, wheat and barley can be raised when by

September the flood has receded, leaving fertile silt on the extensive flood plain (Allchin and Allchin, 1968). Conditions were different at Kalibangan and other southern outposts, where the river system must then have been suitable for irrigation. Traces of rice husks at Lothal (Rao, 1973; Rao and Lal, in press) and Rangpur (Ghosh, 1961; Ghosh and Lal, 1963) do not necessarily point to humid conditions; for some rice may have been grown under irrigation, or wild species gathered from the marshes. A slight decline in rainfall would naturally follow the widening of the temperature range, itself the consequence of the destruction of the natural vegetation.

Has the Climate Changed?

Rainfall and Temperature

Monsoon conditions are said to have become established in India after the Miocene epoch, when the Himalayas rose to prominence. Between that period and the onset of desert conditions in geologically sub-Recent or Recent times, the Western Indian region should in theory have enjoyed a moister climate. The protagonists of a definite climatic shift during the last four millennia claim that a relatively minor climatic adjustment would be sufficient to account for the change in the character of the environment.

Such a change in climate could have taken the following forms:

1. the Atlantic cyclones, which at one time ranged southwards to the latitude of northern Africa and moved across Arabia, Persia and India to nourish the plains of Sind, have receded northwards since the third millennium (Wheeler, 1946; Huntington, 1907);
2. the limit of the area affected by the south-west monsoon has shifted eastwards: formerly the Indus lay within the zone of monsoon rains;
3. the northern storm-belt was deflected southwards by conditions in immediately post-Glacial times, and the effect persisted after the establishment of otherwise "normal" climatic conditions (Piggott, 1950).

The evidence of large-scale movements of populations is often cited, on the hypothesis that, in periods of decreased rainfall, migrations take place from drier to moister areas. In the Arabian region, four great migrations took place, all due to drought, about 4000 B.C., 2000 B.C. (Amorite), 1350–1300 B.C. (Aramaean) and A.D. 700 (Arab). From the Rigvedic accounts it appears that the period of 3000–2000 B.C. was one of increasing drought; at Anau also from 3000–2200 B.C. the climate was very dry. Dispersals and migrations were common during these periods (Brooks, 1949).

The present climate of Sind is extremely arid, the average rainfall being less than 152 mm in a year, with maximum temperatures in the neighbourhood of 120°F, and frosts in winter. That the climate was somewhat kinder in the past cannot be denied, however scanty the objective evidence may be: even if it is conceded that the vegetation was of a scrubby type, and akin to its present degraded remnant, better growing conditions with ampler rainfall and less extreme temperatures must have prevailed. The question is, whether a basic climatic change of the type suggested above took place, or whether the progressive deterioration in the environment in the Indus Valley and nearby areas was the result of human interference, such as burning fuel in brick-kilns, and overgrazing. Interference of this kind would have led to a progressive deterioration in the local climate, by establishing a vicious chain: denudation leading to a harsher climate, this in turn creating conditions unsuitable for the regeneration of plant cover, and finally the reign of aridity.

The combined weight of historical and archaeological studies argues in favour of a great stability of climate, at least during historical time (Tixeront, 1956). There is some evidence of a contrary nature also, which shows on the basis of C^{14}-dating that drastic differences must have existed in some areas less than nine millennia ago, and that there have been significant cycles within this recent period (Kellog, 1956). There have, after all, been wide swings from dry and warm to cold and wet conditions in Europe in the last 2000 years. It is, however, simpler to assume that deterioration in local conditions has been caused largely by local effects which have modified the topography, temperature and humidity: these effects would include seepage and surface drainage, wind movement and insolation, all of which would have had consequences for the local climate. The evidence from Israel and Tunisia as well as India (Pramanik et al., 1952) supports the view that climatic changes due to human causes outweighed those of natural origin.

Deforestation

There is a widespread belief that the destruction of forests has caused a change of climate. There is no doubt that extensive forests do influence the climate appreciably, and may be responsible for a share of the rainfall. A barrier of trees protects the land from desiccation by winds, reduces soil blow, and modifies the régimes of temperature and humidity. If all the vegetative cover were reduced from a large enough tract, remarkable changes would be sure to follow (Tannehill, 1947). The temperature would rise steeply, its range would widen, and the temperature differences between land and sea and land and upper atmosphere would change the pattern of wind circulation both horizontally and vertically, thus disturbing the balance between "wet" and "dry" air currents, and upsetting the distribution as well as the amount of precipitation. This is undoubtedly what has happened, not in one step, but as a cumulative result of the denuding of vegetation over a long period of time.

Conclusions

It would thus appear likely that there has been no real increase in aridity due to natural climatic causes within the last five millennia. Desiccation has certainly taken place to some extent, but it can be attributed to other causes, chief among them being the diminution of the Himalayan glaciers; the diversion of perennial rivers and their cut-off due to the shallowing, widening, and raising of their beds through the deposition of detritus; the erosion in the catchments caused by human activity; the destruction of natural vegetation by man and his roving animals; the collapse of dams and barriers; and the diversion of flood waters for seasonal irrigation. Plundering of vegetation exposes the soil and results in lowered productivity, decrease in surface-water supply in springs, streams and wells, and diminution in underground water resources as the water table sinks. Desiccation under these conditions may be aggravated by the proximity of desert areas from which strong dry winds, hot or cold, usually blow and cause accelerated evaporation as well as the penetration of sand (Stebbing, 1954).

It is evident that such conditions have prevailed, in the Indus Valley in particular, during the last one or two thousand years. Circumstances here are critical, and can with little change bring harsh developments. Strong summer winds prevail, and there is plenty of sand for them to lift. The destruction of even such scrubby vegetation as the area has now, or has had from the beginning, can easily tilt the balance in favour of desert. In such a sequence of events man appears to bear the major responsibility for the present state of affairs.

Except in a narrow fringe where some shifts in patterns of climate may be postulated, namely the southern limits of Makran, Baluchistan, and some parts of upper Sind and western Rajasthan (see p. 299), the desiccation can be attributed directly or indirectly to human activity which can be historically attested. There is definite evidence of the migration of tribes from south Punjab to east Rajasthan and thence to Madhya Bharat in the third century A.D. (Sankalia, 1952). Nomadism became the dominant way of life by the seventh and eighth centuries A.D. in consequence of continued desiccation. The large settlements of the Rangmahal culture in the Drishadavati (the present Shautang) valley may point to a partial resuscitation of the river system during the first half of first millennium A.D., and there are even mediaeval ruins which bespeak a fairly continuous occupation.

Notes

1. Latitude factor is the cosecant of latitude; precipitation factor is the ratio of the difference between maximum and minimum precipitation to average precipitation for a given number of years; and the last term is the mean annual range in °F.
    2. The reason is that, apart from contamination, the pollen diagram is inevitably truncated; for, because only anemophilous pollen is thus transported and preserved, families like Rosaceae and Lauraceae are represented least (Mittre, 1972), and the highest frequency is usually of Graminae. Problems of scale of production, long distance transport by wind and water, differential destruction due to lithological and biological factors, local over-representation, microbial activities and so forth, hamper a faithful reading of the diagram (Chanda, 1971). In a case which may be cited (Roy and Gupta, 1971) the pollen spectrum was found not to represent the adjacent flora (mainly broad-leaved species), and 6% of pine was present, although the latter occurs hundreds of miles away from the area.
    3. Due to the tectonic disturbances which disorganized the drainage in the lower reaches, for example at Allah bund and Khori creek.

References

Abichandani, C. T. 1972. Genetic morphology and management of desert soils of India (Lecture). *Soil reclamation training course.* Haryana Agricultural University.
Allchin, B. and R. 1968. *The birth of Indian civilization.* London: Pelican books.
Auden, J. B. 1950. Introductory report on the ground water resources of Western Rajasthan. *Bull. Geol. Sur. of India,* Ser. B, No. 1. New Delhi.

Banerji, J. 1952(a). The role of vegetation in desert control (Discussions). *Symposium on Rajputana desert, Proc. Nat. Inst. Sciences, India*. New Delhi.

Banerji, S. K. 1952(b). Weather factors in the creation and maintenance of the Rajputana Desert, *Symposium on Rajputana desert, Proc. Nat. Inst. Sciences, India*. New Delhi.

Beal, S. (Translator) Hiuen Tsang, *Indian Travels*. Calcutta: Sushil Gupta Ltd.

Blanford, W. T. 1909. *The Indian Empire–Zoology, Imp. Gazetter of India*. Oxford.

Brooks, C. E. P. 1949. *Climate through the Ages*. New York: McGraw Hill.

Bryson, R. A., Wildon, C. A. and Kuhn, P. M. 1963. Some preliminary results of radiosonde ascents over India. *Proc. WMO/IUGG Symposium on tropical meteorology*. New Zealand.

Chanda, S. 1971. Potentiality and problems of Quaternary pollen analysis in India. *Proc. Seminar on Palaeopalynology and Indian stratigraphy*. Calcutta.

Champion, H. G. and Seth, S. K. 1968. *A Revised Survey of the Forest Types of India*. New Delhi.

Champion, H. G., Seth, S. K. and Khattak, G. 1970. *Forest Types of Pakistan*. Peshawar.

Chowdhury, K. A. and Ghosh, S. S. 1951. Plant remains from Harappa 1946. *Ancient India* **7**. New Delhi.

Dales, G. F. 1966. The decline of the Harappans. *Sci. Amer.* **214**(5).

Das, R. B. and Sarup, S. 1951. The biological spectrum of the Indian desert flora. *Rajasthan Univ. Studies*, Biol. Sr. No. 1.

De Terra, H. and Hutchinson. 1936. Data on postglacial climatic change in NW India. *Current Sci.* **5**.

Geddes, A. 1960. The alluvial morphology of the Indo-Gangetic plain: its mapping and geographical significance. *Transactions and papers*, Publ. No. 28. The Inst. of British Geographers.

Ghosh, A. 1952. The Rajputana desert, its archaeological aspect. *Symposium on Rajputana desert. Proc. Nat. Inst. Sciences India*. New Delhi.

Ghose, B. 1965. The genesis of the desert plains in the Central Luni basin of western Rajasthan. *J. Ind. Soc. Soil Sci.* **13**.

Ghosh, S. S. 1961. Further records of rice from ancient India. *Ind. Forester* **87** (5).

Ghosh, S. S. and Lal, K. 1963. Plant remains from Rangpur. *Ancient India* **18–19**, New Delhi.

Holdich, T. H. 1909. *The Indian Empire–Physical aspects, Imp. Gazetteer of India*. Oxford.

Huntington, E. 1907. *The Pulse of Asia*. Boston: Houghton Mifflin.

Jagannathan, P. 1957. Seasonal oscillations of air temperature in India and neighbourhood. *Ind. J. Met. Geophys.* **8** (2).

Kellog, C. E. 1956. The role of science in man's struggle on arid lands. *In: The Future of Arid Lands*, Am. Ass. for the Advancement of Science Pub. **43**. Washington D.C.

Krishnan, M. S. 1968. *Geology of India and Burma*. Madras.

Majumdar, R. C. 1960(a). *Ancient India*. Delhi: Motilal Banarsidas.

Majumdar, R. C. (Ed.) 1960(b). *The history and culture of the Indian people*. Bombay: Bhartiya Vidya Bhavan.

Manton, S. M. 1954. Biological research and the productive transformation of steppe and desert in the Soviet Union. *In Biology of Deserts*. London: Institute of Biology.

M'Crindle (translator) 1893. *The invasion of India by Alexander the Great* (= Arrian's Alexandri Anabasis). London: Constable & Co.

Medlicott, H. B. and Blanford, W. T. 1879. *A Manual of the Geology of India*. Calcutta.

Mittre, V. 1971. Problems and prospects of quaternary palynology in India. *Proc. Seminar on Palaeopalynology and Indian Stratigraphy*. Calcutta.

Mittre, V. 1972. Plant remains and climate from the late Harappan and other chalcolithic cultures of India—a study in inter-relationship. *Proc. Ind. Arch. Soc.* Session Kurukshetra.

Oldham, C. F. 1893. The Saraswati and the lost river of the Indian desert. *J. Rev. Asiatic Soc. London.* N.S. 25.

Oldham, R. D. 1893. *Manual of Geology of India*. Calcutta.

Pascoe, E. H. 1950. *A manual of the geology of India and Burma*. New Delhi.

Piggott, S. 1950. *Prehistoric India*. London: Penguin Books.

Pithawala, M. B. 1952. The great Indian Desert: A geographic study. *Symposium on Rajputana desert, Proc. Nat. Inst. Sciences India*, New Delhi.

Prasad, B. 1939. The Indo-Brahm or Siwalik river. *Rec. Geol. Sur. India* No. 74.

Pramanik, S. K. and Hariharan, P. S. 1952. The climate of Rajasthan. *Symposium on Rajputana Desert, Proc. Nat. Inst. Sciences India,* New Delhi.

Pramanik, S. K. and Jagganathan, P. 1953. Climatic changes in India–I Rainfall. Ind. J. Met. Geophys. **4** (4).

Pramanik, S. K., Hariharan, P. S. and Ghose, S. K. 1952. Meteorological conditions in and the extension of the Rajasthan desert. *Symposium on Rajputana desert, Proc. Nat. Inst. Sci. India,* New Delhi, also *Ind. Jour. Met. Geophys.* **3** (2).

Puri, G. S. 1945. Some fossil leaves of the *Ulmaceae* from the Karewa deposits of Kashmir. *J. Ind. Bot. Soc.* **24** (4).

Raikes, R. L. 1964. The end of the ancient cities of the Indus. *Am. Anthropologist* **66** (2).

Ray Chowdhury, H. C. 1943. The Saraswati. *Science and Culture* 8 (12).

Rao, K. N. 1958. Some studies on rainfall of Rajasthan with particular reference to trends. *Ind. J. Met. Geophys.* **9** (2).

Rao, K. R. and Lal, K. Plant remains from Lothal (in press). *Ancient India*, New Delhi.

Rao, S. R. 1973. *Lothal and the Indus Civilisation*. Bombay: Asia Publishing House.

Roy, S. K. and Gupta, R. C. 1971. Pollen analytical study of the surface sample from Rasauli pond, Varanasi. *Proc. Seminar on Palaeopalynology and Indian stratigraphy.* Calcutta.

Russell, R. J. 1941. Climatic change through the ages. *In:* Climate and man. *Yearbook of Agriculture,* U.S.D.A. Washington.

Sabnis, T. S. 1929. A note on the ecology of the flora of Sind. *J. Ind. Bot. Soc.* **8** (4).

Sahni, M. R. 1955. Biogeological evidence bearing on the decline of the Indus valley civilization. *J. Palaeontological Soc. India.* **1**.

Sankalia, H. D. 1952. The condition of Rajputana in the past as deduced from archaeological evidence. *Symposium on Rajputana desert Proc. Nat. Inst. Sciences, India.* New Delhi.

Sen, N. 1952. Geomorphological evolution of Delhi area. *Current Science* **21** (6).

Seth, S. K. 1961. A review of evidence concerning changes of climate in India during the proto-historical and historical periods. *Proc. WHO/WMO Symp. on changes of climate,* Rome.

Shamasastry, R. (translator). 1929. Kautilya's *Arthasastra.* Mysore: Wesleyan Mission Press.

Singh, Gurdip. 1971. The Indus valley culture. *Archaeol. Physical Anthropol. Oceania* **6** (2).

Stebbing, E. P. 1922. *The Forests of India* Vol. I. London: John Lane.

Stebbing, E. P. 1954. Forests, Aridity and Deserts. *Symp. on biology of deserts.* London: Institute of Biology.

Tannehill, I. R. 1947. *Drought, its Causes and Effects.* Princeton: Princeton University Press.

Tixeront, J. 1956. Water resources in arid regions. *In: The Future of Arid Lands,* Am. Ass. for the Advancement of science. Pub. No. 43, Washington D.C.

Wadia, D. N. 1926. *Geology of India.* London: Macmillan and Co.

Walker, G. T. 1916. On the meteorological evidence for supposed changes of climate in India. *Mem. Ind. Met. Dept.* **21**.

Wheeler, R. E. M. 1946. Archaeological planning for India—some of the factors. *Ancient India* **2**, New Delhi.

Wheeler, R. E. M. 1953. *The Indus Civilization* (Cambr. Hist. India Suppl. Vol.) Cambridge, England: Cambridge University Press.

19
Climatic Change in the Indian Desert and North-West India during the Late Pleistocene and Early Holocene

Bridget Allchin and Andrew Goudie

Background

In the states of Gujarat and Rajasthan (Fig. 1), investigations into environmental changes have been relatively few, and in particular there is a shortage of precise absolute dating of Pleistocene formations and events; though the researches of the recently established isotopic unit of the Tata Institute (Agrawal *et al.*, 1972), of Singh (1971) and of Hegde and Switsur (1973) have gone some way towards rectifying this situation. In general, however, chronologies tend to be based on archaeological remains. A further handicap is that there has so far proved to be a paucity of faunal and floral remains, with the result that palaeobotanical and palaeoecological studies are rare; though some have been undertaken for the Holocene (Singh, 1971; Singh *et al.*, 1972; Bender *et al.*, 1971).

As a consequence, most studies of Pleistocene environmental changes in this area have been based on the stratigraphy and nature of deposits and on the testimony of landforms. However, reviews of the literary and archaeological evidence for the age of the Thar Desert have been given by Meher-Homji (1973) and by Abichandani and Roy (1966).

River Terraces

In the Plain of Gujarat the tradition has been to undertake studies of the terrace features and river-sections: in Rajasthan, because of the relative

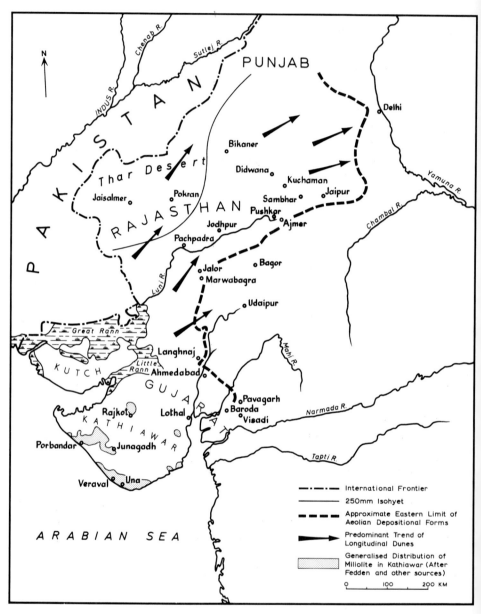

Fig. 1: Landforms of the Desert of Rajasthan.

Table I: Late quaternary chronology in north-western India

Phase	Date	Evidence and effects
Harrapan wet phase of G. Singh	3000–1800 B.C.	Pollen analysis shows conditions of favourable humidity. Archaeological sites in some currently dry areas. Indus civilization.
Pre-Harappan less moist phase	7500–3000 B.C.	Pollen analysis of Rajasthan lakes shows *slight* diminution in rainfall.
Moist phase	Early Holocene (approximately 8000–7500 B.C.)	Freshwater lakes inundated dunes at Sambhar and elsewhere. Arrival of large numbers of mesolithic peoples with their microliths. Start to dune weathering, drainage incision and miliolite solution.
Major dry phase	Late Pleistocene (pre *c.* 8000 B.C.)	Dunes again cover lake basins, block rivers and cause aggradation. Absence of human activity except at margins of desert or at very favoured sites like Pushkar. Upper Palaeolithic tools found in a dune at Visadi, near Baroda. Miliolite laid down.
Major wet phase or pluvial	Middle Stone Age (probably post 40,000 B.P.)	Major phase of soil formation and dune weathering. *Rotlehm* type soils. Widespread human activities even in heart of desert. Through-flowing rivers and deposition of coarse gravels along the Luni and other rivers.
Major dry phase	Pre Middle Stone Age	Major dune formation. Little human activity. Kunkarization of slope wash debris containing Lower Palaeoliths at Pushkar and Marwar Bagra (near Jalor). Some miliolite laid down.

The chronology of Late Quaternary events

Various lines of evidence enable one to establish a tentative chronology of environmental change in North Western India. In the absence of many reliable radiometric dates for the pre-Holocene part of the sequence, the list of events shown in Table I must be regarded as approximate. Overall one can infer that there have been very substantial geomorphic changes in the area during the time-span during which the Last Glaciation affected higher latitudes. Conditions have been both wetter and drier than they are at present, but in general the Holocene seems to have been somewhat moister than the period immediately preceding it, so that the concept of glacial pluvials and of post-glacial desiccation needs to be treated with great reserve in the context of North West India.

absence of incised valleys and associated sections, there has been much less terrace work, and other lines of evidence have had to be followed. Studies by Zeuner (1950), Subbarao (1952, 1955), Wainwright (1964), Allchin and Hegde (1969), and Allchin *et al.* (1970) have shown that the Rivers Mahi, Sabarmati and Narmada possess two major terraces, and that within the Upper (or Ankleshwar) terrace there are fossil soils of wide extent and consistent sequence. The soils have had their calcium carbonate nodules (*kunkur*) subjected to C^{14} dating (Hedge and Switsur, 1973) which shows that they formed over a prolonged period of time extending from 24,000 to 17,000 B.P. The upper terrace (which occurs at up to 30 m above the river bed) and the "old alluvium" of which it is formed are thus relatively young, and the few C^{14} dates so far available for semi-carbonized wood from "old alluvium" in Maharashtra indicate an age of less than 40,000 years B.P. (Agrawal *et al.*, 1972). Thus considerable fluvial aggradation took place in western India towards the end of the Last Glacial, as in many other tropical and subtropical rivers (Fairbridge, 1970).

Lower Palaeolithic artefacts have been recorded in the river valleys of Gujarat, both on the mainland and in Kathiawar and Kutch, stratified below the "old alluvium" (Sankalia, 1965; Subbarao, 1952, 1958; Wainwright, 1964; Zeuner, 1950). This is comparable to the situations in which they occur throughout north and central India and the Deccan. In Rajasthan west of the Aravalli range there is no such geological stratigraphy, and only surface finds had been made prior to our researches.

Middle Palaeolithic industries are apparently absent from mainland Gujarat, but have been recorded in geologically stratified alluvial deposits, and at other sites in Kathiawar (Sankalia, 1965) and Kutch (Joshi, 1972).

Sand Dunes

Fossil sand dunes are widespread in the region and their extent has been mapped by Goudie *et al.* (1973). As in other parts of the world, such as the sub-Saharan zone, the picture has been one of formerly greater aridity that caused a great extension of aeolian activity, even into areas with rainfall in excess of 750 mm today. The dunes were active both in the late Pleistocene period and prior to Middle Palaeolithic times. The last major phase of dune building appears to have been terminated by a humid phase which led to the formation of freshwater lakes (Singh, 1971) and coincided with the arrival of Mesolithic man in large numbers in the area (Allchin and Goudie, 1970).

This period is very well represented in northern Gujarat, where sites have been recorded in large numbers by most of the writers already cited, and in southern and eastern Rajasthan (Leshnik, 1968; Misra, 1971). It is also represented, although less profusely, by a number of sites in Kathiawar and Kutch (Sankalia, 1965; Joshi, 1972). Sites have been found by us as far west as Jaisalmer, and in other extremely dry regions of Rajasthan. (Allchin et al., 1978). All except the last tend to be associated with fossil dunes, which appear to have been favoured camping places. The appearance of Mesolithic industries is associated with the beginning of the Holocene and the onset of climatic conditions approximating to those of the present, and the artefacts are found on the surfaces of the thin soil which has formed upon the fossil dunes. In some cases, such as Langhnaj and other large sites with indications of prolonged or extensive habitation, occupation débris is found up to a metre below the surface. If one looks at the effects of men and animals trampling and breaking the surface around villages in the same localities today the reasons for this will be readily understood: small objects quickly work their way down in the loosened sand. Upper Palaeolithic man appears to have lived in the more favoured localities during the last arid phase, as is witnessed by Upper Palaeolithic tools in a dune at Visadi near Baroda and elsewhere.

Before this stage of aeolian activity, there was a relatively humid phase during which intense sand-leaching and soil-development took place, accompanied by a considerable degree of both Upper and Middle Palaeolithic activity (Allchin et al., 1972; Allchin and Goudie, 1974). The Upper Palaeolithic has only recently been recognized in India, geologically stratified between the Middle Palaeolithic and Mesolithic in extensive sections in the Belan river valley (Sharma et al., 1970), at surface sites in south India (Murty, 1968), and in Rajasthan and Gujarat where it is associated with the buried red soil preceding the last arid phase (Allchin et al., 1972) and with the sands of the last arid phase (Allchin and Goudie, 1970). Its distribution, more limited than that of the Middle Palaeolithic in Rajasthan, confirms its association with arid conditions. At Pushkar and elsewhere Middle Palaeolithic artefacts and working-floors are also clearly associated with the buried red soil intervening between the sands of the two arid phases, and therefore with the prolonged period of increased humidity.

In turn, before this, another deep sand sheet appears to have been deposited over wide areas, and Lower Palaeolithic tools were washed into it by processes of slope-wash. In the Pushkar area near Ajmer in eastern Rajasthan, for example, Lower Palaeolithic artefacts were found in three localities in slope-wash and detritus incorporated into the lower sand-sheet at the foot of rocky hills (Allchin and Goudie, 1974). In each case, gullies had cut through both sand-sheets, exposing the deposits which contained the tools, and the tools themselves were somewhat rolled—an indication that they originated further up the hillside or along the course of the gully.

Other workers have also referred to the fossil nature and palaeclimatic implications of aeolian land forms in South Asia, among them Verstappen (1970) in Rajasthan, and Smith and Snead (1961) and Snead and Frishman (1968) in the Las Bela valley of Pakistan. Verstappen (1972) has provided a useful description of the main types of dune.

Miliolite Deposits (see also Appendix, p. 314)

Related in type to the sand dunes are some controversial deposits called Miliolite or Porbandar Stone. These deposits occur widely in Kutch, and also in Kathiawar where they are of wide extent in the coastal area near Porbandar and Veraval, but are also found at inland locations near Rajkot, Junagadh and Sihor. Miliolite, so called on account of the Miliolid Foraminifera found within it (Carter, 1849) has variously been regarded as a shallow marine facies (Fedden, 1884; Auden, 1952; Shrivastava, 1968a, b) and as an aeolian deposit (Biswas, 1971). Early descriptions occur in Evans (1900) and Chapman (1900), and Biswas, Shrivastava and Fedden all give distribution maps.

Although the Miliolite is made up in large part of the tests of various Foraminifera (mainly Rotalids and Miliolids) and consists largely of calcium carbonate (up to 99%), it is in most inland sites an aeolian deposit. First, it is a very well sorted material with grains of the same size as normal aeolian materials; second, apart from Foraminifera it contains no macrofossils indicative of a marine environment. Foraminifera can be wind-blown and are known as far as 800 km from the sea in some aeolian dunes in inland north-west India. Thirdly, the deposits show cross-bedding of characteristic aeolian type. Fourthly, the deposits occur at heights which are not likely to have been attained by high late Pleistocene stands of sea-level. Fifth, and most convincingly, the miliolite deposits show exactly the same geomorphic effects and relationships as the quartzitic aeolian dune-sands of Gujarat and Rajasthan. Thus it is possible to find very clear instances of deposits located in relation to features of local topography, where natural barriers and traps collect wind-borne sediments, as in valleys and on the windward sides of hills. Moreover, one also finds parabolic dunes composed of cemented miliolite, as near Una in Kathiawar.

These deposits are fossil features resulting from low glacial sea-levels and arid conditions (Glennie, 1970), and are currently being dissolved by karstic processes. Radiocarbon dates (Agrawal, 1969) and the presence of miliolite beneath microliths and above Middle Palaeolithic materials (as in river-sections near Rajkot) indicate a Late Pleistocene age comparable to that of the quartzitic sand dunes of interior north-west India (Allchin *et al.*, 1978).

Fossil River-courses

One consequence of former increased humidity in Rajasthan is that there are numerous old river-courses now blocked by sand and identifiable on air photographs and by the presence of coarse fluvial gravels in the field. Associated with these old courses are lines and clusters of saline depressions such as Pachpadra and Thob (west of Jodhpur), Sambhar, Kuchaman and Didwana (north-west of Jaipur) and certain "ranns" (Kanodwala, Kharowala, Kharia) near Jaisalmer and Pokran (Lawar ka Rann, Dedia ka Rann, and Jhalaria ka Rann). Such river-courses, which are often associated with Middle Palaeolithic artefacts (Misra, 1968), have been mapped by geomorphologists of the Central Arid Zone research Institute at Jodhpur (Ghose *et al.*, 1966). V. N. Misra (1968) found Middle Palaeolithic artefacts at a number of places along the middle course of the Luni, the principal fossil river of South Rajasthan. We also found Middle Palaeolithic sites widely throughout Rajasthan, including the centre and west, and at large factory sites in the Rohri hills in Upper Sind (Allchin, 1976), where it would now be impossible to maintain life without deep wells or piped water. Here they are associated with other fossil rivers, probably former tributaries of the Indus. These old river courses account adequately for the origin of the salt in the "ranns" (Singh *et al.*, 1972), without recourse to the Tethys Sea and other dubious hypotheses (Godbole, 1972). Some of the ranns, however, are largely structural in origin (Pandey and Chatterji, 1970).

Glacial Deposits and Landforms

Virtually no work has been undertaken on late Pleistocene glacial fluctuations in north-west India, and it has so far not proved possible to attempt useful correlations with the stratigraphy and chronology of extra-montane regions. Old moraines at levels more than 1000 m below the tips of present glaciers in northern India were recognized long ago by Hooker (1854) and La Touche (1910), but with the exception of the detailed studies of De Terra and Paterson (1939)—who attempted unjustified correlations with European sequences—and of Joshi (1970), Desio and Orombelli (1971) and Porter (1970), remarkably little is known of the glacial history of the world's highest mountains. Clearly such changes would have had major effects on the alluvial plains and rivers of north-west India, and must stand out as a priority for research.

Acknowledgements

In writing this short survey the authors have drawn largely upon the results of their field work of the last five years, carried out in collaboration with their colleague Dr K. T. M. Hegde, of the M.S. University, Baroda, India, as a joint project for investigating the changing climatic and environmental background of early man in western India. They would like to acknowledge the part played by Dr Hegde in all aspects of the work, and especially in the investigation of the buried soils, and also to acknowledge the various sources of financial support which made it possible for them to go to India, particularly the P. and E. Gibbs Travelling Fellowship, Newnham College, Cambridge (B.A.), Grants-in-aid from The Royal Society (A. G.), and grants from the Smuts and Crowther Benynon Funds, and from Wolfson College in the University of Cambridge.

References

Abichandani, C. T. and Roy, B. B. 1966. Rajasthan Desert—its origin and amelioration. *Indian Geog. J.* **41**, 35–43.

Agrawal, D. P. 1969. *C14date list—June 1969*. Tata Institute of Fundamental Research, Bombay.

Agrawal, D. P., Guzder, S. and Kusumgar, S. 1972. Radiocarbon chronology in Indian prehistoric archaeology.

Allchin, B. 1976. Palaeolithic sites in the plains of Sind and their geographical implications. *Geog. J.* **142**, 471–489.

Allchin, B. and Goudie, A. 1971. Dunes, aridity and early man in Gujarat, Western India. *Man* **6**, 248–265.

Allchin, B. and Goudie, A. 1974. Pushkar: prehistory and climatic change in Western India. *World Archaeol.* (3), (in press).

Allchin, B. and Hegde, K. T. M. 1969. The background of early man in the

Narmada Valley, Gujarat: a preliminary report of the 1969 season's field work. *J. M. S. Univ. Baroda* **17** (1). 141–145.

Allchin, B., Goudie, A. and Hegde, K. T. M. 1970. The background to early man in Gujarat, preliminary report of the Cambridge-Baroda expedition 1970–1971 season. *J. M. S. Univ. Baroda* **19** (1), 15–33.

Allchin, B., Goudie, A. and Hegde, K. T. M. 1972. Prehistory and environmental change in Western India: a note on the Budha Pushkar basin, Rajasthan. *Man* **7** (4), 541–564.

Allchin, B., Goudie, A. and Hegde, K. T. M. 1978. *The Prehistory and Palaeogeography of the Great Indian Desert.* London: Academic Press.

Auden, J. B. 1952. In: *Proceedings of the Symposium on the Rajputana Desert*, Bull. Nat. Inst. Sci. India, 1.

Bender, M. M., Bryson, R. A. and Bearreis, D. A. 1971. University of Wisconsin Radiocarbon Dates IX. *Radiocarbon* **13** (7), 475–486.

Biswas, S. K. 1971. The Miliolite rocks of Kutch and Kathiawar (Western India). *Sedmiment. Geol.* **5**, 147–164.

Carter, H. S. 1849. On the Foraminifera, their organisation and their existence in a fossilised state in Arabia, Sindh, Kutch and Kattyawar. *J. Bombay Branch R. Asiat. Soc.* **3** (1), 158.

Chapman, F. 1900. Notes on the consolidated aeolian sands of Kathiawar. *Q. J. Geol. Soc.* **56**, 584–589.

Desio, A. and Orombelli, G. 1971. Notizie preliminari sulla presenza di un grande ghiaccionio vallino nella medic valle dell'Indo (Pakistan) durante il Pleistocene. *Atti Accad. Nazi. Lin. Radi., Classe Sci. fish., math. nat.* **51**, 387–392.

De Terra, H. and Paterson, T. T. 1939. *Studies on the Ice Age in India and associated human cultures.* Washington: The Carnegie Institution.

Evans, J. W. 1900. Mechanically-formed limestones from Junagarh Kathiawar and other localities. *Q. J. Geol. Soc.* **56**, 559–583.

Fairbridge, R. W. 1970. World climatology of the Quaternary. *Rev. Géog. Phys. Géol. Dynam.* **12** (2), 97–104.

Fedden, I. 1884. The Geology of Kathiawar Peninsula in Gujarat. *Mem. Geol. Survey India* **21**, 2, 73–136.

Foote, R. B. 1898. *Geology of Baroda State.* Madras.

Ghose, B. 1964. Geomorphological aspects of the formation of salt basins in the lower Luni Basin. *Papers from Symposium on problem of Indian Arid Zone*, Jodhpur, 169–178.

Ghose, B., Pandey, S. Singh, S., and Lal, G. 1966. Geomorphology of the Central Luni Basin, Western Rajasthan. *Ann. Arid Zone* **5** (1), 10–25.

Glennie, K. 1970. *Desert Sedimentary Environments.* Amsterdam: Elsevier.

Godbole, N. N. 1972. Theories on the origin of Salt Lakes in Rajasthan, India. *Proceedings, 24th International Geological Congress, Section* 10. 354–357.

Goudie, A. S., Allchin, B. and Hegde, K. T. M. 1973. The former extensions of the Great Indian Sand Desert. *Geog. J.* **139** (2), 243–257.

Hegde, K. T. M. and Switsur, V. R. 1973. Radiocarbon dates of the buried soil in the Lower Narmada valley. *Current Sci.* **42**, 607–609.

Hooker, J. C. 1854. *Himalayan Journals*. London.

Joshi, J. P. 1972. Exploration in Kutch and Excavation at Surkotada and new light on Harappan migration. *J. Orient. Inst.* **22**, (1–2), 98–144.

Joshi, R. V. 1970. The Characteristics of the Pleistocene climatic events in Indian Sub-Continent—a land of monsoon climate. *Indian Antiquary* **4**, (1–4), 53–63.

La Touche, T. H. D. 1910. Relics of the Great Ice Age in the Plains of Northern India. *Geol. Mag.* **7** (5), 193–201.

Leshnik, L. S. 1968. Prehistoric Exploration in North Gujarat and Parts of Rajasthan. *East and West* (N.S.) **18** (3–4), 295–310.

Meher-Homji, V. N. 1973. Is the Sind-Rajasthan Desert the result of a recent climatic change? *Geoforum* **15**, 47–57.

Misra, V. N. 1968. Middle Stone Age in Rajasthan. In: *La Préhistoire, Problèmes et Tendances* (F. Bordes and D. de S.–Bordes, Eds). Paris, pp. 295–302.

Misra, V. N. 1971. Two Microlithic Sites in Rajasthan—a Preliminary Investigation. *Eastern Anthropol.* **24** (3), 237–288.

Murty, M. L. K. 1968. Blade and Burin Industries near Renigunta, on the south-east coast of India. *Proc. Prehist. Soc.* (N.S.) **34**, 83–101.

Pandey, S. and Chatterji, P. C. 1970. Genesis of "Mitha Rann", "Kharia Rann" and "Kanodwala Ranns" in the Great Indian Desert. *Ann. Arid Zone* **9** (3), 175–180.

Porter, S. C. 1970. The Quaternary glacial record in Swat Kohistan, West Pakistan. *Bull. Geol. Soc. Amer.* **81**, 1421–1446.

Sharma, G. R. Stone age in the Vindhyas and the Ganja Valley. In: *Radiocarbon and Indian Archaeology* (D. P. Agrawal and A. Ghosh, Eds), pp. 106–110. Bombay.

Sankalia, H. D. 1965. Early Stone Age in Saurashtra, Gujarat. *Diputacion Provincial De Barcelona, Instituto de Prehistoria Y Arqueologia*, Monografias 16, pp. 327–340.

Shrivastava, P. K. 1968a. A note on the Quaternary Geology of Saurashtra Peninsula. *Q. J. Geol. Min. Metall. Soc. India.* **40** (2), 55–63.

Shrivastava, P. K. 1968b. Petrography and origin of Miliolite limestone of western Saurashtra Coast. *J. Geol. Soc., India* **9** (1), 88–96.

Singh, G. 1971. The Indus valley culture seen in the context of post-glacial climatic and ecological studies in north-west India. *Archaeology and Physical Anthropology in Oceania* **6** (2), 177–189.

Singh, G. Joshi, R. D. and Singh, D. B. 1972. Stratigraphic and radiocarbon evidence for the age and development of three salt lake deposits in Rajasthan, India. *Quat. Res.* **2**, 496–505.

Smith, D. D. and Snead, R. E. 1961. Thick eolian sand prism of probable middle to late Pleistocene age near Karachi, West Pakistan. *Geol. Society Amer. Special Paper* **68**, 274.

Snead, R. E. and Frishman, S. A. 1968. Origin of sands on the east side of the Las Bela valley, West Pakistan. *Bull. Geol. Soc. Amer.* **79**, 1671–1676.

Subbarao, B. 1952. Archaeological explorations in the Mahi valley. *J. M. S. Univ. Baroda* **1**, 33–74.

Subbarao, B. 1955. Archaeology of Gujarat. *Indian Science Congress, 42nd Session, Souvenir volume*, **2**, 44–57.

Subbarao, B. 1958. *The Personality of India*. Baroda.

Verstappen, H. Th. 1970. Aeolian geomorphology of the Thar Desert and palaeoclimates. *Z. Geomorphol. supplementband* **10**, 104–120.

Verstappen, H. Th. 1972. On dune types, families and sequences in areas of undirectional winds. *Gött. Geograph. Abhandl.* **60**, 341–353.

Wainwright, G. J. 1964. *The Pleistocene deposits of the Lower Narmada River*. M. S. University, Archaeology and Ancient History Series. 7. Baroda.

Zeuner, F. E. 1950. *Stone Age and Pleistocene chronology in Gujarat*. Deccan College Monograph Series 6. Poona.

Appendix

Since this chapter was written, the Miliolite deposits, so critical in the climatic and tectonic history of Gujarat, have been the subject of further researches. Lele (1973) proposed a marine origin and an early Quaternary age, and was criticized on both grounds by Sperling and Goudie (1975). Recent studies show that there were several phases of miliolite development (Marathe *et al.*, 1977), and Agrawal *et al.* (1978) provide further radiocarbon dates (between about 35,000 years B.P. and 16,000 years B.P.) for samples which S.E.M. studies show to have had an aeolian origin. Further confirmation of the aeolian origin of inland miliolite deposits comes from evidence provided by Goudie and Sperling (1977) on the wind transport of foraminiferal tests far into the Thar.

New absolute dates have added to our knowledge of the late Pleistocene chronology. For example, studies of ocean cores off Gujarat indicate that large aeolian quartz inputs occurred around 18,000 years ago (Kolla and Biscaye, 1977), an observation which supports the idea that the late Pleistocene was relatively arid. Likewise, radiocarbon dates for Kashmir suggest that deglaciation was in progress at 14,000–15,000 years B.P. (Singh and Agrawal, 1976). The greatly increased amount of archaeological data which is now available for Sind in Pakistan, as well as for Gujarat and

o

Rajasthan, is dealt with at length by Allchin *et al.* (1978) and by Agrawal and Pande (1977).

Appendix References

Allchin, B., Goudie, A. S. and Hegde, K. T. M. 1978. *The prehistory and Palaeogeography of the Great Indian Desert.* London: Academic Press.

Agrawal, D. P. and B. M. Pande (Eds). 1977. *Ecology and Archaeology of Western India.* Delhi: Concept Publishing Co. 255 pp.

Agrawal, D. P., Rajaguru, S. N. and Roy, B. 1978. S.E.M and other studies on the Saurashtra miliolite rocks. *Sedimentary Geology* **20** (1), 41–47.

Goudie, A. S. and Sperling, C. H. B. 1977. Long distance transport of foraminiferal tests by wind in the Thar Desert, North West India. *Journal of Sedimentary Petrology* **47**, 630–633.

Kolla, V. and Biscaye, P. E. 1977. Distribution and origin of quartz in the sediments of the Indian Ocean. *Journal of Sedimentary Petrology* **47**, 642–649.

Lele, V. S. 1973. The miliolite limestone of Saurashtra, Western India. *Sedimentary Geology* **10,** 301–310.

Marathe, A. R., Rajaguru, S. N. and Lele, V. S. 1977. On the problem of the origin and age of the Miliolite rocks of the Hiram Valley, Saurashtra, Western India. *Sedimentary Geology* **19**, 197–215.

Singh, G. and Agrawal, D. P. 1976. Radiocarbon evidence for deglaciation in North-Western Himalaya, India. *Nature* **260**, 232.

Sperling, C. H. B. and Goudie, A. S. 1975. The miliolite of Western India: a discussion of the aeolian and marine hypotheses. *Sedimentary Geology* **13**, 71–75.

20A
Ancient Rivers in the Deserts of Soviet Central Asia

I. P. Gerasimov

Natural Phenomena

Wind and Water Action

The present nature of the desert plains of Central Asia (Turan) is explained by the unusual combination of two sets of phenomena: on the one hand, the destructive activity of the wind—the main sculptor of desert relief—and, on the other, the former accession of water, of which there remain numerous and well preserved traces, to what are now entirely arid territories. These traces consist of a system of dry river beds and numerous lake-basins. As in many other regions of the world, here too nature has shown its inconsistency. The processes of destruction through deflation, which have created large massifs of sandy desert (the Kara Kum, Kyzyl Kum and others) are countered by the creation of hard gravel, salt (gypsum) and clayey crusts which cover all the other deserts with a natural protective armour. Thanks to this surface protection, these deserts preserve many apparently alien relic formations, such as the traces of the former water-courses mentioned above. These so-called *takyrs* and *takyr*-like surfaces evidently play an important role in conserving the traces of ancient fluvial phenomena (Gerasimov, 1954).

The Takyrs

In Soviet Central Asia the term *takyr* implies smooth, bare or almost bare, thin and hard surfaces with a characteristic polygonal (parquet-like) structure (see Fig. 1). Their formation is associated both with the accumulation of elutriated clay alluvium in natural depressions and with

O*

Fig. 1: *Takyrs* in the Karakum Desert.

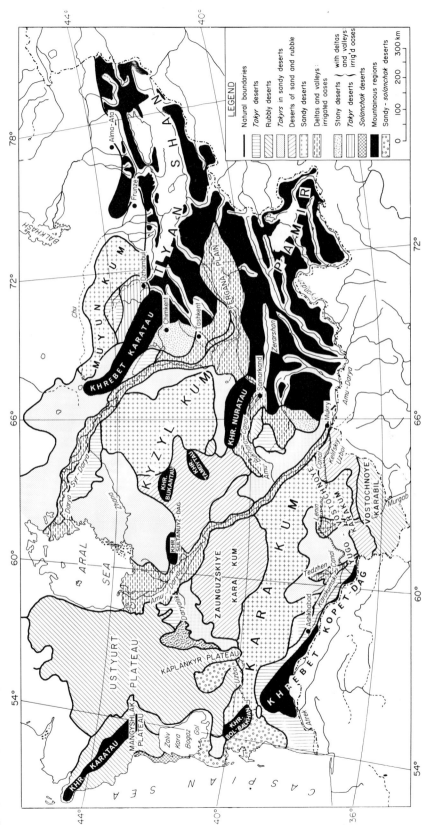

Fig. 2: The major regions of Turan where *takyrs* and *takyr*-like formations are common.

the accumulation of a hard crust of a "dry bread" structure on entirely flat surfaces. Such crusts form not only through the rapid drying under the hot sun of silt suspensions dispersed in alkaline surface water, but also through the cementing of the surface layer by carbonate salts of calcium, precipitated from soil solutions after these have been drawn to the surface by insolation. At the same time, the winds which scour the *takyrs* carry sandy particles quite widely, but these particles are retained only near the sparse shrubs that have here and there managed to fasten themselves to its surface. Small sandy banks or bars form around such shrubs (see Fig. 1).

Extensive strips of *takyrs* in the plains of Central Asia cut across the whole northern part of the interfluve between the Amu-Darya and Syr-Darya (the northern Kyzyl Kum) which lies to the East of the Aral Sea; they cover the present delta of the Amu-Darya with large massifs, stretching far to the west, as far as the Sarykamysh hollow. They also occupy the ancient delta of the Zeravshan River, and penetrate far into the sandy desert of the Kara Kum, both in its south-eastern part (along the ancient deltas of the rivers of Murghab and Tedjen, and also along the so-called Kalif Uzboi) and in its southern part, as far as the foothills of the Kopet-Dag. Moreover, large massifs of *takyrs* cover almost the whole plain between these mountains and the shores of the Caspian Sea in the south-west of Central Asia (the so-called Meshed—Messerian plain and others). Figure 2 shows the main regions in Turan where *takyrs* and *takyr*-like formations are common.

Former Rivers

The whole system of modern *takyrs* in the plains of Central Asia provides convincing evidence of the once high development of drainage in what are now areas of waterless desert. Numerous dry river beds, within which the strips of *takyrs* are situated, confirm this observation. Such is, for instance, the broad bed of Uzboi, which comes out from the Sarykamysh hollow and reaches the south-east shore of the Caspian Sea; and numerous other "worn out" systems of river beds that furrow many massifs and strips of *takyrs*. Of such type are, for instance, the ancient beds in the western (Sarykamysh) part of the delta of the Amu-Darya, which deviate from the present bed of this river in the direction of the Sarykamysh (the Daryalik and others). Of the same character are the dry river-beds which branch out from the modern valley of the Syr-Darya to the west in the northern Kyzyl Kum (the Zhana-Darya and others). When the great "artificial river" of the Kara Kum Canal was constructed in the deserts of Central

Asia, its upper stretch, from the Amu-Darya near the village of Mukra to the village of Karamet-niaz, was laid along the series of dry but clearly preserved basins of the so-called ancient bed of the Kalif Uzboi.

Humid and Arid Places

Quite recently, in the scientific literature on Central Asia, an idea has been proposed regarding the periodic alternation, during the most recent geological period, of pluvial (humid) and xerothermic (arid) epochs (Gerasimov, 1937). The former are considered to be synchronous with continental glaciations in the temperate latitudes of Eurasia; the latter to fall within Interglacial or post-Glacial periods. That very ancient pluvial epochs did occur is proved by the wide spread within Central Asia of thick layers of old alluvial deposits, the upper layers of which have subsequently been deflated and turned into the present sandy deserts. As proof of the occurrence of more recent pluvial periods, some have quoted the traces of a comparatively late accession of water to the territory through the above-mentioned system of old river beds, flooded hollows, takyrs, and the like.

Special Meaning of the term ''Pluvial''

These initial and tentative theories on the palaeogeography of Central Asia have been vindicated by subsequent research. First of all, various geological, palaeobiological and palaeogeographical data hve helped to confirm the great age of the arid natural conditions in the territory of Central Asia which have evidently prevailed at least since the Neogene (see Gerasimov, 1937; Fedorovich, 1956; Korovin, 1961–1962; Sinitsyn, 1962). This is why the general term ''pluvial'' has a quite specific meaning for Central Asia; for by this we do not imply the possibility in the near geological past in the present desert area of true humid climatic conditions such as obtained in the modern forest territories situated further to the north. ''Pluvials'' were rather, in all probability, epochs when the surface water was more abundant than at present in regions which were still nevertheless desert. This was possible through the swelling of the rivers which run from the mountain ridges of the Tien Shan and the Pamirs; also through some increase in the atmospheric precipitation that fed the local closed basins; and finally through a general decrease in evaporation from the water-surfaces.

"Pluvials" Limited to Glacial Epochs

All such hydrological and climatic changes have probably been associated with periodic shifts to the South, that is to sub-tropical or Mediterranean latitudes, of the main trajectories of the eastward movement of air-masses and atmospheric moisture in Eurasia (Gerasimov and Markov, 1939). These shifts, brought about by the development in the north of the Eurasian continent of vast glacial sheets, resulted first in an increase of atmospheric precipitation (increased "interception"), and second in the accumulation of permanent snow and ice in the high-altitude zones of the Tien Shan and Pamirs. Consequently, the run-off of the rivers which fed on the glaciers also increased.

During the most recent Holocene times, that is the last 10,000 to 15,000 years, pluvial changes of this sort were here impossible, because the ice had gone. Periodic moist intervals, involving in particular the water content of the rivers and related to limited changes of climate in historic and prehistoric time, would have had much less marked effects. Conditions of desert climate similar to those of the present (that is, hyper-arid) have evidently prevailed throughout the Holocene on the plains of Central Asia.

Early Irrigation

Direct confirmation of this last conclusion is provided by vestiges of irrigation which used apparently to be widespread on the surface of the clayey (*takyr*) deserts of Central Asia. These vestiges consist of numerous remains of old irrigation structures in the form of half-destroyed canals, water polders bordered by ridges, and once-irrigated soils that contain artefacts (fragments of earthenware and the like). According to some Soviet investigators (Andrianov and Kes, 1967) the total area of desert with remains of ancient irrigation in the plains of Central Asia is as great as 8 to 10 million hectares, which is almost equal to the area of modern irrigation (Fig. 3). If we suppose that irrigation in those early days was practised also on the sites of some of the modern oases, then it would follow that not only was this early irrigation of great antiquity, but that it was also on a quite remarkable scale.

Its Antiquity

Regarding the age of irrigated farming in the plains of Turan, we now have

Fig. 3: Areas of ancient and modern irrigation in the basins of the Amu-Darya and Syr-Darya. 1. Modern irrigated oases. 2. Territory with traces of ancient irrigation.

good archaeological data. Since Palaeolithic remains in Central Asia have so far been discovered only in mountain areas, it appears that pre-historic man did not come down to the foothill plains—and certainly not to the deserts—until the Mesolithic period. In any case, the deserts of Central Asia have so far yielded only isolated finds of Mousterian age (Okladnikov, 1951). However, in the fifth and fourth millennia B.C. there undoubtedly were ancient irrigation structures (as found in the delta of the Tedjen river by Lisitsyna, 1965) and crops cultivated by man (witness the findings of Masson, 1964). In the third and second millennia B.C. the most primitive forms of irrigated agriculture, using land watered by irregular and ephemeral natural floods (supplemented by damming in some areas) were replaced by the first irrigation systems which drew water from permanent water-courses (Gulyamov, 1957; Tolstov, 1962).

If the livelihood of the prehistoric inhabitants of the Turan plains in the Holocene required artificial irrigation, it follows that they were experiencing a desert climate similar to that of the present. At the same time, the great areas of irrigated fields, which at first sight seem to have been even more extensive than those around the modern oases, would appear to indicate that rather more water was available, at least during certain phases of Holocene, than is the case today.

Spurious Extent

An explanation of this contradiction has been provided by the researches undertaken in recent years by Soviet geographers and archaeologists. They show that the remarkable extent of the traces of ancient irrigation on the *takyr* plains of Central Asia is not evidence that these plains were formerly better watered, but is a consequence of the extensive maeandering of the beds of ancient rivers over the Turan plains; for the irrigated oases had continuously to shift in sympathy with the rivers. This general picture has been clearly established in the cases, for example, of the ancient Sarykamysh delta of the Amu-Darya; of the ancient tributaries of the Syr-Darya River in the northern Kyzyl Kum; of the lower reaches of the Zeravshan River; and of the ancient deltas of the Murgab and Tedjen Rivers and the delta of the River Atrek (the Meshed-Messerian plain).

The Sarykamysh Lake and its Phases

We may now proceed to examine in more detail the history of the mediaeval Sarykamysh Lake, as a specific illustration of just such a circumstance of historical geography (see Tolstov *et al.*, 1955; The Lower Reaches of Amu-Karya, Sarykamysh, Uzboi 1960); and, in particular, the relation of the lake to the history of irrigation and to the flow of river water along the Uzboi to the Caspian sea.

It should be remarked in the first place that these features of past geography, namely the Sarykamysh hollow, the dry bed of the Uzboi, and the traces of former irrigation in ancient Khorezm, are very wonderful paleogeographical monuments on the plains of Turan.

The Sarykamysh hollow, which is now completely dry, is the largest depression in Central Asia. Oval in shape, and 90 — 150 km in extent, its floor is 40–45 m below the level of the ocean; in the West and in the North it is bordered by the 80–100 m high scarps (cirques) of the mesa plateau of Ustyurt. To the east of the Sarykamysh lies the so-called ancient Sarykamysh delta of the Amu-Darya River, which rises gradually to the East from 50 m to 80 m above sea-level. This delta is a large plain, with extensive *takyrs* and stretches of sand, and is furrowed by the old river beds of the Daryalik and other streams. In the southern part of the Sarykamysh hollow there is a broad depression (the so-called Upper-Uzboi corridor), within which originates the dry bed of the Uzboi. This depression has the form of a canyon cut in hard mountain rocks and stretching for several hundreds of kilometres between the southern margin of the Ustyurt (the Kaplan-Kyr and other uplands) and the sandy desert of the lowland Kara Kum. The lower reaches of the Uzboi emerge on to the *solonchak* coastal plains on the south-east shore of the Caspian Sea (see Fig. 4).

Various quite fresh traces of former water levels are preserved on the floor and the slopes of the Sarykamysh hollow. These comprise conglomerate ridges and shallow shore-line accumulations of the shells of water molluscs (*Dreissensia polymorpha, Cardium edule* and others), as well as ancient lacustrine benches and terraces. Along the bed of the Uzboi have been discovered prehistoric occupation sites of Neolithic age, the inhabitants of which must have used the water-course which flowed at that time. Finally, on the surface of the ancient Sarykamysh delta of the Amu-Darya, there are numerous remains of ancient irrigation structures, and also ruins of settlements and fortresses, which give grounds for believing that this desert region was once amply populated and well developed.

Ancient and Recent (till Neolithic)

A detailed study of all the above traces of former conditions of

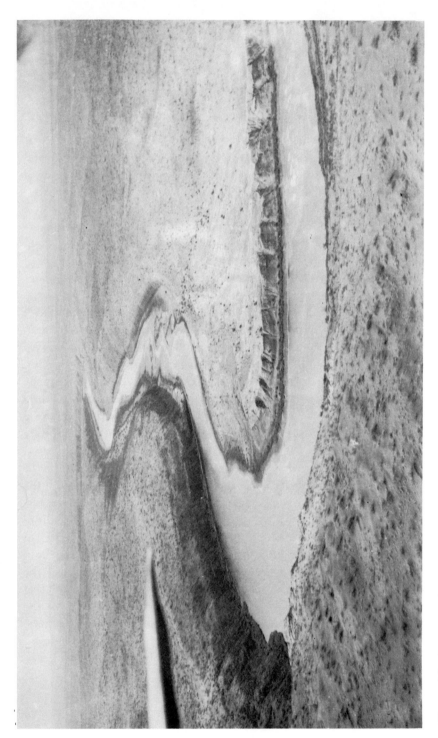

Fig. 4: The lower reaches of the Uzböi.

hydrography, of irrigation, and of rural economy has made it possible to draw significant palaeogeographical conclusions. It has turned out that the Sarykamysh hollow has experienced three phases when water was abundant, separated by epochs of complete aridity. According to the geological data, the first and second floodings took place respectively in Lower and Upper Quaternary times: that is in the Ancient and Recent Pluvial periods. It is quite possible that the latter Pluvial continued into the Holocene (Neolithic and Bronze Ages), as Neolithic finds may indicate (Fig. 5a). At that time some of the Amu-Darya water was flowing along the Uzboi to the Caspian Sea.

However, in the second half of the Holocene and well into historic times (the fourteenth century A.D.) the Sarykamysh lake gradually became dry and the river ceased to flow along the Uzboi (Fig. 5b), as a consequence, doubtless, of the desiccation of those distributaries of the Amu-Darya that earlier flowed into the Sarykamysh. When this happened, the level of the Sarykamysh naturally began rapidly to sink.

Mediaeval (Fourteenth to Sixteenth Centuries)

In the mediaeval period, between the fourteenth and the sixteenth centuries, the waters of the western distributaries of the Amu-Darya again burst into the Sarykamysh and a large lake once more accumulated in the hollow (Fig. 5c). The level of the lake reached 50 to 52 m above ocean level, and irrigation again revived around the lake and on the distributaries of the old delta. However, this last period of access of water did not last long, for according to direct historical evidence after the sixteenth century the Sarykamysh again became dry (Fig. 5d). River flow along the Uzboi probably did not recommence, either during this fluvial phase between the fourteenth and the sixteenth centuries or later.

Causes of Shifts of Rivers

The question now arises of the general reasons for the extensive maeandering of former rivers over the desert plains of Turan, shifts which were evidently influential in the evolution of the present landscape of Central Asia and also in the history of its population. There is probably no single and simple answer to this question. As noted above, there are no grounds for connecting the main maeanderings of the river beds about the territory with significant changes in the general climatic conditions of the

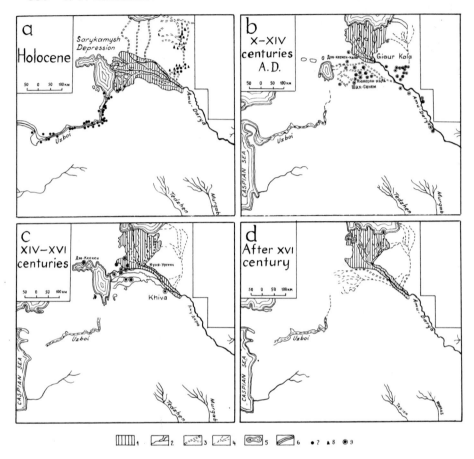

Fig. 5: The four phases of abundant water in the Sarykamysh hollow. 1. Contemporary deltas. 2. River beds. 3, 4. Abandoned river beds. 5. Lake basins. 6. The bed of the Uzboi. 7, 8, 9. Archaeological sites.

whole Central Asian plain, for since very early times these conditions have been characterized by aridity and drought. That is why the most extensive streams of the plains of Turan have long been, and still are, made up of water in transit; in other words, they were and are of alien origin. Having fed on the precipitation of the regions of high altitude in Central Asia, they carried their waters through the desert plains, where, if they did not become exhausted on the way, they reached their terminal drainage basins (the Aral Sea, the Caspian Sea or the Balkhash). That is why the principal probable causes of the observed radical rearrangements of the hydrographic system of Turan were processes of geology or geomorphology, or events of history, which took place within the Central Asian plains.

Increased Access of Water

As noted above, in the period of the Ancient Pluvial the central (lowland) Kara Kum and, probably, the region of the Aral Sea were the main recipients of the river water in the plains of Central Asia. The ancient courses of the ''Great-Amu-Darya'' river went through the Kara Kum, maeandering about the desert spaces and laying down thick alluvial layers. In the Aral region are beds of ancient rivers that came down from the Southern Urals and the mountainous uplands of Central Kazakhstan and flowed freely into the Caspian sea.

Tectonic Effects

In the period between the Ancient and the Recent Pluvial, the general hydrographic pattern of the plains of Central Asia changed radically. The closed Aral Lake took shape, as did the present lower reaches of the Amu-Darya and Syr-Darya, and a whole system of the so-called subaerial deltas that had no exit into the drainage basins (deltas of the Rivers Chu and Sarysu; Zeravshan, Tedjen and Murghab, and others). Such radical changes could have been brought about only by great geological processes, and most probably by extensive wave-like tectonic deformations of the Earth's surface which resulted in the formation of broad downwarps where new basins formed, and of uplifts which became the new interfluves.

The general direction of river drainage on the plains of Central Asia during the New Pluvial already corresponded closely with that of modern times. However, both the subaerial deltas of a number of ''local'' Central Asian rivers (the Chu and Sarysu, Tedjen and Murgab, Atrek, and others) and the beds of large rivers of ''transit'' (the Amu-Darya and Syr-Darya), in those areas where they crossed large flat plains, were very unstable in location, and their wide maeanderings left their marks in the systems of abandoned water courses.

Fan Formation and Eastward Shifts of Channels

It is quite possible that some prehistoric (Holocene) fluctuations of climate influenced the water content of the Central Asian rivers and hence their shifts of course and direction. However, a more important cause of such "migrations" of the river beds and deltas has probably been the processes whereby alluvial detritus accumulated and blocked particular channels and led to the formation of new routes for the run-off. This geomorphic process, which is characteristic of the fans and sub-aerial deltas of streams situated on flat, and particularly piedmont, plains, has certainly been effective in Central Asia. At the same time, it must have operated under the influence of the world-wide phenomenon known under the name of "Ber's Law", according to which there is a gradual shift or undermining to the right, due to the effect of the inertia which follows from the daily rotation of the Earth, in the case of streams that flow in a more-or-less meridional direction. The system of old river beds in the lower reaches of the Syr-Darya, cutting "sidelong" (north-east/south-west) over the whole northern part of the Kyzyl Kum desert, seems to fit this general pattern.

Devastation by Timour

Finally, the Sarykamysh delta of the Amu-Darya and the Meshed-Messerian delta of the River Atrek may serve as excellent examples of the influence of purely historical events on the meandering of river-channels in the deserts of Central Asia. As noted above, between the fourteenth and the sixteenth centuries the waters of the Amu-Darya, which had formerly flowed only to the Aral Sea, suddenly turned their main beds in the direction of the large Sarykamysh hollow and formed there a large lake (Fig. 5c). Historians and geographers believe (see "The Lower Reaches of the Amu-Darya . . ." 1960) that this happened as a result of the conquest by Timour of ancient Khorezm and the resultant widespread destruction of dams and irrigation structures in the conquered territories. The same historical explanation has been advanced by Soviet investigators (see Kes *et al.*, 1970) for the recent changes in the ancient irrigated territories on the Meshed-Messerian plateau, the old delta of the River Atrek.

Conclusion

At the very beginning of this chapter we discussed a paradoxical juxtaposition in the modern deserts of Central Asia of phenomena associated, on the one hand with the wind, on the other with water. Now this paradox seems not only open to explanation, but also entirely to be expected. It follows from the geographical conjunction of the desert plains of Turan with the high-altitude regions of the Tien Shan and the Pamirs which border them to the East. In these mountains, and specifically in their permanent snows and glaciers, originate the great rivers that used to water the deserts. Due to the sharp change of slope between mountain and plain, the beds of such rivers have wandered widely, under the influence of geomorphic processes and climatic fluctuations. However, the concluding stages of the palaeogeographical paradox with which we began were effected by man, who many thousands of years ago started to use the "transit" waters of these large rivers for conquering the deserts of Turan by means of irrigation. Having constructed, in suitable places, his irrigation structures, "tied" to the natural streams, man left them behind when the river beds began to meander; or, sometimes, under different historical circumstances, he destroyed them completely.

References

Andrianov, B. V. and Kes, A. S. 1967. Razvitie gidrograficheskoi seti i irrigatsii na ravninakh Srednei Azii. (Development of hydrographic systems and irrigation on the plains of Central Asia) sb. *Problemy preobrazovaniya prirody Srednei Azii,* Izd. AN SSSR.

Fedorovich, B. A. 1956. Proiskhozhdenie reliefa sovremennykh peschanykh pustyn. (Origin of the relief of recent sandy deserts). *Voprosy geografii.* M.–L., 114–126.

Gerasimov, I. P. 1937. Osnovnye cherty razvitiya sovremennoi poverkhnosti Turana. (The principal features of the development of the present surface of Turan). *Trudy Inst-ta geografii AN SSSR.* **XXV**.

Gerasimov, I. P. 1954. Cherty skhodstva i razlichiya v prirode pustyn. (Similarities and differences in the nature of deserts). *Priroda* **2**.

Gerasimov, I. P. and Markov, K. K. 1939. *Lednikovyi period na terrirorii SSSR. (The glacial period within the USSR).* Izd. AN SSSR.

Gulyamov, Ya. G. 1957. *Istoriya orosheniya Khorezma s drevneishikh vremen do nashikh dnei. (The history of the irrigation of Khorezm since antiquity till our days).* Tashkent. Izd. AN UzSSR.

Kes, A. S. *et al.*, 1970. Istoriya Sarykamyshskogo ozera v srednie veka. (History of Sarykamysh lake in the mediaeval period). *Izv. Akad. Nauk SSSR, ser. geogr.* 1954, No. 1, pp. 41–50.

Korovin, E. P. 1961–62. *Rastitelnost' Srednei Azii i Yuzhnogo Kazakhstana. (Vegetation of Central Asia and South Kazakhstan),* **I–II**. Izd. AN UzSSR.

Lisitsyna, G. N. 1965. *Oroshaemoe zemledelie epokhi eneokhita na yuge Turkmenii. (Irrigated agriculture of the epoch of Aeneochite in the south of Turkmenia).* Izd-vo Nauka.

Masson, V. M. 1964. *Srednyaya Aziya i drevnii Vostok.(Central Asia and the ancient East).* Izd-vo Nauka.

Okladnikov, A. P. 1951. *Drevneishie arkheologicheskie pamyatniki Krasnoviiskogo poluostrova. (The most ancient archaeological relics of the Krasnoviysk peninsula).* Trudy ekspeditsii. Ashkhabad.

Sinitsyn, V. M. 1962. *Paleogeografiya Azii. (Paleogeography of Asia).* M.–L. Izd-vo Akad nauk SSSR.

Tolstov, S. P. 1962. Ed. *Narody Srednei Azii i Kazakhstana.(Peoples of Soviet Central Asia and Kazakhstan).* M.

Tolstov, S. P. and Kes, A. S. (Eds) 1960. Nizoviya Amu-daryi, Sarykamysh. Uzboi. 1960. (The lower reaches of the Amu–Darya river Sarykamysh Uzboi). *Met. Khorezm eksp. vyp.* **3**. Izd-vo AN SSSR.

Tolstov, S. P. *et al.* 1955. *Istoriya srednevekovogo Sarykamyshskogo ozera. (The history of the mediaeval Sarykamysh lake).* Voprosy geomorfologii i paleogeografii Azii. M.

20B
The Past and the Future of the Aral and the Caspian Seas

I. P. Gerasimov

General History and Geography

On the relief map of the world, the Caspian and Aral Seas look like outposts of the broad belt of water of the Mediterranean, which intrudes from the west deep into the Eurasian continent. Such a view of these inland basins can be justified on grounds of geological history; for the whole adjoining territory of Soviet Central Asia was, in the Tertiary period, flooded by the vast sea basin of Tethys, which also engulfed southern Europe. The past existence of Tethys is proved by the many layers of petrified sea sediments which form the plains and plateaux of the Mediterranean region.

However, the relationship of the Caspian and Aral Seas with the present-day Mediterranean cannot be extended beyond such geological considerations; for in respect of the history of their formation, the conditions under which they now survive, and the influence they exert on their surrounding territories, the two seas are unique and have no analogues in the Mediterranean. In particular, nowhere on their extensive Central Asian shores do these basins display such picturesque natural subtropical landscapes as are seen on many European coasts of the Mediterranean. On the contrary, the prevailing landscape here is one of salt (solonchak), sandy, clayey and stony deserts, which come close to the shore-lines of both the Aral and the Caspian Seas. There is here a sharp contrast between the large water basins abounding in lake and sea flora and fauna, and the lifeless desert shores with poor xerophytic vegetation. This contrast creates the impression that the two basins are alien intruders in a hyper-arid natural environment, an impression which is further enhanced when one considers the history of the formation of the Aral and Caspian Basins and their present hydrological peculiarities.

Both the Caspian and the Aral Seas exist thanks exclusively to the influx of river water from afar. The Caspian Sea is, first of all, fed from the whole basin of the Rivers Volga and Ural, that is to say from the greater part of the Russian plain and the western slopes of the ridge of the Urals. The Aral collects water from the high zone of the Tien Shan and the Pamirs, with their permanent snows and glaciers, where originate the Amu-Darya and Syr-Darya. The flow of distant waters to the two seas compensates for their huge losses of moisture through evaporation from their open water-surfaces under hot desert conditions. Thus, the basic condition for the existence of these two water basins is a more-or-less stable balance between the inflow of river water on the one hand and evaporation on the other.

Since they depend so closely on the remoter parts of their catchment areas, the Caspian and the Aral Seas have naturally been regarded as sensitive indicators of many processes within their watershed basins, including first of all a variety of both natural changes and artificial transformations of the natural environment. In the present context, account will be taken not only of the history of the formation of these seas and the conditions under which they have existed in the past, but also of attempts that are being made to forecast their future.

For the time has come to go beyond the study of the basic changes in the regime of our southern inner seas, and to work out practical ways of regulating them in the future. We are indeed faced with the urgent task of rational management of these, our largest, water basins. In what follows, we shall try to present briefly both these related considerations, of the past and future of these seas.

The Caspian Sea

Its Water Balance

As is well known, the water balance of a closed water basin like the Caspian Sea involves the total run-off of the rivers that feed it; the volume of atmospheric precipitation over the water-surface; and the evaporation from this surface. Underground run-off is another factor, but its volume is usually small, and we may therefore ignore it in our argument.

Scientific literature contains many calculations of the water balance of the Caspian Sea, made at different times and with different data. The most recent calculations were published in 1972 by the State Oceanographic Institute (see Present and Prospective Water and Salt Balance of the

Southern Seas of the USSR, 1972). The figures are as follows:

Receipt, km³ (Inflow)		Debit, km³ (Discharge)	
River run-off	291	Evaporation	374
Precipitation	87	Outflow to Kara-Bogaz-Gol	11
TOTAL	378	TOTAL	385

These data show that about 80% of the whole inflow to the Caspian Sea is made up by the run-off of rivers, of which in turn the run-off of the Volga comprises more than 80% (244 km³).

Past Changes

So we may naturally conclude that the level of the Caspian as a closed sea has always been, and still is, unstable and dependent on the state of its water balance. When the inflow of river water increases, even if the general intensity of evaporation remains the same, the level of water in the sea will rise; in the opposite case, it is bound to fall. At the present time, with the water balance shown above, the level of the Caspian Sea fluctuates around 28 m below the level of the ocean. However, on almost all the Caspian shores there are numerous traces (terraces, shore ridges and benches, remains of mollusc shells, etc.) of higher levels of the water basin in past geological and prehistoric periods. Besides, on the basis of many historical data (monuments marking the shore line, flooded structures of different ages and notes in chronicles and old books) we can also define the earlier, usually higher, levels of the sea. Finally, during the last 140 years, special instrumental observations of the sea-level of the Caspian have been systematically carried out. What are the general conclusions from these data?

The Lower and Upper Khvalyn Transgressions

The so-called *Khvalyn* transgression was the last and most profound geological transgression of the Caspian Sea. It is usually divided into two phases; the Lower and Upper Khvalyn. The Lower Khvalyn is conventionally correlated with the epoch of the last continental glaciation (Würm or Valdai, see Gerasimov, 1937; Fedorov, 1957), when the melt-water of the glacier flowed into the Caspian Basin; the Upper Khvalyn, with the beginning of Holocene. Traces of the shore-lines of the Lower Khvalyn Caspian Sea have been recorded at altitudes of 50 to 55 m above sea-level, or even higher. This means that the general area of the Caspian Basin was much greater at that time than at present, and that the water level was as high as 75 m above that of the present (Fig. 1). The maximum

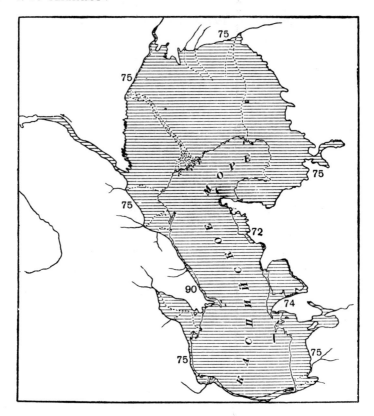

Fig. 1: The Lower Khvalyn Basin. Dated to the end of the Pleistocene (the Late Würm). Heights in metres above the present level of the Caspian.

level of the Upper Khvalyn Basin is supposed to have been 26–28 m above the present, that is, about the same as the level of the ocean. The area of the Caspian was at that time certainly much smaller than in the Lower Khvalyn phase, but still much greater than now (Fig. 2).

Soviet investigators of the geological past of the Caspian Sea are completely agreed that such remarkable rises in the level of the ancient Caspian (at the end of Pleistocene and the beginning of Holocene) were caused not so much by basic differences of water balance between then and now, but rather by purely geological factors. We have in mind the great tectonic movements of the Earth's crust in the region of the Caspian or in the Caspian depression itself, which involved alterations of both form and capacity. In this connection we would like to remind the reader that the present basin or hollow of the Caspian Sea consists of the following three

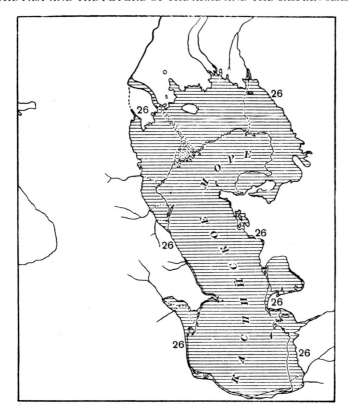

Fig. 2: The Late Khvalyn Basin. Dated to the beginning of the Holocene (*c.* 10,000 B.P.). Heights in metres above the present level of the Caspian.

main parts: the northern shallows (up to 5 m deep); the middle, moderately deep, section (up to 788 m); and the southern, which is the deepest (up to 1025 m). We may easily imagine what profound consequences for the shore lines of the basin may have been caused by a tectonic uplift or subsidence even in only one (for instance, the southern) part of the basin.

The New Caspian Transgression

By the time of the so-called New Caspian transgression, the age of which is believed to be not less than 2000 or 3000 years B.C., the general outlines of the modern Caspian Sea would have been established, although its surface-level was 6–7 m higher than now (Fig. 3).

340   I. P. GERASIMOV

Changes of Level in Historic Times

To A.D. 1760

As noted above, changes during historical time in the level of the Caspian Sea may be defined on the basis of numerous data. A well known investigator of this question, B. A. Apollov (see Fluctuations of the level of the Caspian sea . . ., 1956), has generalized such data as shown in Table I.

Table I: The levels of the Caspian Sea according to historical data

Century (years)	Sources	Level (in m) with reference to the level of the ocean
XII–VIII B.C.	Homer (according to Strabo)	− 25·0
VI B.C.	Gekatei Miletsky	− 26·5
V–II B.C.	Herodutus, Aristotle, Eratosthenes	− 25·0
I B.C.	Josephus Flavius, Strabo	− 14·0(?)
I B.C.	Jafar Zade	− 28·8
	Levels of the Caspian sea in Christian Era	
II	The Map of Ptolemy	− 25·0
VI–VII	Stone quarries of Derbent about	− 26·7
X (951)	Istakhri (The Book of Roads and Kingdoms)	− 25·5
XI–XII	Trees in the region of Lenkoran–Astara	− 31·9
XII–XIII	Stumps in the Kurin spit	− 29·1
1234–1235	Caravansary	− 30·0
XIV	Bakui not less than	− 24·0
1367–1375	Maps by brothers Pitsigani and Katalon less than	− 24·5
1500	Maps of 1500 less than	− 24·5
XVI (1556)	Khanvei	− 26·7
1580	Barro	− 26·2
1604	Tektander	− 26·3
1636	Oleari	− 25·0
1665	Witsen	− 26·6
1668	Strews	− 25·4
XVII (beginning)	Lenz	− 25·3
1715	Bekovich-Cherkasski	− 24·9
1716	John Bell	− 24·8
1714–1720	Van Verden	− 24·6
1719–1726	Soimonov	− 25·3
1723	Sokolov	− 24·0

It follows from the above table that the fluctuations in the level of the Caspian Sea over about the last 3000 years have not been very significant. There is only one eccentric figure (− 14 m in the first century B.C.), and this should be regarded as dubious in view of its isolation. There is, however, definite evidence of the lowering of the level of the Caspian (to 31 m below the level of the ocean, i.e. as much as 5–6 m under the present level) in the eleventh to twelfth centuries A.D. Since which time—that is, in the fourteenth century and later—the fluctuations have been weak (around 1 or 2 m).

Since 1760

Figure 4 shows the fluctuations of level of the Caspian for the period from A.D. 1760 to the present, as confirmed by Appollov. For the period from 1760 to 1900 the curve was drawn by inference from historical data; in 1900 direct observations began to be systematically made on the shores of the Caspian Sea at Baku and elsewhere.

An examination of the curve makes it possible to distinguish three principal phases:

    i. the period from 1760 to 1900, when the level of the Caspian Sea was evidently continuously fluctuating around 25 m below the ocean, with an amplitude of less than one metre;

    ii. the period from 1900 to 1930 when the changes of level of the Caspian have for the first time in history clearly shown a general, though as yet slow, tendency to sink, against a background of reciprocal fluctuations;

  iii–iv. the periods from 1930 to 1950 and from 1950 till the present, when the level has fallen rapidly to reach the present average of 28 m below the level of the ocean, with attendant fluctuations.

Causes of Past Changes

Many Soviet scientists have analysed the reasons for the past fluctuations in the level of the Caspian. They have considered the changes in the run-off of rivers into the Caspian Sea, and, in first place, in that of the Volga, to be the main factor involved. From scientific analysis and correlation of observations of the level of the Caspian, the volume of the run-off of the Volga, indices of solar activity, circulation of the atmosphere, and rhythms of rainfall, it has been possible to detect a certain periodicity in all these phenomena and to establish certain quantitative relations between them. Thus, Berg (1934) found that in periods when the Arctic regions become warmer the level of the Caspian Sea drops markedly, while when the Arctic becomes cooler the Caspian rises. This effect can probably be

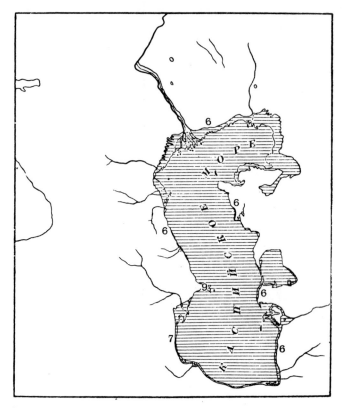

Fig. 3: The New Caspian Basin. *c.* 4000–5000 B.P. Heights in metres above the present level of the Caspian.

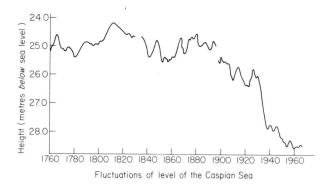

Fluctuations of level of the Caspian Sea

Fig. 4: The fluctuations of level of the Caspian over the period from A.D. 1760 to the present. (Heights in metres below sea-level.)

explained by the consideration that a shift to the North in the routes of the cyclones, which would bring warmer conditions to the Arctic, would thereby result in the prevalence of anticyclone weather in the cold half of the year in the basin of the Caspian Sea. As a consequence, winter precipitation would decrease, and so would the run-off of the Volga.

However, changes in the circulation of the atmosphere are known to be associated first of all with rhythms of humidity in Europe. So it is probable that a complicated combination of factors exerts a still somewhat obscure influence on the level of the Caspian, in respect both of long-term changes and short irregular fluctuations.

There is no doubt that, from the 1930s, intensive economic activity within the catchment basin of the seas began to exert great influence on changes in the level of the Caspian. It fell considerably below its average during the earlier part of the century, following the construction of gigantic dams and of the Kuibyshev, Volgograd and other storage reservoirs, and the resultant increase in the general evaporation from their surfaces, the appreciable expansion of consumption of domestic and industrial water, and the extension of measures to conserve soil moisture, and to improve conditions for farming and forestry over vast areas of the Russian plain. The recent sinking of the level of the Caspian has had diverse natural and economic consequences, and has presented a quite new need—to stabilize the level of this inland Sea.

Stabilization

The considerable lowering of the level of the Caspian during recent decades has effected a marked shift of its shore line and has caused to be formed large areas of new dry land (especially in the north), through the exposure of salinized sections of its bed. Ports and sea canals have grown shallow, spawning sites of game fish have deteriorated, and so forth. The economy on the shores of the Caspian Sea has suffered greatly, and considerable new expenditure (for instance, on dredging) has become necessary. The immediate task for scientists has been not only to find the reasons for the sinking of the level of the Caspian, but also to work out forecasts for the future and to propose remedial measures.

Practical Proposals

As for these last, two suggestions have been quickly put forward for stabilizing the Caspian, originally in scientific (see, for instance, Geller, 1949), and subsequently in technical literature (see, for instance,

"Present and Perspective Water and Salt Balance . . . ", 1972).
These are:

> a. to increase the run-off of rivers into the Caspian Sea by transferring to the Volga Basin some additional water from the basins of the northern rivers (the Vychegda, the Pechora and others);
>
> b. to reduce the general evaporation of moisture from the surface of the Caspian by reducing its area, and in particular by separating from the Sea the Bays of Komsomolets and Kara-Bogaz-Gol.

This latter proposition is especially ingenious and far-sighted. The Bay of Kara-Bogaz-Gol is a large basin divided from the Caspian proper by a narrow sandy dike, through which about 20 km^3 of Caspian water used to leak in one direction each year, representing about 15% of the inflow of rivers; though in recent years only half of this quantity has been involved. As it evaporates in the bay, the water becomes concentrated to the condition of natural brine, and leaves deposits mainly of sodium sulphate. A complete separation of the bay from the rest of the sea should stop the above "loss" and thus help to maintain the main level. However, calculations have shown that this measure alone will not stabilize the level of the Caspian Sea. There remains the possibility of transferring some of the run-off from the basins of the northern rivers into that of the Volga. But how much?

Statistical Forecasts

To answer this question, complicated calculations and experimental projects have been undertaken in the USSR, account being taken of numerous conditions and parameters. It is impossible to consider all of them in this chapter. However, to give a general idea of the essence of the problem, we would like to mention some final figures:

"At the minimum run-off (182 km^3 per year) and maximum water intake (for economic needs 118 km^3 per year) the equilibrium (i.e. stabilization of the Caspian level—Institute of Geography) may be reached only when the level of the sea drops by 22 m as compared with the present level, and the general area of the sea diminishes to 233,000 km^2 (55–60% of the present area—Institute of Geography), which means that the North Caspian area will dry up completely . . . Only if the natural run-off is high (332 km^3), water intake small (up to 85 km^3), the run-off to Kara-Bogaz-Gol only 5 km^3, and if 31 km^3 of water from the northern rivers are brought to the Sea, may the level of the Caspian remain close to the present one." ("Present and Prospective Water Balance . . .", 1972, p. 149).

At the assignment of the Soviet government, several scientific and design organizations are working on this problem and looking for its most rational solution.

The Aral Sea

The Aral Sea, like the Caspian, is a closed undrained basin. Its area is 66,000 km^2; its greatest depth 69 m; its average depth 16·1 m. The present level of the Aral Sea is 51 to 53 m above that of the ocean. Two large rivers flow into it, the Amu-Darya and the Syr-Darya.

Its Water Balance

The present water balance of the Aral Sea is defined by the following broad indices:

Inflow, km^3		*Discharge, km*^{3}	
River run-off	55·3	Evaporation	69·2
Precipitation	9·1		
Total	66·4		

These data show that the run-off of rivers accounts for more than 85% of the total inflow; while the run-off of the Amu-Darya alone makes up 75% of the inflow (42 km^3). Evidently the history of the formation of the Aral Sea and its fluctuations of level are closely related to the history of the Amu-Darya.

Past Changes

According to geological data, the Aral Sea in its more-or-less modern appearance was formed in the Late Pleistocene, that is to say, much later than the Caspian. During the greater part of Pleistocene, the "Great-Amu-Darya" ran through the present desert of Kara Kum into the Caspian. Only as late as the second half of Pleistocene did the water of the Amu-Darya burst into the hollow of the Aral Sea. At the same time, traces of very high lake terraces (75–80 m above ocean level, i.e. 25–30 m above the present level of the Aral) and remains of marine fauna of the Akchagyl (Upper Pliocene) age have recently been discovered in the Aral depression. These finds lead to the conclusion that already in

Pliocene–Pleistocene times there existed some water basins within the Aral area. But there is no doubt that these hypothetical basins could not have been the direct predecessors of the present Aral Sea (Kes, 1969).

The Old Aral Transgression (and a low level)

On the shores of the present Aral there are signs only of a comparatively young, the so-called "Old Aral" transgression. They consist of a well preserved terrace, several metres higher than the present level of the sea, with deposits containing shells of *Cardium edule*. In addition, there are traces of a level of the sea lower than the present, namely old river beds and beach ridges inundated to depths of from 7 to 13 m (Lymarev, 1967). The most likely age of the Old Aral transgression is Holocene, which would allow a Late Pliocene age for the Aral Sea itself.

A Transgression of the Second Millennium B.C.

Proceeding from the connection of some Neolithic remains with Old Aral deposits, Yanshin (1953) has assumed that this transgression took place at the end of the third and the beginning of the second millennium B.C. According to his views, there occurred later another considerable transgression, in the second and early first millennium B.C. Kes (1969), using palaeogeographical and archaeological data collected in the Sarykamysh hollow and the dry bed of Uzboi (see "Ancient Rivers in Present-Day Deserts of Soviet Central Asia"), shows that prehistoric fluctuations in the level of the Aral Sea have been associated with periodic shifts of course of the Amu-Darya, to the Sarykamysh on the one hand, or to the Aral Sea on the other. In the first case, the Aral Sea experienced marked regressions (in the fourth to the middle of the third millennium B.C.; the second to the beginning of the first millennium B.C.; the middle of the first millennium A.D.; the thirteenth century A.D.; the end of the fourteenth century to the beginning of the seventeenth century A.D.): in the second, transgressions. Unfortunately, however, these recon-structions are based only on inference.

Systematic instrumental observations of the changes of the level of the Aral Sea were begun only in 1910. However L'vov (1959), having supplemented these observations with some historical data, has undertaken a review of the fluctuations of the level of the Aral over the last 100 years. According to him (Fig. 5), the level of the sea in the nineteenth century was very low (at most 50 m above the level of the ocean). Then, at the turn of the century, there was a rapid rise, which was followed by a high stand with fluctuations about 53 m above the level of the ocean. After

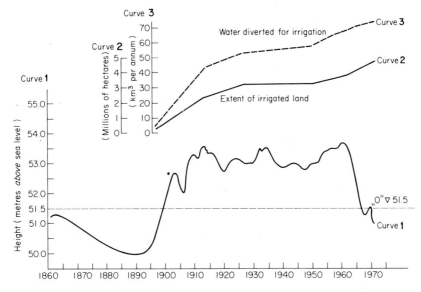

The Aral Sea. Fluctuations of level, and diversion of water from its inflowing rivers

Fig. 5: Recent fluctuations of the level and intake of the Aral. Curve 1 shows fluctuations of level, in metres above sea-level. Curve 2 (also referable to the dates on the horizontal axis) shows the extension of the area of irrigated land in the basins of the Amu-Darya and Syr-Darya. Curve 3 shows the attendant withdrawal of water from these rivers.

1960 the level of the Aral began to decline rapidly, and this process has continued till the time of writing.

The Present and the Future

Stability until the 1960s

The fluctuations of level of the Aral Sea in the period from 1900 to 1960 have undoubtedly been related to periodical changes in the climate of its catchment basin. In spite of a continuous extension of the area of irrigated land in the basins of the Amu-Darya and Syr-Darya (see curve 2 in Fig. 5) and the attendant increasing withdrawal of water from these rivers (curve 3), the level of the Aral Sea did not show any tendency to decline until 1960. Dunin-Barkovsky (1960) was the first to draw attention to this interesting circumstance. He explained the subsequent decline by the additional loss of moisture through transpiration when cultivated vegetation was substituted for the natural, which had been largely restricted to the flood-plains. So, since the 1960s, everything has "behaved to order" in the basin of the Aral Sea, as further extension of the irrigated areas in the basins of the Amu-Darya and Syr-Darya have begun to influence directly, through progressive lowering, the level of the sea.

Recent Fall

It is easy to forecast what will happen as river water is withdrawn for irrigation at different rates. Already the irrevocable use of water, primarily for irrigation, in Central Asia exhausts more than a half of the total run-off of the Syr-Darya and Amu-Darya (about 60 km ^{3}). It is quite possible that the whole run-off will be used for irrigation by the year 2000, and this will inevitably lead to a progressive decline in the level of the Aral Sea (according to some calculations by 20 m in A.D. 2000), to a decrease in its area, and to an intensification of its salinity. If the rivers cease entirely to flow, by the year 2000 the Aral Sea will turn into a small shallow basin of no use either for fishing or for transport. Moreover, in its place there will emerge considerable areas of new desert lands covered with salt crusts and suffering from deflation. It may be assumed that there will be other unfavourable changes in the natural conditions on both the local and the general scale.

Possible Replenishment through Diversion of Rivers

At the same time, even from a purely economic point of view, further development of irrigation in Central Asia seems to be clearly necessary. It is also inevitable because of the growth of population and the need to improve living conditions in the deserts. That is why Soviet planning and scientific institutions are doing their best to prove it possible to save the Aral Sea, even assuming the maximum use for irrigation of the waters of the Amu-Darya and the Syr-Darya. In that event, the principal way of preserving the Aral Sea will be to replenish its basin with additional water from the great Siberian rivers (the Ob, the Yenisei and others). From a technical point of view, such a transference is quite possible, through the central part of Kazakhstan, although considerable expenditure of energy would be needed to pump the water up to the level of the interfluve. Thus the problem under consideration requires comprehensive scientific, technical and economic research which will take into account its many and varied aspects. Such work is now being undertaken in the USSR (Geller, 1969).

References

Berg, L. S. 1934. Uroven' Kaspiiskogo morya za istoricheskoe vremya. (The Level of the Caspian Sea during historic times). *Problemy fizicheskoi geografii.*

Dunin-Barkovsky, L. V. 1960. *Fiziko-geograficheskie osnovy proektirovaniya orositel'nykh sistem. (Physico-geographical bases of designing irrigation systems).* Izd-vo MSKH SSSR.

Fedorov, P. V. 1957. Stratigrafiya chetvertichnykh otlozhenii i istoriya razvitiya Kaspiiskogo morya. (The stratigraphy of the Quaternary deposits and the history of the development of the Caspian Sea). *Trudy Geol. Inst-ta AN SSSR.*

Geller, S. Yu. 1949. K'voprosu o kolebaniyakh i regulirovanii urovnya Kaspiiskogo morya. (Regarding the question of the fluctuations and regulation of the level of the Caspian Sea). *Voprosy geografii.*

Geller, S. Yu. 1969. Nekotorye aspekty problemy Aral'skogo morya. (Some aspects of the problem of the Aral Sea). Sb. *Problema Aral'skogo morya*, Inst Geografii AN SSSR.

Gerasimov, I. P. 1937. Kaspiiskoe morye v chetvertichnyi period. (The Caspian Sea in the Quaternary period). *Trudy sov. serii. Vyp.* **III,** L.-M.

Kes, A. S. 1969. Osnovnye etapy razvitiya Aral'skogo morya. (The main stages in the development of the Aral Sea). Sb. *Problema Aral'skogo morya.* Inst Geografii AN SSSR.

Kolebaniya urovnya Kaspiiskogo morya. 1956. (Fluctuations of the level of the Caspian Sea). *Trudy Instituta Okeanologii AN SSSR.* v. **XV.** (B. A. Apollov).

Lymarev, V. I. 1967. Berega Aral'skogo morya—vnutrennego vodoema aridnoi zony. (The shores of the Aral Sea—the interior basin of the arid zone). L., *Nauka.*

L'vov, V. P. 1959. Kolebaniya urovnya Aral'skogo morya za poslednie 100 let. (Fluctuation of the level of the Aral Sea for the last 100 years). *Trudy Gos. Okeanograficheskogo Inst-ta. Vyp.* **46.**

Sovremennyi perspektivnyi vodnyi i solevoi balans yuzhnykh morei SSSR. 1972 (Modern perspectives on water and salt budget of the southern seas of the USSR). *Gl. Upr. Gidrometsluzhby SSSR.* Gidrometeoizdat.

Yanshin, A. L. 1953.*Geologiya Severnogo Priaral'ya. (Geology of the Northern Aral Regions).*

Synopsis of Part V

It is now apparent that the Caspian and Aral Seas are not such reliable indicators of local climatic change as the lakes of Anatolia and Iran. For one thing, the Caspian draws much of its water by way of the Volga from regions much further north, where a different regimen of climate prevails; for another, the fluctuations of the Aral Sea have depended more on the shifts of destination of the Oxus than on variations of rainfall.

Nevertheless, the level of the Caspian evidently kept falling throughout the Late Glacial period in sympathy with the general desiccation which afflicted the lakes of Iran and Anatolia at that time, and contemporaneously with a very arid phase in Western India. The subsequent major expansion of the Caspian, the Upper Khvalyn Transgression, coincided with a marked wet phase in the Indus Basin, when lakes expanded and Mesolithic settlers moved in; and with a possible pluvial episode in southern Arabia. It will be noted too that the New Caspian transgression of the fifth millennium B.P. happened at the same time as the Harappan wet phase in the Indus region. Since then, both regions have become increasingly arid.

Conclusion

During Glacial times both the atmospheric and the oceanic circulation over the Globe were "sluggish". Transport of warm water from Tropical to Arctic seas became slower; the Trade Winds and Monsoons were less vigorous and extensive, and the Inter-tropical Convergence Zone remained relatively stationary around a mean position south of the Equator; the storm belt at mid-latitudes lay to the south of the Mediterranean, but since the cyclones were not vigorous, they probably brought no more rain than now to North Africa and Northern Arabia; the climatic zones contracted towards the Equator, so that Southern Europe carried cool, dry steppe, and Central and Northern Europe taiga and tundra (Fig. 1).

In a lucid and highly compressed study of 1976, entitled "Environmental and climatic implications of late Quaternary lake-level fluctuations in Africa" (Nature, 261, 385–90), F. Alayne Street and A. T. Grove of Cambridge describe how this state of affairs became changed, in the region which concerns them, through rising temperatures in the Indian Ocean, and increasing rainfall and the release of latent heat over Africa. This wet phase in Africa began about 12,500 B.P. and reached its climax between 9000 and 8000 B.P. By way of confirmation, A. J. Williams and D. A. Adamson (Nature, 12-4-74, 248, 584) have pointed to a rise in level of the White Nile between the years 12,000 and 3000 B.P. approximately.

Figure 2 correlates the African phases with the environmental changes deduced in these studies for various districts of the Eastern Mediterranean and Western Asia. It is now generally accepted that the climax of the Last Glacial was reached about 18,000 B.P. and that the ice-sheets started to melt after that. By about 12,500 B.P. the change to interglacial conditions was evident in Africa, and by 10,000 B.P. these conditions were well established throughout the area of our concern. They are summarized in Fig. 3, which may be checked against Fig. 2. In brief, the Monsoonal

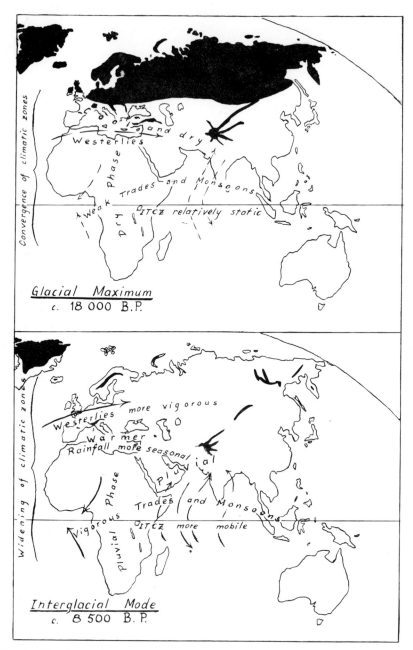

Fig. 1: Wind-circulation under glacial and interglacial conditions in the Old World. (Ice shown in black.)

Synoptic Table

Fig. 2.

B.P. Millennia	15 13	14 12	13 11	12 10	11 9	10 8	9 7	8 6	7 5	6 4	5 3	4 2	3 1	2 B.C.–A.D.	1
European Phases	Older Dryas	Alleröd	Yngr. Dryas	Pre-Boreal	Early Boreal	Late Boreal	Atlantic	Sub-Boreal	Sub-Atl^c	L.I.A
African Terms	= Late Glacial — Glacial Mode — Late Glacial → Postglac^l (Holocene/Recent) Interglacial Mode — Mid-Holocene — Decline from Interglacial conditions

N. and E. Africa (Grove): Max^m aridity —— Lakes rise and reach max^m stand — Reduced flow — Lesser rise — Desiccation — with moister phases (M)

N. Afr.-Arabia (Butzer): Stream-flow increases from dry Late Warm — Pluvial episodes of mid-Holocene —— Onset of drier conditions

Med.- Nr. East (Bottema): Steppe — Some pines — Less trees — Grass — Spread of forest to its maximum

Levant (Turton-Brock): Mingling of Ethiop., Med. and As^c species — Gazelle — Aceramic Neolithic — Gazelle — Caprines

N. Greece (Higgs): Col steppe — Some oak — Return to steppe — Postglac^l forests — Domestication — Erosion and depos^n — Slower — Renewed depos^n.

Peloponnese (Raphael): Domestic^n damages forests — Flandrian transgression — (Subsid^ce)(Coastal)(Coastal) — Subsid^ce — alluv^n of coast prograd^n erosion — (here faced)

E. Aegean (Eisma): Alluvial fans — Valley infill — Valley erosion and extension of deltas — Present s.l. — (Later fill — Eros^n)

Turkey (Erinç): Drying of lakes and less ext^r drainage — Settle^n on Pine-/alluv^m birch — Salt water enters Euxine — Steppe-aridity and sand — Moister — Forest-exploit^d

C. Anatolia (Erol): Desic^n of Pleist. lakes — NE winds / SW winds / Dry spell — followed by ltd extens^n lakes — Tuzgölü becomes salt

Iran (Ganji): Increased evap^n and desic^n of plat. lakes — Climax of aridity → — Moist^r — Drier — Moister — Mod. clim.

Gulf-head △ (Larsen-Evans): c.-80m — Marine — -35m / -10m (stand) / +1m max Sea — transgression — to Hor al Hammar — Prograd^n of 150-200 km

Kuwait Bay (al-Asfour): -100m — Marine — -32m (organic layer) / +25m — Transgr^n over sabkhas — Lower Kuwait terraces

Gulf (Vita-Finzi): Old Fill in Tigris tributaries / Piedmont deposition in Arabia — Rapid rise of water — Delta bldg. off Iran coast — Burial of △ sites — New Fill — Eros^n △ bldg.

Arabia (espec. S.E.) (Stevens): → Pluvial / fans and outwash — Gypsum crusts — 'Neolithic Pluv.' / Eros^n of fans — Aeolian phase — Ltd. Eros^n — Aeolian phase

W. India (McClure-Goudie-Seth): Arid — Fossil dunes — Miliolite dep^s — Mesolt. influx / Freshwat^r lakes — Becoming less moist — Desert conditions

Sambhar Lake (Rajasthan) (Seth): Severe aridity — Wet phase — becoming drier — (Harappan) wet phase → — Dry-Moist-Increasingly arid

C. Asian Lakes (Gerasimov): Caspian falling — U. Khvalyn transgr^n (+7m) — Sarykamysh Recent Pluvial — (New Casp transgr^n (+28m)) — (Old Aral transgr^n (+7m)) — Sar. Pl.

| Millennia B.P. | 15 13 | 14 12 | 13 11 | 12 10 | 11 9 | 10 8 | 9 7 | 8 6 | 7 5 | 6 4 | 5 3 | 4 2 | 3 1 | 2 B.C.–A.D. | 1 |

P

circulation became more vigorous and extensive, so South Arabia and Western India became wetter; while with the deepening of the Mediterranean cyclonic rain belt not only the shores of that sea but the plateaux of North Arabia and Syria would get more rain. As the climatic belts widened polewards, Southern Europe and Western Asia became markedly milder, forest took over from dry steppe, and the inland lakes lost their water through increased evaporation. Only it seems clear that the high plateaux of Anatolia and Iran did not share in the general increase in rainfall enjoyed in Africa, in the Arabian peninsula and evidently too in the plains of Trans-Caspia. It could be that, as at present, the winter cyclones, which are the main springs of precipitation here, were deflected to the north and to the south of the high plateaux, around their reservoirs of cold air, and along the warm winter tracks over the waters of the Euxine

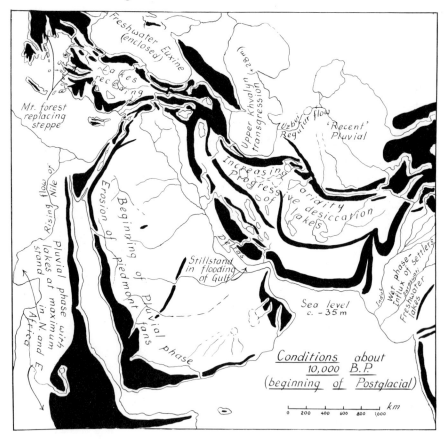

Fig. 3.

and the Caspian on the one hand and of the Gulf on the other. As the Gulf took in sea water, it would certainly exert a stronger pull on the winter cyclones, and by raising local humidity too it would contribute to the rise in the rainfall of East and South Arabia.

Towards the Mid–Holocene the climate seems to have become rather drier in the Indus Valley, but a short fresh wet phase was entered about 5000 B.P. (as also in Africa). These shifts must reflect changes in the vigour of the monsoons, and since Southern Arabia comes under this same wind regime, it seems reasonable to correlate Stevens's first ''post–Neolithic sub-Pluvial'' aeolian phase, and the succeeding phase of limited erosion, with these fluctuations in Western India, as shown in Fig. 2.

Figure 4 is an attempt to reconstruct conditions about 5000 B.P. This was the time when Northern Hemisphere ice was at its minimum and sea-

Fig. 4.

level at its maximum. The Euxine was now flooded, and the Gulf had overflowed regions of Southern Mesopotamia and Eastern Arabia which have since become dry land. The great inland lakes of the Northern Plateaux had retreated to something like their present dimensions, and thereafter all that region seems to have become progressively drier; but, as several writers have pointed out, it is far from easy to dissociate the effects here of climate from those of human depredation on the deterioration and impoverishment of the flora, the fauna and the soil.

Erinç has shown the broad coincidence of glacial advances in Anatolia with those in Europe in more recent historical times— namely during the Sub-Atlantic phase which was most marked in the latter half of the first millennium B.C., and again during the "Little Ice Age" of the fifteenth to the nineteenth centuries A.D. Now the remarkable meteorological record from Alexandria preserved by Claudius Ptolemy in the second century A.D. and analysed by G. Hellmann ("Über die Ägyptischen Witterungsangaben im Kalendar von Claudius Ptolemaeus", Berlin, *Sitzunzsber. preuss. Akad. Wiss.* **13**, 1916, 332) indicates, as E. P. Brooks argues in his synopsis of that study (*Climate through the Ages*, 1926, 372–4) that Lower Egypt was experiencing at that time a climate rather like that of Northern Greece at present, with westerly winds and appreciable rainfall during the summer. All this hints at a tendency then in North Africa towards "glacial" conditions, with a southward shift of climatic conditions and a local increase of rainfall. It would be dangerous to press the evidence too far, but a limited reversion during the first millennium B.C. to the "glacial" conditions shown at the top of Fig. 1 would go some way towards explaining the contemporary cycle of alluviation termed by Vita-Finzi the "New Fill", analogous with the "Old Fill" of Late Glacial times. The Northern Mediterranean countries would in that case have become in some measure cooler and drier as the glaciers advanced again in Europe in the Sub-Atlantic period and later during the "Little Ice Age".

As more data are found and studied, like the Istanbul records referred to by Sirri Erinç (p. 99), it will doubtless be possible to say more about climatic changes in this region through historical times.

Subject Index

A

Abarghoo cypress 155
Abant earthquake 195
  lake 77
Abbasid irrigation system in Iraq 230,
  276
Abhirs, nomads in early India (Class.
  Abiria) 296, 298
Abu Dhabi afforestation 273
  marine platform 238
  palaeosols 269
  sabkha with anhydrite 271
  transgression 252
Abu Dibbis depression with marine
  traces 230, 232, 249
Abu Houreira, Iraq 225
Acacia
  in Pakistan and Rajasthan 284–5,
  287–8
  in Yemen 271
Acarnania earthquake 195
Achaemenid settlements in Sistan 176
Acıgöl 114, 119, 121
  former expansion of 89, 91–2, 95
Aegean
  Dark Age in 1
  seismicity of 194, 198, 212
Aeolian deposits
  in Arabia 245–6, 265, 268, 271
  in Central Asia 319–22, 348
  in Indian desert 312, 317,
  in Iraq 235–6
Aeolianites in Oman 257–8

Aeolis, city in 72
Afghanistan, seismicity of 187, 206,
  208 (*see* Sistan)
Africa
  East, in Würm 11
  fauna and flora from 29, 33, 284
  lakes of 211, 351, 353
  North
    cyclones over 299, 351
    mediaeval drainage of 78
    pluvial episodes in 145, 354
Agra borehole 279
Ağrı mt., volcanic 107
Agriculture, origins of 10, 76, 86
  in dry farming 36–8
  effects on vegetation 46–7
  on fresh alluvium 99, 130, 144, 259
  in Sistan 171
Ahmatli earthquake 197
Ain, al, Abu Dhabi
  afforestation 273
  palaeosol 268
Ajmer palaeolithic 311–12
Akchagyl (U. Plioc.) fauna 345
Akgöl 116
Akşehir-Eber basin 111, 114–6, 120–1
Alabaster in Sistan 180
Alaşehir earthquake 195
Albanian earthquake 202
Aleppo 141, 222
Alexander the Great
  conquests of 77, 278
  in Sind 290, 296
  and Nearchus 228

Alexandria, early climatic records from 356
Alexopoulos, frost action near 44
Algae in soil formation 271
Ali Kosh, Neolithic site 31–2, 35–6
Aliköy lake terrace 135
Allah Bund in Lower Sind 291–2, 302
Allahabad, Gangetic drainage at 295
Alleröd warm period 8
  vegetation of 16, 22–3, 27, 42
Alore (Aror) gorge and bund (barrier) in Indus valley 290–2
Alphaeus river, history of 62, 64
Alpide belt, tectonics of 186
Alpine glaciers 86
  species 143
Altyn tepe (Turkmenia) early settlement 178
Amaliás town and erosion surface (Peloponnese) 52–5, 58–9, 60–1, 63–4
Amanus mts., lions in 141
Amara marshes (Iraq) 230, 234, 237
Ambala ridge and irrigation 295
Amersfoot interstadial 41
Amık lake 112
Ammianus on Syrian lions 141
Amphibians of Sistan 179
Amorite migrations 299
Amri (Rajasthan) rhinoceros relics 289
Amu-Darya drainage 321, 322–3, 325–7, 329, 331–2, 336, 345
  changes of direction 346, 350
  irrigation from 347–8
  region of dunes in 170
  seismicity of 206
Amyntas, king, flocks of 145
Anatolia
  Central (see also Asia Minor, Turkey)
    dunes 106
    karst landscape 104
    vegetation 145–6

desiccation and droughts 98–9, 141–7
early forests 97
glaciation 90
lake basins 111–39, 356
rivers 67–81, 216
seismicity and vulcanism 107, 122, 188, 191, 198, 201–4
snowline 106
Anau (Turkestan)
  cycles of occupation 156
  past climates 299–300
Ankara, drainage features near 77, 93
Ankleshwar river terrace (Rajasthan) 310
Antelope, desert 33–4
Antioch
  former forest near 141
  sedimentation of 212
Anti-Caucasus glaciers 86
Anti-Taurus glaciers 86
Apolyont lake 113
Aquifers in Sistan 177–8
Arab geographers 78
Arabia, environmental history 353
  climates past and present 11, 145, 233, 263–4, 268, 278, 299, 351, 353–5
  coastal changes 231–2, 245–54, 291, 296
  past lakes 10, 278
  past rivers and sediments 248, 255, 257, 267, 275
  past soils 263–74
  tectonic history 203, 207
  vegetation type in India 284
Aragonite deposits
  in Gulf 249–50
  in Qatar 271
Aral Sea and its fluctuations 320–2, 335–50
Aramaean migrations 299

Aravalli range
  archaeology 310
  recent increase in rainfall 283
Archaeological evidence of earthquakes 186
Archaeology and geomorphology 57–62 (see Neolithic, Palaeo-lithic)
Archaic sites in Elis 58, 60
Architecture and earthquakes 208
Arctic species 143
Argaeus, mt., (see Erciyes)
Arghandab river 165, 174
Argissa Magula, neolithic site in Greece 46
Aridity index 282, 302
Aristotle on forestry 65
Armenian documents on earthquakes 189
Aror (see Alore)
Arrian on the Punjab 296
Arta plain (Peloponnese) sediments 45, 47
Artefacts and dating 6 (see Aurignacian, Mesolithic)
Artemisia in Greece 17–8, 42, 82
  Indus valley 287–8
  Iran 25, 27
  Italy 19–20
  Mediterranean 26
  Yugoslavia 21–2
Artemision of Ephesus 102
Ashkabad earthquake 196
Ashoka, climate at time of 296
Asia Minor (see also Anatolia, Turkey)
  deterioration of vegetation 14, 77
  Hellenistic settlement 77
  seismicity 194, 198
  structural plates 208
Aşıklı Hüyük, neolithic site 31–2
Asir (Arabia) soils 271
Aspendos, siltation of 73
Asprochaliko frost-action 44

Ass, African wild 33
  in early Greece (steppe—) 45
  in early India 285, 290
Atabey Ovasi lake traces 120–1, 135
Atali (NW India) early climate 297
Atlantic, Sub-epoch 1, 142, 353, 356
Atoll formation 153
Atrek delta (Turkestan) 320, 326, 331
Aurignacian artefacts (Turkey) 135
Aurochs in early Iran 35
Australia, former sea-levels 250–2
Axylon (C. Anatolian steppe) 145
Aydin earthquake 196
Azalea, Pontic 143
Azarbaijan lake basins 157 (see Rezaiyeh lake)

B

Bafa lake 71–2, 103 (see also Latmic gulf)
Bafra (Turkey) sediments 70
Baghdad
  climate 233
  position 228, 234
Bahama "emergence" 252
Bahawalpur drainage changes 291, 293
Bahla (Oman)
  flow deposits 264–5
  irrigation 273
Bahra, al- (Kuwait) terraces 245–7, 252
Bahrain former higher sea-level 232
  submarine platform 253
Bakır Çay 67–8, 72, 74, 100
Baku measurements of Caspian levels 341
Balat harbour changes 103 (see Miletus)
Balkans seismic zone 191, 194, 202–3
  early vegetation 42
Balkash lake intake 330
Baltic sea-level 238

Baluchistan
    desert 296
    former climates 279, 301
    tectonic plates in? 208
Bamboo, constructional 286
Bananas, Indus Valley 288
Bandar Abbas mountains 151
Bandar Mashur sediments 236–7
Baradiz 132
    mesolithic 91, 134
Barda Balka (Iraq) mid. palaeolithic 257
Barley
    early cultivation of 36, 38
    endemic in Indus valley 288, 298
    in early Sistan 179
    in Turkey 76
Barmer (Rajasthan) early climate 297
Baroda palaeolithic 309, 311
Bartim earthquake 195
Basra bore hole 236
    climate 233
    position 234, 240–1
Batin, al-, wadi, former flow of 248
Batinah west (Oman) reddened soils 268, 270
Batmaz (see Lade island)
Bayhak seismic zone 191, 194, 206
Beaches (see also Terraces)
    raised in Gulf 249
    ridge in E. Arabia 232
    seismic movements of 190
Bears in Indus valley 289
Beas river shifts 291, 294–5
Beaver in early Greece 46
Beech in Turkey 77, 144–5
Beidha neolithic site 31–2, 35
    irrigation at 38
Belan valley (India) palaeolithic 311
Belevi (W. Turkey) alluvial fan 69
Ber, constructional timber 286
Ber's Law 332 (see also ''Northering'', ''Westering'')

Beypazi earthquake 197
Beyşehir 120
Beyşehir lake and its former extent 114, 116–7, 119, 121
Bhangar deposits (Delhi) 279
Bhoj I inscription 293
Bikaner former drainage 293
Bingöl
    earthquake 195, 197
    former forests 141
Binjor drainage shift 296
Biological invasions 29
Birch (Betula) in early Anatolia 97, 143–4
Birds of early Sistan 179–80
Birjand earthquake 188, 206
Bithynian Olympus moraines 142
Black Sea
    connections with Mediterranean 95–6, 100
    former forests at E. end 97
    freezing in Middle Ages 98
    history of 354–6
Boats of reeds in Sistan 180
Bölling phase 42
Boluk lake, former extension 124
Bondone (Italy) vegetation phases 19
Bor depression (C. Turkey) 120
Border seismic zone 191, 194, 202–5
Borings in Lower Iraq 234–7
Bosporus (see also Straits)
    flooding of 100
    freezing of in Middle Ages 98
    in Ice Age 89
Boyabat sediments 70
Boz mts. of C. Anatolia 122
Bozanönü, Aurignacian site near 135
Bozkurt, old channel near 119
Brahmanabad earthquake 290
Bricks at Harappa 285
Broach early climate 297
Bronze Age
    in Central Asia 329

in Messenia, conditions 57, 60
in N. Greece, vegetation changes 57, 60
in Turkey,
    dry later part 77
    lake expansion in early part 130
Brörup interstadial 41
Budh Thakar (Sind) lake deposits 290, 298
Buffalo, water-, in Indus valley 289–90
Buhabad earthquake 196, 206
Buladdah (Oman) reddened soils 268–70
Bulgarian sediments 47
Burdur basin 119–20, 124
    earthquake 195
Burdur lake and its former extension 8, 89, 91–3, 95, 111, 114–5, 117, 120–1, 130–6
Bus Mordeh (Iran) neolithic 31, 35
Bushire raised beach 249
    submerged delta 259
Buyin earthquake 195, 205
Byzantine rule in the Peloponnese 59–60, 63
Byzantine town in Syria 215

C

Çaga lake 113
Calcareous deposits in Sistan 171
Calcrete in Oman 257
Californian desert 282
Calligonum, in Pakistan and Rajasthan 284–5
Camels
    in Indus valley 290
    in Levantine neolithic 33
    in Sistan 177
Camel-thorn in Anatolia and Iran 145
Can Hasan (Turkey) neolithic 31–2
Canals
    Abbasid in Iraq 230, 276
    as indices of seismicity in Iran 189

Caprines, domestication of 36, 38, 46–7, 82, 353
Carbon-14 dating 91, 245, 257, 300, 310, 313, 317
Cardium edule in Aral Sea 346
Carmel mt., cave remains 35
Çarsamba river gorge deposits 117
Caspian Sea
    cyclones over 355
    earthquake near 205
    history of 335–50
    levels 150, 155, 157, 160–1, 278, 353
    New Transgression 339, 342
    solonchak plains 327
    takyrs 322
    Uzboi intake 322, 326–31
Cat in early Indus valley 290
Çatal Hüyük neolithic site 31–2, 35, 76, 93, 127, 144
Catalonia, deforestation and soil-loss in 65
Cattle
    domesticated in early Greece 46
    early hunting of 35–6, 144
    herded in Sistan 172, 179–80
    in Indus valley 289
    wild in Troad 41
Caucasus mts. as refuge for vegetation 144
Cave climates 44
    deposits in Levant 9
    fauna 45–6
    inhabited in Anatolia 104, 135
    in N. Greece 42–4
Çayönü neolithic site 31–2, 35
Cedar in Turkey 97, 143–5
Cellat (W. Turkey) alluvial fan 69
Cereals
    early cultivation of 36–8
    in Indus valley 288
    Oman 273
    Sistan 171

Çeşme wave-cut terrace 75
Ceyhan delta 73, 100
Chagar Burjak (Sistan) 174–5
Chah Nahma depression 170
Chalcolithic of Gujarat 289
Chalkidiki earthquake 196
Chalus valley (Iran) 150, 160
Chaman seismic zone 191, 194, 206
Chemchemal plain (Iraq) deposits 257
Chenab river shifts 291, 294, 296
Chesney, Col. on lions 141
Chestnut in Turkey 77
Chinese, early travellers in India 297
Chios earthquake 196
Chlemutsi headland (Peloponnese) 52–3, 59, 63
Chlorite in Sistan 180
Chronology through earthquakes 208, 212
Chu delta (C. Asia) 331
Cihanbeyli delta (Turkey) 124
Cilician plain 100
Cilo mts. glaciation 88, 142
Cities and earthquakes 208–9
Civilization, birth of 37–8
Çivril earthquake 196
Classical sites in Elis 60
Cliff, lake, in Turkey 135
Climates
    in Arabia 214
    cave 44
    changes of, interest in 5
    with glaciation 152
    in Iran 156
    in mediaeval times 62
    in post-glacial times 211
    and soil erosion 76–8
    in Turkey 77–8, 86–7, 89–90, 97–9
Clover in early Sistan 179
Coastal movements
    archaeological records 51
    seismic 190
Colchic flora 89

Colomb Bechar (Sahara) 282
Commerce in early Sistan 180–1
Compaction of delta sediments 241–2
Cones
    pyroclastic 107
    volcanic on mt. Erciyes 107
    volcanic submerged 198
Conglomerate, Neogene, in Syria 216, 219
Conifers (see Fir, Larch, Pine, Spruce)
Convergence Zone, Inter-Tropical 351–2
Coot in early Sistan 180–1
Copper in Sistan 171, 180
Coriolis effect 175
Corinth
    Gulf of 198
    wave-cut terrace 75
Cormorant of Sistan 180–1
Cotton in early Indus valley 288
Crab fauna in early Iraq 235
Cretaceous rocks in Sistan 170
Crete, deforestation of 65
"Crop-robber" animals 36
Crustaceans of early Sistan 179
Cucurbits of early Sistan 179
Çukur earthquake 197
Cultivation, beginnings of 36
Currents, ocean, in Ice Age 351
Cyclone belt, shift of 299, 343, 351–2, 354–6
Cypress trees, ancient, in Iran 155
Cyprus
    early deforestation of 142
    seismic connections of 56
Cyrenaica
    early cultivation in 14
    vegetation of 284

D

Dalmatian type of coast 100
Damavand mt. 151

Damascus basin deposits 9
Dammam dome (Arabia) 265
Dams
   check 146
   high 146
Daphne 141
Dar-i-Khazineh flood deposits 230
Dardanelles current 73
Dark Age of Aegean 1
Daryalik river bed (C. Asia) 320, 327
Dasht deposits of Sistan 167, 175
Dasht-e-Bayaz earthquake 195, 200
Dasht-i-Kavir 187
Dasht-i-Lut 187–8
Dates in early Indus valley 288
Dead Sea
   former extension 278
   seismic zone 191, 194, 203, 207
   tsunamis 203
Debar earthquake 194, 202
Dedia ka Rann (Rajasthan) 313
Deer
   Indus valley 289
   in early Greece 45
   Turkey 35
Deflation
   in C. Asia 348
   in Turkey 99, 104, 106
Deforestation (see Forests, destruction of)
Deh Luran complex 31,35
Delhi loess 279
   ridge 295
Deltas
   Amu-Darya 320, 326–7, 332
   Atrek 326, 331–2
   in E. Arabia 248
   in Central Asia, shifting 332
   Ceyhan-Seyhan 73, 100
   Chu 331
   Gediz etc. 72, 74, 104
   Göksu 100

Greater Meander, 70–4, 76–8, 100, 103–4
   off Gulf coasts, submerged 241, 251, 259
Hilmand 167, 169–71, 173–6, 178
Lesser Meander 62, 64, 70–4, 77–8, 100–3
Meriç 95
Mississippi 51
Murgab 322, 326, 331
Niger 238–9
Nile 64
Sarysu 331
Sakarya 73–4
Skamander 73
Tarsus 100
Tedjen 322, 326, 331
Tuzgölü 124
Zeravshan 331
Deluge (see Flood)
Demirci earthquake 194
Demography and earthquakes 208
   evolution of in Sistan 165
Dendrochronology 97–8, 155
Deodar in Indus valley 286
Deposition (see Sediments)
Derin göl 72
Dervişinhani mesolithic 127
Desert belt (see also Dunes)
   of C. Asia 319–34, 348
   of Middle East 154
   of Old World 282
Dhba'iyyah, al- (Kuwait) 252
Dibdibba formation of Lower Iraq 235–6
Dibsi Faraj (Syria), environment of 215–25
Didwana (Rajasthan) salt lake 287, 313
Diodoros on Punjab 296
Diorite in early Sistan 171
Divanlar coastal traces 128–9
Diyedin lake terrace 135
Diyala river 234, 259

Dog in Indus valley 290
Dolomite formation in Qatar 271
Domestication
    beginnings of in Greece 46–7, 82
    possible origins of 33, 36, 76, 86
Donau pluvial at Tuz Göl 124
Donkey, early domesticated 34
Dorud (Iran) seismic fault 189, 199
Doves in early Indus valley 289
Drainage, interior, extension of in
    Turkey 93–5
Dreissensia fossils
    in Anatolia 117, 132, 135
    in C. Asia 327
Drishadavati valley (Punjab) mediaeval
    settlement 302
Drought cycles 1
    in Dark Age Aegean 1
    in Iran 155–6
    in Old Kingdom Egypt 11
    in Sistan 171, 177
    in Turkey 98–9, 146
    in W. India 282
Dryas vegetation 16–7, 26–7, 41
Duck in early Sistan 180–1
Dunes, sand
    afforestation of in Arabia 273
    Iran 152, 154, 157, 161
    under Gulf 232, 251, 258
    in Konya basin 93, 129–30, 132,
    145
    Sistan 167–70, 172, 181
Dust storms of Mesopotamia 233
Düver overflow 135
Dvaitvana (Punjab) early desert 296

E

Eagle of early Sistan 180
Earthquakes (see also Seismicity)
    in Greece 56
    and history 208
    incidence and prediction 185–210

    records of 187
    in Sind 290–1
    in Turkey 106, 131
Eber basin 114–5, 121 (see also
    Akşehir)
Echinoid fauna in early Iraq 235
Eclipses and chronology 208
Edessa (Greece) pollen traces 20
Eggs in neolithic economy of Sistan
    180
Eğridir 120
Eğridir lake 114, 119, 121
Egypt
    climate of in Würm 10–1
    in classical times 356
    early domestication of gazelles
    36
    wave-cut terrace 75
Einkorn cultivation in early Levant 38
Elaia (Turkey) Roman bridge 72
Elam in C7 B.C. 228
Elazığ lake basin 112
Elbistan earthquake 197
Elburz earthquake 195
    mountains 151, 154, 157
    glaciation of 160–1
Elephant in W. India 285, 289–90
Elis (Greece) 59, 62
    plain of 51–66
Elm, constructional, in early Indus
    valley 286
Emir lake (Turkey), formation of 94–5
Emir mt. basins 122
Emiralan earthquake 196
Emmer wheat in early Levant 38
Enderes earthquake 196
Eocene rocks 170
Ephesus sediments 62, 70
    wave-cut terrace 75
Epirus (Greece) early conditions 42, 44
    (see also Ioannina, Tenagi Philippon)
Equids in Neolithic 34–5
    in early Greece 45

hunted in early Sistan and Turkmenia 177, 178
Eratosthenes on deforestation of Cyprus 142
Erban earthquake 196
Erciyes mt. vegetation 141, 143–4
vulcanism 107
Ereğli 120
basin 126–30, 135
Eridu near sea 229, 239
Erimanthus mts. (Peloponnese) 52
Eritrea, seismicity of 204
Erosion
cycles of 73, 122, 215
in early Greece 45, 47, 51–66
off Elis coast 61–5
surfaces 158
by wind 146, 159
Erzerum 233
earthquake 196
Erzincan earthquake 196
Ethiopian seismicity 204
zoological region 35
Etruria valley deposits 64
Euphrates
climate and catchment 233, 255–6
delta 227–44
fluvial history 215–25, 257–8, 275
former extension in Gulf 249
Europe, climatic changes in 300
Eustatic changes of sea-level 74–5, 95–6, 231–2
evidence of from Gulf 238, 249, 275
Euxine (see Black Sea)
Evaporation
from Aral and Caspian 336, 344
C. Asian reservoirs 343
W. Asian lakes 354
in Lower Iraq 233–4
Evliya Çelebi on Gediz delta 72
Evolution of tropical species in Levant 30

F

Failaka island off Kuwait 237
Falaj irrigation in Oman 273
Fans, alluvial, in W. Anatolia 68–70
Fao (Iraq) borings 234, 236–8, 275
Farming, early dry 36–8
Farsinaj earthquake 195
Faults in Anatolia 67, 106, 116, 120, 122,
at plate margins 185–6
associated with seismicity 188–90, 193, 198, 202–6, 208
Fauna, neolithic 45
Ferozepur, shift of Sutlej near 291
Fertile Crescent 32, 37
Fethiye earthquake 196
Fiavè (Italy) vegetation changes 19
Fill (see Sediments)
Finiglacial period 130
Fir in Turkey 77, 143–4
Firing of forests in early Turkey 76
Firuzabad earthquake 195
Fishing
Sistan 174, 179, 180, 211
in early Turkey 144
Flandrian transgression
in Elis 58
in Gulf 239, 249–53
in Iraq 236
Floods in C. Asia 326
Biblical 228–30
in Indus valley 286, 288, 290–1, 298–9,
in Punjab 296
in Sistan 172
Flora, Mediterranean and Colchic 89, 96
Fluvial epochs in Iran 156 (see Pluvials)
Flysch zone of Iran-Afghan border 208
Foça sea-cliff 75
Food storage in early Neolithic 30, 33
Forage crops in early Sistan 179

Foraminifera below Tigris 234
Forests
  in Arabia 272
  care of, in classical Greece 65
  creation of 273
  destruction of 65, 76–7, 97, 107–8,
    141–2, 145, 215, 300–1
  in Himalayas 295
  in Punjab and Sind 296–7, 300–1
  riparian of Sistan 173, 178
  spread of 7, 19, 27, 42, 82, 144,
    353–4
  thorn in India 284
  of Yemen 271
Fowl, in early Indus valley 290
Fox, hunted in early Levant 35
Frankish rule in Peloponnese 59–60
Frost-weathering 9, 44–5
Fruit trees in Sistan 173

G

Gabarbands (dams) of Baluchistan
  279
Gadra Road (Rajasthan) wells 281
Ganga (Ganges) river system 293, 295
Garda lake vegetation changes 19
Gardan Reg (Sistan) 170, 175
Gastropods in early Iraq 235–6
Gaud-i Zirrah (Sistan) 167, 174–6
Gaudars (cow-herds) of Sistan 179–80
Gaza wadi environmental changes 83
Gazelle
  hunting and domestication of 35–6,
    38, 82, 353
  in Sistan and Turkmenia 177–8
  speciation of 31
Gebrem Ovasi lake traces 119
Gediz earthquake 195, 201–2
  river and delta 67–70, 72, 74, 100,
    104
Gemlik earthquake 197
Geographers, Arab 78

Geosyncline (C. Anatolia) 122
Gerede earthquake 196
Germany, palaeolithic 46
Gevcek earthquake 197
Ghab valley bore 16, 24–5
Ghazzar plain (Punjab) old channels
  279–81, 292–5
  Harappan sites 298
  river vegetation 286
Gharif plain (U.A.E.) gypsum deposits
  264
Ghidhai (Kuwait) terraces 245–7
Ghir earthquake 195
Gir (Saurashtra) lions 285
Girnar (Saurashtra) lake 296
Glaciers
  Alpine and Anatolian 86
  in Himalayas 301, 314
  in Pamirs and Tien Shan 333
  in Turkey 88–90, 142
Goat, hunted and domesticated 35–6,
  38, 46–7, 76
  in Indus valley 290
  in Sistan 170, 177–9
Göksu delta 100
Gölcük (Turkey) crater lake 120
Golden Horn genesis 100
  freezing 98
Gönen earthquake 195
Gönen river 135
Goose of early Sistan 180–1
Gordion, botany of 97
Graben of W. Anatolia 67
Graeco-Roman colonization of W. Asia
  108, 142, 145
Grain-pounding platforms of Indus
  valley 286
Grazing
  in Arabia 272
  excessive 76–7, 145–6
  in Himalayas 295
  in early India 298, 300–1
  in Sistan 170, 176–7

Greece
    deforestation and soil-erosion 77–8
    environmental changes 14, 41–9
    mediaeval alluvium 74
    seismicity 186, 194, 198
    early vegetation 16, 22–4, 26–7,
        353
Gujarat
    archaeology (palaeolithic—
        mesolithic) 289, 307–8, 310–1,
    climatic changes 307–18
    miliolite deposits 312, 317
Gulf
    catchment of 255–6
    cyclones over 355
    dust storms over 233
    former extension, 270
    recent geological history 214, 239,
        258, 275, 353
    Nearchus's voyage in 228
    origins of 230–2, 239, 248–53
    terraces   230,   245–54
Gulf of Mexico 238
Gulf of Oman 249
Günz-age terraces by Tuz göl 124
    -Mindel sea-level 231
Gurjar invasions of India 298
Gurjardesh (Rajasthan) desert 297
Gypsum in Iraq 235
    in Oman 264–5

H

Hacılar (Turkey) neolithic site 31–2,
    76, 91, 135, 144
Hakra river (Punjab) former channel
    292–3, 295
Halite in Iraq 235
Halophile vegetation in Sistan 177
Hammar marine formation (Iraq)
    235–9, 253
Hamun-i Parian (Sistan) 175
Hamun-i Puzak (Sistan) 167

Hamun of Sistan 155, 165–7, 172,
    174–5, 211
Hanumangarh (Punjab), drainage near
    292–3
Harappa 292, 294
    civilization, environment of 285–91
    decline of 297–9
    wet phase 309, 350
Harbiye (see Daphne)
Harbours, silting of 108, 145 (see also
    Ephesus, Miletus, Tarsus, Troy)
Hardaneh (Syria), drainage near 217,
    221, 222
Hares in early Indus valley 289
Harran, lions once near 141
Hartebeest in early Levant 34
Hasa, al- afforestation 273
    coastal recession 252
    over-irrigation 272
    soils in sabkhas 270–1
Hasan Dağ (Turkey) forests 143
Hasan Khan canal (Sistan), dunes near
    170
Hatay (Turkey), Amık lake 112
Hayotojor valley earthquake 188, 197,
    204
Hazar lake (Turkey)
    former expansion of 89, 91–2, 112, 121
Hazel in Turkey 145
Heat, latent, release of in Post-glacial
    351
Heather in Turkey 77
Helladic sites in Elis in Messenia 57–8,
    60
Hellenic culture in Anatolia 62, 64
Hellenistic sites in Elis 59, 64, 82
    epoch in Turkey 77, 97
Hellespont in Ice Age 89
    flooding of 100
Hemiones
    in early C. Asia 178,
    Levant 34
    Sistan 177–8

Herat, possible seismic zone near 194, 206
Hermus river (*see* Gediz)
Herodotus on Asia Minor 71,
  Caspian 340
  droughts 98
Hilmand
  civilization 165–83
  river 165, 170, 173–5
  possible seismic zone 206
Hindu Kush snow-melt 172
Historical records and remains in Iraq 239, 242, 259
History, social and earthquakes 208
Hiuen-Tsang's travels in India 297
Holocene, start of 87
Homer
  on Caspian 340
  on topography of Troy 73
Honaz earthquake 197
Hor al- Hammar (Iraq) 235-6, 240–1, 275
Hormuz straits 249
Hornbeam in Taurus 144
Horses
  in early C. Asia 178
  in India 285, 290
  Levant 34–5
Hoydos (Turkey) delta traces 124
Human influence on landscape 107–8
Humidity affected by lake (Sistan) 171–2
Hunting
  in early Levant 35
  in Sistan 177, 180, 211
  in Turkey 144
Hyderabad (Sind) former lake 290

I

I-Tsing's travels in India 297
Ibex, Nubian 35
Ice Age, 'Little' 45, 62, 353
  in Turkey 90, 142, 356

Ida, mt., deforestation of 143
Iğdeli (Turkey) erosion surface 131
Ilgin lake (Turkey), former size 116, 120
Incesu valley (Turkey) drainage history 93–5
India
  climate 233, 279–80, 300, 350, 354–5
  Ocean 351 (*see also* Rajasthan)
Indo-Europeans enter Turkey 77
Indus Civilization 285–90
  decline of 297–9 (*see also* Harappa)
Indus river 278, 290–2, 296
  relation to monsoons 299
Insuyu deltaic plain 124
Ioannina 16, 20, 22
  core 42
  lake 42–5
Ionian Sea 198
  seismicity 56, 58
Iran
  coastal features 241, 249, 255, 259
  climatic changes 7–8, 11, 25–6, 149–63, 299
  crustal slab under 207
  earthquakes 187–9, 193, 206–8
  orogeny 230–1, 248
  lake basins 145
Iranshahr mts., 152
Iraq delta 83, 227–44 (*see also* Mesopotamia)
  climate 233
  mediaeval irrigation 276
  Neolithic 31
  seismicity 205, 207
  transgression 248–9
  in Würm 7–8
Irrigation
  in C. Asia 324–7, 329, 333, 347–8
  in Baluchistan 279
  disruption of, by earthquakes etc. 189, 206, 208, 225, 241–2

early 37
excessive 272
in Indus valley 288, 299
in Iraq 230, 234, 276
in Oman 273
in Punjab 295, 299, 301
in early Saurashtra 296
on "slotted" streams 260
Islamic potsherds in Iraqi alluvium 258
invasion of Sind 296
town in Syria 215
Isostatic movements 252 (see also
    Subsidence, Tectonism)
Isparta topography 120, 135
reclamation 146
Israel climatic change 300
forested in last Glacial 9
Istanbul climate 98
meteorological records 98, 356
Italy
early vegetation 15–6, 19, 21, 26
deforestation 77
mediaeval alluvium 74
palaeolithic population 46
seismicity 56
Izmir topography 69, 72, 104
Gulf 104
Iznik lake, expansion of 89, 91–2,
    113–4, 121

J

Jackals in early Indus valley 289
Jacobabad (Sind)
climate 282
marshes 289
Jaipur salt lakes 313
Jaisalmer Mesolithic 311
ranns 313
Jal az-Zor escarpment (Kuwait)
245–6, 248
Jalor (Rajasthan), L. Palaeolithic near
309

Jarmo, neolithic site 31–2, 35
Jarrahi delta (Iraq) 240–1
Jaxartes 278 (see Syr-Darya)
Jebel Hafit (Oman) palaeosol 268
Jebel Tuwaiq sands 271
Jericho
early economy 31–2, 35–6
irrigation 38
Jhalaria ka Rann 313
Jhelum river shifts 291, 294, 296
Jhirak (Sind) lake deposits 290, 298
Jimi, al (Abu Dhabi) palaeosols 269
Jodhpur salt lakes 313
Johi (Rajasthan) lake 289
Jordan valley earthquake 203
lakes 8–9, 278
neolithic sites 31
soil 268–9
Judaean hills, climatic history 83
Julian, Emperor, hunting lions 141
Jullunder (Punjab) early forests 297
Jumna river (see Yamuna)
Junagadh (Rajasthan) dam 296
miliolite 312
Juniper in Turkey 76–7, 144
Yemen 271

K

Kandahar early settlement 165
Kapali cave (Turkey) Aurignacian 135
Kaïkos river (see Bakır Çay)
Kaistros river (see Menderes, Lesser)
Kalibangan (Harappan site) 286, 292,
    294
fauna 289–90
irrigation 299
Kalif Uzboi 320, 323
Kallidromo earthquake 196
Kamyakvana (Punjab) early climate 296
Kanodwala Rann 313
Kautilya's evidence on Rajasthan
climate 297

Kaplan-Kyr (Trans-Caspia) 327
Kara-Bogaz-Gol (Caspian) 337, 344
Kara Kum 178, 319–21, 327, 331, 345
  Canal 320–3
Karaman dunes 106
Karamet-niaz village 323
Karamuk lake basin (Turkey) 115, 121
Karapınar dunes 93, 106, 129–30
  restricted grazing 146
Karataş lake (Turkey) 119
Karina göl (Turkey) 76
Karkheh river 229, 255
Karst phenomena
  in Turkey 89, 104, 111–2, 116–20,
    130, 135
  in Rajasthan 313
Karun delta 227–44
Kash river (Sistan) 173
Kashmar (Iran) cypress 155
Kashmir deglaciation 317
  loess 279
Kastritsa cave (Greece) 42–4, 46
Kastron (Greece) Palaeolithic 58
Katakekaumene (Turkey) vulcanism
  107
Katákolon cape 56, 58–9
Kathiawar
  early settlement 310–1
  miliolite 312–3
Kathma (Kuwait) terraces 245–7
Kato Achaia 58
Kavirs (Iran) 155
  Great 156–9
  earthquakes in 187
Kayacik (Turkey) sediments 130
Kayseri, former forests 141
Kazakhstan
  canals 348
  rivers 331
Kermanshah earthquake 189
Khairpur (Sind) marshes 289
Kharag island raised beach 249
Kharia Rann 313

Kharowala Rann 313
Khasab (Oman) alluvium 257
Khimaditis (Greece) early vegetation
  21
Khiran, al- (Kuwait) terrace 252
Khirbet Kumran fault 203
Khor Musa inundation 230
Khor Zubair inundation 230
Khorezm, devastation by Timur 332
  ancient irrigation 327
Khori creek (Sind) 290–1, 302
Khorramabad alluvium 255
Khur (Iran) kavir 156
Khuzistan
  flood deposit 230
  seismicity 205
Khvalyn
  transgressions of Caspian 353
  Lower 337–8
  Upper 278, 337–9
Khwaf earthquake 206
Kigi earthquake 194
Kırkişla delta 124
Kirmasti earthquake 197
Kırşehir earthquake 196
Kirthar range (Pakistan) 289
Kite of Sistan 180, 182
Kızılırmak delta 100
Kokkinopolis (Greece) Palaeolithic
  44–5
Komsomolets bay (Caspian) 344
Konya
  basin 112, 124–6, 130–1, 135
  lake 89, 91–3, 115–7, 119–21
  plain 31
Kopet Dagh (Trans-Caspia) 320
  earthquake 195
Korouta (Greece) shoreline 55
Kostanjevica (Yugoslavia) pollen
  section 21
Kotíkhi lagoon (Greece) 52–4, 56,
  59–61, 63

Kounoupéli (Greece)
 cape 59
 river 52
Kovada lake (Turkey) 114, 119
Krupnik earthquake 196
Kuchaman salt lake (Rajasthan) 313
Kuh Dinar (Iran) glaciation 154
Kuh-i Khwaja (Sistan) 170
Kuhistan seismic zone 191, 193, 206–7
Kuibyshev reservoir (Trans-Caspia) 343
Kula (Turkey), vulcanism near 107
Kunkur nodules (Rajasthan) 309–10
Kurdistan, Neolithic occupation 31, 76
 seismicity 205 (see also Jarmo, Zagros, Zeribar)
Kurnaköy (Turkey) travertines 130
Kurrulwala (Punjab) early drainage 293
Kursunlu earthquake 196
Kurukshetra river (Punjab) 296
Kuwait marine terraces 237–8, 245–54, 275, 353
Kyzyl Kum (Trans-Caspia) 319–20, 326, 332

L

Lade island (near Miletus) 71–2, 103
Ladik earthquake 196
Lakes (see also playas, Aral, Caspian and other individual names)
 in Africa and W. and C. Asia 86, 350–1, 353, 356
 artificial 146
 brackish, in Iraq 230
 former beds, settled 99, 179
 glacial (general) 8, 144
 in Greece 42–4
 in W. India 310, 313
 formed by land slips 104, 211
 source of sand 106, 161
 tectonic origins 122, 298

 in Turkey 91–3, 111–36, 145
Lamellibranchs 235
Landslides 104, 189, 211
Langhnaj (Rajasthan)
 Mesolithic 311
 rhinoceros bones 289
Lapis lazuli 180
Larch 144, 146
Larissa, Aeolian 72
Las Bela valley aeolian formations 312
Laterization in N. Turkey 89
Latium fish-tanks 75
Latmian (Latmic) gulf, 71, 103
Lava-fields in Sistan 170, Turkey 107
Lawarka Rann 313
Lebanon, loss of forests in Würm 9
Legumes in early Sistan 179
Lenin (Kara Kum) Canal 320, 322–3
Levallois in Peloponnese 58
Liman coasts (Marmara) 100
Limestones (see Karst)
 in Oman 265, 268
 in Rajasthan 280, 310, 312
 in Syria 216, 223
 in Turkey 117, 120
Lion
formerly in Syria 141
 in Saurashtra 285
Lisan lake (former Dead Sea) 278
Livy on vegetation of Anatolia 141, 145
Ljubljanska Barje (Yugoslavia)
 pollen bore 21
Locris earthquake 196
Loess
 of Ghaggar plain 281
 of Iran 154, 157
 of Kashmir and Delhi 279
Londeh earthquake 195
Lothal (Harappan sea-port) 292
 floods 291, 298
 rhinoceros 289
 rice 288–9
 timber 286

Louisiana settlements 51, 59
Louros gorge (Greece) screes 44
Lucerne in early Sistan 179
Ludhiana deserted by Sutlej 292
Luka (Sind) lake deposits 290
Luni basin (Rajasthan) 279, 281, 309
  mid-Palaeolithic 313
Lunkaransar lake (Rajasthan) deposits
  287
Lut desert (Iran) 156–9
  questionably a plate 208
  possible seismic zone 206
Lycaonian depression 122
  sheep flocks 145
Lycia
  coast changes 82–3
  deforestation 143
Lydia, former forests 141

M

Maars near Kula 107
Macedonia, early climate 65
  pollen bore 23
Madhya Bharat tribal migrations 302
Mahabharat times drainage 293
Maharashtra river terrace 310
Maiandros river (see Menderes)
Mahi river terraces 310
Makhus formation (Oman) 257–8
Makran
  climatic change 301
  coastal uplift 249, 291
  desert 292
  mountains 151, 167
Malaria in early Turkey 99
Malwa, early climate 297
Manchhar lake (Sind) 289
Manyas (Turkey
  earthquake 195
  lake 113
Maquis in Turkey 76–7

Maritsa earthquake 197
  seismic zone 193, 202
Marmara Sea 113
  coasts 100,
  earthquake 196
  former lake 95
  freezing in Middle Ages 98
Marshes
  of L. Euphrates 230, 234, 238, 240
  of Indus 286–7, 289, 299
Marwar early desert 296
Marwar Bagra L. Palaeolithic 309
Marwara (Rajasthan) shisham 286
Mass movements
  glacial 104
  seismic 189, 211–2
Massileh (Iran) erosion surfaces 158
Mathura, early vegetation 297
Mazanderan seismicity 206
Meana-Čaača, early site in Turkmenia
  178
Meander alluvium 257 (see Menderes)
Meanders of Çarşamba 117
  of Euphrates 215–25
Mediterranean
  climate in early Turkey 136
  connection with Black Sea 100
  cycles of erosion 73–4, 78, 258
  cyclones 278, 354
  environmental changes 353
  fauna in Levant 30,
  origins of 335
  early sea levels 231–2
  seismicity 188, 198, 204
  scrub woodland 233
Megalopolis earthquake 195
Melons in early Indus valley 288
Menderes
  Greater 67–70
    delta 70–4, 76–8, 100, 103–4
  Lesser 62, 64, 67–8, 70
    delta 70–4, 77–8 100–3
Merdinevli Yayla dunes 130

Meriç delta 95
Meshed mountains 152
Messerian plain 320, 326, 332
Meskene (Syria) river erosion 225
Mesolithic
  in C. Asia 326
  W. India 309–11, 350
  Turkey 91, 127, 134
Mesopotamia (see also Iraq)
  canals and earthquakes 189
  delta 214, 227–44
  in Würm 9, 11
Messenia in Bronze Age 57–8
  early vegetation 65
Metallurgy and deforestation 142
Metals, early trade in 165–6
Mexico desert 282
  Gulf sea-level 238
Microliths
  in W. India 289, 309, 313
  in Turkey 91, 127, 134
Middle Ages lake in C. Asia 327, 329
  sediments in Mediterranean 78
  storm tracks 62
Migrations and climate 1, 299–300,
  302
Miletus 71–2, 103–4
Miliolite deposits in W. India 309,
  312–3, 317–8
Mimosa in W. India 284, 287–8
Mindel-age lake terraces in Turkey
  124
Mindel-Riss sea-level 231
Minerals in early Sistan 180
Miocene formation
  in Iraq 235
  Oman 268
Mirabad lake (Iraq) pollen sequence
  159
Mississippi delta 51, 59
Mogan lake (Turkey) 94–5, 113
Mohenjodaro 292
  floods 290

flora and fauna 285–6, 289
  sedimentation 298
Molluscs of Sistan 179
Monastic records of earthquakes
  187–8
Monastirian sea-level 249
Mongol devastations 206, 276
Mongolian climate 144
Mongoose in early Indus valley 289
Monkeys in early Indus valley 289
Monsoons, mechanism 284, 299,
  351–2, 354–5
  in Himalayas 278
  in Sind and Thar 281, 291
Moraines
  in Himalayas 314
  Iran 154, 157, 160
  Near East 7
  Turkey 90, 111, 142
Mosul climate 233
Mousikanos (i.e. Sind) at time of
  Alexander 296
Mousterian
  in C. Asia 326
  in N. Negev 83
  Peloponnese 58
Mudairah (Kuwait) coastal terraces
  245–7, 252
Mudurnu earthquakes 195
Muhammatabad earthquake 195, 206
Muhipler earthquake 196
Mukra, take-off of Kara Kum Canal
  323
Mule in early Near East 34
Multan
  former climate 297
  river confluence 291
Muminabad earthquake 196, 206
Mundafan, former lake (Arabia) 278
Mundigak (Afghanistan), early site
  165–6
Munhatta (Levant) Neolithic 31
Munzur mts., glaciation 89

Mureibit formation (Syria) 222
Murgab delta 321, 322, 331
    seismicity 206
Muş (Turkey) former forests 141
Musandam peninsula (Arabia)
    alluvium 259
    subsidence 248,
    wadis 257
Musannat, al-, Wadi, Pleistocene
    248
Mysia, former forests 141
Myus (W. Turkey), former port 71, 103

N

Nafud earthquakes 187–8
Nahal Oren (Levant) Neolithic 31–2
Nahr Umr (Iraq) boring 235, 237
Naiwal river courses (Punjab) 292–4
Naizar marshes of Sistan 179
Najaf marine remains (Iraq) 230, 232,
    248
Najd, former drainage of 248
Nara river course (Sind) 281, 289,
    291, 293, 296
Narmada river terraces (W. India) 310
Naulochos, harbour of Priene 71
Naval timber and deforestation 142
Navigation (see Boats)
Nazilli (W. Turkey) river fans 69
Nea Nikomedeia (Greece), early
    domestication 46
Nearchus's voyage 228
Negev forested in last Glacial 9
    landscape history 83
Nemrut mt., (E. Turkey) vulcanism
    107
Néochori (Greece) Palaeolithic 58
Neogene
    cherts (Syria) 216
    deposits (W. Turkey) 69
    deserts (C. Asia) 323
    lakes (Turkey) 111–2, 122

Neolithic origins 33, 38
    fauna, in Greece 45
    pluvial 264–5, 355
        in C. Asia 327, 329, 346
        in Greece 47
        in Indus valley 288
        in Levant 30, 82, 130, 134–5
        in Turkey 91, 130, 144
Netherlands sea-levels 238
Niatak canal (Afghanistan) dunes 170
Niger delta 238–9
Niha earthquake 196
Nile delta accretion 64
    White, high-water phase 351
Nisah-Sahbah wadi (E. Arabia),
    Pleistocene 248
Nisibin, former lion country 141
Nomadism
    in early Greece 47
    mediaeval India 302
    Sistan 177
"Nomadization"
    of Anatolia 145
    of N. India 298
"Northering" of Punjab rivers 290,
    293, 295
Nubian ibex 35

O

Oaks
    in Greece 18–9, 27, 41
    Turkey 76–7, 143, 145
Ob river, possible diversion to Aral
    348
Obsidian artefacts 107
Odderade interstadial 41
Ohind (Sind) timber 296
Olympia
    burial of 14, 62
    games 59
Olympus, mt., of Bithynia (see
    Uludağ)

Oman
    calcrete 257
    Gulf 249
    orogeny 248
    outwash plains 264–5, 267, 275
    sabkha 249
    soils 263–74
    marine terraces 252
Onager in early Levant 34–5
Ophiolitic zone around Arabia 207
Optimum
    climatic 90–1, 145
    secondary 62, 130, 353
Orogeny
    Alpine 56
    Himalayan 293
    Oman 248
    Turkish 136
Orontes
    drainage 112
    sedimentation 211–2
Ostracods of L. Iraq 235
Otter of early Sistan 180
Ovacik lake (Turkey) 120
Oxus river 278 (see also Amu-Darya)

P

Pachpadra salt lake (Rajasthan) 313
Pakistan
    desert vegetation 284–5
    seismicity 206
Palaearctic fauna in Levant 9, 30
Palaeolithic
    of C. Asia 326–7, 329, 331
    of India 309–11, 313
    Syria 222–3, 225
Palaeosols
    of Arabia 263–74
    Egypt 10
Palynology (see Pollen evidence)

Pamir mts. 278
    rivers 323–4, 330, 333, 336
Pamphylia soil erosion 73, 78
Parrots in Indus valley 289
Parthian times in Sistan 176
Partridge hunted in early Sistan 178, 182
Pastoralism (see Grazing, Nomadism)
    in early Greece 47
    in Sistan 177
    in Turkey 144
Pasture in Turkey 142, 145
Pat desert of W. India 281
Patiala drainage 293
Patmos charter on Maeander river 72
Patras Palaeolithic 58
Paul's cosmology 14
Pausanias on Asia Minor 77
Peas in early Indus valley 288
Peat deposits
    in Iran 155
    in Turkey 76–7, 117–9
Pechora river, possible diversion to Caspian 344
Pehova inscription on E. Saraswati stream 293
Pelican in early Sistan 180, 182
Peloponnese
    decline of rainfall 14
    erosion in 51–66
Pelusiac channel of Nile 64
Peneus river (Peloponnese) history 52-4, 59–63
Penjween earthquake 195
Perge (S. Turkey), stranded 73
Peron marine terrace (Australia) 252
Persia (see Iran)
Peshawar, former marshes 289
Pheia, city of Elis 59
Phragmite vegetation in Sistan 171, 179
Phrygana of W. Turkey 77
Pig
    early hunting of 35–6

domestication of 46, 76
   in Indus valley 290
Pinarbaşi lake 119
Pindus mts., early vegetation 18, 82
Pine
   in Greece 17–8, 22–4, 27, 41, 65
   in Turkey 74, 77, 97, 142–4
   Yugoslavia 22
Pipal in Indus valley 286
Pistacia in Greece 18–19, 41
Pitane (W. Turkey) Roman bridge 72
Plaiting in early Sistan 180
Plane, Oriental in Turkey 143, 145
Plate-margin phenomena 185–6
   in Middle East 207
Plato on erosion 44
Playas of Iran 150, 152, 155, 158–60
Pleistocene
   end of 87
   sediments of L. Iraq 235
   of Sistan 167, 171, 175
   tectonism in, 106
   terraces of 106
   vulcanism 107
Pliny on Asia Minor 72–3
Pliny, Younger, on Nearchus 228
Pliocene
   lake terrace in Turkey 112
   sea-level in E. Arabia 248
   sediments in Greece 58
   Sistan 167, 170, 176–7
   Turkey 69
   tectonism in 106
   transgression in Iraq 230
Plovdiv earthquakes 195, 202
Pluvial periods 8, 10–12, 120, 353
   in Africa 351
   in Arabia 248, 263–4, 268, 278, 355
   in C. Asia 323–4,
   in Greece 44–7, 58
   in Iran 157–8, 161
   in Iraq 257

neolithic 264–5, 278
   in Turkey 87, 113–5, 124, 127–8, 130–1, 134–6
Podsolization 89
Pokljuka (Yugoslavia) pollen sequence 21
Pokran (Rajasthan) ranns 313
Pollen evidence
   in Greece 41–4, 46–7, 65
   Indus valley 287–8, 302, 309
   Iran 150, 155, 159
   Levant 9
   Mediterranean (incl. Italy, Yugoslavia) 15–28, 82
   Turkey 76–7, 90, 97, 119
Pontic mts., in Ice Age 88–90, 106, 142
   vegetation, 144
Population movements 1, 299–300
   variations 45, 86, 144, 187
Parbandar Miliolite 312
Porpoises of Indian rivers 295
Ports (see Ephesus, Lothal, Miletus, Myus)
Potash in Turkish lake 124
Pottery, Chalcolithic, of Gujarat 289
Pratihara dynasty (Punjab), drainage at time of 293
Prayag (Allahabad) drainage 295
Prehistoric footprints in Turkish tufa 107
   settlements in Turkey 99–100
   (see also Mesolithic, Neolithic, Palaeolithic)
Priene 70–1, 103
Progradation
   of coast of Elis 61–2
   of Ionia 68
Prosopis vegetation in Pakistan and Rajasthan 284–5, 287–8
Ptolemy
   on Alexandria (meteorological records) 356
   on Caspian 340
   on Punjab 296

Pulses, early cultivation of 36
Pulumur earthquake 197
Punjab
    former climate 296–7
    drainage 278, 290–6
    migrants from 302
Pushkar (Rajasthan) palaeolithic site
    309, 311–2
    lake vegetation 287–8
Puzak (Sistan) lake 167
Pylos vegetation 65
Pyrgos (Greece) Palaeolithic 58
Pyrrha (W. Turkey) near coast 71

Q

Qal'ah Bust (Afghanistan) 174
Qanats, evidence of earthquakes 189,
    208
Qarmat Ali boring (Iraq) 236–7
Qatar
    evaporites 271
    early sea-levels 232, 249, 251–2,
    257
Qayn-Birjand possible seismic zone
    206
Qazvin, Dasht-i 156
Qishm raised beach 249
Qom playa 158, 160
Quetta early civilization 165

R

Rafts of reeds in Sistan 180
Rajasthan
    archaeology 310–1, 313, 317–8
    former climate 279–80, 297, 301,
    307–18, 350
    desert 279, 282
    drainage 293, 313
    fauna and flora 286, 289
    miliolite 312
Rajkot miliolite 312–3

Rajputana desert 154 (see Rajasthan)
Ram Rud (Sistan) dunes 170
Rangmahal (Rajasthan) mediaeval
    culture 302
Rangpur (Harappan site) 292
    floods 298
    horse remains 285
    rice, possibly wild 288, 298
    timber 286
Ranunculus glacialis absent from
    Turkey 143
Raqqa silts 222
Ras al-Jlay'ah (Kuwait) 252
Ras al Khaymah alluvial fans 256–7
Ras al-Mish'ab (Kuwait) 252
Ras Ashairij (Kuwait) 252
Rasula (Punjab) drainage 293
Ravi climate 296
    river shifts 291, 294
Reclamation of forest in early Cyprus
    143
Red Sea
    earthquakes 188, 203–4
    rift 231
Reeds used in Sistan 179–80, 211
Relict species, Tertiary 143
Reptiles in Levant 30
Restoration of damaged terrain in
    Turkey 146
Rezaieh (Urmia) lake 155, 157
Rhinoceros
    in early Greece 45
    in India 285, 289
Rias of Turkey 100
Rice, possibly wild
    in early Indus valley 288, 298
    Punjab 297
Rigvedas 299 (see also Vedic)
Rimah, Tell al (Iraq) late alluvium 258
Rimah—al-Batin watercourse (Arabia)
    248
Riss
    lake terraces (Turkey) 112, 124, 132

moraine (Turkey) 111
pluvial (Iran) 158
vegetation (Greece) 41
-Würm sea-level 231
River capture
Turkey 89
shifts in C. Asia 319–34
Middle East 215
Punjab 290–6
Roads, evidence of earthquakes 189
Rodents, in Levant 30
Rohri (Sind)
drainage 290, 292
mid. Palaeolithic 313
Roman
imperial decline and sedimentation 74–5, 78
sites
in Greece (Elis) 59–61, 63–4, 82
in Syria 215, 218, 223
in Turkey 70, 97, 257
Rome, erosion near 64
Rub' al Khali
former lakes 278
source of sand 265
Rubefication of Arabian soils 265, 268–70
Rud Hilla (Iran) submerged delta 259
Rud-i Biyaban (Sistan) 170, 175–6
Rud-i Parian (Sistan) 171, 174–5
Rud-i Sistan 171, 174–6
Rud-i Zirrah (Sistan) 175–6
Rudradaman inscription on Rajasthan dam 296
Rupar (Punjab) drainage 292
Russian seismic documents 189
Ruyan earthquake 205

S

Sabarmati (Punjab) drainage 291–2
Sabkhas
high, in E. Arabia 248
soils of 270–1
Sabkhat Jabbour (Syria) 222
Sabkhat Umm as-Samin (Oman) 249
Sachia river (Peloponnese) history 53, 55, 59, 61, 64, 82
Sadagh earthquake 197
Sagziabad destroyed by earthquake 205
Sahend earthquake 197
Sahara
aridity 282
in Würm 11
Sahara—Arabian climatic belt 233
Sahul shelf (Australia) 251
Saidmarreh (Iran)
rockfall 211
terrace 255
Sakarya
delta 73–4
river 95, 116, 122
Salda lake (Turkey) 119–20
Salinization of Black Sea 96, 353, 355–6
Salmas earthquake 189, 195
Salt
deposits in Sistan 171, 177
lake in Turkey 124, 126
lakes in W. India 287
playas in Iran 160
plugs in Iraq 276
in Tigris and Euphrates 234
Saltarino (N. Italy) past vegetation 19, 22
Salton (Calif.) aridity 282
Salwah (E. Arabia) raised beach 252
Samarra, possible head of delta 228–9
Sambhar (Rajasthan) salt lake 287, 309, 313, 353
Sana Rud (Sistan) 170, 176
Sand (see Aeolian deposits, Dunes)
Sand-seas of Arabia 272
Sandstone in Iraq 235
Santorin vulcanism 193, 198, 204, 212
Saraswati river (Punjab) 293, 295–6

Sardis sediments 70
Sarıkemer (W. Turkey), on former coast 71
Sarykamysh depression (C. Asia) 322, 326–30, 332, 346, 353
Sarysu delta (C. Asia) 331
Sassanian canals 230
Sat mts., (Turkey) glaciation 88
Saurashtra
  early climate 296–7
  fauna 285, 290
Savalan Kuh (Iran) 154
Scree-formation in N. Greece 44
Scirpus vegetation in Sistan 171, 179–80
Scythian invasions of India 298
Sea-level changes 64, 67, 74–5, 87, 89, 95–6, 99–100, 231–2
  in Gulf 245–54
Seals in early Indus valley 289
Sediments
  aeolian
    India 282–5, 293
    Iraq 233, 239
  recent 45, 108, 356
  in reservoirs 146
  seismic 211–2
  settled 47, 211
    in N. Africa 78
    Arabia 271
    Greece 61–5, 82
    Gulf 249
    India 295, 310
    Iran 159–60, 211–2, 255, 259
    Iraq 230, 275–6
    Mediterranean 45, 47, 73
    Sind 290, 298
    Sistan 167
    Turkey 67–70, 76, 99, 141, 145–6
Sehwan (Sind) tectonic effect 290, 298
Seismic activity
  in S. Aegean 56
  in Near East 86, 185–210
  in Iran 231
  studies and general history 208, 211–2
  in Turkey 87, 106
Selçuk 75 (*see also* Ephesus)
Selenite in Iraq formation 235
Sennacharib, Gulf coast at time of 228
Sera lake (Turkey) 104
Sesamum in early Indus valley 288
Sesklo (Greece) Neolithic 76
Seyhan delta 73, 100
Sha'aib, al- (Kuwait) 252
Shahr-i Sokhta (Sistan)
  early settlement 165–6, 170, 172, 175–8, 180
Shahr-rey (Iran) destroyed by earthquake 205
Shash (Syria) alluvium 258
Shatt-al-Arab 233, 240–1
  former extension 249
Shautang valley (Punjab) mediaeval culture 302
Shedgum (Arabic) landforms 265
Sheep
  Barbary 33
  in early Indus valley 290
  Levant 35–6, 38, 46–7, 76
  Sistan 170, 177–9
  Turkey (Lycaonia) 145–6
Shelagh Rud (Sistan) 174–6
Shisham timber 286
Shughr earthquake 197
Shipbuilding in early Punjab 296
Siberian rivers, possible diversion to Caspian 348
Sicilian sea-level 249
Sicily, alluviation in 62, 64
Sihor miliolite 312
Silakhor earthquake 189, 195
Silifke (Turkey) wave-cut terrace 75
Sillyon (Pamphylia) stranded 73
Silting in Peloponnese 14 (*see also* Sediments)

Simav lake (Turkey) 113
Sinai
  fauna 30
  in Würm 11
Sind (see also Indus civilization)
  former climate 279, 296, 299, 300–1
  desert 282, 297
  drainage history 290–3, 295
  early settlement 313, 317–8
Sinop alluvium 70, 257
Sirhind river (Punjab) 292, 294–5
Sirmur region (Siwaliks) drainage history 293
Sirsa (Punjab) drainage 292–3
Sissu timber 286
Sistan
  early environment and settlement 155–6, 165–83, 211
  possible seismic zone 206
Siwaliks talus fans 293
Skamander river (Turkey) 73–4, 78, 105
Skanda Gupta, dam at time of 296
Skhul, early Levant site 35
Skopje earthquake 195, 202
Skylax on Troy 73
Slovenia pollen cores 21–2
Snow-line
  in Iran 154, 161
  Pamirs 278
  Tien Shan 324, 333
  Turkey 88, 92, 144
  shifted by tectonism 106, 136
Snow melt 172, 216, 293
Soghdian basin (C. Asia) dunes 170
Söğüt mts., (Turkey) 120
Soil erosion
  in Arabia 272
  in Classical times and later 14, 65
  in Punjab 295
  in Sistan 171–2
  in Turkey 74, 76–8, 108, 141

Soil formation, fossil 310
  in Oman 263–74
  in Turkey 89
Söke (W. Turkey) landscape changes 76, 103
Solonchak plains (C. Asia) 322, 327
Sophades earthquake 195
Sor-tepe (Kara Kum) fauna 178
Sotar river (Punjab) 293
Soviet Central Asia hydrology and terrain 319–34
Spits
  of former Turkish lake 124, 127
  and winds 128, 130
Spruce, planted in Turkey 146
Squirrel in early Indus valley 289
Stadion, length of 228
Steppe
  cold in Last Glacial 82
  Greece 41
  in S. Europe 351
  W. India 281
  Sistan 176
  Syria 216
  Turkey 144–5
Stone Age (see Aurignacian, Mesolithic, Neolithic, Palaeolithic)
Stones, trade in early Sistan 165–6
Storm-tracks, shift of 62, 351–5
Strabo, on
  Asia Minor 71, 73, 97, 107, 141, 145
  Caspian 340
  Cyprus 142
  Peloponnese 52, 59
Straits (Black Sea—Mediterranean) formation of 95, 353, 355–6
Süberde
  neolithic site 31–2, 104
  pollen evidence 97
Subsidence
  in L. Iraq 229–31, 236, 238, 241, 259

of Musandam peninsula 248
Sudarshana lake, artificial, in early
   Saurashtra 296
Sudras territory in early India 296
Suğla lake (Turkey) 104, 114, 116–9,
   121
Sukkur (Sind) drainage 290, 292
Sulaimaniya valley alluvium 257
Sulphur in Sistan 171
Sultan mts., (Turkey) dry valleys 95
Sultanhanı (Turkey) sink-holes 130
Suludere river post-neolithic alluvium
   134
Sumerians
   cf. Harappans 288
   near sea 239
Sungassar terraces (Iraq) 257
Sur (Oman) coastal section 268
Sutlej river, old course 289
Swamps
   of Iraq 276
   of Sind 291
Syr-Darya 170, 320, 325–6, 331
   irrigation from 347–8,
   shift to right 332, 336, 345
Syria
   ass 35
   early climate 354
   forests, loss of in Glacial periods 9
   pollen bores 24–5
   seismicity of desert 186–7
   river fill and terraces 215–26, 257
Syrie island, near Ephesus 106

T

Tabun, equid from 35
Tahr, Arabian 33
Tahtaci (''Woodmen'') of Lycia 143
Taiga of Europe in Ice Age 351
Takht-i Sulaiman glaciation 160
Takyrs (crusts) of C. Asia 319–23
Taliqan valley earthquake 205

Tamarisk
   in Rajasthan 284, 286–8
   Sind 178–9
Tarsus delta and harbour 100–1
Tash earthquake 196
Taurus mts.,
   glaciation 89–90
   karst landscape 104, 120, 122
   lions formerly in 141
   vegetation 144
Taxus in early Phrygia 97
Tchihatcheff, de, Russian naturalist
   143–4
Teak at Lothal 286
Tectonic movements
   and alluviation 259
   in E. Arabia 245, 248, 252, 275
   in C. Asia 331, 338–9
   in deltas of Netherlands and Nigeria
      238–9
   Greece 55–6, 61, 64
   Indus valley and Indo- Gangetic
      watershed 290, 295, 298, 302
   Iran 159, 230
   in Iraq 230–1, 238–9, 242, 259,
      275–6
   in Middle East 185–210
   Sistan 170, 175
   Turkey 74–6, 82–3, 87, 106, 112,
      119–20, 122, 124, 131, 136
Tedjen delta 320, 326, 331
Tefenni basin (Turkey) 119, 131
Tehran alluvium 255
Tel Gat, Bronze Age site 34
Tenagi Philippon (Greece) pollen bore
   16, 23–4, 40–2
Tendürek mt., (Turkey) volcanic 107
Terraces
   coastal
      Kuwait and nearby 232, 245–54,
      353
      Iran 230
      Turkey 100, 106

lake
  C. Asia (including Aral and Caspian) 327, 337, 345–6
  Iran 157
  Sistan 171
  Turkey 91, 111–36
river
  India 307–10
  Iran 150, 159–60
  Syria 215–26
Territoriality in animals 36
Tersihan lake (Turkey) 124
Tethys Sea 313, 335
Thar
  desert 154, 295, 297
  lakes 278
  miliolite 317
Tharthar wadi alluvium 258
Thebe (Troad) former woods 141
Theophrastus on deforestation 142–3
Thera eruption 212 (see also Santorin)
Thessaly, early nomadism in 47
Thob salt lake (Rajasthan) 313
Thrace pollen bore 23
Tien Shan rivers 323–4, 330, 333, 336
Tigers in W. India 285, 289
Tigris river
  catchment 233, 255–6
  climate 233
  delta 227–44
  former extension in Gulf 249
  history, alluvial 257
  tributary, former 248
Timber
  in Harappan economy 285–6, 289
  use of in Neolithic 211
  -line in glacial Turkey 89
Timur invades India 291, Khorezm 332
Tmolosschutt deposits (W. Turkey) 69
Tohana (Punjab) drainage 292
Tokat earthquake 197
Tortum lake (Turkey) 104
Torud earthquake 195

Towns
  damaged by earthquakes 205
  by nomads 145–6
Trabzon, landslide near 104
Trans-Caspia, past rainfall 354
Transcaucasia in Würm 8
Transgression, Flandrian 58, 236, 239, 249–53, 356
Transhumance in early Greece 46–7
Travertine deposits in Turkey 130
Tree-rings (see Dendrochronology)
Tribal migrations
  in India 302
  into Turkey 145
Troad, former woods 141
Troy, topography of 73, 104–5
Trstenik (Yugoslavia) pollen core 16, 21
Trucial coast
  shell-beds 252
  transgression 232
Tsunamis (seismic sea-waves)
  in Dead Sea 203
  in E. Mediterranean 193, 204
Tufa in Turkey
  with fossil footprints 107
  wind-eroded 146
Tunceli earthquake 194
Tundra in Ice Age Europe 144, 351
Tunisia climate change 300
Turan (C. Asia) desert, ancient rivers and irrigation 319–34
Turkey
  deforestation 77
  Neolithic of 35, 76
  seismicity 207–8
  early vegetation 76
  in Würm 7–8
Turkish rule in Peloponnese 60–1, 63
Turkish seismic documents 189
Turkmenia, early economy 178, seismicity 206
Turpentine collected in Turkey 142–3

Turquoise in early Sistan 180
Tursa earthquake 189, 195
Tuz göl (C. Turkey)
history of 89, 111–2, 115, 120–6,
131, 135–6
Typha vegetation
in Rajasthan 287–8
in Sistan 171, 179–80

U

Ubaid stratum at Ur 229
Uludağ (Olympus of Bithynia) 142
Umarkot (Sind) drainage 289
Una (Kathiawar) miliolite dunes 313,
346
United Arab Emirates, outwash plains
of 264
United States of America, coastal
population 51
Ur
flood stratum 229–30
near sea 229, 239
Ural mts., 331, 336
Ural river 336
Urbanism, beginning of 47
Urfa, lions once near 141
Urmia lake (*see also* Rezaieh)
once large 161
earthquake near 189, 204
Uruk stratum at Ur 229
Ushturan Kuh (Iran) glaciation 154
Ustukran earthquake 196
Ustyurt plat. (C. Asia) 320, 327
Uzboi overflow channel (C. Asia) 321,
322, 327–30

V

Valdai (Würm) Glaciation and Caspian
337
Valleys, dry, in C. Anatolia 95

Van
earthquakes near 188–9, 204
lake expansion 89, 91–3, 111–2,
114, 121
vulcanism near 107
Varro on wild cattle in Troad 141
Varto earthquake 195
Varves in chronology 153
Vedic times drainage in India 293,
296, 299
Vegetation changes in Turkey 77, 96–7
(*see also* Forest, Steppe)
Veraval (Kathiawar) miliolite deposits
312
Vico lake (Italy) pollen bore 16, 20–1,
24
Villafranchian deposits 69, 122, 127
Vine
in early Sistan 179
high in Turkey 144
Visadi (Rajasthan) V. Palaeolithic site
309, 311
Vlach shepherds (Balkans) 47
Volga river 336–7, 341, 343, 350
Volgograd reservoir 343
Vostiza earthquake 197
Vulcanism in Sistan 170, 175
Turkey 106–7
Vulcanism in Sistan 170, 175
Turkey 106–7
Vychegda river, possible diversion to
Volga 344

W

Wadi el-Mughara (Mt. Carmel) horse
remains 34–5
Wadi-Fallah (Nahal Oren) neolithic
site 31–2
Wadi el Safa (Syria) 220, 223
Wadi Haidha (Oman) 268
Wahibah sands, blown to Oman 265

Wahind river (Punjab) 293, 295
Walnut in early W. Turkey 77
Watar (Punjab) drainage 296
Water-table
  evaporation at in Oman 264
  fall of in W. India 301, and Iraq 259
Wave-cut notches in Peloponnese 56
"Westering" of Punjab rivers 290–1,
  293, 296
Wheat
  cultivated early in Indus 288, 298
  Levant 36, 38
  Sistan 179
  wild in Turkey 76
Willow in Sistan 178
Willow grass absent from Anatolia 143
Wind erosion
  in C. Asia 319
  Iran 159, 161
  Sistan 167, 170–2, 176
  C. Turkey 128–9, 145
Windbreaks in Sistan 178
Wolves in early Indus valley 289
Woods (see Forests)
Wullur (Punjab) drainage 293
Würm period phenomena
  in Iran 158, 160–2
  in Turkey 111–3, 115, 130–1, 134–6

X

Xanthi interstadial (Greece) 41
Xenophon on forests of Armenia 141
Xinias lake (Greece) pollen bore 16–9,
  21–5

Y

Yamuna (Jumna) river, former flow
  293, 295
Yaraşlı basin (Turkey) 120–1, 135

Yaylas (see Pasture in Turkey)
Yemen, soils of 270–2
Yeniçağa göl pollen record 77
Yenisei river, possible diversion to
  Aral 348
Yeşilirmak delta 100
Yugoslavia
  earthquakes 202
  early nomadism 47
  pollen bores 16, 21–2, 26

Z

Zab, Lesser, alluvium 257
Zagros
  drainage 234, 249
  glaciation 161
  mountains 151
  neolithic occupation 29, 31, 38
  orogeny 231, 248
  terraces 230
  vegetation 27
Zard-Kuh glaciation 154, 157
Zardeh-Kuh (E. Iran) 150, 152
Zebu cattle of early Indus valley 289
Zeravshan
  nature of delta 320, 326, 331
  river (C. Asia) 322
Zeribar lake (Iran) and its pollen core
  8, 16, 35–6, 150, 159, 161
Zfat earthquake 197
Zhana-Darya, dry offshoot of Syr-
  Darya 320
Zibar earthquake 197, 204
Zizyphus (ber) timber in early Indus
  valley 286
Zorbat earthquake 196
Zubair (Iraq) anticline and borings
  236–7
Zülfüönü promontory in former Konya
  lake 128–9